BUILDING A BETTER FUTURE

BUILDING A BETTER FUTURE

MEMOIRS OF A CARIBBEAN ECONOMIST

COMPTON BOURNE

First published in 2025 by Hansib Publications
76 High Street, Hertford, SG14 3TA, United Kingdom

info@hansibpublications.com
www.hansibpublications.com

ISBN 978-1-0686993-7-5
ISBN 978-1-0686993-8-2 (Kindle)
ISBN 978-1-0686993-9-9 (ePub)

A CIP catalogue record for this book is available from the British Library

Production by Hansib Publications
Printed in Great Britain

www.hansibpublications.com

Founded in London in 1970, Hansib Publications has played a crucial role in documenting the Caribbean experience and bringing Caribbean perspectives to a wider audience. It is renowned for its extensive catalogue of Caribbean fiction and non-fiction, spanning a diverse range of genres, including historical novels, biographies, poetry anthologies, political commentaries and social narratives. It has also made significant contributions to Caribbean scholarship by publishing insightful works on history, culture, politics and social issues.

Today, Hansib Publications remains a significant force in the world of Caribbean publishing and continues to publish books that reflect the vibrant diversity of the Caribbean region and the global Caribbean diaspora. Its legacy of promoting Caribbean voices and perspectives has made it an invaluable resource for those seeking to understand and appreciate the rich cultural heritage of the Caribbean.

To the memory of my mother, Sylvia, and Grandmother Hutson whose faith and confidence in me never wavered.

To my wife, Pamela, and son, Monty, and to the memory of my son, Tunji, for love, understanding and support through the years.

To my siblings and grandchildren for the joy of life.

ACKNOWLEDGEMENTS

A work of this nature would not have been completed without the encouragement and assistance of my family members, friends and associates.

I wish to thank my family, siblings, colleagues, and friends like Richard Kellman, Dr Marlene Attzs and Professor Emerita Bridget Brereton who encouraged me to undertake the task. Richard Kellman and my sister, Raulda, read every chapter in its initial draft and provided encouraging comments and sound editorial suggestions.

Much of the material about my journeys in political economy and higher education is the result of stimulating and productive professional collaboration and collegial relationships in the Caribbean, Latin America, United States, Africa and the Philippines. I remain grateful for their invaluable assistance and support.

I thank my friends and colleagues Sir Kenneth Hall, Professor Andrew Downes, Dr Arnold McIntyre and Dr Shelton Nicholls for reading the manuscript.

I must thank Nickeisha Wickham who once more responded positively, quickly and efficiently to my call for word processing assistance.

Finally, I wish to thank Hansib Publications, especially Kash Ali, for shepherding this work through the stages of publication and marketing.

ABOUT THE AUTHOR

Compton Bourne is Professor Emeritus of Economics, the University of the West Indies. He is a graduate of the University of London, the University of Birmingham and the University of the West Indies. He was President of the Caribbean Development Bank from 2001 to 2011, Principal of the St Augustine Campus of the University of the West Indies from 1996 to 2001 and Pro Vice Chancellor for Planning and Development from 1990 to 1996.

For various periods, Professor Bourne served as a Director of the National Savings Commission of Jamaica; Commissioner of the Port Authority of Trinidad and Tobago; Vice-Chairman, UNESCO Institute for Higher Education in Latin America and the Caribbean; Director of the Central Bank of Trinidad and Tobago; Director, Trinidad Publishing Company; and Chancellor, University of Guyana.

He is a Fellow of the Caribbean Academy of Sciences, past President of the Caribbean Studies Association, and past Vice-President of the Caribbean Agro-Economic Society.

Professor Bourne is a Member of the Order of Excellence, the highest honour of the Cooperative Republic of Guyana, and is a recipient of the Caribbean Studies Distinguished Service Award, The American Foundation for the University of the West Indies Award for Outstanding Contribution to the Caribbean, and the National Coalition on Caribbean Affairs International Service Award, Honorary Doctor of Laws (LLD) (The University of the West Indies), and the Lifetime Achievement Award for Excellence in Higher Education (Accreditation Council of Trinidad and Tobago).

Compton Bourne has authored or edited numerous books, scholarly papers and research reports and advisory memoranda for Caribbean governments, foreign governments, the United Nations Development Programme, international development institutions and organisations, and regional and international financial institutions.

PREFACE

This book is primarily motivated by the desire to provide policy makers, practitioners and analysts of economic development and higher education management with a record of some of the major issues, challenges and policies in the Caribbean primarily but also in a few African countries and the Philippines at various junctures in their contemporary history. It is expected that scholars and students will also be interested in the succinct summaries of Caribbean economic research and policy briefs on economic development, development banking, rural financial markets, financial sector development and monetary policy prepared by the author and his collaborators.

Spanning almost fifty years, this book deals with issues, problems and policies in major economic sectors, such as agriculture, tourism and finance, as well as policy issues fundamental to the evolution of the Caribbean Community and its institutions, such as the Caribbean Development Bank, the Caribbean Community Secretariat and the Caribbean Court of Justice.

It also presents accounts of engagement in rural financial market reform in Zambia, financing of agricultural rehabilitation in Uganda, preparatory work for renegotiation of the Southern African Customs Union on behalf of Botswana, Swaziland and Lesotho, and central banking in the Philippines.

Much attention is given to major issues, challenges and policies within the higher education sector with primary focus on the University of the West Indies and the University of Guyana.

Commentaries on the national political and social context of developments in the various countries intersperse the book. The book also identifies many of the academics, professional economists and students operating in the Caribbean development and university landscape between 1969 and 2016. Another feature which completes the tapestry of the memoirs are the accounts of the author's family and social life.

The book begins conventionally with reminiscences on early childhood in Georgetown, Guyana, but then rapidly transits into an account of political developments between 1953 and 1964. After a chapter which describes the nature and circumstances of the author's undergraduate and postgraduate training in England, the next three chapters deal in detail with the years 1969-2001 spent at the University of Guyana and the University of the West Indies. These chapters present quasi-historical accounts of academic development, governance issues and challenges at the University of Guyana, planning, university development and tuition fee reform at the University of the West Indies, and an account of a major industrial relations challenge at its St Augustine campus in Trinidad. The succeeding two chapters, spanning 2001-2011, deal with the Caribbean Development Bank, and with Caribbean economic integration, including financing of community institutions and an extensive summary of the Strategic Plan for Regional Development prepared in 2010-2011. The last chapter, written in lieu of an epilogue, deals with some new challenges for Caribbean countries such as the correspondent banking crisis, diminished access to external finance, the issue of tertiary education governance, and the perennial problem of financing higher education.

CONTENTS

CHAPTER SEVEN

CHAPTER EIGHT

CHAPTER NINE

CHAPTER TEN

CHAPTER ONE

CHILDHOOD AND TEENS

THE FAMILY

I was born on 7 October 1943. I grew up in a large extended family consisting of my parents (Sylvia and Cecil), eight siblings (three brothers and five sisters), four grandparents, two aunts and one uncle, and numerous cousins. My brothers are Clement who is one year older than me, Lyndon and Cecil. My sisters, all younger than me, are Janette Raulda, Lynda Helene, Lorna Sylvia and Judith Dian. Another sister, Brenda Anita, who was third in line died in 2016. My siblings and I adored our mother and as children would clamber into her bed and compete for the places closest to her, a practice that continued until near her death in 2019 at 96 years old.

We were a closely knit family, happy together, and supportive of each other. That relationship continued throughout our adult lives. Friends on experiencing a Bourne family gathering would remark that when together we needed no others. While living in different countries, we remained in contact through phone calls and occasional visits and since 2020 started having monthly Zoom meetings which include grandchildren of the siblings. We have also remained close to our cousins despite our now advanced years and our residence in different countries and in different cities even when in the same country.

The families were solidly working class. My grandfather was a stevedore on the Bookers docks and my father was a ship's engineer. The extended family lived in separate dwellings typically in close proximity to each other in Georgetown (the capital of Guyana) but some were rural folk resident on the East and West Banks of the Demerara River, the West Coast of Demerara and the East Coast of Essequibo. In Georgetown were my maternal grandparents, Edwin and Amelia Hutson and their daughters Ivy, who was married to Tobagonian Daniel Hamlet, and Evelyn who was married to Ivelaw Gravesande, and their son, Whitney, who was unmarried.

I saw them almost every day. In the rural areas were several Hutson family units and the Padmore family in Den Amstel, West Coast Demerara and Vergenoegen, East Coast Essequibo. The Cummings family (in which Percy, Herbie and Rosalyn were my contemporaries) lived in Craig Village, East Bank Demerara. Oscar Greene, his wife Ivy (who was my godmother) and daughter Grace lived on Versailles Sugar Estate, West Bank Demerara. Aunt Maybelle MacCleod and her family lived in Pouderoyen, West Bank Demerara, and Aunt Rosa Primo lived and farmed in Buxton, East Coast Demerara.

My mother was a gifted raconteur who would occasionally gather up children of neighbours late in the afternoon and entertain them with a variety of stories, some of which would be ghost stories or something equally frightening, but they would be back next day for more. In British Columbia, where she resided from 1976, she had a large following of devotees from various Caribbean countries who would periodically gather at her residence for her latest tales and jokes. Some of that skill seems to have been transferred to my younger brother, Lyndon, and to my niece, Alexia Duke.

Because I was particularly close to my mother and because my seafaring father who worked on tankers travelling to Europe and other distant parts of the world was frequently out of the country for long periods, some of my evening hours were spent in her company listening to local and Caribbean news and music on the radio. I remember that Frank Sinatra's 'Learning the Blues' was one of her favourite songs. Often, she would read romance novels while I did school homework or read some children's book.

When my father's ship was in the Kingston port, I got the opportunity to wander around on board. My favourite area was the engine room where he worked. I found the gleaming brass fittings, the steaming and hissing turbines and the throb of the engines tremendously exciting. This interest remained with me for many years, causing me to venture into the engine rooms of coastal and river ferries in Guyana whenever possible and even into the engine room of the *MV Begonia* on which I travelled from Port of Spain, Trinidad, to Southampton, England, in 1964 to begin university studies.

My mother, grandparents and aunts must have thought that I could be relied upon from the time I was ten or so years old. I was entrusted to do household grocery and market shopping, run errands for my aunts and pay my grandfather's Friendly Society and Lodge membership dues. In Bourda, Stabroek and La Penitence markets, I learnt to negotiate price discounts

Earliest childhood photograph with my mother, Sylvia, and older brother, Clement.

and reallocate the shopping budget depending on relative prices and scarcities – perhaps an early foundation in applied microeconomics.

I was somewhat enterprising. Out of wood and related materials, I made toy boats, ships, kites and other artefacts for sale to my contemporaries, even going so far as to make a wooden substitute for a miniature plastic toy bomb imported by one of the retail stores in Georgetown. One enterprise which did not pan out was my capture of a couple of baby alligators which unknown to my mother I planned to keep in her wash tub until I found buyers. Confronted by their snapping presence a few days later, she was far from thrilled and insisted I get rid of them which I did by returning them to their natural habitat.

GLIMPSES OF RURAL LIFE

Much of my early childhood years and that of my siblings was spent visiting households of extended family members during school holidays and sometimes on weekends. From cousins in the rural districts, especially the Padmore and Hutson families in West Demerara/East Coast Essequibo, I got my first introduction to small farming by accompanying one uncle to his farm in the "back dam" from early morning to mid-afternoon. For leisure, my brothers, my cousins and I did river fishing, crab catching, canoeing and rafting on makeshift rafts which frequently disintegrated while we were in the middle of the canals. We learnt to carefully examine the surface of canals and ponds for air bubbles which were tell-tale signs of alligators and caimans lurking below the surface. One of my uncles, in addition to his day job, caught snakes and caiman for sale so I also got to know second hand about these reptiles. With the reluctant help of my cousin, Norman Padmore, I also conducted a live experiment to disprove the common belief that pigs cannot swim simply by throwing my uncle's pig into the trench at the back of the residence. The pig protested noisily but it did swim. Had it not, the consequences for me and Norman would have been severe.

I learnt about rural life in general. I observed the close and mutually supportiveness of residents of communities which were racially and culturally diverse. I observed the hardship of small farming and labour on sugar estates, the quest of families to achieve household food self-sufficiency through backyard cultivation and fishing in trenches and canals, and the problem of alcoholism among sugar estate workers facilitated by easy access to credit in rum-selling social clubs operated by the estates. I became aware of how geographically distant villages seemed from each other in rural districts where feet, bicycles and slow trains were the means of transportation.

I also learnt from crossing the Demerara River between Wales Village on the West Bank and Houston Village on the East Bank late one night that river travel at night on small boats was hazardous. It was so dark that one could not see obstacles until the very last moment. I was reminded of this when many years later in the company of my younger son, Tunji, I travelled in the very deep upper reaches of the Essequibo River and saw the huge sizes of boulders in the river and realised that they would normally be invisible at night in high tide. A small boat transporting goldminers at night could easily splinter upon the boulders and cause people to lose their lives in the fierce currents. This to my mind explains the legend of the Massacura Man who would rise from the depths of rivers at night to destroy vessels, leaving no one alive to tell the tale.

LIFE AMONG FRIENDS

My mother, my older brother and I first lived on Carmichael Street but we moved to Duke Street, Kingston when I was five or six years old. Life in my parental home in Duke Street, Kingston, was usually enjoyable. Cricket, football, swimming in the Demerara River foreshore in Kingston (the Sea Wall as it was known to everyone) and in the Cowan Street Forty Feet Canal, fishing in the same canal, and board games with neighbourhood friends filled the daytime leisure hours. My friends were mainly within my age group, namely Oswald "Pats" Gravesande; Winston, Compton and Yvonne Oudkerk; Gordon Narine; Joan Durham; Esther, Daphne and Naomi Taylor; Sylvia and Vesta Lewis; Mackie and Georgie Charles; and Monty Walters but they were older children such as Kingsley Innis, Ulric Pilgrim, Arthur Baird (later known as Arthur Alexander), Patrick Walters, Festus Charles, Yvonne Smith, Gladstone Moses, and George Quintal who befriended and encouraged me. I remember George Quintal presenting me with a proper cricket bat presumably because he detected some batting talent. Winston and Haydock Beveney, another two friends, lived on Parade Street; Eton Wilson and the Rickfords lived on Cowan Street; and Ian Bobb and his older brother lived on Fort Street. The Narines and Gravesandes were our closest family friends.

There are a few incidents connected to swimming in the Demerara River that I remember vividly. We often swam at Fort Groyne at the mouth of the river. It was not safe to do so but many did. One day, a twelve-year-old boy made the newspaper headlines by rescuing three of his older sisters from drowning there. The outcome on another occasion was tragic. One of my group of friends, Georgie Charles, drowned there. He swam too far into the mouth of the river, the strong tide was leaving, and he just could not make it back to shore. We took his clothes home to his mother who on seeing us screamed loudly in pain. She knew instantly what had happened. A third occasion was less stressful. There was a shipwreck on the Atlantic coastline which greatly intrigued us. One day, a group of older boys decided to build a canoe and paddle to the wreck which was close enough to the mouth of the river. They made it to the wreck, loaded the canoe with salvaged metal and started the journey back to shore. Unfortunately, the bottom of the canoe which could not support the added weight dropped out and the boys had to swim back. The last incident was about a thief, nicknamed Eggs, who constantly made his escape to Trinidad and upon his recapture by the Trinidadian police, would be returned to Guyana by boat. On nearing Fort Groyne, he would jump overboard and escape again. He did so one time too many. On his last attempt, he was eaten by sharks which sometimes could be seen at the mouth of the river. The newspaper reported next day that "Sharks had Eggs for breakfast."

There was also an incident in the Forty Feet Canal, the truth about which was not known until many decades later when one of the two Cowan Street boys involved re-visited Guyana and told the story to the newspapers. Until then, everyone in the neighbourhood believed that the two boys had gone for a swim early that Easter morning and that one of them had drowned. The real story as told by the survivor was that they were attacked by a black caiman that killed and presumably ate his friend. He was too petrified to reveal to his parents what happened. As children who frolicked often on the bank of the canal, we knew that alligators and caiman lived in it for we sometimes observed them on the western side of the Parade Street bridge about 200 metres away. I was afraid they would venture on to the bank of the canal at night and for that reason was reluctant to run errands for my grandmother to the police officers housing on the northern bank of the canal. Quite foolishly we never thought they would venture near our part of the canal during daylight hours but evidently they did.

An annual event that we eagerly anticipated was an excursion organised by a church group. It was a family affair attended by many children so there were lots of children of different ages present. The excursions were to various rural districts to which we travelled by train or bus. Food and other delicacies were always abundantly provided. There was inevitably some drama on the eve of departure at the end of the day as parents counted their children and found that one was missing, usually because he or she was still playing with other children.

DUKE STREET CHARACTERS

Duke Street had its adult characters. There was Miss Susan who sought out funerals to weep and wail as well as birthday parties to imbibe rum. Every Sunday, Mr Oscar "sunned" his many flashy suits, cleaned and polished his several pairs of brogue shoes, washed and shined his Triumph motorcycle, dressed and rode off into the evening much to the displeasure of his wife. There was Bajan George who often stole and cooked his neighbours' chickens. Miss Mary, an illiterate woman, who was known to be very jealous of her husband, Papa Willy, thought she had her suspicions confirmed by Cynthia who she asked to read a letter addressed to him. Cynthia read it aloud as a love letter arranging an assignation. The problem, however, was that unknown to Miss Mary, Cynthia was also illiterate and sensing Miss Mary's anxiety, pretended to read the letter and told her what she thought Ms Mary wanted to hear. Papa Willy had to mollify Miss Mary by getting a friend trusted by both of them to read the letter which was actually a job offer. Miss B, a very flirtatious woman, would often drive her husband into fits of jealously during which he would destroy all the glass ware in his home, shed loud tears, beg forgiveness from his wife and then replace all the broken items next day. There was also one lady who when tired of her paramours got rid of them by head-butting them in full view of an assembled company of men which naturally shamed the no-longer loved ones into hasty permanent departure from the love nest.

PRIMARY SCHOOL

I attended Kingston Methodist School, which was located on Barrack Street, a few hundred metres away from my home. Four of my siblings, Clement, Raulda, Lyndon and Lynda, attended the same school. It was one of 269 schools controlled by Christian denominations; only 28 were outside of the control of the churches. The Anglican and Catholic schools were in the majority.

The curriculum included a course in which pupils were taught basic things about the Caribbean, such as names of the various islands, their geographical and population sizes, the names of their capitals and the names of the leaders of their governments. This instilled in my childhood consciousness a sense of the Caribbean which was reinforced by nightly radio broadcasts which included items about Caribbean countries, especially the nearer ones like Trinidad and Barbados. It was also reinforced by the physical presence of people I encountered. For a short while, we had a Trinidadian house guest invariably dressed in jacket and tie. There was a St Lucian on my street; there were at least two Barbadians in my neighbourhood; Trinidad steelbands like Invaders and Casablanca performed on the Georgetown streets occasionally for pre-Christmas celebrations; and Trinidadian calypsonians came to perform at the end of their Carnival season.

There was a small agricultural field at the back of the school. It was used for the cultivation of vegetables and root crops planted from seeds germinated by pupils in the classroom. Pupils were required to tend the crops. Obviously, this was an introduction to the science of plant life but in retrospect I think it served a bigger purpose which was to instil values of patience and care.

I did well in school; made many friends; and participated in many school activities. However, I was not a joiner of clubs and associations and did not last long in boy scouts and church choir. It was not so much that I was a loner, but more a case of me being an independent spirit (which became more evident in secondary school) and a love for quiet times and personal space. Even in my neighbourhood, there would be times when I delinked from the gathering of friends and sat quietly on the fringe observing them or pursuing quite unrelated inner thoughts.

As was usual in those days, there was a Methodist Church adjacent to the school in the same compound. Pupils were required to attend services every Wednesday morning. The priest initially was an Englishman, Reverend Batty. He was succeeded by a young local priest, Reverend Samms. My mother was Anglican. Therefore, my siblings and I would accompany her to Sunday morning services at Christ Church Anglican Church on Waterloo Street. I became a confirmed Anglican and attended that church until at nineteen years old I started my journey from agnosticism to atheism. Before then, I also attended worship sessions at several of the evangelical churches that were springing up in Georgetown.

SECONDARY SCHOOL

In 1954, at ten years old, I entered secondary school. I did not win a scholarship to Queens College, the premier secondary school for boys, but was awarded a partial scholarship to British Guiana Education Trust, a co-education secondary school owned and operated by Co-Principals Aubrey Percival Alleyne and Randolph Emanuel Cheeks. It was one of several privately owned and operated secondary schools in Georgetown at the time. They included Central High School, Tutorial High School and East Indian Education Trust. The schools were established not as elitist institutions but to take up the slack between the demand for secondary school places and the small supply of places in the government schools Queens College and Bishops High School and the Catholic secondary schools St Stanislaus College and St Roses College.

A few boys who started with me, namely Terrence Callender, Oscar Bayrd (deceased) and Eugene (Joe) Lewis (deceased) became lifelong friends. David Peters and Desmond Bandoo, East Indian students from East Bank Demerara taught me the difference between Little Diamond village and Diamond village where they lived. There were two quiet, un-talkative Bacchus brothers whom I befriended. There was Thakur, a pleasantly serious and intent older Indian student who wore short khaki trousers that exposed his very hairy legs about which he was teased mercilessly by co-Principal Alleyne. Peter Holder, a Georgetown boy, and Douglas Moore, who lived in Pouderoyen Village on West Bank Demerara, were popular. So too were Lloyd and Ovid Hercules. Among the boys were also Patrick Wellington, Lennox Browne and Vernon Browne (distinguished by their nicknames Light Brown and Dark Brown), Vernon Kirton whose protective mother vetoed his participation in our planned swimming escapades with the words, "Vernon, you can't go to swim until you learn to swim" and Compton Mitchell from East Bank Demerara who was full of good-natured mischief. Among the girls were Sheila Lucas, Agnes Mercurius, Carmen Kipling, Gwendolyn Northe, Negla Brandis, Pansy and June Sobers, Gloria Headley, Loretta Shepherd, Jean Alleyne, the Principal's fun-loving daughter, and Yvonne George. Yvonne George, who in later years married James Croal, is now a family friend in British Columbia, Canada. Walter Alexander, who graduated in 1957 and started teaching at the school in 1958, became a lifelong friend.

The first year was a bewildering experience. I was much younger than the cohort and knew little or nothing about the topics of their conversation. To make matters worse, I was a good enough cricketer to merit selection to the school team which had a big fast bowler from my class named Fitzroy Dorway. I was just too physically small to be entrusted with bowling or to bat higher than number 9. Nought not out, 1 not out, 2, maybe 3 not out was my fate in the cricket team.

Things changed markedly from the second year. I switched from cricket to football and became a goal scoring fixture in the school team at the inside right position (attacking mid-fielder in the modern parlance). Bertram Prescod, a classmate and fellow Kingstonian, organised the purchase of a pair of football boots at a discounted price. My friends Terrence Callender and Oscar Bayrd were full backs alongside Lennox Kilkenny Harding who had succeeded Julian Rhodius in the central defender role, Ovid Hercules as centre-forward and Ivor Vincent, the right winger with a tendency to overrun the touchline. Peter Holder, another classmate became the team captain when Julian Rhodius graduated. I continued to play cricket in my neighbourhood, but football became my passion. I played almost every day, sometimes early mornings and late afternoons. My last competitive game was in 1970 against a Georgetown Football Club youth team.

Trinidadian Edwin Carrington who had joined the CARIFTA Secretariat was in my team of "oldsters". The youths ran us ragged. There and then I had to make a choice, nightlife or football. Nightlife won out.

Because of football, my social life at school improved. My interest in calypso singing was another plus. I knew Sparrow's songs and entertained the class during breaks. This interest in calypsos was kindled in the home of my maternal aunt, Ivy Hamlet and her Tobagonian husband Daniel where Trinidadian calypsonians like the Mighty Spoiler, Growler, Cypher and Lord Melody ate, drank and sang during their post-Carnival visits to British Guyana.

The school made a week-long sporting tour to Bartica, a town at the mouth of the Mazuruni River in 1958. It was my first visit to Bartica. At that time, it was a town of narrow, unpaved roads, wooden buildings in varying states of disrepair, and a bad reputation. Small, independent miners (known as "pork-knockers") in the Mazuruni-Potaro region would endeavour after long sojourns in the mines to return with their hard-earned money to their families in Georgetown and elsewhere in Demerara and Berbice. Bartica was the transit town, a place of plenty booze and irresistible women. It is said that year after year, miners would get only as far as Bartica, returning to the mines penniless. It was not until late in the 1990s that, en route to Baganara in the Essequibo River with my son Tunji, I visited Bartica again. It looked very much the same with its reputation for badness intact. It was still a booze and booty trap for miners except that there were many more miners and many Brazilian women in town.

The boys competed against local teams in cricket and football. The girls competed in netball. Most of the tour was lively and exciting. Perhaps too exciting for our goalkeeper, who started a hot affair with a local woman. He would sneak out of our lodgings at night and return before dawn next day. We covered for him. She followed him to Georgetown when we returned. The relationship became too powerful a distraction from his studies. He dropped out of school and did not graduate. The tour ended on a sad note. In the last football match, our captain, Peter Holder, had his leg broken in an atrocious foul committed by an opposing player immediately after I had passed the ball to him in an attacking position. I remember vividly his anguished expression when on trying to rise from the ground he realised that his leg was broken. Peter was a very popular student, well-liked by classmates and teachers. Everyone was distraught by his injury. It was not properly treated in the Bartica public health service with the consequence that remedial work was required in Georgetown.

One of the boys in school formed a musical band called Chet and the Diamonds. It was very popular and performed commercially for a few years. I do not recall whether Chet finished school or dropped out to pursue a musical career.

I must admit that the standard high school curriculum was of little interest to me. I read selectively the prescribed literature but delved more deeply and extensively in books not on the list. English medieval and Elizabethan histories were part of the scholastic fare. Shakespeare did not excite much, Chaucer's *Canterbury Tales* somewhat more, but not as much as Jan Carew's *Black Midas* and the *Wild Coast*, Edgar Mittelholzer's *Corentyne Thunder* and the *Kaywana* series, and Sam Selvon's *Lonely Londoners*. I was probably too imaginative. I recall an essay writing assignment where the class was given a list of specific topics and also allowed chose one of our own. To the surprise of the teacher, I wrote a short story on the dog in Sputnik 2 which was launched in 1957. I guess most children would have written about space exploration, but I was more intrigued by the fate of the animal.

Latin, presided over by Principal Alleyne, was a particular problem. I enjoyed reading Homer's Iliad and a couple other works in Latin but hated the formal study of Latin grammar. The problem developed into a contest of will between me and the Principal which I lost in dramatic fashion when I accepted the choice offered to my class to do or not do Latin but was vetoed by him with the words: "Bourne, the offer does not extend to you. You shall do Latin." I accepted my fate, did Latin right up to the final exams in which I topped the class and then promptly jettisoned most of what I had learnt under duress. Or so I thought!

I graduated from secondary school in September1959, five years after I entered, with a University of Cambridge Senior School Certificate and no clue about what to do with my life. With Christmas around the corner and no money to purchase gifts for girlfriends, I accepted an offer from Principal Alleyne to teach the incoming class. I taught Latin, English Medieval History and Religious Knowledge. The stint did not last beyond a term. Principal Alleyne and I had another clash of wills, and I left the job. We encountered each other occasionally between 1961 and 1964. The meetings were always cordial and interspersed with discussions about politics in which by then I had a great interest and in which he was an accomplished political party activist who later won a seat in the general elections held in 1964 and became Speaker of the House of Assembly. In retrospect, with gratitude, I think that Principal Alleyne had taken it upon himself to guide a headstrong boy in whom he detected some potential.

An eighteen-year-old me at home in Guyana.

Co-Principal Randolph Emanuel Cheeks was a different kettle of fish. Unlike most teachers in private secondary schools, he had a university degree. He was self-important and overbearing. He was also unforgiving. This latter personality trait became evident in my last year of school. The boys in my class had learnt the nicknames of both Principals and the Deputy Principal. Co-Principal Alleyne's nickname was "Old Crow" in reference to the greying edges of his hair style. He wisely chose not to hear whenever it was said audibly in his presence. The Deputy Principal, Mr Alexander, was called "Pirate" because he wore a black eye patch. He never seemed offended. We discovered in our final year that Co-Principal Cheeks was nicknamed "Broom" for a reason we did not know. One day, out of annoyance, a boy in our final year class shouted the nickname in his presence. No one would identify the culprit despite Co-Principal Principal Cheeks' insistence over several weeks. As a result, he stopped teaching French Language to all the boys in the class for the duration of the school year and furthermore refused to write the customary letter of commendation for any of us. However, there must have been redeeming features of his character because on entering politics he was elected in 1961 and 1964 and was appointed as Minister of Local Government in 1964.

On 11 November 1999, I gave an address to a British Guiana Education Trust Reunion in Georgetown. I say Georgetown because by then with so many graduates of secondary schools having migrated to Canada, the United States and Britain, it was not uncommon for school reunions to be held in cities such as Toronto, New York and London. I ended my speech with by stating that I was acutely aware of the challenges before us; that when we were the bright young things of the 1950s, we could have taken comfort in Langston Hughes' *Youth* in which he wrote that the future is bright before us like a flame; but that now in the fullness of our maturity, we have a duty to make tomorrow bright like a flame for future generations.

EARLY VENTURES IN TEACHING

Apart from the one term stint at my alma mater, I had two ventures in teaching during my teenage years. One was at Montmartre High School about which I will recount some experiences in the next chapter. The other was an attempt in my mid-teens at teaching basic literacy to a young male several years older than me. The assignment was given to me by my Aunt Ivy whom he had made aware of a particular difficulty he faced, namely his inability to reply in writing to his girlfriend who had migrated to the United States and was understandably becoming very upset by his failure to respond. There were no phones available in those days. My task was to teach him to read and write and most importantly to write and mail his declarations of undying love. I did not really succeed with the first aspect but did spectacularly well with the second aspect, becoming for many months like the commissioned writer of love letters in Mario Vargas Llosa's *Aunt Julia and the Scriptwriter*.

FURTHER SECONDARY STUDIES, THE PUBLIC SERVICE AND THE GUIANA INTERIOR

In 1962, while working as a junior clerk in the Roads Division of the Ministry of Works and Hydraulics, I decided to prepare for the University of London General Certificate of Education Advanced Levels. I opted to do Economics, British Constitution and an eclectic combination of History subjects focussing on the European voyages of discovery in the New World. I ordered the relevant textbooks from a local bookseller, signed up for Wolsey Hall correspondence courses and engaged in self-study.

For a while, I sought guidance on British Constitution from Fred Wills, a prominent lawyer with a scholarly reputation and an avid cricketer to whom Lance McCaskie had introduced me. Fred would usually greet me at his Queenstown residence with the words, "Here comes Compton Bourne with a lean and hungry look". I quickly realised that from him I would learn more about local politics and social issues than about the British Constitution. Wills at the time was not on the best of terms with Forbes Burnham with whom he had shared a legal practice. Perhaps because of this, he spoke disparagingly of Burnham's lack of productivity and excessive claims on the revenues generated by the firm. Wills reconciled with Burnham in the 1970s, becoming Foreign and Justice Minister in 1975 until February 1978 when he resigned and became a Professor at Rutgers University in New Jersey, USA. Tyrone Ferguson (1999) wrote that Burnham requested his resignation in response to criticisms by senior and influential Foreign Ministry staffers like Rashleigh Jackson of his "operating style and personality deficiencies". Other accounts cite inadequate briefings of Guyana's diplomats and criticism of the country's unbalanced foreign policy. Rashleigh Jackson, who was then Guyana's Ambassador to the United Nations, was appointed as his replacement.

The decision to prepare for university education was an easy one made during my first few months in the Public Service. I observed that young people who entered the service with undergraduate university degrees did so at higher salary points than long serving senior clerks who had no university qualifications and that their career trajectory was steeper. In effect, I concluded that clerkship was a dead end which I should avoid. Fortunately, my immediate supervisor, Pryor Jones, was very understanding and supportive of my ambitions, defended me when I was seen studying in my spare time, and gave me intellectually challenging additional work such as abstracting articles on road design and construction in engineering journals. He also occasionally invited me to socialise with him and some of his peers. It was at his home that I first heard the tenor saxophonist Sonny Stitt who was widely regarded as Charlie Parker's heir in the bebop era of jazz.

My time in the Roads Division was interesting in other ways. Preliminary work was proceeding on the bridging of the Demerara River. Joe Holder was the engineer with primary responsibility for that project which was completed successfully with immense economic and social benefits, especially to the communities on the East and West Banks of the Demerara River, West Coast Demerara and East Coast Essequibo. Another major project was the construction of the Soesdyke to MacKenzie Highway. (MacKenzie was renamed Linden in the 1970s) The project was in the land surveying and design stages. On completion several years later, it substantially reduced travel time between Georgetown and the bauxite mining town of Linden-Wismar. Road travel became the norm since the journey was two hours long compared with four hours on the Georgetown-MacKenzie Ferry and because passenger capacity and freight capacity were limited only by the number and carrying capacities of motor vehicles.

I developed two lifelong friendships in the Roads Division. Victor and Noel Thompson were two brothers in training for professional qualification as land surveyors. Over the years, we lived simultaneously in countries other than Guyana, remained in contact when the countries of residence differed, and supported each other in our professional and family lives. It is through the Thompsons that I was first able to satisfy my desire to visit the Guyanese interior. Noel was in charge of a survey camp somewhere in the basically uninhabited territory between Soesdyke and MacKenzie; Victor was in charge of a survey camp on the fringe of MacKenzie. I spent a week in each camp. In Noel's camp, I learnt that the only sure way to avoid snakes sharing your bed at night was to build it a few feet above ground with whatever materials were at hand, in my case crocus bags and forked sticks, and that having live animals, especially dogs, in camp was an invitation to jaguars who ventured close at night. I learnt that on first entry, forests because of their canopy of tree cover always seem dark and that they always seem silent, but after one's eyes and ears adjust, one can see and hear all kinds of creatures. I learnt that the sap of some vines can be very corrosive or poisonous. In Noel's camp, I had a highly unusual experience. The guy in the camp bed next to me kept talking to me all night. He just would not let me sleep. Somewhat irritable next morning, I complained and was asked to be understanding of his situation. He was a reformed commercial assassin who was finally apprehended because he had not properly disposed of the body of his latest victim. It was reported that he tied the corpse onto logs with ropes and dumped it into a river but it became undone and was discovered floating on the surface. He was tried, defended by the famous Sir Lionel Luckhoo, and acquitted. His subsequent bouts of remorse and conscience kept him awake.

In Victor's camp, I learnt that if one's sense of smell is keen enough one can detect in good time the nearby presence of anacondas and boa constrictors, and that the stronger the smell, the bigger and more dangerous the snake. A lot of alcohol was imbibed in Victor's camp. When supplies ran out very late on Friday night, the men simply woke up the nearby vendor for replenishment. On the last night of my stay, I went into the town where I encountered a former student with whom I had had a major disagreement. Wanting to make amends, he invited me to have a beer with him. Much to my surprise, he ordered a full case of twelve bottles, most of which he drank. It made me think that MacKenzie-Wismar was an alcoholic place.

With my mother and sisters, British Columbia, June 2007.
L-R: Raulda, Mom, Me, Lynda and Dian.

My mother and my siblings in British Columbia, June 2017. Mother, seated, and from left, Lorna, Clement, Lynda, Raulda, Lyndon and Dian.

CHAPTER TWO

POLITICAL AWARENESS, 1953-1964

BRITISH TROOPS IN GEORGETOWN, 1953

My political awareness began with the sight of Welsh Fusiliers, a battalion of British troops marching through Kingston, my childhood neighbourhood on 8 October 1953 (one day after my 10th birthday). In retrospect, that event and what followed during the rest of that year and into the next year were the genesis of my anti-colonial sentiments.

The People's Progressive Party led by Cheddi Jagan had won the first elections under full adult suffrage in April 1953. The electoral turnout was massive; 75 per cent of eligible people voted. The PPP won eighteen of the 24 seats. Among its successful candidates were Forbes Burnham, Ashton Chase, Sydney King (re-named Eusi Kwayana later in life), and three women namely, Janet Jagan (Cheddi Jagan's wife), Jane Phillips-Gray and Jessie Burnham (sister of Forbes Burnham). The PPP immediately signalled its intention to seek self-government status, institute transformative changes in the rice industry, restructure the primary and secondary education system by removing church control of schools, repeal the Undesirable Publications Ordinance, and introduce a Labour Relations Bill to allow union recognition by majority vote of workers. The PPP also sought to deepen its relationship with communist countries and organisations.

The British Government responded by alleging that the PPP government, led by a communist clique which included the two Jagans and Sydney King, intended to turn the country into a communist state. On 8 October, the Governor, Sir Alfred Savage, implemented emergency powers granted to him by the British Government on 4 October, by bringing in the Welsh Fusiliers and Royal Marines and terminating the appointments of the PPP Ministers. On 9 October, he prorogued the House of Assembly and the State Council, which actions were tantamount to a suspension of the constitution.

As a young child, I had little knowledge or understanding of the political underpinnings and ramifications of what I witnessed. But I do recall the heated discussions among my parents and grandparents, and indeed in many neighbourhood households about their sense of injustice and imposition by the actions of the British Government. The perception of injustice and oppression were combined with palpable anger with the arbitrary arrests, detentions, geographical and residential confinement, imprisonment and sedition charges against PPP leaders, including Cheddi Jagan, Janet Jagan, Rory Westmaas, Sydney King, Martin Carter, Brindley Benn and Fred Bowman. Forbes Burnham was not among those detained. Jessie Burnham, his sister, in a pamphlet entitled "Beware My Brother" noted that he was the only PPP leader not to be arrested or detained by the colonial authorities and raised the intriguing question of whether he had collaborated with Governor Richard Savage in the suspension of the constitution.

I recall being quite perturbed by the presence of the troops and the assumption of superior status and claims in the society. I was not pleased by their encampment on the Eve Leary Parade Ground where I was accustomed to play cricket and football. I took a dim view of the scramble among the adult population, especially females, for financial and other favours from the troops. In my neighbourhood, I observed several upper middle-class women fraternising with soldiers, even marrying some of them, whose social status would have disqualified them if they were local men. Nonetheless, I was sad when two soldiers drowned while foolishly attempting to swim at the foot of the Kaieteur Falls. Kaieteur Falls, with a single drop of 251 metres and an average flow rate of 663 cubic metres per second, is four times higher than Niagara Falls and twice the height of Victoria Falls. It is evidently a very formidable proposition for even the best of swimmers. The route of the military funeral procession took it past the intersection of Duke Street and Barracks Street, so I was able to observe for the first time the solemnity of the drums and the slow march of the troops.

THE 1957 GENERAL ELECTIONS

General Elections on 27 August 1957 followed the end of the British installed Interim Government which had a record of non-achievement according to the local media and leaders of the business community.

An ironic feature of those elections was the participation of two political parties bearing the same main name: PPP (Jagan) and PPP (Burnham). The PPP of 1953 had split into two parts. Burnham had initiated claims to be leader of the united PPP as early as May 1953 and culminated his attempts on 13 February 1955 to replace Cheddi Jagan by using his position as Chairman to convene a meeting of the Party's Congress contrary to the Executive's decision to hold a conference rather than a congress. The meeting elected Burnham as Leader and Cheddi Jagan as Senior Vice-Chairman while Burnham's supporter Dr Latchmansingh was elected Chairman. It seemed as if Burnham's quest for leadership was accomplished. However, the party reacted by expelling him and his group at a congress in Buxton Village chaired by Sydney King. In March 1956, Burnham established a PPP (Burnham) with himself as Leader and other executive members including his sister Jessie Burnham, Aubrey Percival Alleyne, Jane Phillips-Gray and Lewis Evelyn Bobb (who decades later became my colleague and friend in Trinidad and Tobago). There was much confusion about the split in the PPP among the households in my neighbourhood. Presumably, many across the country were no less confused and perturbed. Most likely, this is one of the factors which led to only a 56 per cent turnout of the electorate.

The political parties contesting the elections in 1957 were the PPP (Jagan), the PPP (Burnham), the National Labour Front led by Lionel Luckhoo, the United Democratic Party led by John Carter and the Guiana National Party. Sydney King, apparently having become estranged from Cheddi Jagan, declined to contest the East Demerara seat on the PPP slate, choosing instead to oppose the substitute PPP candidate as an Independent candidate. Having lost, he subsequently joined the Burnham party.

It was during the elections campaign that I first saw Forbes Burnham. Lionel Luckhoo was holding a moderately attended political meeting on my street in the Georgetown North constituency. The candidates were Percival Cummings (United Democratic Party), who was favoured by my mother because of his work to advance the welfare of seamen, Andrew Jackson, the PPP (Burnham) candidate, and Lionel Luckhoo who headed the National Labour Front. At some point, Burnham turned up with a megaphone and mobilised neighbourhood children to disrupt the meeting by having them shout incessantly, "Luckhoo, you can't win. Licks like peas." I was not favourably impressed.

The elections were won by Jagan's PPP with nine of the fourteen seats. Burnham's PPP got three seats, the National Labour Front and the United Democratic Party one each. Lionel Luckhoo, Percival Cummings and John Carter failed to win the seats they contested. John Carter subsequently merged his party with Burnham's PPP to form the People's National Congress. Sydney King, who had broken ranks with Jagan's PPP and ran as an independent candidate for Central Demerara, lost narrowly with 43.8 per cent of votes compared with 49.7 per cent obtained by Balram Singh Rai, the PPP (Jagan) candidate.

During his period in office, Cheddi Jagan's government proceeded to pressure the commercial banks to change their personnel recruitment practices. The banks and major retail stores had practices which discriminated against Afro-Guianese and Indo-Guianese by restricting employment to people of Chinese and Portuguese ancestry. The government succeeded in getting the banks to hire Afro-Guianese and Indo-Guianese for the first time and changed dramatically the occupational prospects of members of those two ethnic groups.

GHANA'S INDEPENDENCE DAY, 1957

On 6 March 1957, Ghana became constitutionally independent from Britain. The new country named Ghana was formed by the unification of the separate regions/nationalities of the Gold Coast, Ashanti, Northern Territories, and Togoland. The Gold Coast was a British Colony with Kwame Nkrumah as its Prime Minister since 1952, Ashanti was ruled by a British Governor, the Northern Territories were a British Protectorate until when it was annexed under the Ghana Independence Act in 1957, and Togoland was under a British-administered United Nations Trusteeship until 1957 when by majority vote it decided to join Ghana.

Principal Alleyne on the morning of Ghana's independence convened an assembly of the entire school and gave a stirring speech about the significance of the event. He spoke about Nkrumah's struggle for independence, his year-long imprisonment, during which time he was elected as a Member of Parliament, his release from prison to become leader of government business and then Prime Minister of the Gold Coast in 1952. He spoke about how Ghana's achievement should motivate other colonies, especially those in the Caribbean, to pursue their quest for political independence from Britain. Principal Alleyne's remarks resonated with my nascent nationalist sentiments.

SOCIALLY CONSCIOUS READING

Around about 1958, I started participating in an intellectual discussion group started by Alfred Skeete (then known as Alfred Jadunauth), a brilliantly charismatic teacher at British Guiana Education Trust. Outside of school hours, he engaged a select group of students from that school and other secondary schools in wide-ranging discussions of literature and society. We were introduced to fiction with a distinctly socially conscious orientation. From those times, literature for me became a source of entertainment as well as a means of understanding the human condition and society.

The Caribbean writings included the Jamaican Roger Mais's *Brother Man* published in 1954, Neville Dawes' (also from Jamaica) *The Last Enchantment* published in 1960 and Jan Carew's *The Wild Coast* published in 1958. Strangely, Guyanese writer Wilson Harris did not get on my reading list until about 1963 when with considerable difficulty I read his *Palace of the Peacock* published in 1960 and managed with slightly less difficulty his later publications, *The Whole Armour* and *The Secret Ladder*. Prominent among the readings in American fiction were John Steinbeck's *Grapes of Wrath*, *Cannery Row* and *Of Mice and Men* as well as Erskine Caldwell's *Tobacco Road*. These novels dealt with the human costs of the Great Depression of 1929-1933, but it was Horace McCoy's *They Shoot Horses Don't They?* which I had discovered independently that really touched my soul. McCoy told the story of a couple participating in a dance marathon. Dance marathons were a competitive form of entertainment which were popular in the depression years because they provided much needed food and shelter to competitors and spectators and an opportunity for the last couple standing to win a cash prize. A marathon could last weeks. In the story, the female participant having reached the limit of her physical and mental resources asked her partner to end her suffering by shooting her. "They shoot horses, don't they?" was her persuasive response to his initial demurral.

I struggled through the 700 pages of *Crime and Punishment*, the highly regarded novel by the great Russian writer Fyodor Dostoevsky. This novel examined the effects of extreme poverty on an ambitious young man who wished to resume his legal studies, his family and his female friend. The young man murdered a pawnbroker to obtain money to alleviate his poverty, his sister is married off by her father to a wealthy suitor, and his female friend earned her living as a prostitute.

On my own initiative, I read Albert Camus's *The Rebel* with special attention to the sections in the chapter entitled "Historical Rebellion" where Camus dealt with "State Terrorism and Irrational Terror" (exemplified by Mussolini and Hitler) and with "State Terrorism and Rational Terror" focussing on Karl Marx's (and Friedrich Engels) revolutionary prophesy in *The Communist Manifesto*, its antecedents in Auguste Comte, and on Vladimir Lenin's *The State and Revolution*.

I also read Simone de Beauvoir's *The Second Sex*, the classic literary foundation novel on women's rights and feminism. De Beauvoir challenged the conception of woman as relative to man rather than as a person of separate humanity, argued that women's social and economic roles have been determined by the nature of their participation in the economic system, their entrapment in reproductive slavery, and by men's commitment to patrimony. She cited the Church, except for German Lutheranism, as an oppressor of women. Trade union participation, birth control and suffrage were seen as liberating influences. De Beauvoir concluded that men and women will only become equal when they both "unequivocally affirm their brotherhood."

My grandfather Hutson, for whom I usually borrowed Western cowboy novels from the Georgetown Public Library, saw me with *The Second Sex* and decided to read it. We subsequently had several discussions of the radical ideas it contained; me, the secondary school graduate and my grandfather who had not had the opportunity to proceed beyond primary school. That interaction between me and him taught me not to underestimate the wide interests of the uneducated elderly and their capacity to grasp relatively abstract and advanced philosophical ideas.

THE CUBAN REVOLUTION, 1959

In January 1959, Fidel Castro and his guerrilla army overthrew the government of President Fulgencio Batista. Batista fled to the Dominican Republic on 1 January and on 8 January, a provisional government was installed with Fidel Castro as Prime Minister. This was electrifying news in British Guiana, especially to the intellectual group to which I belonged. The defeat of Batista came after an unsuccessful attack on the Moncado Barracks in Santiago on 26 July 1953, the imprisonment and trial of Fidel Castro and his brother Raoul Castro from 1953-1955 when they were granted amnesty, their regrouping in Mexico and enlistment of Ernesto 'Che' Guevara, and the invasion of Cuba by them on 2 December 1956.

During his trial in 1953, Fidel Castro in his defence made an unrepentant speech to the judges which impressed my group tremendously. We listened numerous times to the recorded English language version despite its two hours length. Entitled "History Will Absolve Me", the speech identified five revolutionary laws which would be implemented immediately after the capture of the Moncada Barracks. First, proclamation of the 1940 Constitution. Second, granting of non-transferable and non-mortgageable ownership of land to tenant and sub-tenant farmers, leases, share-croppers and squatters. Third, granting workers and employees the right to a 30 per cent share in profits in large industrial, mercantile, mining and sugar milling enterprises. Fourth, granting all sugar planters the right to a 55 per cent share of sugar production and a minimum grant to all small tenant farmers. Fifth, confiscation of all holdings and illegal gains. Fidel Castro declared: "The problem of the land, the problem of industrialisation, the problem of housing, the problem of unemployment, the problem of education and the problem of the people's health: these are the six problems we would take immediate steps to solve, along with restoration of civil liberties and political democracy." Given the inequities of resource allocation and material deprivation in British Guiana these revolutionary laws resonated with us, however grand and problematic they seem in retrospect.

Fidel Castro referred to ecclesiastical, moral and political philosophers, the English Revolution of 1668, the American Revolution of 1775 and the French Revolution of 1789 to justify rebellion against tyranny and injustice. He quoted the French Declaration of the Rights of Man: "When the government violates the rights of the people, insurrection is for them the most sacred of rights and the most imperative of duties."

He concluded: "I do not fear prison ... Condemn me. It does not matter. History will absolve me."

MONTMARTRE HIGH SCHOOL

Alfred Jadunauth and Walter Alexander started Montmartre High School in 1960. Among its teachers were Desmond Shepherd and Ovid Edwards. I, too, taught there for a couple of years before joining the civil service in 1962.

Its origin was an experiment started in 1959 in providing accelerated education (two years) to General Certificate of Education level to working young men who had not had the benefit of secondary education. It was akin to a human development laboratory. The few students came from a variety of labouring jobs, including on the Georgetown docks. The experiment was successful. Students completed their course of study. Some went on to further studies, ultimately becoming professionals. Montmartre High School was then established, first on Robb Street and subsequently on South Road, Georgetown to provide secondary education opportunities for children from low income and lower middle-income households. With increasingly favourable examination results, it gained popularity. My brother, Lyndon, and my sister, Lynda, attended the school. Graduates, in later life, having established themselves in various professions in Guyana, the Caribbean, Canada and the US, have paid tribute to the school for providing them with an education foundation they might not have been able to obtain otherwise.

The school premises also served as a venue for informal night and weekend meetings of the discussion group which had started since 1958. Members included Alfred Jaddunath Skeete, Ovid Edwards, Sam London, Lance McCaskie, William Brathwaite (Willy Braf to distinguish him from his older brother, the singer Johnny Braf), Peter McDonald and Michael Forde. In 1962, some of them left the country on scholarships provided by the PPP. Alfred, who was newly-wed, went to East Germany accompanied by his wife, Jean. Peter McDonald and Michael Forde went to Cuba. Peter McDonald later became a Marine Surveyor. Sam London became a Civil Engineer and worked at the Caribbean Development Bank in Barbados until retirement. William Brathwaite became a Forestry Manager. Ovid Edwards, who was my close friend, had a variety of occupations, such as educator, information specialist and newspaper reporter in his long career. Walter Alexander another close friend, after departing from Montmartre, went on to establish himself as one of the distinguished educators in the government secondary school system and as an authoritative and well-regarded educational administrator.

THE 1961 GENERAL ELECTION

The general elections on 21 August 1961 were contested by three political parties. The PPP still led by Cheddi Jagan contested 29 of the 35 seats in contention. The PNC led by Forbes Burnham contested all 35 seats. The United Democratic Party which under the leadership of John Carter had fought the 1957 elections and won only one of fourteen seats was integrated into Burnham's PNC in March 1959 and its leaders became part of the PNC's Executive Committee. The third party in the elections mix was the United Force led by a successful businessman, Peter D'Aguiar, which had also won only one seat in the 1957 elections. The United Force contested 34 seats.

There was a falling out in the PNC on the eve of the elections. Burnham had on 15 July 1961 unequivocally expressed support for British Guiana constitutional independence from Britain, regardless of which party won the elections. Sydney King, who had joined the PNC after the 1957 general elections, publicly opposed Burnham's position on the grounds that it was dangerous to the African people and would help Jagan secure British Guiana's constitutional independence from Britain. The PNC leader responded to King's frontal attack by expelling him on 30 July 1961.

Several things struck me about the elections campaign. First, the PPP's slate of candidates was once again more ethnically diverse than the PNC's slate of candidates. My next observation from attending political meetings in various Georgetown constituencies and constituencies on East Coast Demerara/West Coast Berbice was that the PPP attracted very large crowds in the rural areas, the PNC likewise in its traditional Georgetown strongholds, and that the United Force was mounting a strong challenge in a few Georgetown constituencies. Third, the PPP and the PNC parachuted into the elections diaspora people they thought would help their cause. The PPP brought in Ram John Holder, a singer and actor resident in Britain. The PNC brought in Dr Rawle Farley, an accomplished Economics faculty member at the University College of the West Indies in Jamaica. Farley added some intellectual weight to the PNC platform. I am not sure what Ram John Holder contributed to the PPP platform other than his stage presence, but he did capture 24.9 per cent of the votes in a losing cause in Georgetown South. Fourth, as if signalling the underlying ethnic dynamic of the elections contest between the PPP and the PNC, Laurence Mann, an African candidate for the PPP in the Mahaicony/Mahaica/Demerara Coast East constituency was often introduced on the platform as "Lallmansingh", as I myself witnessed at one of those meetings.

The PPP won twenty of the 35 seats, PNC 11, and United Force 4. Among the Afro-Guianese winning seats for the PPP were George Bowman, Victor Downer, Laurence Mann, Brindley Benn, C.R. Jacobs, George Henry, and Gladstone Wilson. Laurence Mann was made a Junior Minister of Education but resigned within a short period of time and left the country under a cloud of suspicion as to whether he had defected to Burnham's PNC. There was one Indo-Guianese among the PNC's successful candidates.

The PPP victory brought to the fore simmering ethnic interpretations and animosities. Some PPP supporters along the routes of victory motorcades could be heard shouting, "We pon top" (We are on top), clearly interpreting the party's victory as an ethnic victory despite the leaders' projection of ethnic inclusivity through the diversity of successful candidates. On the African, pro-PNC side, Sydney King and H.H. Nicholson formed the Society for Racial Equality which in the belief that Africans would become slaves of East Indians, advocated partitioning of the country into three zones: an African Zone for Africans, an Indian Zone for Indians, and a Free Zone for whosoever wanted to live with other races.

After the elections, the PNC held its Annual Congress at my old high school, the British Guiana Education Trust, on Charlotte Street,

Georgetown. I was on the street outside the congress venue the evening when the congress ended in absolute mayhem. Dr Rawle Farley, motivated by his popularity during the elections campaign and his success in mediating among internal party factions, and perhaps encouraged by some influential members of the party, challenged Forbes Burnham for the leadership position. The meeting broke up in disarray without a formal vote being taken. John Carter's motor car which was parked on the street outside the venue was vandalised. This caused me to think that some PNC members loyal to Forbes Burnham associated John Carter with Farley's challenge to Burnham's leadership. Dr Farley left the country, never to be seen again in British Guiana's politics.

THE KALDOR BUDGET, 1962

The "Kaldor Budget" laid in the House of Assembly on 31 January 1962 became a flashpoint for organised urban protests against the PPP government. Nicholas Kaldor, an eminent British economist and fiscal expert, had been commissioned by the Government to assist its budget preparations. He had been invited similarly by Nehru to India in the 1950s and by Nkrumah to Ghana. The budget proposed a wealth tax; a gift tax to prevent evasion of death duties; introduction of a compulsory saving levy; investment of the proceeds of the compulsory savings levy in tax-free, interest-bearing government bonds; and a direct tax on luxuries and semi-luxuries.

The budget proposals were strongly opposed by the opposition parties, by the business community which was allied to the United Force party led by Peter D'Aguiar, by the urban-based trade unions which were closely allied to the Peoples National Congress led by Forbes Burnham, and by many households.

To my knowledge, it was the compulsory savings levy which generated the most disquiet among households. They thought it meant loss of control over the disposition of their incomes and harboured doubts about redemption of government bonds which had never previously been issued for investment by the public in British Guiana.

Street demonstrations became prevalent. Leaders of the opposition political parties and trade unions were visible in some of them. They culminated on 16 February with looting and acts of arson against business premises on major shopping streets in Georgetown such as Regent Street, Camp Street, High Street and Water Street and the Stabroek Market, the largest of the three municipal markets in the city. It was later estimated that

56 buildings were destroyed, 66 damaged and looted, and 21 damaged. Market stalls were also looted and damaged. A few vehicles were destroyed by fire. A senior police officer died from gunshot wounds, four looters were killed, and 41 people injured. As a bystander, I witnessed several of the demonstrations and heard volleys of gunfire, including the events on 16 February ("Black Friday" as it was later named). Order was finally restored late on 16 February when British troops based at Atkinson Field, twenty odd miles distant from Georgetown, arrived at the request of Governor Sir Ralph Grey.

A Commission of Enquiry into the disturbances was established on 11 May 1962. Its members were Sir Henry Wyn-Parry, a British High Court Judge, as Chairman, Ghanian Sir E.O. Asafu-Adjaye, and Justice G. Khosla of India. The Commission conducted hearings from 21 May to 28 June. People interviewed included trade union leaders, Forbes Burnham and Peter D'Aguiar. They concluded that the trade union leaders acted to incite workers against the government and that the Chamber of Commerce exhibited a lack of responsibility. They criticised Peter D'Aguiar for falsely claiming that a child had been killed to inflame public passions. They concluded that: "The real motive behind Mr Burnham's assault was a desire to assert himself in public life and establish a more important and rewarding position for himself by bringing about Dr Jagan's downfall." They concluded that he had roused the crowd to a frenzy and pointed them to unlawful action by declaring on 15 February that, "Government could not be got rid of by merely saying 'Resign' or 'Down with Jagan'". These are useful slogans, but more than slogans are required in the present circumstances." The Commission considered Burnham's explanation of his refusal to assist in restoring order, especially his statement, "We also considered it ill-advised to go and tell the people to desist from what they were doing when we had nothing to do with the starting of it. The man who calls off the dog owns the dog." They concluded that he was, "callous and remorseless".

I encountered Nicholas Kaldor, who was by then Lord Kaldor in the British Houses of Parliament, in Caracas, Venezuela, late in the 1970s and asked him what he then thought about the hostile reaction to his proposals in Guyana, and indeed in India and Ghana. His response is best summarised in the title of the paper he published in the journal Foreign Affairs in 1963: "Will Underdeveloped Countries Learn to Tax?"

THE LONG STRIKE, APRIL-JULY 1963

The PPP Government published on 25 March 1963 a draft Labour Relations Bill which would allow workers to choose their representative trade union by secret ballot. The Bill, unsuccessfully introduced before the suspension of the Constitution in 1953, was patterned on existing US legislation. Despite being on the face of it quite reasonable, it was instantly opposed by the umbrella Trade Union Council which had been an active opponent of the Kaldor Budget the year previously. A plausible reason for their opposition is that they interpreted the Bill as an attempt by the PPP to gain recognition of its favoured trade union, the Guyana Agricultural Workers Union, in displacement of the recognised union, the Manpower Citizens Association whose President, Richard Ishmael, was at that time also President of the Trades Union Council. However, other reasons were publicly given, such as non-consultation prior to dissemination, too much power to control the unions, and that the Bill was communist in character.

A country wide general strike began on 18 April and ended on 8 July. This was the longest strike in the country's history. Many businesses were closed, the public service although remaining in operation, was denuded of staff, international travel and international trade were disrupted. Curtailment of port operations created shortages in the supply of many consumer goods, including food, although supply by Indian farmers who did not support the strike helped to alleviate some of the food shortages. Sugar workers did not support the strike, but production of sugar was adversely affected by closure of the sugar factories. Rice production was severely hampered by reductions in critical inputs such as imported fuel.

The strike was soon accompanied by violent attacks on those who did not support it, invasion and/or dynamiting of some public buildings, and a general atmosphere of intimidation and terror. No event or place was sacrosanct. The funeral service of Claude Christian, the Minister of Home Affairs, at the Brickdam Cathedral was the scene of opposition crowd protests. Matters got worse at his interment in Le Repentir Cemetery where mourners were attacked. A young Indian man known to the group at Montmartre High School was beaten and had to run to us for refuge that evening.

I was at work in the Ministry of Works and Hydraulics on Fort Street one afternoon when it was invaded by a mob, one of whom attempted to relieve me of my wristwatch. I resisted. However, I was more concerned to protect a large can of biscuits that I had purchased with difficulty that morning. The biscuits were essential for feeding my household; I could not afford to lose them. Often during the strike, I would be the one who would succeed in purchasing scarce, irregularly available food item from roadside produce vendors I encountered on my bicycle journey through the city to our home in East Ruimveldt.

By the time the strike ended on 8 July, eleven people were dead, many injured, and nineteen buildings in Georgetown bombed.

ITABO

ITABO was a kind of coffee house established in 1962 sometime after the Kaldor Budget riots. It was the brainchild of Steve DeCastro, a recently graduated engineer from the University of Bristol, England who had returned to take up a job with the Bookers enterprises. Other foundation members, in addition to me, included Brian Rodway, Bonnie Paul, Tom Dalgetty, Lance McCaskie, Clairmonte Taitt, and Clairmonte Moore with whom I played football and in whose apartment on Parade Street, Kingston, I spent countless hours listening to jazz. Helen Taitt, Clairmonte Taitt's sister who danced ballet, was an occasional visitor.

ITABO was a venue for eclectic formal and informal discussions, listening to recorded music (mainly jazz and blues) and talks by local and visiting cultural and intellectual personalities. Rex Nettleford, a University of the West Indies (UWI) academic who was already a distinguished personage in trade union education, extra-mural studies, and dance theatre was an early visitor. ITABO attracted many young people from middle-class Georgetown families initially but after a while its image was damaged by PNC-inspired propaganda that it was a PPP front, or a communist entity absurdly evidenced by the Castro-style beards sported by some of its members (especially Steve DeCastro who looked like Fidel Castro). Attempts were made by unknown people to bomb and set fire to ITABO on two occasions.

During the ITABO period, I began to venture out at night in the company of the older guys into under-class areas of Georgetown, such as Tiger Bay and Albouystown. The world of the lumpen proletariat in the terminology of Andre Gunder Frank was a different world to the one I knew. Economic existence was precarious, revolving around occasional jobs, petty crime and prostitution. People drank hard liquor and Banks beer copiously, engaged in loud, ribald conversations and were easily roused to violence. The social skill-set for survival in those neighbourhoods was quite different from what was required in the middle-class districts in Georgetown. For me, it was a broadening of my education and opportunity to become aware of a generally unacknowledged aspect of life in British Guiana.

Georgetown in those days also had what were called speakeasies in the Prohibition era in the United States. They were outwardly large homes located in residential districts, but their real function was sale of alcoholic beverages and sexual encounters. Rum was served in teacups to maintain the pretence of law-abiding beverages. My childhood friend, Mortimer Walters, was a habitué of one of the establishments located on South Road. The tradition continued into the 1970s.

Engaging in late night expeditions necessitated a practical decision about the route I would bicycle to my home in East Ruimveldt Housing Scheme where we had moved during my middle years in high school. I had made lots of friends in the neighbourhood, including Roland Moe, Michael Blackman, Joy Primo, and Pinky and Claudette Forde, but most of my leisure time was spent in Georgetown. The choice of route home was between the much longer route along Sussex Street adjacent to the Le Repentir Cemetery or the short route proceeding from Cemetery Road directly through the cemetery. Super-rationalist as I then was and unafraid of ghosts rising from their tombs and graves, I invariably took the short route. In the afternoon, I would stop at my Aunt Evelyn and Uncle Ivelaw Gravesande's home on Cemetery Road for food, playful fun with my cousins (Megan, Clyde and Barbara), conversation mainly with Aunt Evelyn, and recorded jazz. By then Uncle Ivelaw trusted me to carefully handle his quite large collection, as indeed I was by Mrs Muriel Walcott (later Lady Walcott), the spouse of cricketing great Sir Clyde Walcott, who was in charge of the United States Information Service and kindly indulged my growing appreciation of jazz by lending me albums from the USIS collection.

There was ample opportunity in Georgetown in those times to listen to all kinds of live performances by visiting artistes from the US. In the Queen's College auditorium, I heard Louis Armstrong and his band as well as Duke Ellington and his band. At the Strand Cinema, I heard the original Platters and at the Empire Cinema, I heard Johnny Mathis in his prime. At the League of Coloured Peoples annual fair at the Malteenoes Sports Club ground in Thomas Lands, I heard Brook Benton who when the local band was making a mess while he rendered his hit song 'Ties that Bind' asked them to desist from playing. "I will sing my song alone", I recall him saying, which he did wonderfully to the applause of the audience. To be fair to the band, it was a difficult musical composition. At the same venue, I also saw

Laverne Baker in her peak R&B years. At ITABO, the music was usually recorded jazz renditions by popular performers like Miles Davis, Stan Getz, and Dave Brubeck but also blues, especially by Bill Bronsky.

Steve DeCastro left British Guiana around June 1963 to study for an MSc degree in Operations Research at the University of Birmingham. Because the Eighty Day General Strike had not ended, he travelled to Port of Spain, Trinidad, on a schooner and then by plane to England. Activities continued normally that year and into 1964. I, myself, departed for England in August 1964, by plane instead of schooner to Port of Spain where I boarded the *MV Begonia* bound for Southampton.

Two unusual events at ITABO engraved themselves on my memory. One is witnessing post-traumatic stress disorder (PTSD) in a veteran of World War II. PTSD did not become a subject for serious medical and sociological analysis and treatment until American soldiers began returning from the Vietnam War in the 1970s. One night, a regular visitor suddenly dropped to the floor and with guttural grunts began propelling himself by his elbows and knees. Initially, I thought he was clowning but when I looked closely at him, I saw his entire body drenched in sweat, his contorted facial expressions and desperation in his eyes. Something, maybe some disturbing noise, had transported him mentally to some battlefield in Europe. He apologised when he recovered but never explained.

The second is visits from a man named Dickey Howard who tried to sell me a camera. Dickey was an inveterate confidence trickster. He was recently out of prison for fraudulently obtaining accommodation and related services from the Tower Hotel located less than 200 metres away from the Demerara Bauxite Company Headquarters on Main Street, Georgetown. Dickey had convinced the hotel management that he was a senior employee of the company, normally resident at the mining operations in McKenzie/Wismar, but temporarily recalled to Georgetown for company business. "You can verify by just phoning the company headquarters next door", he told them. By the time they did get around to phoning, Dickey had racked up thousands of dollars in unpayable debts. It is doubtful that Dickey Howard reformed despite his engagement with ITABO. Much to my surprise, while I was a student at the University of Birmingham, I read in a Guyana newspaper that Dickey (who had never done an honest day's work in his life) had led a delegation of gold miners to see Prime Minister Burnham and had privately convinced him that Guyana troops on the Venezuelan border had faulty intelligence and could not be trusted. I heard that Burnham later enlisted him in the Guyana Defence Force. In 1970/71,

I read about Dickey Howard once more in a Guyana newspaper. His corpse had been found on the coastal road in East Coast Demerara apparently run over by a heavy vehicle. I could not help wondering whether Dickey had tried to flip the Venezuela script and had failed on his last confidence trick.

THE UNDECLARED CIVIL WAR OF 1964

It was almost as if the country had been gradually prepared for increasing levels of political violence. In retrospect, the Kaldor Budget riots in February 1962 seemed like a dress rehearsal for the larger riots and violent demonstrations of 1963 to be followed by a major racial, violent political upheaval in 1964.

The Guiana Agricultural Workers Union which was supportive of the PPP called a country-wide strike on 17 February 1964. By March, this had led to violence between striking Indian workers on sugar estates and African strike breakers hired to protect estate property.

Quite quickly the situation escalated to one in which racially directed assaults and destruction of household and business property were committed by Indian and African ethnic groups against each other in East Coast Demerara, West Coast Demerara, McKenzie/Wismar and in Georgetown. Ethnic minorities in many communities fearing loss of life and arson to dwellings were forced to abandon their homes and resettle in other communities where they were the ethnic majority. Financial losses, losses of jobs and disruption of children's schooling were often immediate consequences of the forced resettlement. People affected by these forced resettlements remained deeply aggrieved decades later as I have learnt from accounts by both Afro-Guyanese (including my spouse) and Indo-Guyanese. There was sporadic violence in Georgetown. One night, as I neared the home of my friend Ovid Edwards at 128 Regent Street where I was a frequent visitor, I witnessed a mob, incited by women, set fire to an Indian man. Casualties were high. The Police Service estimated that by the end of the conflict in August 1964, 176 people had been killed and more than 900 people injured. An estimated 1425 buildings were destroyed by fire. Fifteen thousand people had been displaced.

The disturbances ("The Troubles" the Irish would have termed them) seemed to me like an organised quasi-military operation conducted by both the PPP and the PNC. Some PPP personnel known to me were alleged to be implicated in the bombing of the *MV Chapman*, a Demerara River boat conveying Afro-Guyanese workers to McKenzie-Wismar and in some of the bombings in Georgetown. Additionally, Michael Forde who had returned from his training in Cuba was constantly being arrested and released without charge by the police. He told me in response to my query about this experience that the police believed that he had been trained in explosives and insurgency tactics in Cuba and may have been responsible for some of the Georgetown bombings. On 17July, 1964 Michael Forde died while removing a bomb that had placed by a PNC operative in the Progressive Bookshop housed in Freedom House, the PPP's Headquarters building on Robb Street, Georgetown. It is quite possible that he undertook that task because he had expertise in the handling of explosives. On the PNC side, as early as May 1963, a police raid on the party's headquarters, Congress Place, had unearthed large amounts of arms and ammunition, chemicals which could be used for explosives, and documents, one of which detailed plans for overthrowing the government and identified Comrade Van Genderen as the person in charge answerable directly to Burnham. Furthermore, it was whispered in family circles that a good friend of my grandparents who had retired from the police service as a senior officer was reputed to be the head of the PNC's armed wing under the code name of "The Old Man".

Many activists and combatants on both sides were arrested by the authorities and imprisoned without trial in the remote Sibley Hall Prison on the Mazaruni River. A few, including a young man who the PNC leadership believed had planted the bomb on the MV Chapman, fled the country before the crackdown. The prison was surrounded by a jungle. Escape was not a reasonable contemplation. In 1970, after I returned to Guyana on completion of studies in England, my wife and I held a party at our home in Bel Air Park for friends from the old days. Present were some who had spent time in detention in Sibley Hall. Liberal helpings of rum loosened their spirits and tongues, leading to declarations and denials of who did what in that fateful period between February and August 1964 and who sold out their comrades for favours in the prison.

CHAPTER THREE

STUDYING ECONOMICS AND LIVING IN ENGLAND, 1964-1969

UNDERGRADUATE STUDIES IN LONDON

I left British Guiana in September 1964 to pursue undergraduate studies in England. In 1963, I had been offered a place at Leeds University but did not take it up because my funding plans did not materialise. I had been in discussions with the Ministry of Education about a grant/loan over several months and thought there was agreement. However, when I went to finalise the matter, the cordial Education Officer with whom I had been in face-to-face discussions on several occasions, suddenly could not remember me and when I jogged her memory, my file could not be found. She advised that I proceed to England while matters were sorted out. I had no confidence that if I was not remembered while I was present in British Guiana, I would be remembered when I was in far-away England. I therefore did not accept her advice.

My alternative course of action was to self-finance my studies in the following year with savings from salary earned at the Ministry of Works and Hydraulics. My grandmother pleasantly surprised me with a gift of the money I had been paying her for lunch during the 30 months I worked at the Ministry. She said she had not wanted the money but thought that the time would come when it would be very helpful to me. With a bank draft for the princely sum of one thousand pounds sterling in my possession, I set off for England and entered Woolwich Polytechnic which my maternal uncle, Whitney Hutson, had recommended as a good, inexpensive institution to study for the University of London BSc (Economics) degree. He, himself, was resident in London and studying part-time for his professional qualifications in structural engineering.

I travelled to Port of Spain by air and then embarked the *MV Begonia* to Southampton, England. Cabin mates included Billy Stewart from British Guiana and two Trinidadians Ben and "Stretch". There were a few

Trinidadian young women on board who were on their way to UK nursing schools. There was instant hostility between the Jamaican men who had boarded the ship previously in Kingston and the Trinidadian men, so much so that they had to be reassigned to different decks to minimise conflict. It was perhaps residual antagonisms from the breakup of the West Indies Federation or rivalry for West Indian leadership. The voyage took twelve days with stops in Tenerife in the Canary Islands and Vigo, a Spanish port. We experienced a few days of a tropical cyclone but otherwise the trip was enjoyable, made particularly so by socialising with the Trini girls and drinking cognac with the seamen at their bar in the bowels of the ship.

Woolwich Polytechnic established in 1890 and located near the Woolwich Arsenal was the second oldest polytechnic in England. In 1907, it became an institution with recognised teachers in the University of London. Woolwich Polytechnic became Thames Polytechnic in 1970 and then the University of Greenwich in 1992. Ironically, I was a member of a team appointed by the Accreditation Council of Trinidad and Tobago to evaluate the University of Greenwich in 2012.

I met several West Indians at Woolwich. My seniors by two years were David Fletcher from Grenada and Michael Agostini from British Guiana. My cohort included Carlton Cunningham of Jamaican parentage. David Shorey from Barbados was in the year after me. On graduation, David Fletcher returned to Grenada where he became a senior civil servant before dying prematurely. Michael Agostini returned to Guyana to work as an economist in the government service for many years before accepting employment at the Inter-American Development Bank in Washington, D.C. Carlton Cunningham took up a job with Ford Motor Factory in England before migrating to Jamaica around 1975 to work with the Jamaican government. David Shorey pursued further studies for a professional accountancy qualification and entered the commercial and public utilities sectors in Barbados. In those days, West Indian graduates were highly motivated to return to their native lands.

A non-West Indian classmate with whom I developed a close friendship was George Zis. He was a Greek whose father was exiled as a communist from Greece and settled in Khartoum, Sudan. George himself was a communist nationalist who travelled frequently to Greece and Khartoum. George, upon completing the undergraduate degree, completed an MA degree in Economics at the University of Manchester in 1970. After a stint working as Research Assistant with the Inflation Workshop run by David Laidler and Michael Parkin, he became a Lecturer at the same university.

He moved to Salford University in 1980 and then to Manchester Metropolitan University where he ended his academic career as Professor and Head of Department.

George Zis and I were mentored at Woolwich by the gentlemanly Stephen F. Frowen who taught monetary economics. He was born as Horst Otto Frowein in Germany but migrated to the United Kingdom to escape the Nazi regime. Overcoming what must have been major difficulties of establishing a career in post-War Britain, he became an influential figure in monetary systems and banking, serving for many years as the Editor of *The Banker* magazine, Senior Lecturer at University of Surrey and Honorary Fellow at University of Cambridge and University College London. Stephen Frowen invited us to dinner at his private members club, the Reform Club, one evening. The club at that time was a male-only establishment founded since 1836. It had many leading conservative politicians and literary figures, including Sir Winston Churchill, Joseph Chamberlain, Henry James and even the infamous spy Guy Burgess, as its members. Nonetheless the Reform Club was known to be an institution welcoming of people with progressive political views.

Part I of the University of London BSc degree structure required candidates to take five subjects in their first year. I chose Psychology and English Legal Institutions alongside the three compulsory subjects, Economics, Introduction to Politics and Introductory Statistics. Introduction to Politics taught me much about the Westminster system of government, the organisation of British political parties and voting behaviour. I elected to do a discussion paper on nationalism thinking that it would be relevant to my own nationalist orientation. That was not the case. What I learnt from reading Elie Kedourie's book on nationalism and other material was that several European countries such as Yugoslavia, Czechoslovakia and Hungary were amalgamations of tribes. It is interesting to consider that tribal formations re-established themselves in the guise of new nations such as Estonia and Lithuania when the USSR broke up. For Part II of the degree, candidates were examined in eight subjects at the end of the three years of their study for the degree. There were no examinations in the second year. I studied international economic history, monetary economics, monetary history, microeconomics, macroeconomics, applied economics, economic statistics and Greek and modern political thought.

I spent a fair amount of time reading journals at the University of London Senate House Library. It was there that I discovered Owen Jefferson's comprehensive Oxford University DPhil thesis on the Jamaican economy,

Norman Girvan's highly stimulating University of London PhD thesis on Foreign Capital and Economic Underdevelopment in Jamaica, and Clive Yolande Thomas's University of London PhD thesis "Monetary and Financial Arrangements in a Dependent Monetary Economy: A Study of British Guiana, 1945-1962". William Demas' seminal monograph entitled The Economics of Development in Small Countries was also an important introduction to the economic development literature. These writings started my groundings in the economics of the Caribbean, whetted my appetite for more material and stirred a desire to research the Caribbean myself.

LIFE OUTSIDE THE POLYTECHNIC

My life outside the Polytechnic was both difficult and enjoyable. For the first year until I moved into my uncle's home in West Croydon, I had no settled abode. I lived for a few weeks at a time in bedsitters in Stockwell and Brixton in south London. I must have been a neighbourhood sight walking towards the latest temporary dwelling at night with a big bag of personal effects on my shoulder and an old paraffin heater in one hand. To make matters worse, I ran out of money.

I was employed during the second Christmas break from classes, and the one after, and worked most of every summer vacation. The first Christmas job was for the Croydon Post Office loading and unloading mail trains from 10pm to 5am. The mail bags sometimes had metallic contents which made them heavier than they seemed. The second Christmas job, although with the same post office, was more comfortably indoors sorting mail. My first summer job was in the Philatelic Bureau of the London Post Office in central London. I quickly concluded that while the work was easy and work mates convivial, the pay did not provide a sufficient savings margin after travel and meal expenses were deducted.

The next summer and the following one, I opted for work on the factory floor of Courage and Barclay brewery, a major manufacturer of beer, stout and barley wine where the pay was much better and cafeteria food was not only tasty but highly subsidised. My job, apart from a brief spell in driving a forklift truck (my very first driving experience), consisted of superintending the washing end of the bottling plant, ensuring that the bottles entered the proper way up, did not break and did not spill the caustic soda cleansing agent on workers at the bottling end of the plant. I also had to clean the tubes at the end of the day. The work was extremely boring, but one had to be alert because any mishap would bring the entire operation to a loud, grinding halt. To cope with boredom, I developed the practice of doing memory exercises systematically on every work of fiction I had read, dealing one day with French fiction, another day with West Indian fiction and so on. I practised the same memory exercises with calypsoes.

There were a few points of interest about life in the factory. One is my observation that women were a substantial majority of workers and that they were assigned the more arduous tasks. The second is that despite being provided with some free beer in the cafeteria at lunch time, workers would steal the various alcoholic beverages off the bottling plant. Vigilant patrols by supervisors were especially frequent when barley wine and stout were being bottled. Third, women could drink faster and hold their drinks better than men. Three gulps by a woman would empty a bottle of beer. Several bottles would be consumed with no visible effects on work performance or even marked flushing of faces. All of this I saw from my position high on the bottling plant which provided an excellent view of the factory floor.

The experience of financial stringency, often resulting in inadequate accommodation, was not unique to me. It was a fairly common experience for many West Indian full-time students who, financially unsupported by their governments, were studying social sciences and engineering at several polytechnics across London. Regent Street Polytechnic and City of London Polytechnic (which later became City University) were popular with social sciences students. Croydon Polytechnic was the institution of choice for many engineering students. These students constituted a network for shared experiences and information on part-time job opportunities. Like me, some of the graduates of the polytechnics pursued postgraduate studies at universities in the UK or Canada.

England at the time had many West Indians who had migrated there in search of better employment opportunities. Although being full-time workers, some of them sought to advance their educational qualifications in engineering and allied fields by registering in technical colleges and polytechnics for sub-professional qualifications offered by bodies such as City and Guilds as well as for professional qualifications offered by the various associations of professional engineers. My uncle, with whom I lived in West Croydon, and several of his friends, were in the latter group, studying to become civil engineers and structural engineers.

During my spare time, I continued reading West Indian fiction. I read George Lamming's widely acclaimed debut novel *In the Castle of My Skin* for the first time and also read very carefully three of his later books *The Emigrants*, *Of Age and Innocence* and *Season of Adventure*. I read Edgar Mittelholzer's *Latticed Echoes* which was published in 1960. The fiery suicidal death of an insane character in the book foreshadowed Mittelholzer's own suicidal death by fire in May 1965. Samuel Selvon remained of interest to me with his publications of *Turn Again Tiger* and *I Hear Thunder*. V.S. Naipaul's *Miguel Street* and *The Mystic Masseur* also got my attention. I took notes on some of material in these literary works because I contemplated doing an essay on how being resident outside of the Caribbean affected the writing of fiction on the Caribbean. My plans never came to fruition. After an extended discussion with Gordon Rohlehr who I met at the University of Birmingham, I realised that I would be out of my depth with respect to literary criticism and wisely abandoned the idea. I also ventured into African fiction with three novels of Chinua Achebe, namely, *Things Fall Apart*, *No Longer at Ease* and *Arrow of God* published in 1958, 1960 and 1964 respectively.

My social life included frequent visits to the home of my sister, Raulda, who had migrated to England in 1962. At first, she lived in Stoke Newington in north London, which was far from my lodgings in south London but when she moved to Thornton Heath in south London, I was able to see her and her family much more frequently. I spent a lot of time with my girlfriend, Pamela Telman, who I had met in 1965 at the wedding reception of Phillip Hutson, one of my older cousins. We went to parties, cinemas, theatre, and jazz concerts. In the London theatre district, we saw two James Baldwin's plays 'Amen Corner' and 'Blues for Mr Charlie', the original production of 'Barefoot in the Park' and several other plays. At the Fairfield Hall in Croydon, we heard the fabulous jazz organist Jimmy Smith at the peak of his career, the legendary Dizzy Gillespie, and tenor sax player Ben Webster who was visiting from his base in Europe. We did a lot of walking in public parks and would sometimes visit the homes of her brother Hilbert and his wife Ayleen or her brother Bertrum and his wife Lurline.

Towards the end of my period at Woolwich Polytechnic, my friend Kingsley Innis turned up from Guyana to get married. With my two years or more of London experience, I was able to show him the ropes, including how to successfully satisfy bureaucratic requirements for obtaining employment. It was especially important for Kingsley to be able to rent his own accommodation because he had been sharing his older brother Calvin's single room bedsitter with the kind of obstacles to Calvin's love life and Kingsley's sleep so well described in Sam Selvon's *Lonely Londoners*. Through Kingsley and his betrothed Onel, who was a student nurse, I gained another set of friends comprised mainly of the female student nurses known to Onel. The one I remember the most is a vivacious Indo-

Trinidadian girl named Lucy. The other nurses were convinced she had a crush on me.

I also spent some Saturdays, especially in my first year, hanging out with my uncle and his friends at his home in Brixton and then West Croydon, Surrey. Listening to jazz, especially to Miles Davis's 'Bags Groove' which he loved, and conversing about the experiences of he and his friends were the usual evening fare. There was an interesting incident one Saturday, late in 1964 when he lived in Brixton. The men began a game of dominoes in which I participated. I won six games to nil against my uncle's friend Johnny and instantly remembered him. "I remember you. I six-loved you in Versailles when I was twelve years old." What had happened then was that my godfather's male friends at the Versailles Sugar Estate on West Bank Demerara were short of a domino player and prevailed on me to join them. I had never played dominoes with them before although I had had lots of practice playing with childhood friends in Kingston, Georgetown. I won six games to nil against Johnny. Not once but twice. That night in Brixton, his friends who had been defeated in dominoes many times by a boastful Johnny were delighted by my story of "six-loving" Johnny. He, of course, was far from delighted.

On 7 December 1964, British Guiana had another general election. I had not followed events closely but knew that the PPP won 24 of the 53 seats, the PNC 22 seats and the United Force seven seats. Forty-six per cent of the PPP's successful candidates were non-Indian and thirty-two per cent of the PNC's successful candidates were non-Afro. Despite the protests of Cheddi Jagan, Governor Richard Luyt agreed that the PNC and the United Force should constitute a coalition government. Forbes Burnham was appointed Premier. As a result, it was he and his PNC which led the country into constitutional independence from Britain on 26 May 1966.

I recall Pamela and me attending an Independence Day celebration at a night club in Brixton at which the very popular American soul singer Ben E. King made a guest appearance. He was only supposed to perform for 30 minutes but was so appreciative of the audience's response to him that he sang for hours, belting out song after song as they requested. I also recall a visit he made to Guyana in which he jammed with some of my friends who had a small string band and with whom I had practiced playing the guitar.

The coalition between the PNC and the United Force did not last very long. D'Aguiar, the leader of the United Force, broke from Burnham in September 1967 and even joined with Jagan in protesting electoral fraud in the 1968 elections. D'Aguiar subsequently retired from politics.

BIRMINGHAM UNIVERSITY

In October 1967, I entered the University of Birmingham to do a twelve-month Master of Social Science degree in Economics. I was accompanied by my wife, Pamela. We had married on 9 September 1967 and after a short honeymoon in Paris made our way to Edgbaston, Birmingham where the university was located. The Croydon County Council had provided me with an education grant to cover tuition and living expenses and my wife soon obtained a senior secretarial position in the civil service therefore money was no longer a major problem. Under the auspices of the Victoria League, we rented a furnished studio apartment in a building owned by the League. One of our neighbours was an Australian couple, Noel and Sally Thompson, with whom we became friends. Noel had an Australian government scholarship to do postgraduate work in nuclear physics at the University of Birmingham. He was helpful to me with integral calculus. Another neighbour was a mature Guyanese couple, Claude Gill and his spouse. Claude was a senior public servant sponsored by the Guyana government to pursue postgraduate accountancy studies at Aston University in Birmingham.

The University of Birmingham had developed a reputation for quantitative economics, economic theory and monetary economics. Frank Hahn and Terrence Gorman who were foundation members of the Faculty of Commerce and Social Science had international reputations in the fields of general equilibrium theory, monetary theory, aggregation, duality and demand theory. John H. Wood was the Esmee Fairbairn Professor of Investment from 1962 to 1965. By the time I got to Birmingham, Alan A. Walters was Professor of Econometrics. Professor Walters was becoming Britain's foremost monetarist. He left to become the Cassel Professor of Economics at the London School of Economics from 1968 to 1976, after which he joined the World Bank, and Johns Hopkins University, and then became Economic Adviser to Prime Minister Margaret Thatcher. The quantitative economics tradition was continued. Maurice McManus, whose PhD was supervised by Frank Hahn, was appointed Professor of Mathematical Economics in 1965. One of McManus' early publications was on stability analysis done in collaboration with Kenneth Arrow. The other quantitative academics in the Faculty were Tony Lancaster, an econometrician with expertise in Bayesian theory, a Dutch econometrician A.R. Heesterman who taught applied econometrics and Hans Neudecker, also Dutch, who taught linear algebra and dynamic programming. The academic staff in the non-quantitative fields included Henry Scott, an international economist, C.D. Harbury, a microeconomics and business behaviour specialist, Ingrid Palmer, lecturer in economic development, who had a strong background in the economics of South-East Asia, and David Sheppard who taught monetary economics and was then working on a history of UK financial institutions which in 1971 he published as a book entitled *The Role and Growth of UK Financial Institutions, 1880-1962*. Ingrid Palmer was a kind, encouraging lecturer who hosted me and a few other graduate students to dinner at her home.

Among my classmates were James Bok Abban, an older student from Ghana who had temporarily left his family in his home country, and Nick Lafitte, the son of a Professor who headed the Department of Sociology. Upon graduation, Abban returned to Ghana for an academic appointment at the University of Ghana's Legon campus where he researched and published on West African economic development, including on topics such as Ghanaian Migration to Nigeria and Regional Integration Issues in Africa. Nick Lafitte had mental health challenges which affected completion of his programme of studies. He was very imaginative about economic matters. I recall many discussions with him about the thesis he wanted to write on the economics of outer space, the economics of outer space at a time when space exploration was still in its infancy. Nick was many decades ahead of his time.

I focussed my studies on monetary economics, development economics, mathematical methods and introductory mathematical statistics. The subject listed last was tough, but I succeeded. I had studied basic statistics and economic statistics in my undergraduate degree but concluded that I needed to be versed in econometrics. Dr Lancaster, whose advice I sought, recommended that instead of doing a "cookbook" econometrics course on offer, I should do an alternative econometrics course which turned out to be an introductory course in mathematical statistics. Thrown into the deep end, I had to grapple with conditional probability, stochastic independence, distributions of functions of random variables, limiting distributions, central limit theorem, sufficiency, maximum likelihood estimation, and analysis of variance.

The course in economic development was eclectic. One segment contained the standard fare of the times, dealings with topics such as the classical growth theory, Marxist growth theory, Schumpeter's theory of economic development, sociological dualism, technological dualism, backwash and spread effects, balanced and unbalanced growth and international trade and development.

In this segment, I was introduced to W. Arthur Lewis' famous model of development in his article "Economic Development with Unlimited Supplies of Labour" published in 1954 and his book *The Theory of Economic Growth*, published in 1952, an extraordinarily encyclopaedic dissertation on the process and determinants of economic development. Robert L. Tignor in his book *W. Arthur Lewis and the Birth of Development Economics*, published in 2006, expressed his judgement that the Theory of Economic Growth "masterly merged economic theory with social and political analysis." Previously, I had only known of W. Arthur Lewis as an industrial economist from my reading of his 1949 book *Overhead Costs: Some Essays in Economic Analysis* during my undergraduate studies of microeconomics. I certainly had not heard of him as a major figure in development economics.

The Lewis model has been subjected to voluminous analyses and comments. I recall Professor Dale W. Jorgenson who was on his way from University of California, Berkeley to Tokyo overnighting in Birmingham to deliver a paper on his own work on the Lewis model at 10pm. It was intensely debated by Faculty members and graduate students who attended. Jorgenson subsequently published the paper with the title "Surplus Agricultural Labour and the Development of a Dual Economy" in 1967 in Oxford Economic Papers.

The writings of the Burmese economist, Hla Myint, also merited detailed study. Myint had taken as his starting point a country which was sparsely populated but was endowed with natural resources. In his conceptualisation, economic development starts with the opening of the economy as a natural resource-based exporter in a few specialised primary products with foreign private investment facilitated by government. Myint tried to explain why growth in the primary commodity export sector did not carry over to the rest of the economy. He identified high turnover of labour, worker acceptance of low wages, employers' belief that the supply curve of labour was backward bending, meaning that the supply of labour would decrease if wage rates exceeded a specific level, and insufficiency of industrial skills.

Another issue of the time was the choice between balanced growth and unbalanced growth approaches to economic development. Notable economists like Paul Rosenstein-Rodan and Ragnar Nurske emphasised the need to recognise indivisibilities in production, product demand and savings and to consequently maximise external economies. Ragnar Nurske strongly argued that: "More or less synchronised application of capital to a wide range of different industries ... (would) result in an overall enlargement of the market." In contrast, economists such as Albert Hirschman and Hans Singer advocated strategies of unbalanced growth in which there is selectivity in investment projects instead of a big push across all or many sectors. Their approach was predicated on the observation that critical resources were typically short in underdeveloped countries and that there was competition for those resources.

There was an unorthodox segment to the economic development course. That segment explored economic planning approaches using the Indian and the Soviet economies as case studies. On the Soviet approach, one was introduced to the writing of Evenii Preobrazhenski who argued that the plan must systematically disrupt society by altering the balance between the economic sectors. For India, we focussed on the Second Plan (1956-1961) which operationalised the model developed by Prasanta Chandra Mahalanobis in 1953. It was intensive in its use of operations research and optimisation techniques to guide allocation of investment among productive sectors. The segment of the course also dealt with China's economic development model. The main text was Audrey Donnithorne's *China's Economic System*, published in 1967. After graduating from Birmingham, I continued my reading on China to extend my knowledge.

Early in February 1968, Ota Sik, the Czechoslovakia Vice-Premier with responsibility for reforms in the economy visited the University of Birmingham and made a presentation on the Czech economic reforms then in train. He was accompanied by a colleague whose name I do not recall. Czechoslovakia had elected Alexander Dubcek as the reformist First Secretary of the Communist Party of Czechoslovakia. Ota Sik had published in 1967 a book *Plan and Market Under Socialism* which contained in full his ideas which underpinned the reforms. Section I set the stage by briefly reviewing critically socialist market theory and its practical applications in Czechoslovakia. Section II on the Planned Economy and Market Relationships expounded in detail his innovative thoughts on the social orientation of labour, socialist production and planned management of economic activity, socialist market relationships, organisation of management, the character of labour, consumption and commodity relations, and material and moral incentives. Sections II and IV dealt with socialist price formation and money under socialism. The economic reforms were to be accompanied by reforms intended to democratise the political process. Within months after Sik returned to Czechoslovakia, the Soviet Union invaded Czechoslovakia. The invasion on 20 August 1968 effectively ended the Prague Spring. Gustav Husak, who had been appointed Vice-Premier in charge of the political reforms, assumed leadership in the Normalisation Period and reversed the economic decentralisation and democratisation introduced under Dubcek.

I came to the course in monetary economics well prepared. I had delved deeply into the subject during undergraduate studies and was quite familiar with the issues debated on topics such as liquidity preference, demand for money, supply of money, open market operations, interest rate theory, and rediscount rate policy. I had developed a strong interest in the debate surrounding Milton Friedman's restatement of the quantity theory of money and his work with David Meiselman on monetary velocity and the investment multiplier. I also studied the monumental *A Monetary History of the United States*, published by Milton Friedman and Anna Jacobson Schwartz in 1963. An essay on the Friedman-Meiselman model which I presented to faculty and graduate students in my first term at Birmingham was well received. Given this background, I was able to spend much more time during graduate studies focussing on some advanced theoretical writings. A major work for study was Don Patinkin's *Money, Interest and Prices: An Integration of Monetary and Value Theory*. Six hundred and sixty-three pages long, the book published in 1965 was exhaustive in its coverage of monetary theory. Another important work was Boris P. Pesek and Thomas R. Saving *Money, Wealth and Economic Theory*, published in 1967.

I did not confine myself to monetary theory. I began to investigate the role of money and banking in economic development. A paper by John S. Gurley and Edward S. Shaw entitled "Financial Aspects of Economic Development" published in the American Economic Review in September 1955 had stirred my interest. At the time, there was little written explicitly on this subject so that a good deal of my time was spent combing through economic histories of industrially developed countries. Rondo E. Cameron's publication *Banking in the Early Stages of Industrialisation: A Study in Comparative Economic History* was helpful. Because I had read the PhD theses by Owen Jefferson and Norman Girvan on the Jamaican economy and knew something of the workings of that economy, I decided that my own thesis would be on commercial banking and economic development in Jamaica. David Sheppard was my supervisor. Charles Goodhart at the London School of Economics served as External Examiner. Sheppard was hard to pin down for regular consultations on my thesis. Typically, he would suggest meeting late afternoons in the bar in the Students Union Building where he would be perpetually distracted by the legs of the mini-skirted students. "Look at those legs" would be his frequent interjection into my remarks about commercial bank behaviour in Jamaica. David Sheppard accepted appointment as Professor of Economics at the Cave Hill campus of the University of the West Indies late in the 1970s. After a short, reportedly unhappy stay, he moved to Australia where he prematurely died.

It was not until 1973 with the publication of two influential books by Ronald I. McKinnon and Edward S. Shaw that the role of money and finance in economic development took centre stage. McKinnon's book was entitled *Money and Capital in Economic Development* and Shaw's was *Financial Deepening in Economic Development*. Rondo Cameron in the preceding year had published another book *Banking and Economic Development: Some Lessons of History* which as the title makes clear sought to distil what could be learned from history of the connection between banking and economic development.

When I was getting to the end of my studies and trying to decide on the next steps in furthering my economics education, a classmate encouraged me to write and seek the advice of the renowned monetary and international economics theorist Professor Harry G. Johnson who was teaching at the London School of Economics. Emphasising Harry Johnson's stature in academic economics, Nobel Laureate James Tobin was later to say that the third quarter of the 20th century was the "Age of Johnson". To my surprise, within a week or two I received a hand-written reply from Professor Johnson detailing several options, pointing out their pros and cons, and wishing me well whichever choice I made. My surprise at getting a reply was because I had a notion of how busy Johnson had to be. At that time, he occupied Professorships at the University of Chicago and the London School of Economics, published books and many papers annually, and was a frequent conference presenter and discussant. I learned much later from the following statement by Harry Johnson's collaborator and friend Professor Jagdish Bhagwati that I should not have been surprised. Professor Bhagwati in a tribute to Johnson after his death from a stroke at age 53 had this to say: "Countless numbers of manuscripts would reach him from aspiring students of international economics and somehow Harry found the energy and time to read them carefully and write back to the authors promptly." The world of economics and indeed the world of scholarship would be a much better place if there were many more like the great Harry G. Johnson.

THE WEST INDIAN PRESENCE AT BIRMINGHAM

There was a fair number of West Indian students at the University. The ranks in 1967/1968 included Gordon Rohlehr who was wrapping up a PhD dissertation on Joseph Conrad. Aggrey Burke from Jamaica was studying medicine and Brian Morgan also from Jamaica was studying dentistry. Guyanese Trevor Sue-a-Quan was a PhD student in chemical engineering, and Trinidadian Winston Akong was also studying chemical engineering. Elliot Bastien from Trinidad, who graduated from Birmingham in chemical engineering, had returned with his wife Glenda for postgraduate studies in operations research. Egbert (Bert) Carter, a Guyanese, was studying for an MSc in transportation engineering. Guyanese students John Dow and Horace Nurse were pursuing undergraduate studies in electrical engineering and civil engineering respectively. Perry Christie from The Bahamas was doing law, and Elvin McDavid from Guyana had switched from civil engineering to undergraduate studies in political science. Cynthia Massay, a Guyanese, was being trained as a physiotherapist. I do not remember what Owen Leach, a Barbadian, was studying; it might have been something in the field of literature.

The University was a lively place. The West Indian students had formed Birmingham University West Indian Society (BUWIS) which formed a West Indian Folk Singers group and established a steelband, both of which performed country-wide as Trev Sue-a-Quan describes in Story 14 in his *Cane Rovers: Stories of the Chinese-Guyanese Diaspora* published in 2012. I visited Birmingham City in 1994 while on a Commonwealth Secretariat assignment on education policy and was told that an amphitheatre had been created in the city and that a West Indian steelband had pride of place in the Saturday evening performances. The BUWIS also organised lectures and discussions on West Indian matters. On one occasion, I presented on economic development making liberal reference to William G. Demas's *The Economics of Development in Small Countries*. At various times, West Indian students would also gather in the Students Union armed with guitars and cuatros and entertain themselves and whoever wanted to join them. Sometimes there was a kind of Pied Piper effect as female students would depart with them, not always with their English boyfriends, to wherever the fun would continue. We struck up friendships with Lance Gibbs and Rohan Kanhai, the famous West Indies off-spinner and batsman respectively, who were playing professionally for the Warwickshire County Cricket Club located in Edgbaston not far from the campus. My friendship with Lance continued through the years though our paths rarely cross. I tried unsuccessfully to recruit Rohan Kanhai to be Sports Director at the University of the West Indies St Augustine campus when I was Campus Principal in the latter half of the 1990s.

There were many parties and luncheons among the group. Some men tried their hand at preparing a variety of dishes. A favourite venue for parties was the Holbourne Road apartment shared by Gordon Rohlehr and Aggrey Burke. John Dow replaced Gordon Rohlehr after he departed from Birmingham. The apartment was very convenient because it was on a commercial street above a greengrocer or butchery so there was no risk of disturbing neighbours late on Saturday nights. Parties were organised on a "sub" basis, each invitee contributing by bring some drink or food. Aggrey Burke's black book of female names and telephone numbers was an invaluable asset. Aggrey with his imposing presence and friendly smile had this technique of walking up to strange women and saying, "Who are you? I don't know you. Introduce yourself", which they almost invariably did. Elvin McDavid's links with the female freshers, as first year students were termed, was another useful asset for the party planners. Furthermore, both Aggrey Burke and Elvin McDavid were prominent athletes in the University and Elvin was President of the Students Union. They were very popular among students. A grand time was generally had by all.

Despite the fullness of social life in the West Indian circle, Pamela and I engaged in some of our accustomed travel and sightseeing activities, including a visit to Killarney in the Republic of Ireland, and in checking out the music scene in Birmingham City where we were able to see performances by the Modern Jazz Quartet, Miriam Makeba and blues singer Robert Cray.

Several members of the West Indian student group achieved professional prominence after graduating from the University of Birmingham. Gordon Rohlehr, a Guyanese, who I saw frequently since those times and became my close friend, became the foremost scholar of Caribbean cultural expressions in poetry, fiction, 1960s Jamaican reggae music and Trinidad calypsos. He had joined the University of the West Indies in Trinidad straight out of Birmingham, achieved the rank of Personal Professor and retired in 2007 as Professor Emeritus. Among his major works are *Calypso and Society in Pre-Independence Trinidad* published in 1990, *My Whole Life is Calypso: Essays on Sparrow* published in 2015 and *Projected Fables Now: A Bookman Signs Off on Seven Decades* published in 2019.

Aggrey Burke, a Jamaican friend to this day, specialised in Psychiatry. He became an authority on mental illnesses and psychiatric disorders of coloured immigrants in Britain, especially Black West Indians who he demonstrated were racially discriminated against in diagnosis, treatment, hospitalisation and court reports prepared by psychiatrists. He showed that young Black men are five times more likely than young men from any other group to be diagnosed with severe schizophrenia. Commenting on the court reports, he concluded that they have an "obsession with blacks being bad, big blacks somewhat worse, and big black males ... as the most dangerous of all cases." With co-author J. Collier, he did a landmark study which demonstrated empirically that the London Schools of Medicine discriminated against Black applicants and students. Aggrey Burke was awarded the Royal College of Psychiatrists President's Medal in November 2020.

Perry G. Christie upon completing his legal studies entered Bahamian politics as a Senator in 1974 and became Prime Minister from 2002-2007 and then again from 2012-2017. Elvin McDavid upon graduation also became an active politician in his native Guyana. We had become friends when I first assisted him with some of his undergraduate courses at Birmingham. We remained good friends despite me not sharing his political views and loyalties. He became Minister of Information and Culture 1971-1972 and should be credited with the organisation of the Guyana National Service, construction of the still much used Guyana Cultural Centre Building and the successful organisation of the first Caribbean Festival of Arts hosted by Guyana in 1972. Elvin McDavid served as Political Advisor to President Forbes Burnham and as Ambassador to the USSR when Desmond Hoyte succeeded Forbes Burnham as President.

My very good friends, John Dow and Horace Nurse established professional engineering careers in several countries. John Dow worked as an engineer in the sugar industries of Guyana, Zambia and Jamaica and ended his career as Manager of the Andrews Sugar Factory in Barbados. Horace Nurse, who had returned to Birmingham for postgraduate studied in town planning, at first was a senior engineer in the City Engineering Department of the Georgetown City Council and later in town planning in Botswana. He ended his career as a civil engineer with the Caribbean Development Bank in Barbados. Elliot Bastien first went to Canada where he became Personal Assistant to the President of Sun Oil Corporation and then re-migrated to Trinidad to work in the establishment of the Point Lisas Industrial Estate which was intended to make Trinidad and Tobago a major player in the global petrochemical industry. Cynthia Massay returned to Guyana and became the driving force in the provision of rehabilitative physiotherapy in Georgetown.

Egbert (Bert) Carter worked as an engineer with the Georgetown City Council before becoming an industrialist. I had first met Bert in his then trademark striped pop star jacket at a wine and cheese reception that the University of Birmingham hosted for incoming postgraduate students. I had already dined at home and therefore was drinking the wine and discarding the cheese with which each glass of wine was paired. Bert had been observing me and came across to make a trading proposition. "Banna, I notice that you are drinking the wine but not eating the cheese. Me, I am not interested in the wine but would like the cheese. Can we trade?" I discovered that for Bert whose education grant had not yet come through, the cheese was his dinner that night. Bert and I have remained close friends and know each other families from the very beginnings.

LEAVING THE UK

My wife and I left Birmingham in December 1968 to reside temporarily in her mother's house at 47 Ribblesdale Road in Streatham, London, while we awaited the birth of our first son, Clairmonte, who was born on 22 December. While in Streatham, I ran into a former high school classmate, Compton Mitchell. He had married a Guyanese-Indian woman which led to the ostracisation of both of them from their respective families. They had recently migrated to England when I met him. We agreed to meet again but he died suddenly soon after.

On 16 December 1968, Guyana held a very controversial election which attracted considerable media criticism in the United Kingdom. The controversy centred on irregularities in the lists of eligible voters. The Burnham government had introduced overseas voting which was theoretically intended to allow Guyanese resident in the United Kingdom, the United States, and indeed in other countries the opportunity to vote. Granada Television, however, broadcasted a damaging documentary entitled 'The Trail of the Vanishing Voters' which showed that many of the listed voters in the United Kingdom were non-existent at the addresses listed and that some of the listed addresses were demolition sites, derelict buildings, building yards and railways. They concluded that fifty per cent of the voters listed in England did not exist and that the overseas voters' scheme was a device for electoral fraud. The Institute of Race Relations in London weighed in with the suggestion that there were as many as 20,000 fraudulent names. Granada Television also raised the question of voter padding in Guyana itself. Forbes Burnham's sister, Jessie, was perhaps prophetic when on the eve of the election, she warned potential voters about his unprincipled quest for power. She wrote, "His love for personal power is so great he will trade anything to achieve it ... Nothing is safe, no person, no liberty that stands in his way." As it turned out, the PNC, which was in office, won 30 of the 53 seats, the PPP nineteen and the United Force four seats thus eliminating the need for a coalition government between the PNC and the United Force.

My search for professional employment developed in unexpected ways. I had been exploring opportunities with The University of the West Indies, the University of Guyana, and the Government Planning Agency in Guyana. I had initially received from Mr Winston King, the head of the Guyana Government Planning Agency, a very enthusiastic response to my general enquiries about job prospects. He encouraged me to apply to the Ministry in charge of recruitment. I did so and there was follow up correspondence until suddenly I no longer heard from the Ministry. I learnt from them after I had returned to Guyana in April 1969 that they thought I would be returning in any case and that they decided to wait until then before making me an offer in order to avoid paying my airfare to Guyana. My application to the ISER, University of the West Indies, was accepted but the letter of acceptance was long delayed in the mail by the Rodney Riots which had broken out in Jamaica when the Jamaican Government denied Walter Rodney permission to re-enter the country. Rodney, an academic historian at the University of the West Indies, was a prominent social activist. Student demonstrations quickly spread and there was considerable violence and destruction of property. Because of its delay in the mail, the offer from UWI reached me after I had received an offer of employment with the University of Guyana. After consideration of events in Jamaica, I accepted the University of Guyana offer and soon departed for Georgetown, Guyana.

CHAPTER FOUR

UNIVERSITY OF GUYANA YEARS, 1969-1971 and 2009-2012

RETURN TO GUYANA

In April 1969, together with my wife and infant son, I returned to Guyana to take up an appointment as Lecturer in Economics at the University of Guyana. I was received by Mr Maurice Odle, the Head of my Department, who introduced me to Dr Bertram Collins, the Dean of the Faculty of Social Sciences and to other colleagues. Initially, the university housed us in an extremely large house on Durban Street in Georgetown. After a short residence there, we were relocated to a better situated house on Rupert Street West, Bel Air Park, an upscale suburb of Georgetown. There are only two memorable things about the premises. First, it was at the opposite end of the street where my old school friend Oscar Bayrd and his family lived. Second, there was a harpy eagle, absolutely unbothered by my presence, which perched in the guava tree in our backyard.

THE UNIVERSITY OF GUYANA

The University of Guyana was a part-time institution when I arrived. It was still a part-time institution when I left in August 1971. It was started on 1 October 1963 without premises of its own. Offices for academic and administrative staff were in premises borrowed from the Queen's College secondary school and academic programme delivery was in the school's classrooms and laboratories at night. Utilising a gift of 50 acres of unused sugar cane lands from the Bookers Group of Companies, the University was able to construct a campus at Turkeyen, East Coast Demerara and began operations there in October 1969. Sister Mary Noel Menezes, an eminent Guyanese historian and a foundation member of the university, was to note on the 50th anniversary of the University of Guyana Ordinance that 1969 was an important landmark for the university for several reasons, notably the move to Turkeyen with 1000 students, many visiting scholars, many new staff members, the first Open Entrance Examinations, United Kingdom approval of the university and the arrival of Professor Denis Irvine as the new Vice Chancellor. The campus was formally opened by Prime Minister Forbes Burnham on 24 February 1970.

The Turkeyen campus required a pioneering spirit. The roads were unsurfaced which made pedestrian and vehicular passage muddy and slippery during the rainy season. Mosquitoes were a constant irritation, especially at night. Snakes might occasionally slither across one's path at night in the vicinity of the Staff Club. Alligators could be glimpsed from time to time. Library resources were limited and computers non-existent. However, in those days there was dependable supply of water and electricity.

Despite these arduous conditions, the University of Guyana did well in scholastic terms. It was a dynamic institution. Its Chancellor was Sir W. Arthur Lewis, a foremost development economist who would a few years later be awarded the Nobel Prize in Economics. Dennis Irvine joined as Vice Chancellor in 1969 and started to provide clearer academic direction. In a paper entitled "The University of Guyana (1969-82) A Vice Chancellor's Perspective in a collection of retrospective essays entitled *The University of Guyana: Perspectives on The Early Years* published by the University of Guyana Guild of Graduates, Ontario, in 2002, he indicated that he perceived there were five major issues to be addressed: (i) establishing credibility locally, regionally and internationally; (ii) gaining government support, given their antagonistic posture; (iii) breaking down racial barriers that "had polarised the student body and infected staff relationships"; (iv) establishing broad-based participation in policy making and decision-making; (v) winning public trust and confidence.

Guyanese, Caribbean and international academic staff in those days were committed to both teaching and research. In the Natural Sciences, there was Harry Drayton as Professor of Biology, Omawale (then Walter Greene) and Joshua Ramsammy as Lecturers in Biology, Lyttleton Ramsahoye as Professor of Physics along with Frederick Campagne, who had distinguished himself in Europe in nuclear physics, and Neville Trotz in Chemistry. In the Humanities, faculty members included Marilyne Trotz and Jocelyn Loncke in foreign languages and Derek Bickerton and Bill Carr in linguistics and literature. In the Social Sciences faculty, there was Professor Bertram Collins, Harold Lutchman and Paul Singh who taught and published in the fields of political science, local government, and public administration. Pat Commissiong, Tom McCann and Maurice St Pierre taught sociology. Wilfred David, Maurice Odle, Clive Thomas, who had joined after being denied re-entry into Jamaica to resume his academic post at the University of the West Indies, Isidore Jainarine and I taught economics. There was also a sub-department of business administration in which the only full-time academic member of staff was Aubrey Armstrong who changed his name to Akintunde and then back to Aubrey Armstrong when he took leave to pursue doctoral studies in the United States. There were able administrators like Registrar David Karran, Bursar George Williams, Librarian Yvonne Stephenson, and Valerie Holder, a Registry officer. Students were anxious to learn, engage in discussions and develop their intellectual capacities even at the end of their workdays. There was a sense of common mission and purpose among academic and non-academic staff made achievable by people like Faye Gaskin from among the ranks of non-academic staff.

I felt that University of Guyana was a good place to be. So much so that when around the middle of 1969, I indirectly received a proposal from Prime Minister Burnham that I leave the university for the government service, I respectfully declined on the grounds that I felt morally committed to the university which had brought me back to Guyana and that I was satisfied that I could make a valuable contribution there. His response, also indirectly, was astonishing to say the least. Early one Sunday morning while I was still residing on Durban Street, my doorbell rang. I opened the door to find a senior government employee who I knew personally with an obscene oral message he had been asked by the Prime Minister to deliver to me.

TEACHING AND RESEARCH

My primary teaching responsibility was economic statistics which was an unenviable task since the minds of the students were hardly fresh after a day at work. One student would fall asleep within fifteen minutes of taking his seat.

I developed a research agenda quickly. I authored a paper on supply behaviour in the rice industry of Guyana for the 1970 Conference of the West Indian Agricultural Association which was held in Georgetown, Guyana. Because there were no computer facilities in the university, I had no choice but to do the computations on a Friden electronic calculator which had been procured for the teaching of the statistics course. The paper which was published in 1971 is still cited by international scholars. Three other agriculture sector exercises which I undertook were forecasts of demand for pork and pork products for the Guyana Marketing Corporation whose Chairman was Eusi Kwayana, preparation of a conference paper on agricultural finance in Jamaica, and a survey study of small farm financing in Guyana. In the paper on agricultural finance which I presented at the Regional Programme of Monetary Studies conference in Barbados in 1971, I stated ten propositions and provided theoretical and partial empirical justifications for them. Two propositions pertained to the small volume of institutional credit to the farming sector and its explanation in terms of production risks, absence of adequate collateral and differences between the preferred loan maturity preferences of lenders and those of potential demanders of credit. Five propositions pertained to non-institutional lenders such as moneylenders, traders and shopkeepers. It was observed that the greater part of agricultural finance was supplied by non-institutional lenders, that non-institutional lenders impose less stringent formal loan security requirements than institutional lenders, that their credit is expensive, and that they behaved monopolistically. One proposition observed the significant use by farmers of hire-purchase and other credit-sale facilities for purchase of farm equipment and supplies. The remaining three propositions dealt with the bias in credit supplies towards some crops, mainly exports, the low volume of internal finance utilised by farmers, and the dependence of farm-household savings on farm incomes.

The survey study of small farm financing in Guyana was not completed before I left the University of Guyana to join the University of the West Indies, but I arranged to continue it. John Browman, a senior official in the Ministry of Agriculture, kindly agreed to supervise the field work. I entrusted the analysis and write up of the data to one of my UWI graduate students, Gladstone Lewars. The exercise was completed as his thesis for his MSc degree in Economics under my supervision. The thesis was subsequently published by him as a monograph entitled Small Farm Financing in Guyana.

Outside of the agricultural sector, I did a study of business financial behaviour which I presented at the Regional Programme of Monetary Studies conference in The Bahamas in 1972. It was a cross-section study which not only analysed data from the credit system but entailed interviewing companies and obtaining pertinent company data from them. The study revealed that most firms, especially the smaller and medium-sized ones, relied on internal financing, mainly through profit retentions and reserves. Bank credit was the principal source of external finance, followed by trade credit. Financing patterns differed between local firms and foreign firms, with the former utilising retained profits and bank credit more extensively. The study also found that commercial banks were more inclined to lend to large firms than to small firms and that safety and liquidity were the decisive credit considerations. In surveying the business landscape and conducting the interviews, I was struck by how many indigenous producers of consumer goods like soft drinks, margarine and soap had been become insolvent because their domestic markets had been displaced by imported substitutes.

ECONOMICS NETWORKS

My research in the finance field was done under the auspices of the Regional Programme of Monetary Studies (RPMS), a programme financed by the Caribbean central banks and administered by the Institute of Social and Economic Research at the Mona campus of the University of the West Indies. Its Director was Alister McIntyre. The RPMS held its annual conference at the University of Guyana in 1970. Attendees came from the UWI campuses in Jamaica, Barbados and Trinidad and Tobago and from the central banks and monetary authorities in several Caribbean countries. One highlight was Maurice Odle's presentation of a voluminous paper on non-bank financial intermediaries on which he had been working feverishly until the last day of the conference. It was published as a 200-plus pages book. As we learnt from his later publications on public expenditures and pension funds, Maurice Odle is a big book man.

The RPMS and the annual West Indian Agricultural Economics conferences provided welcome and rewarding opportunities for professional interaction with scholars and public officials across the Caribbean. In Barbados, there was Frank Alleyne at the UWI Cave Hill campus; in Trinidad, Jerry Hospedales at the Central Bank of Trinidad and Tobago and Nugent Miller and Lloyd Rankine at the UWI St Augustine campus. The University of Guyana Economics Department also had good working relationships with economists in the Guyana government sector. Colleagues at the Bank of Guyana included Wilbert Bascom, Clarence Ellis, Haslyn Parris and Cargill Alleyne. At the Ministry of Finance was Donald Augustin I developed close friendships with Frank Alleyne, Lloyd Rankine, Jerry Hospedales, Wilbert Bascom and Clarence Ellis. I got to know Donald Augustin a lot better when we were international consultants in Swaziland in 1989.

The professional careers of some professional associates and friends took different directions subsequently. Wilbert Bascom became the Managing Director of the Guyana National Cooperative Bank which was established in February 1970. Clarence Ellis did double duty as Deputy

Governor of the Bank of Guyana and Chairman of the State Planning Commission, another 1970 creation. Also at the State Planning Commission as Chief Planning Officer was Carl Greenidge who had lectured briefly at the university in 1970 before leaving to join the State Planning Commission. Haslyn Parris in 1971 left the Bank of Guyana to become the Chief Executive Officer of Guyana Bauxite Company which was the name given to the newly nationalised Demerara Bauxite Company.

SOCIAL LIFE

On returning to Guyana, we caught up with my parents, siblings and my maternal grandmother who had remained in the country. My wife's mother and her brother Hilbert returned to Guyana shortly after as did my Uncle Whitney. It was a period when skilled nationals were strongly motivated to re-migrate and contribute to the country's development. I reunited with old friends from the Montmartre High School days, such as Ovid Edwards, Walter Alexander, Lance McCaskie, Peter MacDonald and Desmond Shepherd. John Dow and Horace Nurse were already back from Birmingham. Elvin McDavid returned in 1970. New friends like Reynold Burrowes who was the Prime Minister's Personal Assistant, Berkeley Wickham, a former Montmartre High School student who had returned from Canada with an engineering degree, and Fairbain Liverpool, a Captain in the Guyana Defence Force, became part of interchangeable groups engaged in leisure activities.

Pamela and I made a day trip to Kaieteur Falls at the tip of the Potaro River on a Guyana Airways plane. Pamela had obtained a job as Secretary to the Managing Director, Ernest Christiani and we decided to visit the Falls with one of her colleagues. My unease about plane trips to the Guyanese interior on Guyana Airways began on that trip. We were seated behind the pilot on departure from the Timehri Airport. We taxied out and before take-off returned to the ramp. I overheard the pilot telling the engineer that the plane was not lifting off as quickly as it should. The engineer replied that it was not a serious problem; the pilot should simply travel a longer distance on the runway. The pilot replied that the suggestion could work at Timehri because the runway was sufficiently long but might be impracticable at Kaieteur where the runway was much shorter. Some adjustments were made to the plane on the ramp and we departed for Kaieteur and returned without incident. I overcame my apprehensions sufficiently for Pamela and me to travel again with Guyana Airways for a day trip to the Orinduik Falls near Monkey Mountain and Paramakatoi in the North Rupununi District. We were accommodated at a Guyana Defence Force camp headed by Captain Oliver Hinckson, a friend of my friend, Horace Nurse. The army camp was there presumably to prevent smuggling from Brazil. We took a canoe trip across a narrow river dividing the country and visited a very small shop where I was surprised to see not only groceries and other household items but also rifles on sale.

My wife and I hosted parties for old and new friends. Late in May 1970, we held a party at which Walter Rodney, who was in Guyana for a set of lectures on the history of West African-European confrontations, was present. Our home was also the venue for lunching on venison prepared by Reynold Burrowes' dad or the wild ducks and fish caught by me and my hunting and fishing buddies. Horace Nurse and Berkeley Wickham also hosted parties and Elvin McDavid provided the venue for a suckling pig barbecue evening. Visits were paid occasionally to John Dow's residence in New Amsterdam, Berbice and to the rivers and creeks in various rural districts. On a duck shooting trip in a Berbice paddy field, Reynold initially provided amusement and later irritation by falling repeatedly into the swampy fields with a loud splash whenever we reached within shooting range of the ducks which of course then flew some distance away. We finally solved the Reynold problem by parking him on the embankment to await our return with birds in hand. We tried our hand at cast net fishing with limited success on one occasion.

I visited Trinidad a few times in this period. John Dow, Horace Nurse and I decided to go for Carnival. We were graciously accommodated by Gordon Rohlehr in St Augustine. On a subsequent trip, I socialised with Elliot Bastien who introduced me to Henry Jeffers, my lifelong friend. I met Wally Looklai who introduced me to Earl Lovelace, a novelist who had just published his second novel *The Schoolmaster*. On one of those visits, I met Eddie Greene who lived next to Edwin Carrington in North Valsayn which at the time was a new, mosquito infested housing development. Both Eddie and Edwin were Research Fellows at the UWI St Augustine branch of the ISER. I also met and became a friend of Adlith Brown who taught economics at UWI St Augustine. She introduced me to Carlos Hee Houng and Maritza Pantin with whom I became good friends as well.

One visit to Trinidad was for the purpose of arranging the funeral of my maternal grandfather who had died while on an extended vacation with my aunt Ivy and her husband Daniel. My friend Gordon Rohlehr had called me in Georgetown late at night to inform me of my grandfather's death. It was my sad duty to awaken my grandmother to inform her of her husband's demise. She knew before I uttered a word. A few days later, I flew to Trinidad to arrange the formalities of burial.

NETWORKING IN JAMAICA

During my stay at the University of Guyana, I attended a Caribbean statisticians' conference in Kingston, Jamaica. The leading figures in Caribbean statistics then were George Roberts, Professor of Demography at the University of the West Indies, Dexter Rose, Head of the Jamaica Statistical Bureau, and Jack Harewood, Director of the Central Statistical Office in Trinidad and Tobago. Up and coming Jamaican statisticians included Carmen McFarlane, Dexter Rose's deputy and Fay Sylvester who with her husband Otto became my good friends when I joined the University of the West Indies in Jamaica in 1971. On a visit to the Mona campus in 1970, I met George Beckford who had established himself as a leading agricultural economist in the Caribbean. I was the house guest of Woodville Marshall, a UWI historian and his wife Dawn on University Close, a street in a private residential complex owned by the university. That house might well be the same one my family and I occupied when we moved to Jamaica in 1971.

RATOON

Soon after my return to Guyana in 1969, I formed the opinion that apart from political commentaries by political parties, there was little public discussion of government policies, actions and behaviour in Guyana. That state of affairs changed when a group of us at the university started a quasi-political pressure group and published a monthly newspaper called RATOON. The newspaper published commentaries on politics, government policies and culture. For most of its early life, Joshua Ramsammy and I edited and wrote most of its content. Maurice Odle authored a long article on the termination of national railway services and Clive Thomas published a short monograph on the sugar industry with the RATOON imprimatur. I wrote a satirical column called 'Nuff Rass' which poked fun at various statements emanating from Prime Minister Burnham and members of his Cabinet. I had long discerned that politicians were vulnerable to people laughing at them. The column was liked by many, but not by the Prime Minister, I am sure.

Joshua Ramsammy, Clive Thomas, Maurice Odle and I travelled about the country selling the newspaper and making speeches. On one trip in

Blairmont, Berbice, I got a reminder of the problem of adult illiteracy when a willing purchaser, a sugar estate worker, asked me to read from the front page because he could not read. On a subsequent trip to the Essequibo Coast, we experienced the vagaries and dangers of river transportation and life without electricity. We crossed the turbulent Essequibo River from Parika to Wakenaam in a small boat powered by an outboard engine, taking in water from time to time much to the trepidation of Maurice Odle. At Anna Regina on the Essequibo Coast, we attended a party without electricity; the music player was battery powered; and the venue dimly lit by lanterns. Outside was pitch dark. Nonetheless, we had a good time. On the return journey from the Essequibo Coast, we missed the ferry at the designated crossing and had to go to another point where we were obliged to wade about fifty metres out to the point where the ferry paused to take us on board. Maurice Odle had to be persuaded to venture into the water of unknown depth. On a trip to Tain in the Corentyne, Joshua Ramsammy, Clive Thomas, Maurice Odle and I also discovered that even when invited by respectable, authority figures in the community, radical looking, bearded men could be viewed with great suspicion and hostility and forced to make undignified departures. We had been invited by a school principal to address members of the community in the school hall. During the proceedings, we could hear loud voices which eventually turned hostile. Our host was forced to interrupt the proceedings because it was evident that the hostility was directed against us and could become violent. He provided us with safe escort out of the district. We understood that there had been a kidnapping of a village child by bearded men a few days before and that was the reason for suspicion and hostility towards us.

One evening, a few of us, including Clive Thomas, Maurice Odle and Joshua Ramsammy, visited Cheddi Jagan at his home in Prashad Nagar to discuss the political situation. He and his wife Janet were hospitable. At some point, one person in the group made the absurd suggestion that both Cheddi and Forbes Burnham should withdraw from active politics and leave the field to a new, upcoming generation of political aspirants. Cheddi, being Cheddi, was polite but firm in rejecting what was clearly an unreasonable proposition for a career politician who had been central to Guyana's political life since 1949.

At some point, RATOON morphed into the Movement Against Oppression (MAO). MAO was a more overtly political movement with a membership larger and different from RATOON. It ventured into socially and economically deprived Tiger Bay to provide various community services. It therefore elicited more politically partisan support and criticism. It was severely damaged in May 1970 by the visit of Stokely Carmichael, the well-known Trinidad-born American Black Power activist, whose visit to Guyana it sponsored. Omawale, a member of both MAO and the Guyanese Africanist organisation African Society for Cultural Relations with Independent Africa (ASCRIA), at the instance of ASCRIA's leader Eusi Kwayana, had approached MAO about sponsoring the visit. I did not agree with the rationale that it would help to strengthen MAO, but my views did not prevail. Plans were made for Carmichael to first address a public meeting in Georgetown, then participate in a panel discussion at the University of Guyana on the following day and to be on a platform of speakers in the National Stadium on the day after. Lunch was arranged for Stokely Carmichael and his group at my home soon after his arrival. He behaved in the manner of some African leaders. He had an entourage and security detail. He ate before them and had some of his men taste the food first to ensure it was not poisoned.

Stokely Carmichael's first speech was explosive. He declared that Black Power was only for people of African descent. Other ethnic groups had no place in it and should attend to their concerns separately. This view was in sharp contrast to the multi-ethnic philosophy espoused by MAO. It threw the MAO leadership into disarray especially since it attracted widespread condemnation in the country, including from the Maha Sabha which accused the movement of foisting Carmichael on the country and stated that it should be blamed for any consequences of his visit. The MAO leadership tried to distance itself from Carmichael's position during the panel discussion at the University of Guyana next day. After Carmichael had spoken at the panel, Clive Thomas made a speech extolling the West Indian contribution to the anti-colonial struggle in Africa, articulating RATOON's/ MAO's position on the definition and issue of Black power in Guyana, and by allusion denouncing Carmichael's speech of the day before. Thomas said that RATOON's position was different and that there would be no uncritical acceptance of the United States variant of the Black Power ideology. He went on to state that RATOON's position was based on Afro-Indian solidarity. Stokely Carmichael was quick to see Thomas's remarks as criticism of him, turning immediately to me on the platform to declare, "He is attacking me; he is attacking me!" It was a raucous session with several people walking out before the end.

Matters were worse in the National Stadium the following night. The designated Chairman of proceedings had declined to perform his duties, therefore I did. Clive Thomas wanted to deny Carmichael an opportunity to speak but I insisted that we could not properly do that to our sponsored guest whom we had advertised as the featured speaker. As Stokely Carmichael spoke, I could hear loud, hostile voices from the huge audience but in the glare of the platform lights could not clearly see any of them. One of the platform members grew increasingly fearful, constantly asking me to end the proceedings. I ignored him, calmed the crowd and allowed Carmichael to finish his speech without any crowd disruption or subsequent unrest.

RATOON/MAO did not recover easily from Stokely Carmichael's visit. The financial expenses were large and took some time to be cleared despite special fundraising efforts over several months. Stokely Carmichael, while he remained in Guyana, was embraced by the People's National Congress. Prime Minister Burnham hosted him and his entourage to lunch and on other occasions had him address PNC political gatherings.

GUYANA'S POLITICAL ECONOMY

COOPERATIVE SOCIALISM AS DEVELOPMENT STRATEGY

In April 1969, Prime Minister Burnham began to articulate a new development strategy. In a document entitled *Towards a Cooperative Republic*, published by the People's National Congress, he stated the following: "In moving towards our goal of exploiting our resources and giving the masses economic power, we shall have to fashion new institutions ... and put new content into others which already exist. One such latter is the Cooperative. It has to be expanded and adapted and given a new purpose." He spelt out the distributional implications of his reconceptualisation of the cooperative model in a speech to his party's Regional Conference on 24 August in the same year. "The cooperative is the means through which the small man can become a real man, the means through which the small man can participate fully in the economic life of the nation, and the means through which the small man can play a predominant part in the workings of the economy." On 23 February 1970, he declared Guyana to be a Cooperative Republic.

As Kempe Hope has documented in a paper "Cooperative Socialism and the Cooperative Movement in Guyana" published in Review of International Cooperation, Volume 68, No.2, 1975, there was considerable expansion in cooperative activity after the cooperative development strategy was made formal. The expansion occurred mainly among savings, thrift and credit cooperatives and to a lesser degree among those in housing, industry and transport and those in commerce and marketing. Despite the expansion of the cooperative movement, it was evident that economic life for individuals and country was dominated by large corporations in the sugar industry, in the bauxite industry and the wholesale and retail industries. Little wonder that critics scoffed at the proclaimed objective of making the small man a real man.

An important institution for operationalising the cooperative development strategy was the Guyana National Cooperative Bank which was established in February 1970 with government majority shareholding but with provision for shareholding by registered cooperatives, trade unions, friendly societies and public corporations. The provisions for non-government shareholdings did not take effect. In 1991, the government held 97 per cent of the Bank's shares.

Wilbert Bascom was made the Managing Director of the GNCB. He was knowledgeable about the operations of cooperative credit banks in the country having written in 1968 a short history of cooperative credit banks for the period 1914 to 1954. Bascom was quite astute in anticipating the challenges and formulating a strategy. In a promotional address given in Berbice prior to the actual establishment of the bank, he stated that it would be the policy of the Bank to make sound loans, supervise them adequately and obtain repayment on schedule. He pointed to factors which would affect repayment performance by cooperatives such as honesty and integrity, financial condition of the cooperatives, efficiency and productivity, and product market opportunities. He pointed out that the Bank would require collateral on most loans. He noted that agricultural credit was more susceptible to loan delinquency than credit to manufacturing enterprises. Prime Minister Burnham had envisaged the GNCB as a means of "miniaturising" the foreign banks. The foreign banks in operation then were Barclays, Chase Manhattan, Royal Bank of Canada and Bank of Nova Scotia. In an address to the Guyana Council of Churches on 2 January 1970, Bascom implicitly endorsed the strategy of "miniaturisation" while making it clear that he did not favour nationalisation of the foreign banks. "The answer to the problem of increasing the impact of commercial banking on the Guyana economy cannot to my mind, be found in the nationalisation of these banks."

The GNCB was attractive to Guyanese depositors. Its deposit balances grew faster than in the rest of the commercial banking industry. The foreign banks began to close branches. By 1991, only the Bank of Nova Scotia remained in Guyana. In that year, the GNCB had 40.4 per cent of banking sector assets and 75 per cent of bank loans.

An unintended consequence of the "miniaturisation" of the foreign banks was the reduction of experienced senior bank officers in Guyana as several of those employed with the foreign banks emigrated to take up employment in their branches in Antigua, Barbados, Jamaica and Trinidad and Tobago.

NATIONALISATION OF BAUXITE

On 23 February 1971, the Guyana Government announced the nationalisation of the Demerara Bauxite Company (DEMBA) which was fully owned by the Aluminium Company of Canada (ALCAN). The announcement was the sequel to negotiations between the government and the company which started on 7 December 1970 and ended in a breakdown on 20 December 1970. At the heart of the irreconcilable difference between the government and ALCAN was ownership and operational control over the enterprise. The company could not have been unaware of Prime Minister Burnham's earlier public statements on the issue of ownership and control of Guyana's natural resources. In an address to his political party's 13th annual congress in April 1970, he had stated that Guyana must own and control the exploitation of its resources because, "foreign owned extractive industries prosper while the native population remained poor and destitute." On 20 November 1970, the Prime Minister delivered "Guyana Bauxite-Broadcast Address to the Nation" in which he announced that the government was inviting ALCAN to negotiate, prefacing his remarks with the following statement: "A nation cannot achieve economic independence unless the decisions with respect to the exploitation, use and disposition of these resources are taken within its own borders." He said that the government's goal was, "meaningful participation" not confiscation or expropriation.

Norman Girvan in a paper entitled "The Guyana-Alcan Conflict and the Nationalization of Demba" published in the New World Journal (Vol V, No. 4, 1971) provided an informative account of the preparations for the negotiations, its conduct and eventual outcome. Girvan was one of a team of technical advisers that included William Demas, Alister McIntyre, Kari Levitt, George Beckford and Maurice St Pierre in the early preparations. Guyanese officials on the team included Minister Hubert Jack who led the negotiations, Haslyn Parris and Laurence Mann. The Guyana government had the benefit of detailed technical advice which drew upon the experience of Zambia and Chile no doubt informed by Girvan's knowledge of the two cases, St Pierre's analysis of the acute social and income disparities between DEMBA's expatriate management and the Guyanese workforce, and the intimate knowledge of geology, taxation, accounting and DEMBA's operations possessed by senior Guyana government officials on the technical preparatory team.

This advice informed Burnham's statement of the government's non-negotiable points in his December 1970 broadcast to the nation: majority government participation by means of share purchase; the use of the company's written down book value on 31 December 1969; payment for government's share acquisition out of future after-tax profits; effective control by the government as majority shareholder; effective date of acquisition to be 1 January 1971.

ALCAN counter-proposed that the government and ALCAN enter into a partnership arrangement for a new company in which the Guyana government would contribute $50 million financed by a World Bank loan and ALCAN would contribute DEMBA. The government's contribution would be used to finance an expansion of calcined bauxite production. The new company would repay ALCAN for the value of DEMBA's asset from funds in the company's depreciation reserves. Operational management of the new company would be vested in a Chief Executive Officer nominated by ALCAN. The new company would be exempt from taxation and foreign exchange control and its after-tax profits would be allocated 70 per cent to ALCAN and 30 per cent to the government.

No wonder Prime Minister Burnham concluded in his 23 February1971 Address to the Nation that negotiations could not end with agreement. "We have offered partnership and have been threatened with continued domination. Our choice is between being men or being mice."

The decision to nationalise met with qualified support from the RATOON group. After all, prior to the start of the negotiations, the group had published a version of Girvan's paper "Why we need to nationalise bauxite and how to do it" in its monthly newspaper. Clive Thomas was also advocating not only the nationalisation of DEMBA but also the nationalisation of Reynolds Bauxite Company. The trade unions and civic groups, including the University of Guyana Staff Association and Student Association, welcomed the decision. Cheddi Jagan, while not opposing, criticised the government for not confronting the US by nationalising Reynolds Bauxite Company as well. Further afield, there was endorsement from UWI economists.

Alister McIntyre in his memoirs, *The Caribbean and the Wider World*, published in 2016, reports that he and William Demas had warned during the preparatory negotiation stage that management capacity implications needed to be carefully considered but their counsel was not heeded. Haslyn Parris, who had no experience at any level in the industry, was appointed Chief Executive Officer. Some of the difficulties ahead manifested themselves early. Unionised workers went on strike, particularly over concerns about the safety of their pensions. In addition to expatriate management and technical personnel, some Guyanese professional staff migrated to parent company subsidiaries in Jamaica and Trinidad and Tobago. Production decreased substantially almost instantaneously.

EXTERNAL TRADE BUREAU

The government in 1970 restructured the arrangements for international trade. It established an External Trade Bureau which would have sole responsibility for licensing merchandise imports. This meant that private enterprises which would have previously managed the entire sequence of transactions with foreign suppliers now had to channel their orders through the government agency. The Ministry of Foreign Trade oversaw the operations of the External Trade Bureau. Laurence Mann, who had returned from an extended stay in the United Kingdom, was appointed Permanent Secretary of the Ministry of External Trade. Soon there were public allegations of corruption in allocation of import licenses and procurement which ultimately led the Prime Minister in 1971 to dismiss the head of the External Trade Bureau and assign Laurence Mann to the post of Guyana Ambassador to Europe stationed in Brussels.

THE ASCRIA-PNC SPLIT

Events at DEMBA even prior to nationalisation had begun to strain the relationship between the leadership of ASCRIA and the leadership of the PNC. The PNC seemed to have formed the view that a strike by DEMBA workers in July 1970 was organised and managed by ASCRIA. Concerned by the decision to nationalise, DEMBA workers agitated about provisions to safeguard their pensions under the RILA scheme. ASCRIA went on record as sharing their concerns but was not supportive of the work stoppage. Matters between ASCRIA and the PNC came to crunch point on the issue of ministerial corruption. Eusi Kwayana specifically made corruption complaints against Hamilton Green and David Singh, two senior Cabinet members, to the Ombudsman in 1971 and criticised Prime Minister

Burnham for inaction in the "all-out war against corruption" which he had announced in January 1971 when he had dismissed the PNC's Chief Parliamentary Whip. The Prime Minister responded by dismissing Kwayana from his post as Chairman of the Guyana Marketing Corporation. Kwayana's public response to his dismissal was something to the effect that, "The Lord giveth and the Lord taketh away." It was disappointing to me that several public officials, whose appointments Kwayana had facilitated, acquiesced in his subsequent ostracisation by the government. I recall asking Wilbert Bascom, Managing Director of the GNCB, and Hugh Saul, who had been recruited to the post of General Manager of the Guyana Marketing Corporation, if they would maintain contact with Kwayana. Both men said they could not. Much later, Kwayana would chart a multi-ethnic course by collaborating with Moses Bhagwan's Indian People's Revolutionary Associates and join with the Movement Against Oppression to form the Working People's Alliance political party.

DISCORD IN THE PNC

In 1970/71 there were signs of discord in the PNC leadership. One instance pertained to local government reform. A commission established by the PNC government had submitted its report which was believed to have recommended greater democratisation of local government and more autonomy from the central government. After a long period had elapsed without the release of the report or any action by the government, Rickey Singh, a senior journalist with the widely read Guyana Graphic, published an article which extensively revealed the main recommendations of the commission's report. It was felt that the Minister of Local Government, Lewellyn John, had leaked the report to Rickey Singh to put pressure on his own government to act. Rickey Singh was taken by two very senior police and security officers to the Minister of Home Affairs, Desmond Hoyte, who demanded information on the source of the leak. Rickey Singh did not comply, whereupon he was physically assaulted by Hoyte. The subsequent possibility of legal action by Rickey Singh and potential political damage was averted by Miles Fitzpatrick, a radical lawyer, who arranged for Hoyte to apologise to Rickey Singh in the presence of the Prime Minister. Another instance of discord arose when Hamilton Green, the incumbent General Secretary of the Party was challenged for the post at the annual congress of the PNC in 1971. The Congress ended in disarray, much like the one in 1961 when Rawle Farley challenged Forbes Burnham for leadership of the party, and Hamilton Green retained his office as General Secretary.

DEPARTURE AND RETURN TO UNIVERSITY OF GUYANA

By the start of 1971, it had become evident that the University of Guyana was becoming politicised along party lines. The student body was split into PPP and PNC factions. The elections for the student union executive in 1971 resulted in an all-Indian executive to which the Afro-Guyanese students responded by establishing their own all-African student executive. The government had restructured the governing council of the university to give it a majority and had appointed members of Cabinet, such as Hamilton Green and the Prime Minister's wife, Mrs Viola Burnham, to the Council. It did not seem a place for me to develop professionally. I therefore made the decision to seek employment at the University of the West Indies in Jamaica.

I returned to the University of Guyana on several subsequent occasions to deliver guest lectures and to render service as an external examiner. In 1987 for instance, I lectured on "Monetary Relations in the Guyanese Macro-economy" and on 22 February 2002, I lectured on "Caribbean Development at the Start of the New Century". On 15 November 1997, I delivered the Graduation Address. My speech noted that university education provided both private and social rates of returns and stressed the contribution of higher education to economic growth, identifying channels of influence such as positive effects on labour quality and labour performance, the influence of knowledge and ideas on national productivity, ability to acquire, assimilate and adapt improved technology, and the role of education in social stability. I noted that the University of Guyana was underfunded and urged a major fiscal effort directed at expanding access and improving the quality of university services, highlighting what I considered to be the components of an enlightened fiscal approach, components such as investment in electronic technology infrastructure, faculty research and international academic cooperation and networks. I also urged private sector contributions to the University.

In 2009, I accepted an invitation by the government to become Chancellor of the University which had established a second campus at Tain, Berbice. My recently retired UWI colleague, Professor Lawrence Carrington, had been appointed Vice Chancellor in April 2009. At a cocktail reception in Guyana later that year, he broached the idea of me filling the post of Chancellor which had been vacant since Dr Bertram Ramcharan demitted office in 2007. I was the eighth in a line of Chancellors which included distinguished personages such as Sir Arthur

Lewis (1967-1973), William Demas (1975-1981) and Sir Shridath Ramphal (1987-1992).

I delivered my Installation Address on 3 December 2009 to an audience which included Prime Minister Samuel Hinds, several Ministers of the Guyana Government, members of the Diplomatic Corps, the Vice Chancellor, Pro Chancellor, other members of the University community, and people from the business community and wider society. My address used Sir Arthur Lewis' 1974 paper on "The University in Less Developed Countries" as my point of departure. Lewis had identified four roles: "Bearer of Culture", "Trainer of Skills", "Frontier of Knowledge", and "Service Agency". I elaborated on the ways in which universities can contribute to economic growth and development and pointed to the potential importance of university education in improving social relations, fostering social cohesion and instilling social responsibility, all of which seemed critically lacking in Guyana. I also returned to the issue of expanding university access with which I had dealt when I gave the Graduation Address in 1997. I quoted from Alfred Marshall's Principles of Economics to make the point that there need not be conflict between equity objectives and economic growth objectives, that, "Equality of educational opportunity is a social justice principle which combines positively with the economistic human capital justification." Marshall had written: "They, (the children of the working class) go to the grave carrying underdeveloped abilities and faculties which if they could have borne fruit would have added to the material wealth of the country ... many times as much as would have covered the expense of providing adequate opportunities for their development." I concluded my address by identifying cost-drivers in universities and appealing for government and business sector financial support to the University of Guyana.

I found the University to be even more conflict-prone than when I left 28 years ago. The Council was so factionalised that more of my time in the Chair was spent making peace and maintaining a framework for civil discussion than in getting the Council to focus on development matters. Some members of Council were appointees of the government and in a few instances held senior positions in the governing political party. The staff union representative on Council was a newspaper columnist who opposed the government and was the defendant in a libel suit filed by the Guyana President. At least two other leaders of the staff union were activists for the opposition political party and in all likelihood, there were also union members supportive of the governing political party.

The financial situation was precarious. The facilities were dilapidated with major buildings like the George Walcott Lecture Theatre in need of refurbishing. The library was sinking into the ground. The Turkeyen campus flooded frequently when it rained. Academic staff were not as well-qualified since many of them had not obtained doctoral degrees. There was no evidence of a research and publication culture. These problems were well recognised by Vice-Chancellor Carrington. In his several reports to the Council, he drew attention to inadequacies in the regulatory and management structures and systems which militated against efficiency and effectiveness; he pointed to infrastructural deficiencies; he noted the insufficiency of a research culture among academic staff; and he constantly drew attention to the inadequacy of government funding both in terms of budgetary approvals and timeliness of disbursements.

The Strategic Plan for the period September 2009-August 2012 stated that, "The greatest weakness by far is the underfunding of the University resulting in major deficiencies (material, human, technological, etc.) as well as a number of negative secondary effects." Accordingly, strategic goals included broadening of the university's financial base, enhancing its ability to recruit and retain high quality staff, and improvement of the teaching and learning environment. Infrastructural requirements receiving attention by the planners fell into four broad categories: educational technology; water, sewerage and drainage; electricity generating capacity; expansion, rehabilitation and refurbishment of physical facilities for teaching and learning.

On my first visit to the campus, I was accompanied by my wife who observed that the aesthetics of the campus was in need of improvement. She formed a committee which included Mrs Lorene Grant, Dr Marlene Cox, Mrs Indra Chandrapal, Mrs Yvonne Stephenson, Mr Charles Nelson and others for a tree planting beautification project which was successfully implemented. Sponsors of the project included private business entities and individuals. Donations were also received from friends of the university in the Caribbean, Canada, the UK and the US. Unfortunately, maintenance became a problem when project funds were re-allocated to other purposes by the university management.

In the Graduation Address which I delivered in 2010 to an audience which included the President of Guyana, as well as the Prime Minister and the Minister of Finance, I commented on the financial stringency under which the university operates and its effects on capital development, ability to offer attractive compensation and research facilities to high quality academic and professional staff, and on the quality of the learning environment. I also intimated the likelihood of a comprehensive independent review of the University's governance system and arrangements.

On the matter of the regulatory framework, it must be recognised that the University operated under the framework enacted in the University of Guyana Act which dated back to 1963. The Council itself is unwieldy with provision for 26 members, of which the governing political party effectively selects nine people, the university eight people and the opposition political party one person. The Trade Union Council and the University Staff Association each provide one representative. University officers, a representative of Deans and representatives of the student body and alumni comprise the remaining five members. My experience was that this structure and composition of the Council easily lent itself to factionalism in its deliberations. No revisions to the Act had been undertaken since 1963. Furthermore, there had been no comprehensive review of the university's governance structures and systems. The Strategic Plan for the period September 2009-August 2012 spearheaded by the Vice Chancellor identified improvement of "institutional governance, administration and management by statutory and structural adjustments" as a strategic goal. In March 2011, some progress was envisaged when, on my recommendation, the University initiated a Caribbean Development Bank consultancy project to strengthen its regulatory framework. The project was designed to review the effectiveness and efficiency of the university in the context of its mission and current regulatory structure; recommend processes, systems, structures and procedures; and examine the operational framework between the Turkeyen campus and the campus which had been recently established at Tain, Berbice. In addition, it was mandated to assess the University's budgetary and financial structures, its current methods of funding, and resource mobilisation structures.

Governance structures in modern universities clearly demarcate the boundaries between the functions and responsibilities of their Council or Board of Governors as the highest decision making and policy making and review body and the functions and responsibilities of executive management and academic management entities. Appointment of university officers such as members of the executive management and Faculty Deans would be a matter reserved for the governing body. Academic staff appointments, performance assessment, contract renewals and approval of leave would be matters within the remit of committees chaired by the Vice Chancellor or other designated university officers as would be the myriad micro-decisions normally required with respect to financial management, personnel management, facilities management, and security. Not so at the University of Guyana. Almost everything came to Council. To compound matters, government-nominated members of Council were members of the Appointments Committee and often referred matters to Council for final decision. This proved to be dramatically problematic in a matter of appointment beyond retirement age. Because it essentially sought to micro-manage the university, Council convened many times each year in Special and Extra-Ordinary Meetings. This is in stark contrast to modern universities where the governing body would rarely convene apart from its annual business meeting.

The outdated nature of the University's statutes combined with understandable problems of institutional memory lapses due to changes in the membership of the Council and University officers may have led to some inconsistency in approaches and decisions on at least two critical set of matters. The first was the appointment of a Registrar at the end of the contract of the incumbent, Mr Vincent Alexander, whose term of office would have ended on 31 March 2012. The second was appointment beyond retirement age for Mr Frederick Kissoon, an academic staff member in the Faculty of Social Sciences.

In relation to the post of Registrar, in my capacity of Chancellor, I wrote members of Council on 29 August 2011 to say that because the Registrar's current appointment would end on 31 March 2012, consideration should be given to the renewal of his appointment. I suggested a process which would start with a formal assessment and recommendation by the Vice Chancellor in his capacity as immediate supervisor, followed by the constitution of an ad hoc committee which would receive the report, deliberate on the matter and make recommendation to Council for reappointment or otherwise. The next stage would be Council's consideration and decision. I suggested that the ad hoc committee could be comprised of the Chancellor as Chairman, a named Government's representative on Council, the Ministry of Education representative on Council, a representative of the Deans, and a business sector representative.

To my surprise, Pro Chancellor Dr Prem Misir responded to my memo on 1 September 2011 stating that he had culled the views of some members of Council and that in the view of many members of Council my proposal was "highly irregular" and represented "a serious departure from the basic legal groundings of UGC appointments of senior officers, possibly and inadvertently constituting an attempt to pre-empt the entire appointments process of UGC appointments." He went on to state that they felt that Council could appoint a sub-committee but that my proposal that the Vice Chancellor provide an assessment report on the Registrar would be "ill-advised" and place the Vice Chancellor in an "invidious" position since he is also appointed by Council. The letter further stated that the process should "enable existing officers to reapply for their positions" and provide others with an opportunity to do so.

I took mental note of the fact that the Pro Chancellor did not identify how many and which Council members he had consulted but claimed that he was reporting "the view of many members", and that the wording of his letter implied an input by some member of Council with a legal background. Nonetheless, I responded to him in a memorandum dated 2 September 2011 in which I expressed my astonishment at the contents of his letter and stated specifically that as Chancellor I had been party to renewal of two senior University of Guyana officers, namely the Bursar and the Director of the Berbice campus and that in each case, an assessment and recommendation was made to Council by the Vice Chancellor as the immediate supervisor of the officer concerned. I stated that it could not and should not be otherwise in fairness to Council which has no direct knowledge of the performance details of the officers and in fairness to the officers who would be disadvantaged by less well informed and fact-based comment and that in my view it is an essential requirement for full and proper assessment and quite in keeping with international best practice. I also pointed out that the University's basic appointment procedures do not require UGC-appointed senior officials to re-apply for the positions they currently hold, that the contracts of the Registrar and the Director, Berbice campus explicitly made provision for renewal and furthermore, that no application for renewal was made in the case of the recent renewals of the Bursar and the Director, Berbice campus. I stated that it would be at variance with standard human resource management practice to require an incumbent to re-apply. Normal human resource management practice is to assess the person's performance as a basis for considering renewal or otherwise. I ended by noting that my proposal emphasised the pre-eminence of Council in deliberating and making a final decision on the Registrar's appointment.

On request of nine members of Council communicated on 6 September, an Extra-Ordinary Council Meeting was convened on 23 September 2011 to discuss appointment policy and other urgent related matters. Only three members were absent. On the matter of appointment of the Vice Chancellor and the Registrar, the Council decided that the Chancellor should write to them asking them to indicate in writing if they were interested in another contract of employment for the respective positions. Council also decided that the supervising officer of the Registrar, namely the Vice Chancellor, would prepare and submit a performance appraisal report on the Registrar, as was done for the Bursar and the Director of the Berbice campus. Eventually, the post of Registrar was advertised on insistence of some Council members who asserted that non-advertisement of the posts of Bursar and the Director of the Berbice campus was an aberration and that international best practice of first evaluating the incumbent and making a decision to renew or not renew his contract was inapplicable to Guyana.

An ad hoc Joint Committee of Council and Academic Board was established. It was comprised of the Chancellor as Chairman, the Vice-Chancellor, four Council members and four Academic Board members. On 31 May 2012, the Committee interviewed three of four applicants for the post of Registrar and decided that it was not necessary to interview the incumbent because there was sufficient prior knowledge of his service in the post. The Committee with one dissent recommended that the incumbent be offered a three-year contract. On 1 June 2012, a Special Extra-Ordinary Meeting of Council by majority vote approved the offer of appointment to the incumbent, Mr Vincent Alexander, thereby bringing the matter of renewal of the Registrar's appointment to a conclusion.

The matter involving Mr Federick Kissoon should have been straightforward but turned out to be complicated because many of the actors seemed unfamiliar with extant policies and procedures. Kissoon was due to be retired on 31 August 2011 and in anticipation of this offered his service to the university in a letter dated 25 July 2011.

Consideration of his offer should have been guided by the procedure set out by the then Registrar, Dr David Chanderbali, in a 20 February 2007 memorandum to Deans and Heads of Department. The memorandum headed "Process-Retention of University of Guyana Retired Staff" stipulated seven steps in the process. Step 1: Finish processing the applications for people below the retirement age. Step 2: Personnel Division must forward expressions of interest from retirees to the relevant academic department. Step 3: Departments/Faculties apply retention and assessment criteria as approved by the Appointments Committee at its meeting on 11 December 2006 for retention of rehired staff and submit justification. Step 4: The Vice Chancellor, in keeping with approved criteria, considers justification by Departments and advises whether recommended candidates should go forward to Appointments Committee for staff assessment.

Step 5: Where appropriate, Personnel Division requests faculties to submit academic staff assessment forms to Appointments Committee. Step 6: "Where appropriate, Personnel Division submits decision of Appointments Committee to Council for ratification." Step 7: Personnel Division and Registry will implement the decisions of Council.

The criteria to which the Registrar's memorandum referred were formulated by a committee comprised of the then Deputy Vice Chancellor, the Dean of Technology, a government appointed Council member, and the University Librarian. The committee stipulated in its report to the Appointments Committee that academic staff who have attained retirement age of 60 may be offered temporary contracts "in circumstances and on conditions that now prevail provided that they have healthy academic profiles". "The assessments should take into consideration their research, professional activities, lectures, course work and examinations."

The first issue was the absence of any evidence that the vacancy to be created by Mr Kissoon's impending retirement was advertised and that candidates under the retirement age had been processed in compliance with Step 2 of the process outlined by Registrar Chanderbali in February 2007. The second issue was the basis for the Dean's recommendation to the Special Meeting of the Appointments Committee held on 2 November 2011 that Mr Kissoon be appointed. The minutes of that meeting record him as making the recommendation "in light of the staffing situation in the Department." There was no explicit reference to the quality and intensity of Mr Kissoon's academic profile, that is, the "healthy academic profile" proviso in the criteria approved by the Appointments Committee. Mr Kissoon's curriculum vitae did not reveal a record of peer-reviewed research and publication that would satisfy the criteria of healthy academic profile. In fact, there was only one paper published by a reputable press, certainly unimpressive for an academic career spanning twenty-five years. Also, he had not been promoted beyond Lecturer II. The third issue is that like on so many occasions, the Appointments Committee accepted a motion by representatives of Council to refer the matter to Council instead of deciding to accept or reject the Dean's recommendation and forward its decision to Council for ratification.

However, prior to that decision by the Appointments Committee on 2 November 2011, the Registrar, Mr Vincent Alexander, had written to Mr Kissoon on 30 August 2011 informing him that, "the Vice Chancellor acting on behalf of the Appointments Committee" had approved a temporary appointment for one year beginning 1 September 2011. Mr Kissoon accepted the offer of appointment on 31 August 2011. The Appointments Committee was on 2 November deliberating on a matter that perhaps unknown to it had already been determined by the Vice Chancellor.

On 6 September 2011, seven members of Council, all of whom were appointed by the government, invoked Statute 13(5) to request an Emergency Extraordinary Meeting of Council attended by statutory members only to discuss "the UG appointments policy and procedures inclusive of the rehiring of retirees' policy and procedures". The Emergency and Extra-Ordinary Meeting of Council was convened on 23 September 2011. Council decided that all positions must be advertised, that retirees would be considered only after the consideration of eligible applicants, and that consideration of retirees would involve performance assessment of their service with the university to the point of retirement. These decisions meant that Mr Kissoon should not have been offered an appointment before those steps had been completed (and possibly might not merit appointment) and that the appointment made on 31 August 2011 should be terminated.

The staff union responded to the decisions of Council by organising strike action and protests in support of Mr Kissoon which ultimately failed to reverse the decisions even though the university's operations were severely disrupted, and its reputation damaged by politically biased and uninformed commentary by the union and its supporters.

The process of selecting a new Vice Chancellor was in train by October 2011. In response to my enquiry as mandated by Council, Vice Chancellor Carrington had indicated in writing on 4 October 2011 that he was willing to continue until a new appointee is identified and a date for assumption of duty is determined but would prefer to do so on a month-to-month arrangement so as not to have his personal plans compromised by the length of the recruitment process. On 1 May 2012, I informed Council members in writing that seventeen applications had been received by the closing date of 30 March 2012 and proposed that Council appoint an ad hoc committee of Council and Academic Board to conduct the initial review and shortlisting of applicants for final consideration and decision by Council. I recommended that the ad hoc committee be comprised of six or eight people, equally drawn from the membership of Council and the membership of Academic Board. The duly constituted Ad Hoc Joint Committee met on 31 May 2012 with me (as Chancellor) in the Chair and recommended five people for consideration by Council. That meeting was my last involvement in the process because I decided against a renewal of my tenure as Chancellor.

My term of office extended from July 2009 to 29 June 2012. The Council unanimously decided to re-elect me to serve a second term of three years but in a letter dated 25 June 2012 I declined. In my letter to members of Council I pointed out that at the outset of my term of office I had hoped to bring perspectives of modern university governance, performance requirements, performance standards, financial management and standards of collegial behaviour to deliberations in the Council and the wider university community. I indicated that I expected progress to be gradual given the low morale among staff and students, widespread pessimism about the university, the poor academic calibre and low research productivity of many of its staff and the associated need for a substantial staff development programme, and the acute financial difficulties faced by the University. I noted that what I was witnessing in 2012 was retrogression (rather than progress) evidenced by an unending series of strikes and protest demonstrations, deliberately inaccurate public statements, internecine anonymous memoranda, widening mistrust and antagonism between various segments of the University community and a marked diminution of willingness to engage in civil, rational discussion of issues and differences of opinion. I regarded this trend as inimical to effective transformation of the University into an institution that can command respect through the quality of the work of its academic staff and the achievements of its graduates. The Academic Board of the University met on 10 July 2012 and determined that the publicly expressed sentiments of some academic staff members which prompted my resignation "were not supported by the majority of academics whom it represents." It expressed appreciation for my "effective contributions ... to the functioning of the institution" and noted that I had spent an "unprecedented amount of time working on behalf of UG both on and off campus, in and out of Guyana." In the opinion of the Academic Board, "In Chancellor Bourne, UG has a committed and sympathetic Officer with international reputation and influence. His conduct is both dignified and erudite." The Academic Board hoped that the Council would prevail upon me to withdraw my resignation, but my decision had already been made. There would be no turning back.

I revisited the Turkeyen campus in October 2016 for the pleasurable purpose of seeing a street that bore my name. I was unaware of this development until at a chance meeting in the Georgetown Pegasus Hotel the then Vice Chancellor Professor Ivelaw Griffith informed me that the University had decided to honour past Chancellors by naming streets on the campus after them and that I was welcome to visit the campus to see the street named in my honour.

Reversal of the trend towards damaging internecine strife is a challenge still before the University. Strikes, demonstrations and adverse media interviews by union leaders and individual staff members have continued. Vice Chancellor Jacob Opadeyi who assumed duties early in 2013 to replace Vice Chancellor Carrington was the object of actions by the University of Guyana Senior Staff Association and the Workers Union, culminating in a no-confidence petition to Council and an appeal to the President of Guyana and the Minister of Education for intervention. Opadeyi's contract was not extended beyond its end in 2016. His successor, Professor Ivelaw Griffith, was appointed in June 2016 for a term of three years ending in June 2019. He had an encouraging and expansive start to his term of office but ultimately was the subject of criticisms and protest by both sets of unionised staff as well as adverse media interviews by the leadership of the Senior Staff Association. Vice Chancellor Griffith subsequently withdrew his request for renewal of contract.

CHAPTER FIVE

UNIVERSITY OF THE WEST INDIES, JAMAICA, 1971-1981

SETTLING IN

I took up an appointment as Lecturer in Economics at the Mona campus of the University of the West Indies on 6 September 1971. I was accompanied by my wife and our son, two-year old Clairmonte. We were welcomed by Vice Chancellor Sir Roy Marshall at one of the receptions he usually hosted for new academic staff members. We were greatly assisted in becoming settled by Adlith Brown, a colleague who had transferred from the St Augustine campus of the university a year previously, Eddie Greene who had also transferred from St Augustine, and John Gafar, a Guyanese lecturer in the Department who together with his wife, Bibi, was a source of useful information on procurement of household effects and a motor car. Adlith Brown, Eddie Greene and the Gafars were quite hospitable to me and my family.

Obtaining suitable housing was not easy. The department responsible for allocating residences seemed to reserve the best for expatriate non-West Indian faculty even when those recruits, having not arrived as yet, had no idea of what was available. The first residence we occupied was on the fringe of a noisy district some distance away from the campus. Our second, which we were able to secure because a departmental colleague Nugent Miller had surrendered it, was more suitable, located in a quiet neighbourhood close to the campus but maintenance problems developed, including a collapsing ceiling which the landlord failed to remedy. We were then allocated a house on University Close in an academic and professional staff housing development owned by the university. It is situated across from the campus. We settled there for most of our years in Jamaica. In later years, we resided briefly in Beverly Hills close to the campus and on Long Mountain Road in the same housing development as University Close.

University Close was remarkable for its occupants while we resided there. In our early years, our neighbours included political scientists Trevor Munroe, Eddie Greene, Ralph Gonsalves and Vaughan Lewis, economists Norman Girvan and Owen Jefferson, and sociologists Herman and Hermione McKenzie. There were also natural scientists like Dunbar Steele and Ronald Young who lived in houses adjacent to ours. Later in our stay, political scientists Carl Stone and Rupert Lewis, sociologist Bernard Coard and economists Dwight Venner and Claremont Kirton became residents in the Close. Close friendships were developed with these colleagues and maintained with a few even when the career paths of some took them out of the university environment. For instance, Dwight Venner relocated to St Lucia to become Financial Secretary and then to St Kitts-Nevis to assume duties as Governor of the Eastern Caribbean Central Bank from 1989 to 2015.

My wife and I attended Dwight Venner's 70th birthday celebration in St Lucia in 2015, the year before he unexpectedly died. Ralph Gonsalves transferred to the Cave Hill campus before entering representational politics as a member of the St Vincent and Grenadines Parliament in 1994. He became Prime Minister in 2001, remaining in office at the time of writing. Owen Jefferson went to the Jamaica Ministry of Finance in 1977 before becoming Deputy Governor of the Bank of Jamaica. Eddie Greene remained at the university until 1995 when he joined the Pan American Health Organisation as a Senior Adviser for four years and then the Caribbean Community Secretariat as Assistant Secretary-General from 2000 to 2010. Norman Girvan left the university in 1977 to become Director of the National Planning Institute of Jamaica, returned to the university as Director of the Consortium Graduate School and Director of the Sir Arthur Lewis Institute of Social and Economic Research, and then left again to take up the position of Secretary-General of the Association of Caribbean States when it was established in 2000.

FACULTY OF SOCIAL SCIENCES: COLLEAGUES AND ACTIVITIES

The composition of the Faculty of Social Sciences was mainly Caribbean. Among the people listed were eleven Jamaicans, five Trinidadians, six Guyanese, four Grenadians, one St Lucian, one Barbadian, one Dominican, two English, and one Sri Lankan.

In the Department of Economics initially there was George Cumper (English/Jamaican) who was Professor and Head of Department, Robert

Davidson (English)who taught labour economics, five Jamaicans namely, George Beckford (known popularly as 'GBeck') who taught agricultural economics, Alfred Francis who taught econometrics, Adlith Brown who taught international economics, Norman Girvan, and Owen Jefferson. Steve DeCastro who I had known from the ITABO days in Georgetown, Guyana, and John Gafar were from Guyana. Nugent Miller was from Grenada. Colleagues who entered the Department subsequently included Jamaicans David Wong, Michael Witter, Omar Davies, Colin Bullock, Mark Figueroa, Patricia McClean and Donald J. Harris (the father of Kamala Harris who became Vice President of the USA). Trinidadian Herman Brann joined as did Guyanese Claremont Kirton and Wilberne Persaud. Simon B. Jones-Hendrickson, a St Kittitian economist by profession and "poet by avocation" as he described himself, joined in 1973. Mark Figueroa was later to establish himself as a foremost authority on the work of Sir Arthur Lewis.

Three especially charismatic members of the faculty were Carl Stone, George Beckford and Steve DeCastro. Carl Stone commanded attention with his prodigious work ethic and research output on Jamaican political behaviour, his octane-charged debating style and his intimate knowledge of the Jamaican urban and rural lumpen-proletariat as he often termed the lower working class. George Beckford was folksy in dress, demeanour and speech. He was the sensitive guru of the Economics Department. Steve DeCastro was somewhat eccentric in cobbling his own leather shoes, using a necktie instead of a belt to hold up his trousers and starting a restaurant in Irish Town where he was the chef and sole worker. He would dash up the mountain to Irish Town to fulfil advance dinner requests of the few people who dared to dine there. Steve DeCastro left the Department late in the 1970s to lecture at the University of Brasilia where he had spent his three -month study leave previously.

There was a prominent older generation of social scientists in the faculty. Alister McIntyre was Director of the Institute of Social and Economic Research and Dean of the Faculty, Gladstone Mills was Professor of Public Administration and Head of the Department of Government and George Roberts, Professor of Demography, was in charge of the Caribbean 1970 Population Census.

The political scientists included Ann Spackman, Trevor Munroe, Carl Stone, Edwin Jones, Locksley Edmundson, Louis Lindsay, Vaughan Lewis, Eddie Greene, Ralph Gonsalves and Rosina Wiltshire. The sociologists and behavioural scientists were Sarah Graham, Frederick Nunes, Elsie LeFranc, Wilma Bailey, Herman McKenzie, Hermione McKenzie and

Bernard Coard. Sarah Graham left the university about two years after my arrival but not before loudly denouncing from the second-floor balcony some of her male colleagues who had withdrawn their friendship because of their new Black Power beliefs. The economists in the Institute of Social and Economics Research were Wallace Joefield-Napier, Ramesh Ramsaran, DeLisle Worrell, and Huntley Manhertz. Dhiru Tanna of Uganda origin, Asgar Ally, and Helen McBain joined later. Marshall Hall was recruited to head the new Department of Management Studies, the academic legitimacy of which was doubted by many members of the older social sciences disciplines, especially when it introduced a degree option in tourism and hotel management. The Department of Management Studies at its inception included Randolph Williams, Uriel Salmon, Christopher Ross, George Wadinambiaratchi (Wadi for short), Raphael Swaby and K.D. Edwards. They were soon joined by Dhiru Ramjeetsingh.

There was fluidity of academic staff between the teaching departments and the Institute of Social and Economic Research. Alister McIntyre was excellent in garnering research grants from the Ford Foundation and other such entities and from the International Development Research Council of Canada. The grants enabled the recruitment of academics to the ISER and facilitated full-time and part-time research by people whose substantive employment was in the teaching departments. A few of the projects were large and multi-disciplinary. One of them was the Caribbean Public Enterprise Project led by Adlith Brown in which academics from the UWI campuses and the University of Guyana participated. It produced book length publications which included papers on the role of the State in public enterprises by Edwin Jones and Carl Greenidge, a paper on the rationale for State ownership by Raphael Swaby and one on the administration of public enterprise in Jamaica and Trinidad and Tobago by Gladstone Mills, as well as many papers dealing with public enterprises in general or with specific ones in Barbados, Jamaica, Guyana, Trinidad and Tobago, and the West Indies Associated States, including one by me on the Jamaica Development Bank. There were also two papers on legal aspects of public enterprises in Guyana and the Commonwealth Caribbean authored by Arthur Alexander and Ralph Carnegie respectively.

The second large, multi-disciplinary and regional project was the Caribbean Technology Transfer Project led by Norman Girvan. Girvan was ably assisted by Owen Arthur who later moved with him to the National Planning Agency of Jamaica before returning to Barbados where he had a successful political career, including being Prime Minister.

Several university people outside of social sciences commanded attention. There was Professor Rex Nettleford whose talents were omnibus – political thought and political behaviour, trade unionism, West Indian history, culture and dance, among others. The Faculty of Arts and General Studies had Professor Roy Augier, the dean of Caribbean historians, Professor Douglas Hall, also a leading historian, and Edward Kamau Brathwaite, known more as a poet than a historian. Sir Harry Annamunthodo, a Professor of Surgery, was distinct for his white beard, white shirt and black suit, black shoes and no socks. Norris Melville and Sam Wray, Professors in the Faculty of Medical Sciences from the mid-1970s were noticeable not only for their youthfulness but also for their ostentatious consumption. Sam Wray had turned up with two identical sky-blue Jaguar motorcars and Norris Melville with a Mercedes Benz when few academics could aspire to such luxuries.

In the Faculty of Natural Sciences were Professors Wilfred Chan and Gerald Lalor in Chemistry, and Professor Leslie Robinson in Mathematics. Augier, Lalor and Robinson were subsequently appointed Pro Vice Chancellors. Carl Jackman in the post of University Registrar was a powerful administrator. Mr Ashton Preston was the University Bursar. He later successfully competed for the post of Vice Chancellor against several of his senior colleagues in the academic ranks, an outcome that was not favoured by many academics who saw him as merely an accomplished financial manager. In my judgement after having observed his performance as Chairman of the major academic committees, Ashton Preston, who often deprecatingly described himself as a "statutory academic" had a keen appreciation of academic values and traditions and exhibited strong commitment to the advancement of scholarship.

My initial teaching assignments were undergraduate monetary economics, a graduate course in public policy and an undergraduate course in social survey methods. When the department introduced a postgraduate optional paper called Directed Readings, I also supervised students wanting to specialise in money and finance.

I was fortunate to have many outstanding students at both undergraduate and postgraduate levels. In my first monetary class were Richard Byles who became a leading member of the Jamaican and Caribbean business community and now serves as Governor of the Bank of Jamaica, Jamaica's Central Bank. In that class too was Colin Bullock who upon completing his postgraduate degree became a member of the Department and then moved on to distinguish himself as Jamaica's Financial Secretary and

Director-General of the Planning Institute of Jamaica. Another member of the class was Gladstone (Tony) Lewars who subsequently pursued a career in accountancy and rose to a Partnership in PricewaterhouseCoopers, a leading accountancy firm in Jamaica.

People completing my graduate course in public policy included Byron Blake who became Assistant Secretary-General of the Caribbean Community and Jamaica's Permanent Representative to the United Nations and the Organisation of American States; Alan Slusher who became Governor of the Central Bank of Belize, Director of Economics at the Caribbean Development Bank, Economic Adviser to the Prime Minister of Belize and President of the University of Belize; Claremont Kirton, who became Professor of Economics in the same Department many years later; and Swinburne Lestrade who held a variety of top level governmental positions in Dominica, United Nations Commission for Latin America and the Caribbean, the Organisation of Eastern Caribbean States where he was Director-General, and also was Dominica's Ambassador of the United States and the Organisation of American States.

These former students are just the ones from my first year who excelled in later life. Many other subsequent generations of students did exceptionally well in their careers. I think of Michael Howard and others who became academics themselves; Richard Bernal who after stints in academia and at the Bank of Jamaica became an outstanding Jamaica Ambassador to the United States of America and later returned to UWI as Pro Vice Chancellor for Global Affairs; Carlene Francis who became Governor of the Central Bank of The Bahamas; Mignon Guishard and Laurel Bain who became senior officers at the Eastern Caribbean Central Bank; Derick Latibeaudiere who became Governor of the Bank of Jamaica; William "Billy" Marston who became a senior officer at the Bank of Jamaica and then joined the IMF where he rose to a very senior position; Omri Evans who became a senior professional in the Jamaica National Planning Agency; and Herman Grant, who after a stint at the Bank of Jamaica, joined the Caribbean Development Bank.

For a short while, the publications on plantation economy, especially Beckford's book, *Persistent Poverty*, attracted a few international graduate students from Africa, Pakistan and the Pacific Islands to the department. They all did well and upon completing their programme of studies returned to positions in academia in their home countries. There was no effort by the university to transform these beginnings of international student recruitment into a sustainable component of its overall student body.

THE FACULTY OF SOCIAL SCIENCES ENVIRONMENT

The Social Sciences Faculty at Mona was a place of intellectual ferment. There were almost non-stop discussions in the Institute of Social and Economic Research tearoom and seminar room, along the corridors in the building which housed teaching faculty offices, in the Faculty seminar rooms, and under the trees in the open spaces in front of the Faculty buildings. There were Saturday morning reviews of books published by staff members and others and presentations of research papers. The work on plantation economy which had centre stage late in the 1960s was in its final stages with only George Beckford and Norman Girvan working in that field. The rest of the economists were busy applying more orthodox concepts to their analyses of microeconomic and macroeconomic behaviour in Caribbean economies. In the Faculty in those days, one listened to Louis Lindsay's trenchant review of Trevor Munroe's recently published book on the politics of Jamaican constitutional decolonisation, Donald Harris' critique of plantation economics as dead end economics, Alfred Francis' presentation on natural resource taxation and economic growth, Steve DeCastro on turnpike growth models and on air transportation in the Caribbean, Randolph Williams on taxation of cement, my own presentation on the political economy of indigenous commercial banking in Guyana, Huntley Manhertz's presentation of his econometric model of the Jamaican economy, and Eddie Greene's presentation on race and electoral behaviour in Guyana. There were discussions of current public policy issues such as agricultural land reform, bauxite nationalisation, financial sector reform, public enterprises, minimum wages, and inspired by Carl Stone's work, sometimes heated discussions on political behaviour, especially voting behaviour.

Political developments in Jamaica provided a compelling context for much of the discussions about social and economic policy. The People's National Party (PNP) led by Michael Manley had won a major victory over the Jamaica Labour Party (JLP) led by Hugh Shearer in the general elections held on 29 February 1972, bringing an end to ten years of governmental administration by the Jamaica Labour Party (JLP). As Michael Manley stated in his book, *Jamaica: Struggle in the Periphery*, published in 1982, the PNP had embarked on a reformist agenda which included land reform, notably through Project Land Lease which was started in 1972 and redistributed idle lands to more than 23,000 small farmers with complementary provision of agricultural inputs, credit and technical advice. The reformist agenda also included rationalisation of foreign investment, government participation in the bauxite industry, expansion of the public sector by public ownership of commercial banks, and direct government involvement in foreign trade through creation of a State Trading Corporation for importation of basic items. The policy was extended to the labour sector by introduction of minimum wage legislation. The government further added to the policy agenda early in its life by initiating an adult literacy campaign, deciding to finance tuition fees for secondary and tertiary education, and introducing a National Youth Service.

As might be expected of a vibrant university, there were also lectures by visiting intellectuals. C.L.R. James, the noted Trinidadian intellectual and author of *The Black Jacobins*, gave a most stimulating lecture about the interplay of politics and economic change in Trinidad and Tobago during the time he worked with Prime Minister Eric Williams. Sir Arthur Lewis visited and gave several lectures after the award of the Nobel Prize in Economics to him. I remember debating him on some trade statistics at the end of one lecture. I had read a recently published paper by a UK economist John Spraos which challenged the accuracy of data used by Lewis in his own work. Lewis demurred politely when I sought to use Spraos' paper to press him on the subject. He eventually won the argument by turning to his wife, Lady Gladys, and saying: "Gladys, do you remember John Spraos? He was my student. His statistics were always bad."

Two practices were fundamental to the intellectual environment at Mona. One was the presence of Faculty members most of daylight hours from Monday to Saturday. This was in stark contrast to the St Augustine campus where I observed on visits that academic staff in economics were noticeable by their absence outside of classroom hours. The other practice, also missing at St Augustine, was interchange between staff and students. At Mona, there was even an annual seminar held at the university's Blue Mountain vacation building solely for the purpose of presentation of research papers by selected final year students to their peers and academic staff. Some Faculty members, including me, would also arrange social functions with their final year classes and the classes together would do likewise.

There was a short-lived crisis within the Faculty in 1972. It pertained to appointment of someone to the newly created Chair in Applied Economics. Among the candidates were Donald J. Harris, Albert Hines, Havelock Brewster and Alfred Francis. Donald Harris was then a Professor at the University of Wisconsin in the US. Albert (Bertie) Hines was a professor at the University of Durham in the UK who was well regarded for his seminal publication on the link between trade unionism and inflation. His life story was a particularly interesting one: labouring on the Kingston docks as a teenager, working as a bus driver in London while pursuing secondary education part-time, and undergraduate and graduate study at the London School of Economics. Havelock Brewster, who was previously in the Department, was then at the Commonwealth Secretariat in London, England. Departmental colleagues favoured the selection of Alfred Francis, but it was reported that the university's Selection Committee recommended the appointment of Hines. Departmental members objected strongly. A Faculty meeting was convened at which the Dean, Alister McIntyre defended the process but was unable to quench the fires. In the end, Alfred Francis was appointed Professor of Applied Economics. Brewster later was appointed to the Departmental Chair in Economics at the Cave Hill campus but left after a short while.

PERSONAL ECONOMIC RESEARCH

PHD STUDY ON MONETARY BEHAVIOUR

My career as an economist gathered significant momentum when I joined the UWI at Mona. In 1972, I started to work on a PhD thesis under the supervision of Alfred Francis who was then Professor of Applied Economics. After a period of indecision, I decided to do an econometric study of monetary behaviour in Jamaica. Professor Francis was everything I could hope for in a research supervisor. He was extremely thorough and knowledgeable in the fields of statistics and econometrics, often extending me by insisting that I delve into relevant chapters in Stuart and Kendall's Advanced Theory of Statistics, by probing my knowledge of new topics such as first-order certainty equivalence, principal components, dynamic simulations, linear interpolation of times series and regression by related series which I had discovered independently, and asking searching questions about the monetary and financial aspects of my theoretical and historical frameworks. He was always encouraging and gentle though frank in his appraisals. When the time came that the computer facilities at Mona were inadequate for my work, he arranged with Nobel Prize winner Professor Robert Solow and Professor Edwin Kuh for me to access the facilities at the Massachusetts Institute of Technology (MIT) during the summer of 1973. What started as a collegial relationship between Alfred Francis and me developed into a close friendship that lasted until his demise in August 2015.

Wallace Joefield-Napier who was working under Professor Francis's supervision on a PhD thesis on consumer behaviour in Jamaica was also of great assistance to me in the early stages of the computational work. He introduced me to the old IBM 360 or 1620 mainframe computer which utilised punch cards and kept my company many nights when I struggled with its fits and starts. The computer facilities at the MIT were far superior to those at UWI. I was able to access a powerful mainframe not by going to the Yale University campus in New Haven, Connecticut, where it was located but by inputting my data and running my regressions on terminals in MIT's National Bureau of Economic Research branch office or in the department of economics. Economists located in Tokyo and Rome were able to do likewise.

While I was doing the further econometric computations at the MIT, I was accommodated by my Guyanese friend, Reynold Burrowes, who was pursuing graduate studies towards a PhD degree in international relations at the Fletcher School of Law and Diplomacy at Tufts University in Massachusetts. He lived in campus housing for postgraduate students. He shared a two-bedroom apartment with another student who was out of the country for a few months, therefore, I could be comfortably housed for the duration of my stay.

Despite a tight schedule, I made time to catch up with Colin Nurse, a brother of our friend Horace Nurse, who was doing a PhD programme in marine biology at Harvard University, and attend the Boston Jazz Festival to hear Stevie Wonder and Rahsaan Roland Kirk, and to visit New York City. In New York, we visited museums, historical sites, and Columbia University where we met Monica Jardine, and caught up with some other friends at parties in Brooklyn. I returned to Jamaica at the end of summer 1973 but got distracted for the better part of twelve months by other research and conference commitments and did not complete my PhD until 1975.

MONEY AND BANKING

I continued to research and publish on money and finance. Among the topics were demand for money functions, money stock determination, savings behaviour and mobilisation, central banking, commercial banking, government domestic and foreign debt financing, development banking, economic aspects of life insurance, inflation, and rural finance.

I drew on my PhD thesis to publish journal articles on demand for money and money stock determination. A paper written in 1976 on central bank rediscount policy also drew on material in the thesis. It started with Havelock Brewster's view (Brewster 1973) that central banks in the Caribbean were mainly of symbolic importance rather than having any real influence on the economies. I elucidated two facets of that view, namely that the policy instruments were inadequate or that structural dependence on metropolitan financial centres nullified expressed domestic policies. I chose to analyse central banking policy action in the first decade of Jamaica's constitutional independence and concluded that the Jamaica rediscount rate was influenced more by the UK rediscount rate than by Jamaican economic growth and foreign reserves.

On the commercial banking industry, I published a paper in CSO Research Papers in 1979 on "Commercial Bank Interest Rates in Trinidad and Tobago" which contained a profit maximising model of deposit and loan pricing and concluded that the level of national income and the rate of price inflation were strong push factors on bank loan rates of interest and that the deposit rate is positively but weakly sensitive to changes in income and the price level. Two years previously, I had formulated and tested a model of commercial bank portfolio behaviour in Jamaica which concluded that deposit liabilities were the main determinant of short-period changes in bank portfolios, that interest rate changes were not quantitatively significant influences on portfolio allocation, and that exposure to foreign exchange risks influenced portfolio behaviour.

Aspects of the commercial banking industry in the Eastern Caribbean Currency Area were analysed in two papers. One written in November 1977 dealt with structural features of the industry. It noted that there were thirty commercial banks in operation and that some of them were new entrants. Commercial banks were predominant in the financial sector because of their control of the payments mechanism but building societies and life insurance companies were emerging as serious rivals. Thirty of the banks were totally foreign owned. Branch banking was uncommon in the area but because there were no restrictions on transfer of funds between banks in different islands, commercial banks could draw upon the liquid reserves of sister banks when warranted. The commercial banking industry in the ECCA was highly concentrated with the largest bank having between 50 per cent and 66 per cent of industry assets in the seven countries, except Antigua and Barbuda and St Lucia. Savings and time deposits were the major components of total deposits. Assets were mainly short term, consisting of cash, balances due, investments, and short-term loans and advances.

The second paper "Commercial Bank Costs and Earning in the ECCA" was presented to the annual conference of the Regional Programme of Monetary Studies conference in St Kitts and Nevis in 1979. The paper presented information on sixteen banks. Foreign-owned banks controlled between 38 per cent of industry deposits in the case of Dominica and 100 per cent in the case of Grenada. The main elements in the cost structure of the banks were labour costs and interest costs. The banks operated conservatively and therefore needed to make only minimal provision for loan losses. The cost structures were similar across the ECCA but dissimilar within countries. The dissimilarities among banks in individual countries was attributable to differences in interest charges on balances due to other financial institutions and to control offices, and to administrative charges paid to control offices. Interest on loans was the major component of earnings by commercial banks in the ECCA. Foreign exchange earnings were also substantial. The structure of earnings was similar across the region but dissimilar within countries.

The study also examined the profitability of the banks utilising three profitability indicators, namely, operating margins measured by total earnings as a percentage of total operating costs; gross profits as a percentage of total current earnings; and after-tax profits as a percentage of total current earnings. It was concluded that the industry was a low risk, high return one and that there was no profit incentive to innovate.

Comparisons were made with the banking industry in Jamaica and Trinidad and Tobago. One finding was that the cost structures were similar even though for some years there were differences in a few cost elements. Secondly, the earnings profiles were quite different because of the greater extent of investment in government securities in Jamaica and Trinidad and Tobago and because of the higher ratios of loans to total assets in those two countries. Thirdly, operating margins were higher in the ECCA compared to Jamaica but lower than those in Trinidad and Tobago.

In 1977/78, I started a book length study on the Jamaica Development Bank and completed the first draft but never managed to revise it for publication. One chapter served as the basis for presentation at the Caribbean Studies Association conference in Martinique in 1979. I presented on "Public Sector Financing of Industrial Development: The Case of Jamaica". In that presentation, I explained the emergence of public sector supply of industrial credit as part of comprehensive support policies for industrial development and examined the operations of the Jamaica Development Bank in that context for the period 1970-1977. The topics analysed included the trend in loan approvals and loans outstanding both of which increased greatly, the sourcing of loanable funds by the JDB, of which foreign funds were a substantial proportion until 1976, loan rates and other credit conditions, size and industry characteristics of the loan portfolio, and finally the matter of repayment performance and long-run viability. On this last aspect, the paper documented high loan delinquency towards the end of the period.

My analysis of the domestic debt of Caribbean countries was presented to the Regional Monetary Studies conference in Barbados in 1976. The paper "Current Trends and Problems in Domestic Debt Financing" was published in Public Finances in the Caribbean edited by me in 1977. It dealt with the growth and structure of internal public debt in Barbados, Guyana, Jamaica and Trinidad and Tobago. It showed a large expansion of the debt in nominal terms between 1965 and 1976. The growth in internal debt was explained in term of public policy response to social pressures, build-up of the military capacity, investment in physical infrastructure, and weak fiscal revenue capacity. It pointed to several market constraints on the public internal debt, namely, commercial bank portfolio rigidity, limitations on portfolio demand of other types of financial institutions, personal sector liquidity preference for bank deposits, the absence of secondary securities markets, and the public lack of confidence in government's ability to honour debt obligations. The paper went on to examine macro-economic issues, notably the crowding-out effects of government borrowing on private sector access to credit, debt servicing costs, and monetary expansion.

Outside of the money and finance field, I researched and published on a variety of subjects, including agricultural economics, land reform, and wage price policy and wage determination.

AGRICULTURAL ECONOMICS

In 1980, Colin Weir, Elsie LeFranc, Frederick Nunes and I did a study on Small Farming in the Less Developed Member Countries of the Caribbean Development Bank under a consultancy contract granted to Weir's Agricultural Consultancy Services by the Caribbean Development Bank. The report was published as a 335-page book by the Caribbean Development Bank. Eight countries were studied: Antigua and Barbuda, Belize, Dominica, Grenada, Monserrat, St Kitts and Nevis, St Lucia, and St Vincent and the Grenadines. Each country chapter began with an introduction to the physical features of the country, its infrastructure, population and work force, and the economy. The rest of the chapter then dealt with the overall agriculture sector before analysing in detail the situation of small farming with attention to the size of holdings, farming systems, cropping patterns, productivity, livestock farming systems, marketing, agricultural credit and government policies. I wrote the country chapters on Dominica, St Kitts and Nevis, and Montserrat. Colin Weir and I wrote the chapter on the aggregate summary and analysis as well as the chapter on recommendations.

In 1981, I again teamed up with Weir's Agricultural Consulting Services which had been awarded a contract by the Caribbean Development Bank to report on Commercial Tree Crop Production in the Caribbean Region. The main technical people on the engagement were Colin Weir and Egbert Tai but I wrote the section on marketing in which I reviewed previous studies before examining the situation with respect to international and regional trade in fresh fruit and processed fruits and import substitution in those types of fruits. With respect to international trade, the major non-regional purchasers of fresh fruit were the European Economic Community, Canada and the United States. The scope for exports depended greatly on personal incomes in the importing countries, consumer acceptability and marketing efforts by suppliers. I noted that Caribbean Community countries were minor players but that unit values of exports were remunerative. The main obstacles to expansion of fresh fruit exports, apart from marketing effort, were the small quantities of domestic production compared to world output, the mismatch between the quality preferences of buyers and the quality of fruit offered by Caribbean suppliers, and tariff and non-tariff barriers. There was market potential in the case of processed fruits given the growth in world consumption, but the Caribbean would need to satisfactorily address deficiencies in scale of production, processing facilities, and marketing capacity and effort. Tariff barriers and health and safety regulations applied by purchasing countries also needed to be considered in fashioning export strategies. In the case of regional trade, a considerable amount of fresh fruit was traded. The commodity composition was diversified. Marketing was mainly in the hands of informal traders and small shippers. The regional trade in processed fruit consisted mainly of citrus-based product with Jamaica, Trinidad and Tobago, Belize and Dominica being the main exporters. The marketing section of the study ends with observations about the scope for import-substitution in processed fruits.

LABOUR ECONOMICS

At the invitation of Carl Stone who was editing a special issue of the *Journal of Social and Behavioural Sciences* in 1974, I wrote on "Structure, Power and Wage Price Policy in the West Indies" and for the International Labour Office in 1977, I wrote on "Wage Determination in the Caribbean Countries: Trends and Issues". The invitations provided opportunities to analyse trade union behaviour and wage price policy in the Caribbean. The insights gained from these academic efforts served me well in a major labour dispute at the St Augustine campus much later in my career.

In the Structure, Power and Wage Price Policy paper, I stated reasons why wages and prices are of macro-economic importance, namely, the dependence of the economies on foreign trade and the influence of wages and prices on trade performance; the absence of domestic control over import prices which made domestic prices and wages the only policy levers; the influence of wages and prices on national savings and long-run economic growth; and economic welfare effects generated by trends in wages and profits. I identified two forms of wage-price policy which are direct wage-price restraint and State intervention in production, distribution and trade and noted that the sufficient condition for successful wage-price policy is that wage (price) increases lag appreciably behind price (costs) as happens when there are lengthy bureaucratic delays in wage and price negotiations. The paper extensively discussed worker resistance, power and effectiveness of wage restraint policy. It identified the issues which motivate trade unions and other worker representatives as maintaining or enlarging real incomes, their perceptions of relative deprivation, and their perceptions of class alliances between the business community and governments. The paper discussed labour's power as a factor in wage negotiations and wages policy, making the point that its strength derives from the adverse consequences of disruption of labour services for businesses or governments, the ability of businesses to pass on wage increases by raising prices to customers, the strategic importance of the industry or enterprise, the longer-term prospect of labour replacement through technology changes, and labour's political influence. There were also costs of seeking to exercise power, especially loss of labour income during strikes and loss of jobs from company closures.

Producer resistance, power and the failure of price restraint policy were also explored. I argued that the strength of producer resistance depended on the nature of the market, employers' belief about how labour markets work and the extent to which production relied on imported inputs. I suggested that producers might have social power emanating from their role in supply of goods and services and employment of labour, as well as from their contributions to the finances of political parties. Moreover, faced with resistance to wage-price policies, governments sometimes resorted to policy subterfuges such as direct tax concessions and subsidies, and in extreme cases foreign exchange rate devaluation.

The paper on wage determination for the International Labour Office detailed some features and trends in the collective bargaining environment such as the growth of trade unionism, recognition of bargaining rights as a recurring problem, and the decline in real wages despite trade union actions, including strikes, sit-outs and go-slows. It addressed the issue of public sector wage determination in the context of government being one of the largest employers, the different positions of blue-collar and white-collar public service employees, and the absence of applicable measures of labour productivity and market valuations of services. It noted that labour was more successful in negotiating wage increases in State enterprises and government commercial agencies and pointed to the resultant thorny issue of wage increase transferability to other parts of the public service. Returning to the matter of incomes policy, the paper commented on the exclusion of worker organisations from policy discussions at preparatory stages, the need to be mindful of urban-rural income differentials, the role of price controls, price indexation, and the links to foreign trade and economic development.

COLONIAL PUBLIC ECONOMIC POLICY IN GUYANA

In March 1978, I made a solitary venture into Guyanese economic history with a presentation titled "Public Economic Policy and Colonial Underdevelopment: British Guiana, 1900-1020" to the 10th Annual Conference of Caribbean Historians in the US Virgin Islands. I posited that the budget was the main instrument of public economic policy, that budget debates in the Combined Court were the occasion for expression of development ideas as well as partisan interests, and that revenue and expenditure decisions were the means of resolving them. The central thesis advanced was that the conflicting interests of the legislative groups shaped public economic policy with respect to the two main development ideas contending for fiscal support, namely the further development of the sugar industry as the leading sector and economic diversification through peasant agriculture and import-substituting manufacturing industry.

Joseph Chamberlain, British Colonial Secretary, had articulated a "great estates" development concept which held that colonial development meant the development of both the British Empire and British industry. For British Guiana, he envisaged the resuscitation of the sugar industry and the expansion of the mining industry and rejected the idea of economic diversification and establishment of an independent peasantry.

In British Guiana under the 1891 constitution, public economic policy was made in the Combined Court which was an all-inclusive grouping of the Court of Policy and the College of Financial Representatives. The Court of Policy solely endowed with legislative powers was comprised of the Governor, the Government Secretary, the Attorney General, two or three other senior public officials and three unofficial members nominated by the Governor. The College of Financial Representatives was comprised of the Governor as President, four ex officio members, three appointed public officials, and eight elected unofficial members consisting of two representatives from Georgetown, and one each from New Amsterdam, East Demerara, West Demerara, Berbice, North West Essequibo and South West Essequibo. The Combined Court determined budgetary policy. In terms of class and interest group profiles, the elected members of the Combined Court were more representative of the middle class based in commerce and the professions and of urban and rural workers and the peasantry than of the planter class.

Some elected members of the Combined Court were supportive of economic diversification and an enlarged peasantry. Various contributions in the debates proposed a land settlement scheme, creation of an agricultural bank, government investment in drainage and irrigation for the benefit of the peasantry, establishment of an agricultural college, and establishment of centralised sugar factories to purchase sugar cane from peasant farmers. Recommendations for manufacturing development included provisions of fiscal incentives and production of wheat flour substitutes utilising rice, cassava, plantains and tannias. The latter innovative proposal for flour substitutes was the first recorded instance of such and was not put on the policy agenda until the 1970s by President Forbes Burnham.

The development ideas differed considerably in their public economic policy requirements. The sugar industry which was already well capitalised needed support for export prices in the UK market (which was opposed by Hicks-Beach, the Chancellor of the Exchequer in the Chamberlain government), the maintenance of demand in the UK, and cheap labour in British Guiana, none of which required substantial fiscal resources in the colony. Expansion of the mining industry was more demanding because it required massive infrastructural investment which was not forthcoming from private investors. Expansion of the peasantry was also a fiscally expensive prospect because of the costs of infrastructure, introduction of credit facilities at affordable rates of interest, costs of technical assistance to farmers, and grants of land. Manufacturing development required support through fiscal incentives.

The public policy response which played out in the Combined Court rested heavily on a few basic economic beliefs, preconceptions and class interests. The most constant element in resistance voiced by the representatives of the planters to the economic diversification proposals was fiscal stringency and the need to balance the budget. This fitted well with the balanced budget philosophy to which Prime Minister Chamberlain adhered. Examples of the specific cases where the objections were made are the proposal for a Courentyne Coast Railway, a proposal for coastal drainage and irrigation expenditures, and the construction of an agricultural college. The opposition to economic diversification also took the form of resistance to budgetary switches of expenditures which would have created the fiscal space to finance the proposed projects without violating the balanced budget maxim. There was resistance to de-earmarking of the sugar acreage tax which was intended to finance the costs of importing labour. De-earmarking would have expanded the amount of fiscal revenues available for other uses and required the sugar planters to absorb those costs. Colonial Secretary Chamberlain weighed in on the side of the planters by asserting that de-earmarking would be inequitable since the entire colony benefited from immigration of indentured labourers. Underlying the position of some planter representatives and the colonial authorities was a deep-seated objection to the growth of an African peasantry. Hodgson, a member of the Court dismissing the idea of African land settlers, felt that Africans should accept indentureship under the same conditions as Indians, and that they were incapable of satisfying "the necessity of giving continuous labour", a view to which Colonial Secretary Chamberlain subscribed when he wrote to Hodgson to say that Blacks in British Guiana have an aversion to plantation work and display no industry elsewhere. Another line of resistance, although implicit, was under-provision of financial resources for projects which were approved like the agricultural banks which the Combined Court had agreed in November 2011 to foster. In the case of the centralised sugar factories proposal, the objection was based on a presumed competition between government as owner of the factories and the planters and an anticipated conflict between peasant cultivators and estates over price of sugar cane.

The ideas for manufacturing development fared better in the Combined Court. Approval was granted for reduction of import duties on raw materials used in soap manufacture and of excise duties on locally made matches. When it came to the sugar industry, the Combined Court was entirely supportive. It increased budgetary expenditures on infrastructure beneficial to it and opposed a proposal that states should bear more of the health costs burden of Indian indentureship and the full costs of immigration and repatriation since in Chamberlain's words, "the colony as a whole derives benefits, financial and otherwise, from coolie immigration as being in large measure State-aided colonisation." It also resisted de-earmarking of the acreage tax as previously indicated and increased taxation of sugar production.

GERMAN VOLUNTEER SERVICE

Somewhat outside my normal fields of enquiry was an evaluation of the German Volunteer Service which I did in 1977 with Elsie Le Franc and a German consultant Uwe Luck. We interviewed volunteers and their employers or supervisors throughout Jamaica, sometimes in quite remote locations. On the whole, there was strong commitment among volunteers to development of the communities and institutions in which they worked but good intentions were not always matched by achievement because of several complicating variables such as clashes with authoritarian supervisors, lack of timely material support from the Volunteer Agency and the Jamaican government, and romantic entanglements of volunteers and their family members.

EASTERN CARIBBEAN AND BELIZE

EASTERN CARIBBEAN

My first work sortie in the Eastern Caribbean apart from conference attendance was in the company of Dwight Venner in January, March and April 1974. Alister McIntyre had arranged for us to do a report on foreign exchange control in the Associated States. The assignment necessitated travel to each member country in the Windward and Leeward Islands and Barbados where the East Caribbean Currency Authority was located, but our visit to Grenada had to be cancelled. We interviewed senior officers of the East Caribbean Currency Authority; Financial Secretaries in the Associated States; Exchange Control officers; managers of commercial banks, cooperative banks, insurance companies, development corporations and other pertinent institutions. These interviews enabled an initial understanding of the economic workings of their economies. We were surprised to learn from the British Financial Secretary in Montserrat which was still a Crown Colony of Britain that all the records of foreign exchange application, approval and transaction were kept in a black notebook which he removed from his back pocket and showed us. The system in the other islands was not as unstructured as in Montserrat.

My next work visit to the islands was the following year when I was contracted by the Caribbean Development Bank to evaluate its Farm Improvement Credit Scheme in operation in the Windward and Leeward Islands and Belize. I visited the development banks or development finance corporations which administered the loan portfolio in their country, interviewed their management and credit officers and analysed their loan documents and financial records. I also visited and interviewed selected loan recipients. An important lesson about ensuring the completeness of credit appraisal was provided by the case of a loan for commercial fishing in St Lucia. The recipient who was a very experienced ship captain successfully met the projected targets for landed catch per single voyage but failed to have as many voyages as projected because adequate marketing arrangements were not in place for quick sales of the catch and the ship consequently spent more time in port than projected. The project failed. The field visit to Belize yielded an insight in the burden of collateral requirements on loans to small farmers. One farmer, after itemising and estimating the value of every physical asset he owned, satisfied the collateral requirement only by placing a monetary value on his wife. I was sufficiently curious to visit that farm-household.

In 1977, I was invited by the Eastern Caribbean Central Bank to join a small team comprised of George Theophilus, the Deputy Governor of the Bank, Errol Allen, Director of Research, and an IMF expert to review and make recommendations on the alignment of the Eastern Caribbean dollar with the United States dollar. We worked intensively over a weekend but without the participation of the IMF expert who failed to appear after the first working session. Our recommendation of a parity rate was accepted by the governing body of the Bank. It remains the official exchange rate between the US dollar and the Eastern Caribbean dollar.

BELIZE

I was fascinated by Belize. The accent of most Belizeans was so close to the Guyanese accent that on my first encounters with Belizeans at UWI, Mona, I thought they were Guyanese. Belizeans are among the most hospitable people in the Caribbean. Belize is rugged and sparsely populated like Guyana and has large rivers. It had a population of jaguars and other cat species which attracted foreign hunting parties. Jaguars could be seen at night crossing the highway connecting the new capital "city" of Belmopan and the old capital, Belize City. Perhaps for that reason, some men travelled with shotguns and revolvers, although I was informed by my liaison on a field trip which we started early one evening that the shotgun he carried was for protection against bandits not animals. Belize City itself had wooden houses and office buildings very much like Georgetown, Guyana, but uniquely had a river running through it.

On a visit to Belize a few years later for the purpose of giving a lecture, Irving Holder (the brother of Peter Holder, a former high school classmate) who was then residing in Belize took me to Orange Walk which I liked so much that I decamped from a comfortable hotel in Belize City and spent the rest of my stay in Orange Walk sleeping in a hammock I bought in the absence of a bed. From Orange Walk, I visited Corozal near the Belize-Mexico border. In Orange Walk, I made friends with sugar cane farmers who were then benefiting from buoyant international sugar prices. With them late one night, and with the permission of the Mexican border guard, I crossed over the Mexico-Belize border to Chetumal, Mexico as an honorary Belizean.

I visited Belize many times subsequently, travelling across the country to places like San Ignacio, San Antonio, Dangriga and Punta Gorda to get an appreciation of the diverse spatial features, ethnicity, languages and cultures. I developed an interest in the history and music of the Garifuna peoples who originated from St Vincent and the Grenadines. The Garifuna are descendants of Black Caribs in St Vincent who having lost the Second Carib War against the British in 1796, were expelled to Roataan in Honduras, and gradually settled in other Central American countries, namely Belize, Guatemala and Nicaragua. At the annual conference of the Regional Programme of Monetary Studies in 1980, I first met Carla Barnett and Dorla Humes who were young economists at the Central Bank of Belize. Carla Barnett, after career stints as Vice President of the Caribbean Development Bank and Deputy Governor of the Central Bank of Belize, is now the Secretary-General of the Caribbean Community. Dorla Humes later joined the Caribbean Development Bank and the World Bank. The latest visit was in 2013 for a meeting of CARICOM Central Bank Governors. I was accompanied by my wife, and we took the opportunity to visit one of the Mayan ruins, do a river boat cruise and explore a cave.

CONFERENCES AND NETWORKS

REGIONAL PROGRAMME OF MONETARY STUDIES

Conference attendance and participation in scholarly and professional networks were critical. In the fields of money and finance, the Regional Programme of Monetary Studies (RPMS) was a major stimulant and supportive entity. It was located administratively in the ISER under the overall guidance of Alister McIntyre, the Director of the ISER. It was established in 1968 as a regionally collaborative effort by the central banks and monetary authorities in conjunction with the University of the West Indies to fill knowledge gaps. It was fully financed by the central banks and monetary authorities. Governors of the central banks and monetary authorities and their senior economics staff participated with academic economists in the annual research conference held in various Caribbean countries such as Bahamas, Barbados, Belize, Guyana, Jamaica, Trinidad and Tobago and St Kitts-Nevis. In that environment, a scholar could benefit from the technical insights of academic colleagues as well as from the professional knowledge and experience of the central bankers. Participation in the RPMS also facilitated access to statistical data on the monetary and financial system collected by the central banks and monetary authorities, subject to acceptable confidentially conditions on publication of data. I attended all the annual conferences between 1970 and 1991.

The network of professional contacts in the central banks and monetary authorities was extensive. Patricia Robinson, who was Director of Research at the Central Bank of Trinidad and Tobago, was a model of intellectual engagement on a wide range of money and finance topics and macroeconomic policy in addition to being supportive of the work of the academic researchers and facilitative and hospitable when they visited her Central Bank. Courtney Blackman, who was Governor of the Central Bank of Barbados, was another standout person in the network. He too was exceptional in his willingness to debate, submit his own technical propositions for frank consideration by the conference attendees at the many RPMS conferences he attended between 1972 and 2011 without regard to office or status, and never deviated from a policy of support and encouragement of young economists.

The network included many economists. There was William Allen, Warren Rolle, Julian Francis, Carlene Francis and Wendy Craig from the Central Bank of The Bahamas; Euric Bobb, Jerry Hospedales, Henry Jeffers, Genevieve Vincent, Lucille Best Mair, Joan John and in later years Terrence Farrell, Hazel Marcelle and Annette Najjar from the Central Bank of Trinidad and Tobago; George Theophilus, Errol Allen and Eustace Liburd from the Eastern Caribbean Central Bank; Clarence Ellis, Haslyn Parris, Winston Barton, Gem Fletcher, and Fay Housty from the Bank of Guyana; DeLisle Worrell, Marion Williams, Daniel Boamah, Carlos Holder, Mary Zephirin, Cleviston Haynes and Roland Craigwell from the Central Bank of Barbados; Asgar Ally, Owen Jefferson, Eric Shaw and Winston Carr from the Bank of Jamaica; Ralph Fonseca, Alan Slusher, Yvette Alvarez, Carla Barnett, Dorla Humes and Maydia Luben from the Central Bank of Belize.

From the universities, there was Simon Jones-Hendrickson from the College/University of the Virgin Islands; Helen McBain, Claremont Kirton, Carl Parris, Eric St Cyr, Frank Alleyne, Wendell McClean and Terry Somersall from the University of the West Indies; and Clive Thomas and Maurice Odle from the University of Guyana. Economists based outside of the Caribbean were also part of the network. Karl Bennett from Waterloo University in Canada presented regularly at the annual conferences.

Other occasional contributors included Wilfred Whittingham from UNECLAC, Neville Mitchell from the OAS; William Demas and Roy Jones from the Caribbean Development Bank; Suphan Andic from the University of Puerto Rico; Dinesh Dodhia from the Commonwealth Secretariat in London; Flavia Rodriquez from CEMLA in Mexico; Lance Busby from the Trinidad and Tobago Central Statistical Office; and Edwin Carrington and other senior professionals from the CARICOM Secretariat. I developed close friendships with many of these colleagues.

It was the tradition of the RPMS that its annual conference would end with a party. On one occasion in St Kitts, the official function came to an early end leaving some of us to consider other entertainment. Eustace Liburd solved the problem. He bundled several of the female attendees, including Joan John, Wendy Craig and Mary Zephirin (my close friend until she left Barbados to take up an appointment with the IMF in Washington, D.C.) into his small car, took them to his house and then returned for the guys.

The ensuing party lasted into the wee hours of the next day. I remember to this day the shell-shocked look of Wendy Craig in the airport around 6am. She told me subsequently that it was her first exposure to a Caribbean all-night party.

In 1975, Alister McIntyre requested my secondment from the Department of Economics to the ISER to be Coordinator of the RPMS. His invitation came two years after the university had granted me a special pay increase "on the grounds of exceptional merit". I was appointed Senior Research Fellow from 1 October 1975 to 30 September 1977. In the UWI context where academic staff would wait longer than ten years for promotion from lecturer to senior lecturer or its equivalent and many ended their careers in the same grade, my elevation was unusually rapid. I returned to Department of Economics as Senior Lecturer on 1 October 1977 and served as Acting Head of Department from 1 October 1978 to 30 September 1979. Nonetheless, I continued to serve as Coordinator of the RPMS until 1979 when I was succeeded by Adlith Brown. It was during that period that Ramesh Ramsaran came to the ISER from Trinidad and Tobago to start working on his PhD thesis on The Bahamas monetary and financial system. McIntyre, who was his formal supervisor, asked me to do the initial reading of the chapters and in so doing Ramesh and I became good friends. I was again asked to assume duties as Coordinator in 1984 when Adlith Brown became terminally ill. I did so until 1987.

McIntyre gave me license to propose a substantial increase in the budget to the funders of the RPMS. He had agreed to accompany me on the negotiation visits but on the eve of my departure could not. I experienced no difficulty securing the agreement of all the institutions except the Central Bank of Trinidad and Tobago. The Director of Research at the Bank, Mrs Patricia Robinson, had readily lent her support but the Governor, Mr Victor Bruce, kept me waiting several days for an audience before agreeing to the proposed increase.

NATIONAL SAVINGS COMMITTEE

Another valuable network in the finance field was developed when I was appointed to the Board of Directors of the National Savings Committee from 1975 to 1980. Two years previously, I had published in their journal National Savings Review a paper on generating household savings which might have captured the attention of the Chairman Mr Oliver Jones and his Board colleagues. It was in the company of Oliver Jones that I first visited the Cayman Islands on business and started the practice of a cognac after dinner. Oliver recommended that one drink was good, but no more than one, he warned. On Grand Cayman, I was tempted sufficiently to eat turtle steak which had the taste and texture of veal. My conservationist reluctance was overcome by the knowledge that the Cayman Islands farmed turtles and periodically would even release some into the sea.

At the National Savings Committee, I was able to collaborate with Huntley Manhertz who had become its General Manager, and with Joe Bailey with whom I published a technical paper on economic aspects of life insurance in Jamaica. The purpose of the paper was to demonstrate the importance of the life insurance industry in mobilisation of savings and financial allocation in Jamaica and to engage in a theoretical and empirical analysis of socio-economic influences on the demand for life insurance. We showed that one in eight members of the labour force and one in every six employed people were holders of life insurance policies in 1972. Policies were held by people of all educational levels and that most policy holders were urban, though not by a large margin. Life insurance policies were a significant instrument for savings mobilisation and life insurance companies were major participants in the housing finance market, in the market for long-dated government securities, and in the consumer credit market through provision of policy loans to policyholders. With respect to the demand for life insurance, we found that disposable personal income was the primary determinant. I also authored a paper evaluating institutional arrangements to mobilise personal savings in a book published by the National Savings Committee in 1977.

During that period which coincided with the early years of the global petroleum price boom, Paul Chen Young and I attended a conference in Caracas, Venezuela. We stayed at the Melia Caribe where the manager in compensation for an unacceptable room allocation mistake by a front desk clerk had no option but to offer me the Presidential suite, all marbled and gilded with gold fittings. Participants at the conference included Lord Nicholas Kaldor, Professor Robert Mundell who subsequently was awarded the Nobel Prize in Economics, and Professor Larry Sjaastad who like Mundell was from the University of Chicago. The four of us along with a few others had a long post-dinner economic discussion over drinks on the last night of the conference. Paul Chen Young and I had been invited to join a private dinner party hosted by the head of one of the large enterprises in a restaurant in the hotel. Towards the end of dinner where we had been lavishly supplied with champagne, the host invited a few of us to continue our lively conversation in a private suite and ensured that the restaurant supplied a case of champagne. The session ended in the wee hours of the next day. I believed then what a Chicago economist had told me previously: if they cannot win the argument with logic, they will win by drinking you under the table.

AGRICULTURAL ECONOMICS NETWORKS

WEST INDIAN AGRICULTURAL ECONOMICS ASSOCIATION

I was active in the West Indian Agricultural Economics Association, attending the annual conference in various countries, collaborating in special studies and eventually becoming Vice-President of the Association in 1985, by which time it had changed its name to the Caribbean Agroeconomics Society.

The conference in Grenada in 1972, as Professor David Edwards, Head of the Department of Agricultural Economics and Farm Management (DAEFM) at St Augustine observed, was being staged for the second time in a country without a university campus. I do not recall whether Vincent McDonald from Howard University and Ridwan Ali from the World Bank, regular attendees of the annual conference, were present on that occasion. Osbourne Nurse from the department was one of the main organisers. The theme of the conference was Issues in Land Reform. Sir Arthur Lewis, then President of the Caribbean Development Bank, gave the Plenary Address on the Caribbean Development Bank and its role in financing agriculture, deprecatingly prefacing his lecture by remarking that he was "old hat" and unsure that the current generation of economists would want to hear his views. Among the presenters were Cave Hill economist Frank Alleyne on "Financing Agrarian Reform in the Commonwealth Caribbean", George Beckford on "Land Reform for the Betterment of Caribbean Peoples", George Buckmire on "Land Use and Agricultural Development in the Commonwealth Caribbean", and Acosta Santana on "Cuba's Agrarian Revolution and Economic Development".

I presented a paper "Land Reform in a Sparsely Populated Country with an Indigenous Population: The Case of Guyana". In one part of the paper, I analysed static reasons for land reform with a focus on land utilisation patterns in Guyana and relative productivity of small farms and large holdings. I concluded that comparisons of yield per acre did not support reallocation of land from plantations in the sugar industry but that there were slight diseconomies of farm size in the rice industry. I then proceeded to examine some dynamic considerations usually advanced in discussions of land reform, such as agricultural diversification, capital stock flexibility, and technological innovation, and touched briefly on social and political factors. The paper was the first to deal extensively with the issue of Amerindian land rights. It described the low population density of lands occupied by Amerindians, their system of land ownership, and their pattern of economic activity, especially agriculture, and argued for a more comprehensive approach to the question of Amerindian land tenure and land use.

In preparing the paper, I had also researched the matter of land expropriation from Africans in Northern and Southern Rhodesia by the colonial authorities, white settlers and the Christian churches. I can well understand how compulsory land transfers by President Mugabe in Zimbabwe decades later could attract support among indigenous Africans. It is also to be understood that his inability to provide monetary compensation for seized lands was the result of the British Government reneging on a promise it made to provide Zimbabwe with funds to do so. I recall a private lunch in Montego Bay in July 2003 with former Commonwealth Secretary-General Sir Shridath Ramphal, Jamaica's Prime Minister P.J. Patterson and President Thabo Mbeki of South Africa when the issue came up. There was clear recollection by Ramphal and Mbeki of the British commitment.

A matter of some significance in Grenadian politics occurred outside the framework of the agricultural economics conference. Maurice Bishop, who had been leading the political opposition to Prime Minister Eric Gairy, came to see George Beckford and me one night at the CARIFTA cottages in Grand Anse. He was accompanied by his colleague Lynden Ramdhanny. Elsie Le Franc and Herman Brann who shared the cottage with Beckford and me were both at some event that night. By the time they returned the meeting had ended. Bishop said that he and his colleagues had decided to form a political party and were in search of advice on how to proceed. Bishop, on his return from legal studies in England, had been part of several progressive groups. He had started the National Action Front, teamed up with Unison Whiteman and others in the Joint Endeavour for Welfare, Education and Liberation (JEWEL), and was one of the leaders of the Movement of the Assembly of the People (MAP) whose other leaders included Unison Whiteman, Kenrick Radick, Jacqueline Creft, Francis Alexis, and Franklyn Harvey who was implicated of involvement in the unsuccessful 1970 army mutiny and Black Power protest demonstrations in Trinidad and Tobago.

I do not know that we were of much help to Maurice Bishop. Suffice it to say that the political party, the New Jewel Movement, was established in 1973, with Bishop and Unison Whiteman as Joint Coordinating Secretaries. The New Jewel Manifesto published in 1973 listed many social problems which stimulated the formation of the political party: economic inequality; inadequate supply of housing; lack of affordable medical treatment; inadequate provision of potable water; poor sanitary facilities; inflation; and police abuse. The NJM was socialist oriented. Maurice Bishop, during his student days in England, had visited the Republic of Czechoslovakia and the German Democratic Republic. In an interview with Pedro Pablo Rodriguez published in the Cuban weekly, *Bohemia*, Bishop said, "Our party began to develop along Marxist lines in 1974, when we began to study the theory of scientific socialism."

After Grenada, the West Indian Agricultural Economics Association held its annual conference in Dominica. That was my first opportunity to visit that island. The main organisers were Tom Henderson, a Dominican from the UWI St Augustine campus, and Bernard Yankey who was Dominica's Director of Agriculture, assisted by Ossie Riviere from the Ministry of Agriculture. By then, Hayden Blades, a St Augustine graduate student, was a fixture at the annual conferences, helping matters along.

DOMINICAN REPUBLIC

A small agricultural economics network came out of a consultancy assignment in the Dominican Republic. The Ford Foundation engaged Reed Hertford from Yale University and me to do review of its agriculture research and training grant to the Instituto Superior de Agricultura (ISA). We visited ISA's offices in La Romana for discussions with Louis Crouch and Blas Santos and also visited Santo Domingo and Santiago. It was my first time in the Dominican Republic. I was surprised by the presence of heavily armed soldiers lining streets in Santo Domingo but was told this was not an unusual sight during the Presidency of Joaquin Balaguer. My next involvement was in a Caribbean Consultation on Energy and Agriculture organised by the Instituto Superior de Agricultura, Pontificia Universidad Catolica Madre y Maestra and the Caribbean Association of Universities and Research Institutes in 1979. Wilberne Persaud and I presented a paper on "Financial Implications of the Energy Crisis for Dependent Underdeveloped Countries" which was published in the conference proceeding in 1980 as well as in the journal, Microstates Studies, in 1982. Vaughan Lewis and Oliver Headley were two UWI colleagues who also made presentations at the conference: Vaughan Lewis on "World Politics, the Petroleum Crisis and the Underdeveloped World" and Oliver Headley on "Domestic Applications of Solar Energy". My paper, co-authored with Wilberne Persaud, contrasted the polar cases of the oil-producing underdeveloped economy of Trinidad and Tobago and the oil-importing underdeveloped economy of Jamaica. We showed how the oil price shock worked its way through the balance of payments to financial markets, distorting credit markets, stimulating excessive expansion of money supply, retarding growth of traditional exports, and generating inflationary pressures.

RURAL FINANCIAL MARKETS GROUP

The largest and most productive agricultural economics network in which I participated was undoubtedly the rural financial markets group led by the Department of Agricultural Economics and Rural Sociology at Ohio State University (OSU) in the US. The group was institutionally and internationally diverse. In addition to OSU Faculty members such as Dale Adams, the leader of the group, Richard Meyer, Douglas Graham, Donald Larson, Edward Kane and Warren Lee, it included Robert Vogel from Syracuse University, Jerry Ladman from Arizona State University, Ronald Tinnermeier from Colorado State University and Carl Liedholm from Michigan State University. The international members included Claudio Gonsalves-Vega from the University of Costa Rica, Joao Sayad from Sao Paulo University in Brazil, Arnaldo Mauri from Milan University in Italy, Fritz Bouman from the Agricultural University of Wageningen, Netherlands, B.M. Desai from the Indian Institute of Management, and Christina David from the Philippines. Michael Lipton and Barbara Harriss from the UK also participated at an early stage in the work of the group. There was a cadre of postgraduate research students drawn from the US, Ghana, Ethiopia, Colombia, and Jamaica.

My association with the group began when I was at the ISER. One day, Dale Adams and Douglas Graham who I did not know came to my office unannounced to discuss with me some of the work I had done on savings behaviour and financial markets. A few months later, I received a letter of invitation to coordinate their rural financial markets project in Jamaica to which I replied in the affirmative and that then led to an invitation to become a Visiting Associate Professor in their Department at The Ohio State University. B.M. Desai from India received a similar invitation which he accepted. I spent January to September 1980 at OSU. It was a very productive period. My only formal teaching duty at the OSU campus was to organise and manage a weekly graduate seminar in agricultural development policy in which the presenters were government ministers or senior officials from Latin America and US agricultural economics scholars.

I worked on several aspects of Jamaican development banking and rural financial markets with Douglas Graham and presented at conferences and seminars at Wye College, University of London, England and the American Agricultural Economics Association in Indianapolis, Indiana. With the group, I also participated in conferences in Banff, Canada; Georgetown, Guyana; and St Kitts-Nevis. Douglas Graham and I presented a paper on Agricultural Finance and Rural Progress in Jamaica at the Wye College conference in 1980 which was sponsored by OSU and the Overseas Development Institute (ODI) of the UK. The paper, which was published by the ODI later that year in a book *Borrowers and Lenders* edited by John Howell, surveyed the growth and institutional change in the system for agricultural finance and overall performance, including loan repayment problems.

I gave guest lectures at the University of Notre Dame in Indiana where I renewed relations with Professor Leo Depres, a former University of Guyana colleague, and at the University of Florida in Gainesville where I reconnected with Professor Terry McCoy, a fellow member of the Caribbean Studies Association and Professor Carlton Davis. McCoy and Davis responded favourably to my request many years later that the University of Florida provide a visiting academic position for my friend and former colleague, Vaughan Lewis, who at the time had recently lost office as St Lucia's Prime Minister.

Another valuable feature of academic life in the Department of Agricultural Economics and Rural Sociology was a weekly brown bag lunch time seminar at which there would be presentations by faculty and graduate students. This ensured that academic staff and graduate students were knowledgeable about the research being undertaken in the Department and that the latter did not fall behind in their thesis preparation.

I actively engaged in fieldwork in Jamaica in 1980 where Douglas Graham and I with the assistance of graduate students Stephen Pollard, Peter Heffernan and Girma Begashaw researched farm-household credit behaviour and the supply of agricultural inputs. One early product of the fieldwork in Jamaica in the 1970s was a report to USAID (Jamaica) on Recent Economic Growth and Rural Financial markets in Jamaica: Analysis of Performance, Problems and Recommendations" authored by me, Douglas

Graham and Girma Begashaw in October 1978. Chapter II provided an analytical review of the real economic performance of the economy and developments in agriculture between 1965 and 1978 which paid particular attention to the importance and structure of agriculture and to macroeconomic factors such as foreign trade and payments, employment and labour incomes, profits, capital formation and finance, and prices and credit. Chapter III detailed the national network of agricultural credit in Jamaica and examined its structure, sources of funds, credit subsidies, farm size and agricultural credit use. Chapter IV dealt with the role of commercial banks and Chapter V with the role of the Jamaica Development Bank, describing and appraising the pattern of their credit activity in relation to agriculture, maturity and size characteristics of loans, and credit risks. Chapter VI covered in detail the performance of three institutional vehicles for small farm credit: the Peoples Cooperative banks, the Self-Supporting Farmers Development Programme, and the Crop Lien Program. The penultimate Chapter appraised public financial policy and the report ended with conclusions and recommendations. Most if not all of the issues raised and discussed in the Report became the topics of later research papers by me and Douglas Graham and PhD dissertations by students working under our supervision.

The report to USAID was followed by field surveys in 1979 on farm-household credit experience. A survey of 283 small farmers in St Catherine and 184 small farmers in St Elizabeth was conducted in late July/early August by a team comprised of me and Douglas Graham as team leaders, Peter Heffernan and Stephen Pollard (OSU graduate students), Michael Salmon (UWI graduate student), and Lester Boyne and Roy Russell (Jamaica Ministry of Agriculture). An interim report "Farm-Household Credit Behaviour: A Case Study of the Jamaican Experience" was submitted to the Jamaica Ministry of Agriculture. It examined input expenses, revenue and credit categorised by farm size and type of credit, farm production characteristics, marketing activities, the income distributional profile of farmers and self-employment activity. It then dealt with some specific aspects of formal and informal credit activity within the farming communities.

A more extensive survey of 120 farmers was conducted late in August and early September. We were ably assisted by Roy Russell, former Director of the Ministry of Agriculture Data Bank and Evaluation Unit, and Lester Boyne, the current Director of the Unit and eight numerators. The final report "Farm-Level Survey and Analysis of Selected Clients of the Crop

Lien Credit Program in St Catherine, Jamaica" was submitted to the Ministry of Agriculture in April 1982. It dealt mainly with the institutional performance of the Crop Lien Program, the quality of credit service provided to farmers, including transactions costs in obtaining loans, technical assistance, marketing channels, off-farm employment, savings activity, and the income transfer dimensions.

Interviews of farmers in Jamaica had its challenges of terrain, difficulty in locating respondents in reasonable daylight hours, and suspicion of the motivation and reasons for the surveys, especially when questions about income were posed. On one occasion, a farmer armed with a shotgun made us beat a hasty retreat because he thought we were agents of the Manley "socialist" government.

I joined Dale Adams and Donald Larson on a week-long visit to Haiti in 1980 to assess the prospects for several innovations in its rural financial markets, including the possibility of group lending. It was my first visit to Haiti. We had many discussions with Haitian officials and visited markets in Port au Prince and rural districts. I was astounded by the physical evidence of the level of poverty and unsanitary conditions which coexisted with upscale restaurants and a vibrant artistic culture. In the main market in Port au Prince, the Iron Market, I observed slabs of beef lying on the bare ground and commodities being purchased in minute quantities. In one rural market, I observed rice and other grains being purchased by the handful. At the other extreme, there were elegant restaurants with well-attired staff and fine menus.

We met with the USAID Director over dinner at his residence. Among the dinner guests was Elsa Cheney who was in the process of establishing herself as an intellectual leader on matters of gender equality. I found it necessary to gently disabuse her of the notion that Commonwealth Caribbean women needed to be empowered to own and manage farms since they were already doing so in Jamaica to my certain knowledge from recent fieldwork. An unexpected by-product of that quite pleasant dinner session was an invitation to the University of Georgia's Bicentennial Conference in Athens, Georgia in 1985. I did not know until the last day of the conference that it was the USAID Director from Haiti who had remembered me from the occasion of the dinner party and arranged the invitation. On the last morning, a Sunday morning, I was invited to join the feature speaker, former US Ambassador to the United Nations, Andrew Young for breakfast. He turned up bible in hand and discoursed lucidly about his efforts as ambassador and as a member of the Congressional

Black Caucus to normalise relations with Cuba and the need for the Reagan administration to pursue that objective.

Apart from working on rural financial market matters, I delved deeply into the economic development strategies, policies and experience of Asian and Latin American countries. I studied very closely publications on Taiwan, Japan and South Korea. But what got most of my attention were the analyses of politico-military dictatorships in countries like Argentina, Brazil and Chile which were being promoted even by Western countries with strong democracies as an appropriate model for developing countries. In time, the failure of the dictatorships to sustain economic growth for even moderate periods of time and the evidence of the enormous human costs in terms of lives lost and disappearance of large numbers of people in the repressive political regimes thoroughly discredited the New Authoritarianism as an economic development model. The Cuban economy also got my attention which is perhaps not surprising given my exposure as a teenager to Fidel Castro's famous "History Will Absolve Me" speech.

Life in Columbus, Ohio, was good. My colleagues, especially Douglas Graham, Dale Adams and Robert Vogel, were very hospitable and welcoming to me and my family. Douglas Graham ensured that we were comfortably housed in a nice townhouse development with a river at the back of it and wild ducks swimming or strutting around, ensured that our sons were suitably placed in school, and lent us a car before we acquired our own. We spent many pleasant hours with the Graham family in our home and in theirs. The informal luncheons which Dale Adams organised at various small restaurants and even at a bowling alley were occasions for more relaxed exchange of ideas on economic issues but more important were occasions to socialise and cement friendships. While in Columbus, my family and I made a few trips to Cincinnati, Baltimore and other cities and towns, sometimes just to explore them and on other times to visit friends like Winston Barton and his family who we had not seen for a long time. On other occasions, we socialised with Patricia McClean and Ohene Nyanin who introduced me to the music of Fela Kuti. Sometimes we picnicked on the bank of the river in our housing complex and sometimes we took our sons to the movies and fair grounds.

We also indulged our tastes for live musical performances. We were able to attend performances by musical legends Sammy Davis Jr, Count Basie and his Orchestra and Joe Williams, and the rising star Al Jarreau. The Sammy Davis concert also featured the vocalist Billy Eckstine, who was a favourite of my Uncle Whitney in the 1960s, and his daughter Gina

Eckstine who was beginning to make a name for herself. Ohio State University had a vibrant music studies programme and would organise Sunday performances by jazz luminaries which provided me and my wife with opportunity to enjoy performances by pianist Dave Brubeck, trombonist Gerry Mulligan and drummer Gene Krupa. We also attended the almost obligatory college basketball home games. They were full of excitement and fun and we got to see many players who emerged to be majors stars in the professional leagues, players like Magic Johnson from Michigan, Larry Bird from Purdue, and Ralph Sampson from Texas.

My association with the rural financial markets group lasted long after the end of my visiting professorship. The university contracted me in September 1980 as an Adjunct Professor at half salary with the proviso that I supervise the Jamaican fieldwork of three PhD students and with the understanding that I do not accept an appointment in another US university. They were aware that Howard University had been making efforts to recruit me. I returned to UWI, Mona and supervised the fieldwork of Ohene Nyanin whose dissertation was on the Jamaica Development Bank, Girma Begashaw whose dissertation was on farm-household credit, and Stephen Pollard whose dissertation was on agricultural production and supply functions. I continued to serve as Adjunct Professor until 1985.

Some of the Jamaica research was presented at a Senior Management Workshop of the Caribbean Agricultural Credit Training Committee in Georgetown, Guyana, 17-18 November 1980. The conference was sponsored by the USAID Regional Office in Barbados and the Guyana Cooperative Agricultural and Industrial Bank. It was well attended by representatives from government ministries and other agricultural agencies, development finance institutions, and commercial banks from countries across the Caribbean, including the Dominican Republic, Haiti, the UK Dependencies in the Caribbean, and the Caribbean Community member countries, and representatives from USAID, the IDB, and the University of the West Indies. Among the participants was Ann Bramble who at the time was at the Caribbean Food Corporation but a few years later joined the Caribbean Development Bank.

Colleagues from the Rural Financial Markets Group attended and presented papers. I, myself, presented two papers, one on "Economy Wide Influences on Rural Financial Market Performance" and the other on "Issues of External Funding and the Viability of Rural Development Banks". The paper on Economy Wide Influences argued consistent with an earlier paper by me and Douglas Graham on Economic Disequilibria and Rural Financial

Market Performance in Developing Economies that developments in the wider economy outside of rural financial markets such as price level changes, factor costs, product prices, credit restrictions, changes in foreign exchange market conditions, and monetary policy are potent influences on the performance and viability of rural credit suppliers and that policy approaches to the financial sector should incorporate them.

My second paper on issues of external funding and viability maintained that the methods by which rural development banks were funded contributed to their operational problems because of conditionalities or restrictive guidelines about term structure of loans, beneficiary groups, interest rate policies, and the currency of repayment of foreign loanable funds. It argued that credit policies which limit or discourage farmers attempts at output diversification, exclude short-term loans which might be warranted to overcome temporary depression of farm incomes perhaps because of adverse weather, and which transfer foreign exchange risks to credit clientele could ultimately impair the loan portfolios of rural development banks. The primary challenge then was to ensure that funding patterns were compatible with efficient credit operations and institutional viability. The paper canvassed several proposals for funding that were in vogue, such as savings deposit mobilisation by rural development banks and bond financing and concluded that it seemed more promising to incorporate a development banking window into a well-established commercial banking institution. In the same year, Douglas Graham and I published a more formal treatment of the subject in a paper on "Funding and Viability of Rural Development Banks" published in the Savings and Development journal.

UNIVERSITY OF THE VIRGIN ISLANDS

My good friend and colleague, Simon Jones-Hendrickson, moved to the College of the Virgin Islands (later upgraded to the University of the Virgin Islands) in 1976. That move ushered in collaborative relationships with a new set of academics. At the University of the Virgin Islands were Norwell Harrigan, the Director of its Caribbean Research Institute, Frank Mills, Jerome McElroy, Malcolm Kirwan, and Orville Kean. I presented a paper entitled "Structural Methods of Forecasting the Monetary System" at a seminar Jones-Hendrickson organised on Forecasting in Microstate Economies in April 1978. A conference in St Thomas, Virgin Islands, organised by him the following year attracted me and several Mona colleagues, including Adlith Brown. I think it was on that occasion that I first met Cora Christian, Simon's wife who was warm and welcoming and also met her parents and other family members. My association with the University of the Virgin Islands has lasted many years, anchored by my close friendship and professional collaboration with Simon Jones-Hendrickson but buttressed by relationships with successive Presidents of the University, including Orville Kean, Frank Mills and Laverne Ragster.

CARIBBEAN STUDIES ASSOCIATION

Encouraged by Simon Jones-Hendrickson, who held the post of Secretary-Treasurer in the fledgling Caribbean Studies Association, I joined the association and attended many of its conferences in the 1979-1990 period. I participated in conferences in Martinique in 1979, Curacao in 1980, St Thomas, US Virgin Islands, in 1981, Jamaica in 1982, Caracas in 1986, Belize 1987, Guadeloupe 1988, Trinidad and Tobago 1989 and Barbados 1990.

At the conferences of the CSA, I interacted with US and Canada based Caribbean academics like Hilbourne Watson, Vincent McDonald and Ransford Palmer from Howard University, Ivor Mitchell, Roy Bryce-LaPorte, Lynn Bolles, Jacqueline Braveboy-Wagner and Rudolph Grant. Beverley J. Anderson was one of the US based academics. I first met her at the CSA conference in Martinique. BJ (Anderson) and I developed a close friendship through meetings at subsequent conferences in Curacao, Jamaica and Caracas and in Brockport and Cape Cod, Massachusetts where I provided some guidance on her Boston College PhD dissertation on Friendly Societies in the Caribbean. It was in Curacao when called into service that I discovered BJ's penchant for late night street dining, a practice that a few years later repeated itself in Kingston, Jamaica where at least I knew where taxi drivers found good curry goat and rice at midnight. Ivor Mitchell who was a Professor in the Business School at Florida State University in Tallahassee also became a good friend.

Attendees at CSA conferences also included academics from the University of Puerto Rico, notably Professors Fuat and Suphan Andic and Angel Calderon Cruz, Jean and Louis Crusol from the University of the Antilles and Guyana in Martinique, Andres Serbin from Venezuela, Jorge Heine from Chile, Leslie Manigat from Haiti but based at the Institute of International Relations at UWI, St Augustine, and Wendell Bell from Yale University, Vera Rubin from the US, and many of my UWI colleagues including Selwyn Ryan, Eddie Greene, Vaughan Lewis, Stephen DeCastro, Carl Parris, and Rosina Wiltshire. Jean Crusol was very much a part of the wider Caribbean with academic stints at the Institute of International

Relations in Trinidad, the UWI campuses in Jamaica and Barbados, and in Haiti. The focus of his studies and research was economics of dependency and plantation economics. He later became a prominent political figure in Paris as a Deputy in the French Parliament. Many of the regular CSA conference attendees became Presidents of the Association, including Fuat Andic, Edward Greene, Alma Young, Simon Jones-Hendrickson and Cora Christian, Jorge Heine, Andres Serbin, Selwyn Ryan, Vaughan Lewis, Jacqueline Braveboy-Wagner and Hilbourne Watson.

Initially, the conferences were not of a uniformly high intellectual standard as some of the US-based Caribbean participants did not make the effort to prepare formal presentations, treating the conference more like a Caribbean vacation financed by their universities. Presidents like Anthony Maingot, Fuat Andic, Simon Jones-Hendrickson, Jorge Heine and Eddie Greene in later years of the CSA's existence made successful efforts to raise the intellectual calibre of the conferences and to attract serious scholars of Caribbean society, economy and culture. The annual conferences, however, did provide good opportunities for cross-disciplinary learning and camaraderie.

At the Curacao conference, some delegates discovered that suitable accommodation was not readily available. I remember Charles Carnegie, a very Christian gentleman, having to settle for a room in a brothel where in response to my enquiry a few mornings later he told me he was well treated. Curacao seemed to have a real problem with hotel accommodation at short notice. A few years after the CSA conference, my friend, Victor Thompson, passing through Curacao on his way back to Jamaica had the same experience as Charles Carnegie. Strange coincidences do happen. I, myself, several years later was stranded in Curacao one night but could not find a room to sleep anywhere. I ended up staying in a bar near the airport until closing time and sleeping on an airport bench for the rest of the night.

I became President of the CSA in 1985 and continued until 1986. Vera Rubin had been elected President to serve the 1985 year but died suddenly therefore I had to complete her term and also serve out the one for which I had been elected. I scheduled the 1986 annual conference in Caracas, Venezuela. It was the first time the conference was being held in the Hispanic Caribbean. Andres Serbin, Leslie Manigat and Yolande Manigat did a marvellous job in the local organising committee and the Universidad Central provided excellent conference facilities.

My term as President was preceded by Simon Jones-Hendrickson who was President in 1983-1984. Cora Christian became President in 2000-

2001, making her and Simon the only couple to have held the Presidency of the CSA. Some of my most treasured memories are of times spent with them in their home in St Croix. Mainly due to Simon Jones-Hendrickson, I became close to Fuat and Suphan Andic who were very hospitable, caring and mentoring. A very pleasurable obligatory component of any visit to Puerto Rico was time at their residence in Condada, San Juan for breakfast, lunch or dinner and their enquiries about my personal and professional wellbeing.

In 1990, the annual conference was held in Barbados. Professor Joycelyn Massiah from the UWI Cave Hill campus was Chair of the Local Organising Committee. The highlight of the conference was the tribute to Sir Arthur Lewis in whose honour the conference was held. Professor Massiah on behalf of the CSA presented him with a beautifully bound collection of his papers. Sir Arthur was so moved that he waived his prior stipulation that he would not speak and told a short story, the import of which was that he who had loved and shown love to the peoples of the Caribbean all his life was finally being shown love by them.

INTERNATIONAL INSTITUTE OF PUBLIC FINANCE

In 1976, I decided that I needed to update my knowledge of public finance and that I could make a quick start by attending specialist conferences. In September of that year, I attended a conference held at the University of Stirling in Scotland where I met Professor Morris Beck from Rutgers University and Ved Ghandi, a fiscal expert from the IMF. One night, we drove to Glasgow which none of us had visited previously. We got there soon after the pubs had closed and were amazed by the large number of inebriated men and women we saw staggering on the streets. I was subsequently informed by a medical colleague that Glasgow, like Moscow, Boston and Nairobi, was a city with one of the highest rates of alcohol addiction.

At the end of the conference at the University of Stirling, I proceeded immediately to the 32nd Congress of the Institute of Public Finance at the University of Edinburgh in Scotland. My friend and colleague Simon Jones-Hendrickson who had attended the 31st Congress of the Institute in Nice was there in Edinburgh with his wife Cora Christian. The theme of the Congress was Secular Trends of the Public Sector. Most papers presented were on long term trends and their influences in Western Europe, Eastern Europe and Japan. It was a good opportunity to discuss such matters with acknowledged experts in the field. Simon and I decided that we would offer a paper at the 33rd Congress in Bulgaria which had as its theme Subsidies, Tax Reliefs and Prices. We collaborated by mail and in the final stages wrote the paper entitled "Subsidies, Tax Reliefs and Public Policy – the Development Aspects" at Simon and Cora's home in St Croix. It was published in 1981 in the Proceedings edited by Karl Hauser and also by a publisher in Bulgaria.

The Congress provided an opportunity for renewal of relations with international colleagues such as Victor Halberstadt, then Professor of Public Finance at the University of Leyden, Jack Wiseman, Professor of Public Finance, University of York, England, Alan Peacock, Professor of Economics, University of York and colleagues from the University of Tokyo.

There were six working groups. One dealt with principal theoretical aspects and featured presentations by Jack Wiseman and Victor Halberstadt. The second dealt with institutional aspects with papers on the Federal Republic of Germany, the Netherlands, the Czech Republic and Japan. The third working group was on price aspects. The fourth working group focussed on development aspects and featured the paper by me and Jones-Hendrickson as well as papers on Israel, Romania and Italy. The fifth working group was on distributive aspects with presentations on France and Hungary while the sixth working group focussed on foreign trade aspects with papers by Richard Goode on balance of payments effects and H. Weise from the Federal Republic of Germany on transfer problems of developing countries.

The paper I co-authored with Simon Jones-Hendrickson dealt with the case of dependent underdeveloped economies and outlined two broad approaches to development, namely, a focus on capital formation as an enabler of development and a primary focus on equity, basic needs and human development as the objectives of economic development. It examined the role of subsidies, tax reliefs and public policy. It discussed some problems of operationalising the second approach in public policy, particularly those emanating from the narrowness of fiscal structures and the tax base, tax evasion and avoidance, and resistance to increasing taxes on capital. It then explored how these objectives are pursued within socialist economic systems and the difficulties that might be encountered in applying those policies in the Caribbean context, such as internal resistance, size of the economies, and external forces against ideologically oriented changes.

It was my first visit to an Eastern European communist country. I arrived in Varna, the conference town, before my colleagues and friends and therefore dined alone at the designated restaurant. I discovered then and at each subsequent meal session during my stay that there was little choice of menu items or beverages. At breakfast, one could choose how the eggs were prepared; one could have coffee or tea but no milk, no toast, or no fruit of one's choice. At lunch, it was a chicken drumstick, boiled potatoes, a large bottle of beer and white grapes. At dinner, it was steak, boiled potatoes, a bottle of red wine for each diner and red grapes. The alcohol beverages were obligatory; one could not refuse. My Japanese colleagues who were teetotallers resolved their problem by giving their bottles to others at our table. We soon noticed that locals were served apricots and put in a request for some instead of grapes only to be told that it was not permitted. This was the first instance of the restrictions on personal choice and on the minutiae of official restrictions on worker discretion in Bulgaria.

Simon Jones-Hendrickson, Cora Christian and I witnessed several other instances of the seemingly ubiquitous "not allowed", "not permitted" because "it is written" responses in Varna and in Sofia where we spent a few days. In one restaurant, the waitress produced a huge book of rules to show us that it was indeed written. This is not to say that there no breaches of rules. In a conversation with the daughter of a high-ranking political person, I was told that birth control was illegal because the official policy was to promote population growth. I inferred from the experience of she and her husband that some couples did not comply.

My curiosity was greatly piqued by what seemed to be an open disconnect between an officially regulated foreign exchange market with punitive restrictions and informal foreign exchange purchasing on the streets of Sofia by some who operated at tables with wads of foreign currency purchased by agents on the street. I concluded that this type of activity had to be sanctioned by the economic authorities.

I was impressed by the political commitment to addressing the deficiency in household levels of living, especially with respect to infant and child nutrition which explained the preferential allocation of butter and milk to children and its denial to adults, the ready availability of public transport, and provision of public education.

Despite these achievements, Bulgaria had a problem of defections of its citizens to the West. Censorship of mail was an important instrument for discouraging illegal emigration. In trying to mail a letter and postcards to my wife and friends in Jamaica, I discovered how mail censorship was practiced. On one occasion, I went to the post office to mail a letter. First, I had to purchase the stamps and affix them to the envelope. I then handed it to the postal official who opened it and read its contents before resealing it for onward transmission. Presumably it would have been detained and destroyed if the contents were deemed unacceptable. On my departure at the airport in Sofia, my neutrally written postcards had to be destroyed in front of an official because it was forbidden to take postcards out of the country. I think that the system was designed to severely reduce the ability of family members and other related people left behind in Bulgaria to communicate with those who migrated illegally and to be a deterrent to prospective illegal migrants.

EVENTS IN JAMAICA AND GUYANA

TRADE UNIONISM AND POLITICS ON THE MONA CAMPUS

On 25 January 1972, the West Indian Group of University Teachers which had been established since October 1958 became a registered trade union representing academic, senior administrative, and library professional staff. Some of the older generation of academics did not welcome this development. The mathematician Leighton Henry was its President. The union was granted sole bargaining rights for its categories of membership on 16 July 1973. This was completely in accord with Jamaican labour laws. An immediate issue before the union was staff remuneration. The University had commissioned a review of salaries by a team nominated by its contributing governments. The report of the Cato Salaries Commission in 1973 incensed many of the WIGUT membership not only by its recommendation of minor increases of salaries but by its assertion that non-pecuniary incomes which it deemed intrinsic to working in a university environment were a sufficient remedy for inadequate monetary incomes. Strike action in support of the Union's salary claims took place in October 1973. There was a more prolonged strike in October 1975 over salaries claims for the 1975-1978 period. That strike lasted for seventeen days and briefly shut down the campus. Trade union militancy among the WIGUT membership became the norm in the University.

Other staff members were not far behind in seeking to advance their interests through trade union activity. Trevor Munroe had taken the initiative in organising workers at the campus and established the University and Allied Workers Union in 1972. They too resorted to strike action which lasted three weeks. The UAWU ventured off campus to challenge the trade union hegemony of the People's National Party-affiliated National Workers Union and the Jamaica Labour Party-affiliated Bustamante Industrial Trade Union. The path was not smooth for them. In one incident widely reported in the daily newspapers, the UAWU's leader, Trevor Munroe, was severely wounded by an attacker on the Kingston docks.

After the 1976 general elections at which the People's National Party was once more victorious, some academics became 'Manleyists' or 'non-Manleyists', their synonyms for "socialists" and "capitalists" respectively. Trevor Munroe, who had founded the Workers Liberation League in 1974, founded a new political party, the Workers Party of Jamaica (WPJ) in December 1978 together with colleagues Rupert Lewis, Mark Figueroa and Don Robbotham. The WPJ was widely perceived as being far-left of the PNP which was considered to be democratic socialist.

The Workers Liberation League and its successor the WPJ strived unsuccessfully to be a party of influence on the PNP. One night in 1977, the University group which was working on the Jamaica Emergency Production Plan was invited by Trevor Munroe, in his capacity as leader of the Workers Liberation League, to meet with him at his home. I was present as a member of the group. Munroe sought an intermediary role between the PNP and the group but this overture was rejected by the group. A subsequent public declaration by the WPJ on 22 December 1979 that it would ally with the PNP was not welcomed by Michael Manley, presumably because such an alliance would give credence to emerging public apprehension about a shift from democratic socialism to an Eastern European type of socialist economic policy. Manley would later denounce the notion of any covert alliance between the two political parties.

The WPJ was more successful in forging a relationship with the People's Revolutionary Government (PRG) in Grenada. After two physical assaults by the Grenadian security forces on the leadership of the New Jewel Movement in November 1973 and January 1974 in which Maurice Bishop sustained a broken jaw and his father was fatally shot, the New Jewel Movement, most likely with the assistance of a few Cuban personnel and some arms and ammunition, staged a successful coup against the Eric Gairy government on 13 March 1979. Bernard Coard, a UWI social sciences faculty member who had lived on University Close before moving to the Institute of International Relations at the UWI St Augustine campus was deeply involved in the coup. Two Mona economist colleagues, Claremont Kirton and Mark Figueroa, left Jamaica to boost the technical cadre of the People's Revolutionary Government. The PRG imploded in 1983 with the arrest, release from custody and subsequent execution of Prime Minister Maurice Bishop by a faction of his government. This led to defections from the WPJ which ultimately became defunct in 1992. Bernard Coard was to explain in a Grenada Broadcast Network from his prison cell in Grenada on 24 September 1999 that, "the manner of taking power created a militarised context and a militarised culture within which the Revolution functioned."

JAMAICA EMERGENCY PRODUCTION PLAN

One night early in January 1977, my UWI colleague Louis Lindsay came to my home to seek my participation in some work he was doing on an alternative to a macroeconomic programme under discussion with the International Monetary Fund (IMF). The talks between the IMF and the government were at that stage supposed to be secret but he, George Beckford and Norman Girvan had learnt about them and met at the home of D.K. Duncan, Minister of National Mobilisation, on 18 December 1976 to warn against any IMF agreement. It was known that the Bank of Jamaica in a supposedly secret letter to a ministerial team headed by Manley himself had outlined the Jamaican policy action that would be necessary to secure IMF financial assistance. The actions included a substantial devaluation of the foreign exchange rate, wage freeze and a balanced budget, all standard IMF policy prescriptions. Out of the meeting at Duncan's home came a decision to organise a small group of UWI academics to develop an economic programme that would obviate the need for an IMF programme. I agreed and became a full participant with Beckford, Girvan, Lindsay and Michael Witter in what emerged as Jamaica's Emergency Production Plan, 1977-1978 signed by Prime Minister Michael Manley on 28 April 1977.

The forerunner to the start of the process was a series of government economic and social reformist policies and initiatives started in the PNP's term of office from 1972-1976 and continued more intensely in its next term which began on 15 December 1976. In 1973, the government decided to make secondary and tertiary education tuition-free. It eschewed nationalisation of the bauxite industry as a policy because in Manley's opinion such a move would create an "impossible financial situation" and because the requisite technical expertise to manage the industry did not exist. Instead, it decided "to negotiate tax and royalty arrangements and get Jamaica into the industry". The Jamaica government's approach contrasted with that of the Guyana government several years previously. Negotiations with the American companies started on 18 March 1974. Alister McIntyre, Pat Rousseau, Richard Fletcher, Meyer Matalon, Trevor Byer and Carlton Davis (not the one at University of Florida) were part of the Jamaican team. Having failed to reach an agreement with the companies by the end of April, the government on 15 May enacted the Bauxite (Production) Levy Act (1974) which imposed a levy on the average realised price per ton of primary aluminium. Bauxite and alumina tax revenues initially increased steeply but ultimately decreased when output contracted.

On 8 October 1975, the government announced a series of socio-economic policies including notably a national minimum wage policy, the establishment of a National Housing Trust, comprehensive price controls, reduction of house rents, and freezing of profits. Later in the month, it announced additional measures including new price and rent controls, government price subsidisation of basic foods, new foreign exchange controls, and government purchase of idle lands for redistribution to small farmers. These measures in their totality were consistent with the government's declared commitment to democratic socialism.

Meanwhile, macroeconomic pressures were building. The economic growth rate had become negative in 1974 and continued negative in each succeeding year to 1980. Unemployment remained high. Government total external debt increased precipitously, and debt service was taking up a larger share of foreign exchange earnings from exports of goods and services. Net foreign exchange reserves, vital to highly open economies, had decreased by more than two-thirds in five years.

The government tried to stem the tide by setting out some measures in an Emergency Stabilisation Plan announced on 28 February 1976. The measures included more foreign exchange controls, tax increases on personal incomes, and wage guidelines. Prime Minister Manley in January 1977 made another effort to avoid the IMF. After announcing that Jamaica was not for sale earlier in the month, he announced in Parliament on 19 January an austere economic package which while excluding foreign exchange rate devaluation, drastically reduced permissible foreign exchange allowances for vacation travel to a virtually meaningless US$55, introduced stricter import licensing, imposed a six-month freeze on wages and prices, sharply increased petrol prices, and raised income taxes. He also announced the intention to nationalise three banks, a leading private radio station and the Caribbean Cement Company, and the establishment of diplomatic and trade relations with the Soviet bloc countries. The ideological signals were certainly not pro-capitalist and coming after Manley's speech in Montego Bay on return from a visit to Cuba in 1975 in which he is reported to have said, "For anyone who wants to become a millionaire, we have five flights a day to Miami", the alarm bells rang very loudly.

A few months before the completion of the Emergency Production Plan, international political factors came into play. The Jamaican government sent a Ministerial delegation led by Foreign Minister P.J. Patterson to Cuba.

Richard Fletcher and D.K. Duncan were members of the delegation. The Cuban delegation was led by Vice President Carlos Raphael Rodriquez. The purpose was to explore via Havana the possibility of Soviet aid if Jamaica broke with the IMF. I was in attendance when they reported on the outcome of the mission. Essentially, the Jamaican team was advised that no assistance was likely from the Soviet Union, that Jamaica should maintain the peace with the IMF, and that Jamaica should do everything to avoid causing large scale emigration as happened in Cuba.

During the same period, while I was visiting Trinidad and Tobago, I received a phone call from William Demas, President of the Caribbean Development Bank, asking me to stop over and see him in Barbados on my way back to Jamaica. I did as he asked. Demas wished me to deliver a message to Prime Minister Manley from Cyrus Vance, the US Secretary of State in President Jimmy Carter's administration. Vance wanted to assure Jamaica of the friendship of the US but warned that if Jamaica broke with the IMF the US government would be obliged to not only suspend all its aid to Jamaica but would also veto allocations from all other institutions, including the Caribbean Development Bank, that derived financial resources from the US government. I delivered the message to the Prime Minister in a session in Jamaica House much to the displeasure of the radical members of the government.

The preparation of the Emergency Production Plan was intellectually led by the UWI team. I was the lead on financial and fiscal topics, including the development of proposals on property taxes, and chaired the Task Force on Foreign Budgetary Management. We had many meeting at Jamaica House with the Prime Minister separately as well as with his Cabinet. Manley, himself, was intellectually acute, open to novel ideas and quick to grasp them, and charming and respectful in his interactions with us and his Cabinet colleagues. P.J. Patterson, David Coore and Vivian Blake were calm, deliberative and insightful. At the other extreme was D.K. Duncan who tended to be disruptive.

We often worked well into the night in Louis Lindsay's townhouse in Hope Pastures where on occasion D.K. Duncan, Hugh Small and Paul Robertson would come to get a progress update and see what assistance we needed from them in dealing with a not uniformly cooperative public service. On one such occasion sometime after midnight when we were trying to prepare proposals for property taxes, Duncan asked how we were progressing and on being informed that we were experiencing difficulty in obtaining some necessary data from the senior public servant, telephoned the man, demanding his immediate presence. The public servant turned up shaking in his boots. It transpired that it was his Deputy not he who had possession of the data, whereupon Duncan phoned the Deputy's home. His wife answered the phone and said her husband was not home. Duncan then asked where he was, to which the wife replied that is what she would like to know. I found this treatment of public officials so unacceptable that I declined an offer of appointment with the government, saying quite frankly that I did not like the way public servants were being treated and would not expose myself to the possibility of such treatment. Instead, I accepted an appointment as a member of the Board of Directors of the Bank of Jamaica. I resigned from that position after a few months because I thought that major decisions, especially in relation to ownership of the commercial banking industry, were being made without reference to the Board of Directors.

The approach taken in preparation of the Emergency Production Plan was to evaluate existing productive capacity, set production targets, estimate foreign exchange, manpower and capital requirements for meeting the targets, and identify the implications for implementation by the government. Six committees were constituted to deal with individual production sectors or industries, namely agriculture, manufacturing, construction, tourism, bauxite and fuel and energy. Four other committees dealt with employment and manpower utilisation; financial, monetary and foreign exchange matters; foreign economic relations; and mobilisation and implementation. The public service was formally involved through the National Planning Agency which was assigned the responsibility of producing on the basis of the reports prepared by the committees an integrated and internally consistent overall Emergency Production Plan document for Cabinet consideration.

The Plan was detailed and specific. The component on Emergency Food Production 1977-1978 provided a very detailed listing of crops, production districts, planting material requirements, labour and machine requirements, inventory of machines, and fertiliser requirements. The same level of detail and specificity was conducted for livestock production, fisheries, forestry, manufacturing and construction.

The Emergency Production Plan document signed by Prime Minister Manley on 28 April 1977 restated the government's commitment to a mixed economy within the framework of democratic socialism. It stated that the overriding objective of the strategy was maximisation of production of goods and services consumed by the masses and that the Plan was oriented towards low-income groups, conserving foreign exchange and earning foreign exchange. A novel institutional feature identified was the development of Community Enterprise Organisations for rural reconstruction and development. "The CEOs will seek to answer the social problems of job opportunities, the economic problems of concentrating a complex of production activities within a rural community, and the political problem of decentralisation and democratisation of ownership and control."

On 27 April 1977, I received two letters signed by Prime Minister Manley. One thanked me for "the tremendous job of work on the Emergency Production Plan ... over the last three months." He identified "the tremendous tasks" ahead of operationalising the Community Enterprise Organisations, to establish the State Trading Organisations, and "to monitor the financial resources that we have to raise to ensure that they are used as intended and do not leak back out of the system." He ended by saying that determination, confidence and unity displayed during the year can be used to lay a foundation for the Five-Year Plan. The other letter began: "I write to let you know how deeply the Government and I appreciated your work in presiding over the Task Force on Foreign Budgetary Management" and continued by expressing the hope that I am now prepared to monitor the implementation of the Emergency Production Plan and assist in preparing the "Five Year Plan which will embody the hopes, aspirations, strategies and tactics of the next stage of the struggle."

There were two significant appendixes to the Plan laid before Parliament. One appendix headed "Ministry Paper Incomes Policy 1977" signed by the Minister of Finance, David Coore, on 21 April 1977, announced the implementation of an incomes policy which established guidelines on dividends and profits, froze professional fees, established wage and salary guidelines and instituted a six-month pay moratorium. The other appendix headed "Ministry Paper Multiple Exchange Rates" signed by David Coore on 22 April 1977 announced the implementation of a dual foreign exchange rate system. There would be a basic exchange rate of the Jamaican dollar to the US dollar and a special exchange rate which essentially substantially devalued the Jamaican dollar. The basic rate would be applicable to all government foreign exchange transactions, all basic foods, essential medical and pharmaceutical products, petroleum imports, animal feeds, fertilisers, foreign exchange purchase by bauxite and alumina companies, and commercial bank swap arrangements. The special rate would be applicable for all other foreign exchange transactions. With the benefit of hindsight, I have come to the conclusion that the policies announced in the two Ministry

Papers and the restatement of the social class and democratic socialism emphases of the Plan reduced the chances of its acceptance by many segments of Jamaica's population.

Be that as it may, the Jamaica government, soon after publication of the Emergency Production Plan, began further discussions with the IMF and started a rapprochement with the United States. Jamaica's Foreign Minister P.J. Patterson visited the US Secretary of State on several occasions in 1977. US First Lady Rosalyn Carter paid a two-day visit to Jamaica at the end of May 1977. US Ambassador to the United Nations, Andrew Young, visited in August of the same year and was reported by the *Washington Post* to have expressed respect for Prime Minister Manley's search for a third way between capitalism and communism.

In July 1977, Jamaica signed a two-year IMF Standby Agreement and in November the US government reinstated an aid package. In December, the Standby Agreement was suspended because Jamaica failed to satisfy the net domestic assets performance criteria. New negotiations with the IMF led to agreement in May 1978 on a three-year Extended Fund Facility programme which imposed quite stringent conditionalities. Even though Jamaica had devalued the basic exchange rate by 13.6 per cent and the special rate by 5.2 per cent in January 1977, the government was required to unify the exchange rate and devalue the unified rate by 15 per cent. A crawling peg was instituted for an additional 15 per cent exchange rate depreciation over twelve months. Ceilings were imposed on wage increases. Government expenditure cuts and charges on selected government services were required to achieve a targeted reduction. General government revenues were targeted to increase. General government deficits were targeted to fall by more than a third and government outstanding arrears to be reduced by more than two-thirds. Non-price restrictions on trade and payments were to be dismantled. This was a sweeping set of economic policy stipulations which effectively derailed the Emergency Production Plan.

While a Visiting Professor at the Ohio State University, I wrote a paper entitled "Jamaica and the International Monetary Fund: The Economics of the 1978 Stabilisation Program" in which I attempted to elucidate the economic factors that led to the program, the fundamental differences between the Jamaican government's economic philosophy and that of the IMF and the design of the programme. I analysed the underlying economic model employed by the IMF and ended with a brief assessment of its applicability to Jamaica. Former Barbadian Prime Minister Owen Arthur, who was employed in the Jamaica National Planning Agency during the preparation of the Emergency Production Plan, often complimented me on the paper but never failed to point out that it won me no fans among my radical UWI colleagues.

KEEPING ABREAST OF GUYANA

Although settled at the UWI Mona campus, I followed developments in Guyana. Some got more of my attention than others.

POLITICAL VIOLENCE

On 4 October 1971, an attempt was made on the life of Joshua Ramsammy, my Guyanese Ratoon associate and University of Guyana colleague. He was shot as he exited his car outside the Guyana National Cooperative Bank in Georgetown. He survived bullet wounds to his abdomen, liver and lungs. The news sent shock waves through me and many of my colleagues at the Mona campus. I organised a protest letter which was sent to Prime Minister Forbes Burnham. The attempt on Ramsammy's life ushered in a new and different period of political violence in Guyana. Unlike in the 1960s when violence was ethnically focussed, in the new period specific people believed to be sources of threat to the political appeal of the governing party were the targets. An organisation called the House of Israel, led by American fugitive David Hill but self-styled Rabbi Washington, acted as political enforcers for the PNC. Father Darke, a Jesuit priest, was murdered by its members on 14 July 1979 while he was photographing a WPA demonstration in Georgetown. It was not until July 1986 that Rabbi Washington and other members of the House of Israel were tried and convicted of the crime.

The fanaticism of PNC supporters was palpable. One night when I was relaxing with a group of friends at Elvin McDavid's home in Nandy Park, East Bank Demerara, the conversation turned to then current attempts to glorify Prime Minister Burnham by investing him with omniscience and perfect planning and implementation of political strategies. In my usual way in such conversations, I poked fun at the views expressed by McDavid and his comrades until one person, unknown to me, who had hitherto been silent blurted out that if Burnham gave him the orders next day to shoot me, he would do so. McDavid promptly reprimanded him by saying that I was his friend and that no conversation among friends in his house was to be the cause for harmful political action.

The next major violent occasion in Guyana was in 1980 when Walter Rodney, one of the leaders of the Working People's Alliance, was killed by a handheld explosive device he carried, believing it to be a walkie-talkie for communication purposes. The device was supplied to him by Gregory Smith, a Guyana Defence Force operative who was provided with a new identity and Guyana passport by the government and flown to Cayenne, French Guiana, in a military aircraft. Rodney's death was widely protested by radical political movements internationally and in Guyana, not least by leading figures in the Working Peoples Alliance. Thirty years elapsed before a Commission of Inquiry into the circumstances of his death was established by President Donald Ramotar, leader of the PPP government. During the Ramoutar Presidency, Maurice Odle, Bert Carter and a few others combined their own financial resources with that of other people to construct a Rodney Monument on Hadfield Street in Georgetown.

The Commission's Chairman was Sir Richard Cheltenham, a Barbados Queens Counsel. The two other members were Seenath Jairam, a Trinidad Senior Counsel, and Dr Jacqueline Browne, a Jamaica Queens Counsel. The Commission had 66 sessions over eleven sittings and took evidence from thirty-one witnesses. Among the witnesses were prominent WPA members like Eusi Kwayana, Omawale and Nigel Westmaas, all three of whom travelled from the US to testify, and Tacuma Ogunseye and Jocelyn Dow. Conspicuously absent were co-leaders of the party, Dr Rupert Roopnarine and Professor Clive Thomas. President David Granger, who succeeded Donald Ramotar as President on 11 May 2015, instructed the Commission to conclude its hearings and submit its report by 15 December 2015. President Granger was the leader of a merged political party, A Partnership for National Unity (APNU), formed in July 2011 to contest general elections that year. The WPA was one of the merged entities. The report has not been publicly released in Guyana, but the Rodney Foundation arranged for internet publication of a hard copy in its possession. The voices of the WPA leadership were silent on President Granger's action.

NATIONALISATION

In 1974, the Guyana government proceeded to nationalise Reynolds Bauxite Company which was American-owned. Prime Minister Burnham had evidently overcome the apprehension of the likely US reaction he had at the time of nationalisation of the Canadian-owned Demerara Bauxite Company. He stated then: "There is reason to believe that all American aid to Guyana will be cut off."

The next target for nationalisation was the sugar industry. First, the smaller Jessel Securities were nationalised in 1975. This was followed by the nationalisation of the Bookers Group of Companies in 1976. At the time, the Bookers Group was comprised of twenty-two companies, directly employed 29,000 people, produced 80 per cent of Guyana's sugar, and accounted for 40 per cent of exports and 35 per cent of foreign exchange earnings. Its contribution to gross domestic product was in the order of 30 per cent. The nationalisation of the sugar industry must have met with the approval of the Working Peoples Alliance, the successor to the RATOON group for Clive Thomas in a RATOON study entitled, *Sugar Economics in a Colonial Situation: A Study of Guyana Sugar Industry*, published in 1970, had concluded that, "The only long-run solution to sugar and the plantation structure in Guyana ... is to bring these enterprises under direct national control". Acquisition of the Bookers Group not only made Guyana Sugar Corporation, the umbrella company which combined the Jessel and Bookers sugar enterprises into one corporate entity, the monopoly producer of sugar in Guyana, it also gave the government a dominant position in the general consumer retail business through Guyana Stores, the government entity which was created to handle that component of the nationalised Bookers portfolio. As happened with the nationalisation of bauxite, sugar production contracted drastically immediately and remained below the 1976 peak output level for the next ten years.

In 1976, Jamaica's Prime Minister Michael Manley proposed a Caribbean regional joint production arrangement for the bauxite-alumina industry in which Guyana bauxite and Jamaica alumina would be processed into aluminium in Trinidad and Tobago utilising Trinidad and Tobago's lower-cost petroleum and gas energy resources in aluminium smelters jointly owned by the countries. The deal never materialised because of Prime Minister Burnham's personal indiscipline in dealing with his counterparts. A meeting was convened by Prime Minister Eric Williams in Port of Spain on 10 June 1976. I became aware of what transpired in a conversation with James Moss-Solomon, a leading Jamaican businessman, at the UWI Senior Common Room in 2019. His account of events was subsequently corroborated by Overand Padmore, a member of the Williams Cabinet, and Ferdie Ferreira, a confidant of Prime Minister Williams, in a conversation at the home of Selwyn Ryan in Trinidad in 2022. All three people were present at the meeting in 1976.

Prime Ministers Manley and Williams awaited the presence of Prime Minister Burnham who they knew had dis-embarked at Piarco. Prime Minister Burnham joined the meeting hours later, excusing his lateness on his decision to socialise with a friend in Valsayn, a residential neighbourhood en route from Piarco, before joining his waiting Prime Ministerial colleagues. I was informed that Prime Minister Williams was furious and quickly terminated the meeting with no commitment to any future discussions of the collaborative venture.

JONESTOWN

In November 1978, a Guyana horror story made the international headlines. An American religious cult called the Peoples Temple Agricultural Project led by Jim Jones, had established itself in Guyana's hinterland near Port Kaituma. On 18 November, 918 cult members died by cyanide poisoning and/or gunshot wounds. It was a combination of mass suicide and murder which did the reputation of the government and people of Guyana no good.

Jim Jones went to Guyana with a record of high-level contacts in the American political establishment. Present at a testimonial dinner for him in California were First Lady Rosalyn Carter, California Governor Jerry Brown, Vice-Presidential Candidate Walter Mondale and Lt Governor Mervyn Dymally. There is evidence that the People's Temple was facilitated in its Guyana operations by the government. They were allowed duty-free importation of goods. Compliant customs officials might have facilitated importation of contraband drugs and arms.

It is known that Jim Jones requested status as a foreign dignitary and that he and Lt. Governor Mervyn Dymally met with Prime Minister Burnham and Foreign Minister Fred Wills. Laurence Mann, Guyana's Ambassador to the US from 1975-1981, was romantically involved with Paula Adams, a senior member of the People's Temple. He married her and together they had a son. Mann's relationship with Paula Adams ended tragically on 24 October 1983 when he fatally shot her and their son, and then himself, in her New York apartment.

I recall a luncheon meeting with Laurence Mann and Richard Fletcher in the Dover Convention Centre in Barbados a few weeks before that event. Fletcher was assuring him that arrangements for a consultancy contract with the Inter-American Development Bank were progressing. Mann had mood swings which alternated between joviality and trenchant personal criticism of Forbes Burnham with whom he had maintained a very close relationship over many years.

A curious incident occurred on the morning of the mass suicide at the People's Temple. I was breakfasting with Clarence Ellis in the Trinidad Hilton Hotel and Conference Centre when he received a phone call from Guyana on the tragic news breaking in Georgetown. He informed me that the caller told him that the Prime Minister's wife, Viola Burnham, was on the first plane out to the People's Temple site near Port Kaituma. I could not understand why the wife of the Prime Minister, instead of establishing political distance from the People's Temple, would choose to be among the first to arrive at the gruesome site. Charles A. Krause, a Washington correspondent, on 24 December 1978 hinted at an explanation. He reported that on 20 November 1978, a plane with Deputy Prime Minister Ptolemy Reid and Mrs Burnham left Port Kaituma loaded with more than US$1 million in currency and gold and jewellery. The Guyana government later confirmed the reported plane trip but denied any implied impropriety with respect to the disposition of money, valuables and documents removed from the People's Temple site.

ECONOMIC DECLINE

Economic growth started on a downward trend in Guyana from 1976. The annual growth rate of Gross Domestic Product which was 8.5 per cent in 1975, possibly attributable to the short-lived surge in world sugar prices in 1974, decreased to 1.2 per cent in 1976, -2.64 per cent in 1977, and -1.8 per cent in 1978 and 1979, recovering slightly to 1.5 per cent in 1981. Over the same period, there was a quadrupling of government gross external debt. Gross foreign reserves began to contract and became as little as US$7 million in 1981. The negative trend in foreign exchange availability combined with the government's policy of substituting local agricultural and agro-industrial products for imported products served to depress total imports of goods and created shortages in the economy which led to the so-called "Guy Lines", i.e., long lines of consumers seeking to make purchases of scarce commodities. It also contributed to the emergence of inward smuggling of commodities from Suriname to accommodate the demand for scarce items as well as outward smuggling of jewellery and precious metals to earn unreported foreign exchange for discretionary use by the smugglers. Another consequence was the start of significant emigration of the Guyanese population. Whereas between 1975 and 1978, emigration averaged 14,100 people annually, between 1979 and 1981, it increased to average 18,276 people annually.

FAMILY AND SOCIAL LIFE

It was not all work and no play for me in Jamaica. Either with my family or alone, I enjoyed countless relaxing and happy days in Jamaica. In addition to friends at the university, there were several friends outside of the university community. They included Victor Thompson, a friend from the 1960s in Guyana, and his family, and Carlton Cunningham, a friend from student days in London, and his family. My individual circle of close friends included Fay and Otto Sylvester. I had first met Fay when I attended the Caribbean statisticians' conference in Jamaica in 1970. I became a friend of her family and saw much of them until I left Jamaica for Trinidad and Tobago in 1981. Another close non-UWI friend was Claire Forrester to whom I had been introduced by my Guyanese friend Horace Nurse when he visited Jamaica briefly a few years after my arrival. Another set of non-university friends was Benny Holder and his wife Maureen Casserly. Benny, who taught at the Jamaica School of Agriculture, was the brother of Valerie Holder, a former colleague and friend at the University of Guyana, and Maureen was a dancer with the National Dance Theatre Company of Jamaica.

Our sons, Monty and Tunji, were doing well at Hope Valley Experimental School in Mona. Monty was doing so well that he won the Jamaica scholarship for secondary school entrance in 1979 and was admitted to Campion College, a top school for boys. The university housing development was excellent for children. All the parents were academic or senior administrative staff members. The children knew the parents of their friends. They roamed the compound freely. At our home we kept ample supplies of beverages in the refrigerator in anticipation of random appearances by the roving boys and girls. Just before our departure from Jamaica to Trinidad in 1981, we had a farewell party for our friends at which Vice Chancellor Ashton Preston's son was contracted to provide recorded music. Early in the proceedings, I noticed several teenage sons and daughters of colleagues slipping in uninvited to the party. With my wife's agreement, I responded by allowing them to stay provided they obeyed my ground rules: remain and have their fun in an empty room that I allocated to them; no mingling with my guests; and no imbibing of alcoholic beverages. Everything went smoothly and I earned the reputation of being a "cool dude" as Eddie Greene's son, Abi, one of the neighbourhood teenagers told me decades later.

As a family, we spent a lot of leisure time at various beaches in the country such as Lyssons, the university's private beach in St Thomas parish, Runaway Bay, Hellshire, Ocho Rios, Blue Waters and Negril. Negril in those days was not the overdeveloped tourist district it became in the 1990s. The only hotel facility was T-Waters Cottage, a self-service rental cottage property owned by Dr Ken McNeil, a Minister in the PNP government. We stayed there a few weekends together with Carlton Cunningham, his wife Beverley and children Carl and Tanya. It was fun catching crabs on the beach at night and frolicking in the sea during daylight hours. Lyssons Beach was usually visited in the company of various colleagues from the Faculty of Social Sciences. Runaway Bay was another favourite of ours. The university owned a small cottage close to the beach which we would book for as long as one week. Cleaning and cooking services were provided by a university employee. All we had to do was take our supplies and of course pay rent to the university. In Ocho Rios, in addition to the beaches, climbing Dunn's River Falls was an exciting adventure for the family. We spent a lovely holiday weekend at Blue Waters with our friends Victor and Yvonne Thompson and their children Lisa and Andrew. A highlight of that weekend was on the penultimate morning buying the entire basket of a fisherman's lobster catch because the deal he offered us was all or nothing. Our share had us eating lobster for dinner many evenings after our return to Mona.

We enjoyed the rich, diverse culture of Jamaica. We saw theatrical performances at the Barn Theatre, including the original production of Smile Orange written by acclaimed playwright Trevor Rhone. We went to the Little Theatre to watch pantomimes and to see the famous National Dance Theatre Company of Jamaica led by Rex Nettleford and featuring him, Barry Moncrieffe, and Patsy Ricketts. We attended several Jamaica Song Festival competitions and were present when Eric Donaldson won for the first time with Cherry Oh Baby. On some Saturdays, I would visit a small record shop at Half Way Tree and listen to new 45 rpm roots reggae records by hopeful artistes played by the dealer, leaving usually with purchases that puzzled my wife. Of course, we took in live performances by Toots and the Maytals, Ernie Smith, Ken Boothe, John Holt, Pluto Shervington, Delroy Wilson and several others, but regrettably not by Bob Marley and the Wailers or Jimmy Cliff. However, seeing Jimmy Cliff starring in the path-breaking movie *The Harder They Come* on its debut in Kingston was a must do event. We began to sample Jamaican art: first with the prints of Ras Daniel Heartman, then the oil canvases of Ralph Campbell, Ken Spencer, and George Rodney. In time, I added to our collection with canvases by John Watters and Osmond Watson.

We also travelled occasionally outside of the Caribbean. In London, while visiting relatives, we took the opportunity to view theatrical performances in central London. One of the stand-out performances was 'Ain't Misbehaving', the musical play about the life of the famous jazz pianist, Fats Waller. Stellar roles were played by the legendary trumpeter,

Doc Cheatam, pianist Luther Henderson, actor André De Shields and vocalist Nell Carter. We visited British Columbia where I was a Visiting Research Associate at the University of British Columbia in 1976. We resided at my sister Lynda's home and together, with her and her husband, Michael, and children, Stuart and Ebonne, did a lot of sightseeing of the province's famous parks, lakes and mountains.

A great deal of time was spent socialising with friends and colleagues at their homes and ours for lunch, dinner or drinks. Sometimes the occasion would be a child's birthday party or an adult party. Among the friends were Adlith Brown, Elsie LeFranc, Dwight and Linda Venner, Norris Melville, Sam Wray, Eddie and Gloria Greene, Huntley and Pat Manhertz, Kemp and Brenda Skeffrey, Joe and Wilma Bailey, Sam and Joan Rawlins, and Brian Morgan (a Birmingham University student mate from 1968/69) and his wife Beverley who lectured in Spanish at UWI. Brian and Beverley lived in Stony Hill, some distance away from our residence but we enjoyed the scenic drive. I dropped in on Adlith Brown one evening when she lived on the university campus only to discover that she and her house guest Maritza Pantin had been confined home for several days because Adlith's car was in the service garage. They asked me to accompany them to a New Kingston restaurant. There I discovered that I was not appropriated dressed in jacket and tie to satisfy the restaurant dress code. At the time I was unaware that some Jamaican restaurants had formal dress codes. The maître d' assured me that a jacket would suffice and offered to lend me one. To satisfy my friends, I reluctantly accepted the loan.

We also did a bit of night clubbing, usually with Carlton and Beverley Cunningham. We would go the clubs at Halfway Tree or on the Red Hills Road. Devon House was a favourite venue for relaxation. One night, we and the Cunninghams imbibed perhaps a bit too much of the enticing but powerful Devon Duppy drink and danced so late into the night that Ernie Smith, a very popular reggae singer who was performing pleaded with us to go home: "People, please go home. Don't you have a home to go to?" The Social Sciences guys would go without spouses to the Go-Go clubs on Slipe Pen Road and on the Red Hills Road, usually after researching and writing in our offices late at night. A younger member of the faculty eventually married one of the performers, following in the footsteps of Professor Gabriel Coulthard who was reputed to have had done something similar in the 1960s. I paid my last visit to a Go-Go club during the 1980s in the company of Colin Bullock (now deceased) and Wilberne Persaud from the Mona campus, Ranjit Singh from St Augustine, and Sonny, the

Mona SCR bartender. There we encountered Carl Stone, who evidently well-known by the dancers, insisted on introducing me to one of them in her full nudity. Evidently, the Go-Go club tradition was still going strong.

A favourite campus venue for socialising among academics was the Senior Common Room. The topics of conversations were typically very wide, ranging from scholarly matters to literature, art, sports and politics. The in-crowd of which I was a part included Eddie Greene, Vaughan Lewis, Elsie LeFranc, Madge Greenfield (a zoologist), Brenda Skeffrey (a senior administrator), Adlith Brown and Ann Spackman (who fell fatally ill from a brain aneurysm in the middle of a lecture). Other regulars at the Senior Common Room included Carl Stone, Alfred Francis and Wilberne Persaud from Social Sciences; Leo Wilson from the Bursary; Roy Augier, Locksley Lindo, and Rene Coulthard from Arts and General Studies; John Shepherd from the Seismic Research Institute; Wilfred Chan and Basil Burke from the Chemistry Department; Martin Aub, Kenny Small, Zaffar Ali and Leighton Henry from Mathematics; and Sam Wray and George Nicholson from Medical Sciences.

We had visits from several family members and friends while we were in Jamaica. Horace Nurse and Cynthia Massay spent time with us, as did my mother and my wife's mother. Pamela's sister, Valerie, with her husband Winston and sons Patrice and Fidel visited simultaneously with her brother, Compton, and his wife Andrea. We had a wonderful time. We spent a few days in the university's house in Cinconia, a few days in the house in Runaway Bay and a few days in a house in Montego Bay owned by my colleague and friend Norris Melville. From Montego Bay we journeyed to Negril. The family group was able to enjoy a varied Jamaican experience of beaches, mountain atmosphere, Dunn's River Falls, and Jamaican cuisine, and meet many of our friends.

Claremont Kirton introduced me to his Rastafarian friends in East Kingston, Central Kingston and Bull Bay, St Thomas. He, Dwight Venner and I would visit Ras Negus in East Kingston some nights. It was from Ras Negus that I first learnt about the South African apartheid government's ongoing attempts to build a nuclear bomb and the American resistance to regime change on that count. We would also venture to the Bobo Ashanti community in Bull Bay to listen to the wonderful music of Count Ossie and the Mystic Revelations of Rastafari. The band in which Count Ossie played drums and Cedric Im Brooks and Ronald Nambo Robinson starred on tenor saxophone and trombone respectively played a fusion of Nyabinghi and jazz music. One introduction by Claremont to his Jamaican connections had a humorous twist. I needed a tailor; therefore he took me to his tailor located downtown. The tailor turned out to be a Chinese immigrant who had converted to Rastafarianism and spoke Jamaican roots language with a mixed Jamaica-China accent which I found somewhat incomprehensible. I noticed that the length of his trousers stopped about three inches above his ankles, Chinese style. I then understood why Claremont's trousers always stopped short of his ankles and decided I would not suffer the same fate. No Chinese Rasta tailor for me!

Together with Al Francis, George Beckford, Claremont Kirton, Dwight Venner and Ralph Gonsalves, I indulged my passion for cricket. We always could be found at Sabina Park, the test cricket venue, come rain or blazing hot sun, when the West Indies were playing a visiting team. At Sabina Park, I saw matches with New Zealand, India, Australia, England and Pakistan. There I also saw the greats of West Indian cricket in varying stages of their career, players like Rohan Kanhai in the closing stages of his career, Roy Fredericks, Clive Lloyd at the start of his as well as in his best years, Lance Gibbs, Michael Holding as a teenage fast bowling prodigy and during his most fearsome and devastating years, the unsmiling Andy Roberts likewise, Garfield Sobers towards the end of his career, and the incomparable batsman, Vivian 'Viv' Richards. I particularly remember a West Indian innings against England with Garfield Sobers and Bernard Julien at the crease facing up to John Snow. Sobers kept playing late and missing, the ball thudding into his pads. At the other end, Bernard Julien played some glorious drives with impeccable timing. I thought sport was no respecter of age: Gary's batting prowess was waning, and Bernard Julien was in his ascendancy. I also remember Majid Khan, the great Pakistani batsman, and Viv Richards on his way to becoming the most accomplished and feared batsman in the world, displaying their majestic forward defensive strokes, neither ball or air having a chance to pass between bat and pads. And, of course, I remember young Michael Holding reducing the great Sunil Gavaskar to embarrassed discomfiture and ultimate dismissal. I also remember the pain of watching Australian batsmen like Ian and Greg Chappell, Keith Stackpole and Doug Walters pile up tons of runs against shaggy dog West Indian fast bowlers like Vanburn Holder. Some of us also attended the regional competitive games which showcased emerging talents like Alvin Kallicharran and Lawrence Rowe whose late cut was a stroke to behold. I was there at Sabina Park in February 1972 when Lawrence Rowe made his entrance to test cricket with a double century against New Zealand. He followed up with a triple century against England at the Kensington

Oval, Barbados in March 1973. On debut, Alvin Kallicharran followed with centuries at Bourda and Queen's Park Oval in April.

Sabina Park was a great place for making new friends. The ebbs and flows of a cricket match extending over four or five days were not conducive to the kind of prolonged competitive antagonisms among supporters of rival teams that one witnesses in football competitions. Humour and hope prevailed in situations where the tide could easily turn favourably or adversely for one's team. It was at Sabina Park that I met the Jamaican sportswriter Tony Becca and would often encounter Clare Forrester. Clare Forrester, who died in September 2014, was an excellent repository of sports information. She was an authority especially on athletics which she knew in its many dimensions in Jamaica, including the annual all-island secondary schools' athletics championships, Boys Champs and Girls Champs. She covered the Olympic Games in Atlanta, Athens, Beijing and London and in 1996 published the authorised biography of the great Jamaican international sprinter, Merlene Ottey.

I also attended a few football games at the National Stadium. Tensions tended to run high at football. One memorable occasion was an aborted championship game between Boys Town Football Club from Trench Town and Tivoli Gardens Football Club. I went with Claremont Kirton, Dwight Venner and Maurice Odle. We were late to the ground and could not sit in the bleachers as was our habit and had to settle for seats in the grandstand. Boys Town supporters were beating their Rasta drums as the flow of play favoured their team. Suddenly Tivoli scored. One-nil. The drums became silent. After ten minutes, Tivoli scored again. Two-nil. A few gun shots rang out in the bleachers. Then another round of gunshots. People started to flee the bleachers and head across the field to the grandstand where police officers used their batons to turn them away. It was a choice between bullets and batons. When we exited the National Stadium, we could see men on motorcycles discharging firearms in the air even though Jamaica had extremely severe punishments for illegal possession of firearms. That was my last football experience in Jamaica.

I travelled extensively in Jamaica just to know the country. I would deliberately set out to visit places I had never been, sometimes on roads that petered into impassable tracks for motor cars. Widespread political violence in 1980 and 1981 made it hazardous to continue such forays. One could easily end up in the wrong place at the wrong time, driving the wrong colour car or wearing the wrong colour shirt. The colour green was like a red flag to a bull in a PNP area as was the colour orange in a JLP area.

Even the university housing development was not entirely safe as I realised one day when I saw army personnel taking up shooting positions facing away a few metres across from my residence. My concern mounted on realisation that their expected targets could well be shooting back in the direction of my house. Nonetheless, by the time we migrated to Trinidad and Tobago at the end of September 1981, I knew many nooks and crannies in Jamaica; where to go and where not to go. Not so anymore!

UWI Economics Department colleagues at Mona Campus in 1979. Standing (L-R): Claremont Kirton, Jean Francis, Steve DeCastro, Desiree Tucker, Colin Bullock, Cynthia Hines and Pat McLean' s sister. Crouching (L-R): Wilberne Persaud, me, Patricia McLean and Michael Witter.

Ohio State University Colleagues and Pamela, Columbus, 1980. Academics L-R: B.M. Desai, Dale W. Adams, Douglas H. Graham and Donald Larson.

CHAPTER SIX

UNIVERSITY OF THE WEST INDIES, TRINIDAD, 1981-1989

SETTLING IN

My family and I moved from Jamaica to Trinidad and Tobago at the end of September 1981. I was taking up my new appointment as Professor of Economics in the Department of Economics at the UWI, St Augustine campus. The University had appointed me in July. At 37 years old, I was the youngest person appointed Professor in those days. A member of the selection panel subsequently told me that my comparative youthfulness was the subject of debate which one member of the panel ended by asking if a grey beard was a selection criterion.

We were greeted on arrival in Trinidad by Eric St Cyr, the Head of Department. He and his wife Jo were welcoming to me and my family, had us to lunch at their home in St Anns, and provided much appreciated advice about settling into a new country. Eric St Cyr insisted on my occupation of a spacious office in the main Faculty building that he occupied until a few days before my arrival. Soon after our arrival, Professor Lloyd Braithwaite, the Principal of the campus, and his wife Ursula hosted us to dinner at their home. Lloyd Best, his wife, Christiane, and a few other people from the university were there.

We were temporarily housed in a townhouse complex off St John's Road that the university used to accommodate recently arrived staff before more permanent accommodation could be arranged. Our neighbours in the townhouse complex were Tony Falloon, his wife Dorett and their two children and Colin Benjamin and his wife Claire. Tony Falloon had arrived to take up a post in the Campus Registry and Colin Benjamin to take up a lectureship in the Faculty of Engineering. After a few weeks, we were able to move to a house in Maracas Valley where our immediate neighbours were Selwyn and Joy Ryan and their two children, Michelle and Kwame. Kwame even as a pre-teenager displayed extra-ordinary musical talent which ultimately crystallised in him becoming a prominent conductor of philharmonic orchestras in the UK, Europe and the USA, thereby fulfilling a dream I had about him one night when according to his mother most likely his late night/pre-dawn piano playing had filtered into my subconscious. The Falloons and Selwyn Ryan and his second wife, Jan, became our close friends.

Settling into Trinidad in 1981 was not an easy process. The country as a petroleum exporter was in the middle of an international oil price boom which conferred great wealth, distorted values as was evident in a surge in conspicuous consumption especially of imported luxury items and led to inflated wage rates and poor work attitudes in both the private and public sectors of the economy. The public utilities, especially water supply and telephone services were deplorable, so much so that possession of a working telephone landline was a prized asset. To compound matters, Trinidad and Tobago had introduced a policy of promoting local assembly of motor cars with imported components and severely restricted imports of motor vehicles for private use. This resulted in a huge backlog in private demand for motor cars and waiting lists extending for more than two years for the models deemed by consumers to be more efficient and serviceable.

We were fortunate that the house we were allocated had a telephone landline that worked initially but when it broke down it was not fixed for so many months that I was startled one day when it rang. The situation with provision of telephone services was deplorable. In 1982, there were only 4.26 connections for every 1000 people in Trinidad and Tobago and in 1985 only 7.34 connections per thousand people. Businessmen were reported to travel to Barbados to make important business calls. Significant improvement began in 1986 when the number of connections per thousand people increased to 10.32 and rose steadily to 14.15 in 1992.

Getting a motor car was a more formidable proposition. We had been compelled by Trinidad and Tobago import restrictions to sell our relatively new Mazda 626 car in Jamaica. Try as much as we did, we could not get a new car to purchase in Trinidad. After some months of futility, we gratefully accepted the offer of a second-hand Mitsubishi Galant from John La Guerre, a colleague in the Faculty of Social Sciences. In the meantime, we were greatly assisted in transporting our sons to and from school in Port of Spain by our friend Rosina Wiltshire who had relocated from the Faculty of Social Sciences in Jamaica to the Institute of International Affairs at the St Augustine campus. It was really an immense contribution by Rosina to our settling in because under the dense traffic conditions and the distance between her residence in Valsayn and ours in Maracas Valley, it was an extremely difficult and tiring Monday to Friday commute.

Transportation was one challenge; another was getting the boys appropriately placed in schools. Here, too, Rosina was a great help. When the University School denied admission to Compton Olatunji, our younger son, for the spurious reason that he was too close to the date of high school entrance exams for his age cohort, Rosina was instrumental in his admission to Trinity Junior School which had a connection to her high school alma mater, Bishops High School in Port of Spain. My friend Jerry Hospedales at the Central Bank of Trinidad and Tobago assisted with the placement of our older son, Clairmonte Erlin, in Fatima College. He was able to use his connection with the Principal Gerry Pantin and Deputy Principal Mervyn Moore to surmount what I later discovered was a major problem faced by many parents who had migrated to Trinidad and Tobago at that time. We remain eternally grateful to Rosina and Jerry for their efforts on our behalf.

A third challenge was encountered in getting our modest household belongings from the Trinidad ports. A kindly customs broker employed by the university offered to help me with the formalities and procedures alongside his work at the Port of Spain Port for the university. Getting through the procedures required first getting a very early morning brief from the Customs official in charge as to the documentary requirements, then proceeding to relevant government offices in several buildings to have the completed documents processed and stamped, then returning to the Port to pay for the container to travel to my residence for delivery of the household effects and to pay for Customs officers and guards to inspect the un-stuffing of the contents of the container when it arrived there. The whole process at the Port lasted from about 7am to 3pm. The container and officials duly departed before me. Much to my dismay, when I turned into my neighbourhood, the container was parked on a street which had been made impassable sometime after I left home that morning by a Water and Sewerage Authority (WASA) work crew that had dug a wide drain across the street. The prospect facing me was one of restarting the final stages of the process the next day. Fortunately, I had two resourceful friends, Wallace Joefield-Napier and Ramesh Ramsaran, from my Mona days with me. They borrowed shovels and spades from residents on the street, and with my help refilled the drain (probably to the consternation of the WASA crew next day), enabling the container to reach my residence where it was duly un-stuffed.

My Aunt Ivy Hamlet and her husband Daniel had re-migrated from Guyana to Trinidad many years ago and were well placed to offer some advice and reassurance to aid the settling process. We saw a lot of them at their home in Arima and at our homes in Maracas Valley and St Augustine.

One year after arrival in Trinidad, my wife completed the BSc Management Studies degree for which she had done the first two years of studies at the UWI Mona campus. She, after some initial work permit difficulties requiring the intervention of UWI Vice Chancellor Preston and Trinidad and Tobago Minister of Education Overand Padmore, obtained employment as an auditor at John Hunt, Coopers Lybrand, an accounting firm in Port of Spain. About the same time, we moved from Maracas Valley to a rented house on Santa Margarita Circular Road, St Augustine. By then, our younger son had passed his high school entrance examination and joined his older brother at Fatima College. We still had only one car. The daily commute into and out of Port of Spain remained the same. We had to be on the road no later than 6.30am in order to get to Fatima College by 7.15am. I had to get the boys from school at 2.30 or 4.00pm depending on their extra-curricular activities and pick up my wife when she finished work at 4pm.We rarely made it back home before 5pm. It was enormously tiring for me, especially because I attended to my usual university duties between 9am and 1.30pm, but no less so for the boys who invariably fell asleep during the morning commute. It was a great relief when we finally were able to acquire a second car and the boys were old enough and sufficiently familiar with Trinidad to take public transport from Fatima College in Mucurapo to our residence in St Augustine.

It was in that house that we experienced the only robbery we have had. The robbers came in the afternoon while my wife was at work and our sons at school. I had been home all morning but left around about 1pm for the airport. They broke the burglar bars, went through the ceiling to enter rooms where doors were locked, and ransacked the house, taking everything of value that they could find. It must have been a very noisy operation. The domestic staff of our next-door neighbours, Chanka Seeteram and his family, who heard what was happening did not raise an alarm or summon the police.

UNIVERSITY COLLEAGUES

Many of my academic colleagues at St Augustine were known to me before I joined the campus mainly because of their participation in mutual networks or because of the frequent travel between the campuses necessitated by the university's organisation and modus operandi which favoured face-to-face consultations and decision-making in academic matters such as course design and implementation, examinations and determination of graduation results, as well as on administrative matters such as staff assessment and promotions and finance.

In the Department of Economics, my colleagues initially were Eric St Cyr, Carlton Bruce, Roy Thomas, Trevor Farrell, Ralph Henry, Patrick Watson and Dev Gupta. Winston Dookeran, who I had known from my Mona days, had recently left to become a Member of Parliament. Karl Theodore returned from leave the following year and Dennis Pantin, Godfrey Martin and Elizabeth Parsan joined soon after. The academics in the Department of Management Studies included George Wadinambiaratchi, who had transferred from the Mona campus, Ainsley Mark, Gordon Draper, Vishnu Ramlogan, Suruj Rambachan, Azard Hosein, Nurul Islam, Jagmohan Seghal, and John Eckstein. Gwendolyn Williams joined a few years later. Lewis Bobb, John La Guerre, Najmul Abedin and Carl Parris were in the Department of Government where they were later joined by Victor King and Ralph Premdas. In the Department of Sociology there was Acton Camejo, Susan Craig, Ramesh Deosaran, Maureen Cain and Marcus Balintulo. It was quite a mixed Faculty in terms of nationalities, 21 of the 32 members being Trinidadian, three Guyanese, one Barbadian, one British, two Indian, two Bangladeshi, one Sri Lankan, one South African, and one Sierra Leonean.

Lewis Bobb was not heavily published but was a splendid teacher, the value of which became evident when upon his retirement, former students, some resident as far away as the African continent, arranged and financed a valedictory ceremony at which they paid tribute to his contribution to their intellectual and subsequent professional development. The tributes made me realise that the university did not sufficiently recognise the importance of excellent teaching and mentorship in its assessment and promotions criteria. Student assessment of teaching is now standard practice but is still not systematically incorporated in the decision calculus.

Social Sciences shared a three-storey building with the Faculty of Arts and General Studies. There was a lot of mingling on the corridors which facilitated cross-disciplinary discussions and general camaraderie. In History, there was Keith Laurence who was Professor and Head of Department, Bridget Brereton, James Millette, Brinsley Samaroo, Selwyn Carrington, Fitz Baptiste, Kelvin Singh and Kusha Haraksingh. In Languages and Literature, there was Gordon Rohlehr, Patricia Ismond, Helen Pyne-Timothy, Vishnu Singh, Vere Knight, Denis Solomon, Randy Hezekiah, Lloyd King and Sylvia Moodie.

On the western side of the campus was located the Institute of Social and Economic Research (ISER) and the Institute of International Relations (IIR). The ISER was headed by Jack Harewood, an eminent statistician/demographer who was previously Director of Trinidad and Tobago's Central Statistical Office. Other academic staff included Norma Abdullah as Deputy Director, Selwyn Ryan and Wallace Joefield-Napier. On the academic and professional staff of the IIR were Basil Ince who acted as Director until 1981, Anthony Bryant who was appointed Director in 1983, Rosina Wiltshire, Ramesh Ramsaran, Anselm Francis, Anthony Peter Gonsalves, Yola Alleyne, Wendy Sealy and Herb Addo who I had met a few years previously when he taught at the University of Guyana.

There were many notable academics in other faculties on the campus. In the Faculty of Engineering could be found Professor of Electrical Engineering Kenneth Julien, Professor of Civil Engineering Harry Phelps, Professor of Chemical Engineering George Maxwell Richards, Professor of Construction Engineering Desmond Imbert, Professor of Petroleum Engineering Percy Bruce, Professor of Food Technology George Moonsammy, Professor of Electrical Engineering St Clair King, Professor of Industrial Engineering Avvari Ramasastry and Professor of Mechanical Engineering Suppramanian Satcunanathan.

In the Faculty of Natural Sciences, Professor of Chemistry Wilfred (Willie) Chan headed a strong team including Baldwin Mootoo and Compton Seaforth in natural products chemistry, Marvington Sweeney, Dyer Narinesingh, and Oliver Headley who concentrated on solar energy. Ramsay Saunders was Professor of Physics; Julian (Jake) Kenny was Professor of Zoology. In the Department of Mathematics were Professor Bhu Dev Sharma, Harold Ramkissoon working on fluid dynamics, and Ed Farrell working on exponential series.

The Faculty of Agriculture had Professor of Livestock Science Holman Williams, Professor of Soil Science Nazeer Ahmad and Professors of Crop Science John Spence and Lawrence (Laurie) Wilson; Professor David Edwards had recently left to join the new University of Bradford in England. In that faculty there were several other outstanding professionals: Frank Gumbs in Soil Science, Charles McDavid and Julian Duncan in botany and plant science, Peter Bacon in zoology, P.I. Gomes in agricultural extension, Lloyd Rankine, Ranjit Singh and Carlisle Pemberton in agricultural economics, and Yasmin Baksh-Comeau who developed and brought status to the National Herbarium.

On the west of the campus, with offices also in Port of Spain, the Extra-Mural Department, led by Esmond Ramessar, was on its way to becoming a major enterprise. Close to it was the Computer Centre headed by Ken Cazabon. On the northern side of the campus could be found the Faculty of Education whose leaders included Lawrence Carrington, Innocent Beddoe, Edrich Gift, Jeanette McMorris and Verna Jules.

The Faculty of Medical Sciences was becoming established at the new Mount Hope campus. The leading figures in the faculty were Professors Alan Butler, Norris Melville, Rolf Richards, Courtenay Bartholomew, Michael Beaubrun, Dave Picou, James Cross, Eugene Ward, Syam Roopnarine Singh, S.R. Prabhu, Hylton McFarlane and Jim Kaminjolo. Alan Butler and Norris Melville, ably assisted by administrators Wilfred "Pidge" Permell, Angela Garcia, and Maylin Soo Ting, were the main driving force in the establishment of the faculty, overcoming financial challenges, administrative challenges, as well as technical and personnel challenges. At an early stage in the efforts of the Faculty of Medical Sciences to gain approval for start of operations at Mount Hope, I worked with Norris Melville, Alan Butler and Wilfred "Pidge" Permell on a self-financing plan for the Faculty which persuaded the University Council to give the go-ahead.

On the St Augustine campus, there were also standout personalities in administration. The Campus Principal was Professor Lloyd Braithwaite who had distinguished himself as a sociologist. The Campus Registrar was Hugh Gibson, ably assisted by Marion Fraser, Carmen Redhead and Zaffar Ali in posts of Senior Assistant Registrar, Will Iton, Victor Cowan and Robert Henry. Dr Desiree Wilson and Merle King were the senior members of the Campus Health Services Centre. The Bursary was headed by Byron Williams as Campus Bursar with Sooknath Lackhan as his Deputy and other professionals including Lylla Bada and Genevieve Vincent. Major figures in the Main Library were the distinguished Campus Librarian, Dr Alma Jordan in whose honour the library was later renamed the Alma Jordan Library, Yvonne Stephenson, Barbara Commissiong, Dr Margaret Rouse-Jones, Kasuma Rankine, Reggie Clarke, Marva Henry and Annette Knight.

The campus had its fair share of colourful and eccentric characters. Roger Barnes, an Englishman in the Faculty of Agriculture, always dressed in shirts made of a typical English lime-green plaid, dark short pants and knee-high woollen socks. Vere Knight, a former hockey player, in the Faculty of Arts and General Studies, invariably wore athletic shorts, perhaps to remind people of his sporting history or because of vanity about his thighs or perhaps merely to keep cool in the tropical heat. Vishnu Singh, also from Arts and General Studies, having failed at electoral politics with one incarnation of Basdeo Panday's political parties, turned successfully to university trade unionism. Ralph Premdas, despite being comfortably housed near to the campus by the university, often preferred to take up residence in his office, or so it seemed when days would pass before the early morning cleaners had access to it. Pascal Osuji from the Caribbean Agricultural Research and Development Institute located on the campus was always in search of a monetary bargain and once persuaded me and Frank Gumbs to join him in the purchase of a young cow to economise on the price of meat.

I enjoyed cordial collegial relations with so many people on the campus that it is impossible to list any without being invidious to those omitted. However, there are some who with their families became close friends of me and my family. They include Gordon and Betty Rohlehr, Marion Fraser, Frank and Barbara Gumbs, Lloyd Rankine and Kasuma Rankine, Charles and Gemma McDavid, Karl and Val Theodore, Willie and Audrey Chan, Eric and Jo St Cyr, Norris Melville, Fitz and Katherine Baptiste, Will and Monica Iton, and Lewis Bobb in whose home I had stayed on previous visits to Trinidad and who I had reciprocally housed in Jamaica. Lewis Bobb was especially kind to me and my family. He and I remained very good friends long after he retired from the university. Together with Professor Woodville Marshall and Sir Keith Hunte, both Cave Hill colleagues who were also his close friends, I was a pallbearer at his funeral in Barbados. Friendships started in Mona with Rosina Wiltshire, Carl Parris, Ramesh Ramsaran and Joefield-Napier continued in Trinidad.

I travelled frequently to Jamaica and was therefore able to maintain collegial and friendly relationships with many of my Mona colleagues and through visits to their homes expand the range of non-university friendships, notably with John and Maureen Allgrove who with their two daughters lived across the street from Elsie LeFranc. Their son, Zickie, was an engineering student at the St Augustine campus. From 1990-1996 when I was Pro Vice Chancellor of Planning and Development for the university, Maureen Allgrove served as a senior professional in my office on the Mona campus which facilitated more frequent contact and a closer, lasting friendship with she and her family.

TEACHING AND STUDENTS

My initial teaching assignments were Advanced Economic Theory and Economic Development at the graduate level and Monetary Economics at the undergraduate level. After a year, I was relieved of the Economic Development course and was able to take on supervision of MSc research students. Several members of my undergraduate class in monetary economics continued to do graduate work with me, either just the course in advanced economic theory or also research in money and finance. The outstanding students in the graduate classes were Shelton Nicholls, Juliet Melville, Nigel Baptiste, Roopnarine Oumade Singh, Terrence Clarke, Lyndon Guiseppi, Glenn Khan, Kelvin Sargeant and Laurel Bain. Among the research students, those who excelled were Cleopatra Crawford, Arnold McIntyre, Ronald Ramkissoon, Shelton Nicholls, Roopnarine Oumade Singh, Kelvin Sargeant, Sandra Beckles, Terrence Clarke and Glenn Khan.

Under my supervision, Michael Howard, a member of the Economics Department at Cave Hill completed his University of the West Indies PhD thesis on the Economic Development of Barbados in 1985, Laurence Clarke, a staff member of the World Bank, completed his PhD thesis on Banking Distortions in the Financial Sector of Post-War Economies in 1986, and Gem Fletcher, a staff member at the University of Guyana, completed her PhD thesis on Productivity in the Guyana Rice Industry in 1991. The two Ohio State University PhD students I continued to supervise completed their PhDs in 1982: Stephen S. Pollard on The Performance of the Agricultural Sector in Jamaica and Ohene S. Nyanin on Cost of Agriculture Lending, Institutional Viability and Lender Behaviour in Jamaica. I was asked by the University of Surrey to assist in the supervision of Marion Williams' PhD thesis for that university. Some of my students were granted access to my home library and use of my study and my personal computer to supplement the resources of the campus.

The range of thesis research topics done by my students was wide. For instance, Ronald Ramkissoon's thesis was on commercial bank asset portfolio behaviour in Trinidad and Tobago. Cleopatra Crawford's was on agricultural credit in Trinidad and Tobago with special reference to the Agricultural Development Bank, while Sandra Beckles' was on the loan repayment problem of development banks with particular reference to the St Lucia Development Bank. Arnold McIntyre wrote his MSc thesis on finance, growth and the balance of trade in the Organisation of East Caribbean States countries. Shelton Nicholls' thesis was on external debt and balance of payments adjustment in Trinidad and Tobago. Roopnarine Oumade Singh wrote on capital market development in Trinidad and Tobago, and Glenn Khan wrote on the performance and structure of credit unions in Trinidad and Tobago. Laurence Clarke's thesis was on banking distortions in the financial sector. These theses contained a considerable body of research findings which improved empirical knowledge and understanding of several important aspects of financial behaviour in Trinidad and Tobago and in other Caribbean countries.

All of my graduate students excelled in the world of work. Roopnarine Oumade Singh, Terrence Clarke, Glenn Khan, Lyndon Guiseppi and Nigel Baptiste went to very successful careers in the banking and finance industry in Trinidad and Tobago. Shelton Nicholls, Cleopatra Crawford, Ronald Ramkissoon and Kelvin Sargeant did likewise at the Central Bank of Trinidad and Tobago. After completing a PhD degree in Economics at Queen Mary College, University of London, Nicholls became a member of the academic staff at St Augustine before returning to the Central Bank as Deputy Governor and later joining the International Monetary Fund assigned firstly as Director of the Caribbean Regional Technical Assistance Centre and then as a senior staff member at IMF headquarters.

After some years, Cleopatra Crawford left the Central Bank's Research Department to pursue a legal career; Kelvin Sargeant was appointed General Manager of the Small Enterprise Development Company, before taking up a senior position with the International Labour Office. Ronald Ramkissoon joined Republic Bank as Chief Economist. Juliet Melville completed a PhD degree in Economics at the University of Kent in Canterbury, England, began lecturing in the Department of Economics at St Augustine, and later joined the Caribbean Development Bank as a country economist. Sandra Beckles took up a senior position at the St Lucia Development Cooperation before moving to the Eastern Caribbean Central Bank where Laurel Bain was also employed.

After further graduate study at Yale University and the University of Toronto, Arnold McIntyre joined the economics faculty at UWI Cave Hill and after working with the Regional Trade Negotiating Machinery in Barbados joined the International Monetary Fund in a senior capacity. Lawrence Clarke, after a stint as Director of the Caribbean Centre for Money and Finance, resumed his appointment at the World Bank where he rose to the position of Resident Representative in several African countries. It was rewarding and a pleasure to tutor and mentor such an outstanding set of students, many of whom have endeavoured to maintain contact with me, even organising social functions in my honour when circumstances permitted.

I also formally supervised a few graduate students from the Department of Agricultural Economics and Farm Management. Ronald Ramkissoon registered for his PhD in that Department and was supervised jointly by me and Lloyd Rankine. Another student I recall is Vincent Lyttle who wrote his MSc thesis on "Resource Productivity and Profitability of Cassava Production in Selected Areas of Jamaica" under my supervision. There were other students in that Department, like Edward "Gilly" Evans, who I advised informally on their graduate research and sometimes read the entire thesis before final submission.

FACULTY OF SOCIAL SCIENCES ENVIRONMENT

After the heady atmosphere of the Faculty of Social Sciences at Mona, the environment at St Augustine seemed almost sonorous. Several of the academic staff in Economics were rarely present outside of their lecture and student consultation hours. There was not much discussion on non-departmental matters. Trevor Farrell focussed on the Trinidad and Tobago energy sector and technology policy, Roy Thomas on labour and industrial relations, and Eric St Cyr on plantation economy. Karl Theodore researched fiscal issues and the public utilities. There did not seem to be much interest in economic topics without a Trinidad and Tobago focus.

Two seminars I organised on current economic issues which would normally be expected to get the attention of professional economists anywhere were not well attended except by students. One seminar was on supply-side economics which was in vogue as part of the Washington Consensus and Reaganomics. One of the speakers I had invited was Ved Ghandi, an expert from the IMF who I had got to know at a public finance conference at the University of Stirling in Scotland. The other seminar was on industrialisation and trade in Latin America and the Caribbean. The speakers, who included Latin American scholars, were members of my network on Latin American and Caribbean economics. The pattern of attendance was the same: few academics and many students. In retrospect, it does appear that poor conference and seminar attendance by St Augustine academic staff is a strong characteristic for I have witnessed similar patterns of behaviour at many events through the years extending to present day.

Not much went on in the other academic departments in the faculty where staff seemed to concentrate on teaching and whatever research a few of them were undertaking. I say "a few" because there was not much evidence of published research coming out of the Department of Management Studies, or Sociology, or in Government apart from Ramesh Deosaran and John LaGuerre until the arrival of Ralph Premdas. Some academic staff were involved in party politics, like Suruj Rambachan and Vishnu Ramlogan in the United Labour Front and Gordon Draper and John Eckstein in the People's National Movement.

Livelier and lucid discussions on wide-ranging topics were more likely to be enjoyed at the Senior Common Room whose habitués included Willie Chan, Baldwin Mootoo, Vere Knight, Will Iton, Denis Solomon, Pat Ismond, Helen Pyne-Timothy, Barbara Commissiong, Gloria Baptiste (Main Library) and her sister Cynthia Baptiste (IIR), Wendy Sealy, Irma Burkett (CARIRI), Zaffar Ali, Herb Addo, Anselm Francis, Selwyn Ryan, Kusha Haraksingh, Vishnu Singh, Lloyd Rankine, Pascal Osuji, Reggie Clarke, Pidge Permell, John Shepherd (Seismic Research Institute), Eugene Ward, Marvington Sweeney, Alex Mutani, and myself. In addition to the deepening of collegial relationships and friendships at the Senior Common Room, one got the benefit of perspectives from many disciplines and professional backgrounds and repeated opportunities for deepening understanding and appreciation of the role and work of the university's component parts. The Senior Common Room was closed in the 2000s without provision for any substitute facility by a campus administration unfamiliar with its contribution to these valuable aspects of university life.

In contrast to the desultory intellectual atmosphere of the Faculty of Social Sciences and the Faculty of Arts and General Studies, there was lively, cordial and cooperative relationship between academic and non-academic staff in the two buildings that the faculties occupied. Mavelyn, an elderly office attendant, ran a sou-sou [a cooperative loan club] in which both academics and non-academics participated. Members of the non-academic staff like Margaret Adams, Ava Seaton, Lyra Kendall, Patricia Marcano, Lyn Sheppard, Elizabeth Marcano (from Arts and General Studies), Everold Sampson, and Scott Ramjattan did much to ensure not only that academic matters were efficiently managed but also that conviviality prevailed among all ranks. All this was made much easier by the tradition of Faculty of Social Sciences Christmas parties financed by contributions from the entertainment allowances of Heads of departments in the Faculty. Lasting friendships were developed, particularly with Patricia Marcano, Ava Seaton and Lyra Kendall.

RESEARCH, CONERENCES, NETWORKS

My own research and other technical economic activities continued apace when I joined the St Augustine campus.

RURAL FINANCIAL MARKETS

I continued to participate in the work of the rural financial markets group. With Stephen K. Pollard, I authored a report to USAID/Kingston on "The Supply of Agricultural Inputs in Jamaica: 1960-1980" in 1981. That Report described and appraised the structure of input use, trends in input supplies, the distribution system, and trends in input prices. The conclusions noted the adverse effects on agricultural performance of several factors: input supply difficulties; import price inflation; restrictions on prices of farm products; unequal access to imported inputs; and urban concentration of distribution. As described in Chapter 5, together with Douglas H. Graham and Stephen K. Pollard, I wrote a report to Jamaica's Ministry of Agriculture in 1982 on a "Farm Level Survey and Analysis of Selected Clients of the Crop Lien Program in St Catherine, Jamaica".

A Special Issue of the journal Social and Economic Studies which I edited was published in March 1983. It presented more of the findings from the research on Jamaica's rural financial markets to Caribbean and international readerships. The Issue entitled "Rural Financial Markets in Jamaica" contained papers by Ohene Owusu Nyanin on "Lending Costs, Institutional Viability and Agricultural Credit Strategies in Jamaica", Girma Begashaw on "Evaluation of a Supervised Credit Project in Jamaica", Peter J. Heffernan and Stephen K. Pollard on "The Determinants of Credit Use among Small Farmers in Jamaica" and "Agricultural Productivity and Credit Use of Small Farmers in Jamaica", and Douglas H. Graham and Stephen K. Pollard on "The Crop Lien Programme: Implications of a Credit Project Transformed into an ad-hoc Income Transfer Programme". I, myself, contributed two papers: the lead paper on "Structure and Performance of Jamaican Rural Financial Markets" and "Effects of Subsidised Credit on the Size Distribution of Farm Household Incomes". The first of the two papers concluded that Jamaican rural financial markets were fragmented with institutions and programmes differentiated by their clientele, loan maturity structures, loan pricing policies, operating cost structures, source of funds, and degree of financial viability. The second paper identified and quantified two channels by which credit subsidies affected the size distribution of farm household incomes in Jamaica.

Major explanations of the poor performance of specialised agricultural finance institutions were faulty assumptions and major defects in design and operation, as Douglas Graham and I argued in our paper "Problems with Specialised Agricultural Lenders" in a book *Undermining Rural Development with Cheap Credit* edited by Dale W. Adams, Douglas H. Graham and J.D. Von Pischke published by Westview Press in 1984. We challenged the assumption that credit is an appropriate instrument for development in situations of distorted commodity markets; noted that contrary to prevailing views the unsatisfied demand for credit was at the short end of the finance spectrum rather than at the long end; and noted the high opportunity costs of treating farm financial problems through the credit system. Design and operational defects included narrow liability structures of credit institutions, high lending costs, high borrower transactions costs, low interest rate ceilings, and discontinuous injections of loanable funds. We proposed realistic interest rates, diversification of sources of loanable funds, and maintenance of a stable macro-economy.

I continued this line of analysis in my address in September 1983 to the Caribbean Agricultural Credit Association Senior Management Workshop in Montego Bay, Jamaica. I spoke on "Prospects for Viable Agricultural Credit Institutions Based on Historical Structures". I began by noting the short life cycles of specialised agricultural credit institutions in which, having been started with substantial foreign funding and much political fanfare, they rapidly transited from considerable activity to prolonged periods of dormancy. I listed the elements of historical structures, namely, traditional credit delivery systems, inherited agrarian structure, and policy conceptions and rigidities, and linked them to the crippling problems faced by specialised agricultural credit institutions. These problems were identified as high loan administration costs, high loan delinquency costs, narrow and unsustainable funding patterns, low interest rate ceilings, fragmented and miniscule farm units, and insufficiently remunerative product prices.

On the matter of a stable macro-economy, I had concluded based on my observations of synchronous trends in the Jamaican economy that a big part of the performance problems of rural financial institutions was the wider economic environment in which they operated. I pursued this idea in a paper "Economic Disequilibria and Rural Financial Market Performance in Developing Economies" co-authored with Douglas Graham. It was published in the Canadian Journal of Agricultural Economics in 1983. We used a model of the transmission process to demonstrate how the severe effects of macroeconomic disorder are transmitted to rural financial markets through their impact on costs of farm production and consumption relative to agricultural product prices which together determine changes in farm savings and debt transactions. We applied the model to Jamaica to illustrate its applicability.

I participated in a major policy conference at the World Bank which together with USAID was interested in the Rural Financial Markets Group's empirical findings, policy conclusions and recommendations on the design and implementation of rural financial market programmes and mobilisation of rural savings. Sometime in the 1990s, the Ohio State University received a prestigious award from the American Agricultural Economics Association for its analytical contributions to policy on rural financial markets. As time elapsed and my responsibilities and career took a different direction, I had less contact with the Rural Financial Markets Group.

Nonetheless, I made time to engage in a few rural financial market projects. In May1982, I was engaged by the World Bank to be the financial market specialist consultant on an agricultural rehabilitation project for Uganda, and the following year I led a small team on a USAID/Zambia Project on Zambia Agricultural Financial Markets in September 1983. More will be said about these two project experiences later in a section of this chapter dealing with Africa.

OTHER AGRICULTURAL ECONOMICS ACTIVITIES

I remained active in the Caribbean Agro-Economic Society, participating in the annual conferences, seminars and research projects. At the Annual Conference in 1987 in San Ignacio, Belize, I presented a paper on "Macroeconomic Framework for Food and Agriculture Policy in the Commonwealth Caribbean". In 1986, I collaborated with a team from the UWI Department of Agricultural Economics and Farm Management which included Lloyd Rankine, Ranjit Singh, Suresh Birla and Carlisle Pemberton on a major report on Incentives and Support Systems for Food and Agriculture in the Lesser Developed Countries of CARICOM for the Caribbean Agro-Economic Society.

DEVELOPMENT BANKING

I began to approach the topic of development banking more generally with a paper on "Scope and Prospect for Financial Innovations in DFCs in the Caribbean" which I presented to the Caribbean Development Bank Senior Management Seminar for Development Finance Corporations in Ocho Rios,

Jamaica in June 1988. I started the presentation with a brief statement on the rationale for development banking and then identified several characteristics or operational modalities of development financial corporations, namely, allocation of funds for capital investment, long maturity of loans, use of benefit-cost criteria, clientele targeting, provision of technical assistance, and interest rate subsidisation. I pointed out that DFCs rarely intermediated domestic savings or raised funds on the domestic capital market. Defining financial innovation as the introduction of new financial instruments, institutions or services or discontinuous changes in financial service production technology, the paper notes that there were already facets of financial innovation, such as creation of new institutions and modalities like finance companies, mutual funds, and stock markets to fill identified gaps, new instruments mainly on the liabilities side, and new technologies like automated banking in the Caribbean financial sector. Several ways in which DFCs could innovate were suggested. These included indirect intermediation through borrowing from domestic financial institutions, issue of bonds and shares locally, tapping into the statutory reserves of commercial banks, investment in client equity, and making short maturity loans in addition to long maturity loans.

MONEY, FOREIGN DEBT AND ECONOMIC GROWTH

Problems in the Caribbean monetary and financial system took centre stage on my research agenda. Development finance corporations were in serious difficulty in several countries. Private financial institutions were on the verge of collapse in Trinidad and Tobago. Foreign debt burden was crippling some countries. Capital flight was a problem in Guyana, Jamaica and Trinidad and Tobago. Exports, other than tourism services, were not buoyant.

TRINIDAD AND TOBAGO DOMESTIC FINANCIAL SYSTEM

Between 1982 and 1989, I prepared and published seven papers on the Trinidad and Tobago financial system. Three of them were reproduced in the book entitled Money and Finance in Trinidad and Tobago that Ramesh Ramsaran and I produced in 1988 under the auspices of the Regional Programme of Monetary Studies. In 1982, I had written a paper surveying and analysing financial changes in the economy in the 1966-1978 period. That paper chronicled the financial structure in terms of assets, liabilities and institutions. It concluded that debt expansion was too rapid and financial management unsatisfactory. The imminent dangers to which it alluded became obvious in later crises in the commercial banking industry and the non-bank financial intermediary industry. Three banking institutions, namely the National Commercial Bank, the Workers Bank and the Cooperative Bank experienced such severe solvency problems that their operations were suspended, and they were ultimately reconstituted by the Central Bank of Trinidad and Tobago into a new bank, First Citizens Bank, under a lengthy period of supervised management by the Central Bank. My paper "Banking in Boom and Bust Economies: Lessons from Trinidad and Tobago" in 1985 analysed some perils of commercial banking in the periods of petroleum boom and collapse.

During the economic boom, asset quality became impaired as the banks responded to unprecedented increases in deposits and a build-up of liquidity by extending loans to riskier customers engaged in speculative investment and by financing more consumer expenditures on durable goods. Bank profits rose in the boom. The slump, however, reversed the upward trend in personal incomes and expected rates of return on speculative ventures and impaired the quality of bank assets by increasing loan arrears and delinquency, ultimately undermining financial viability of the banks.

A companion paper "Potentials and Pitfalls of Rapid Financial Innovation in Less Developed Countries: The Case of Trinidad and Tobago Finance Companies" published in 1986 dealt with the crisis among finance companies. My professional interest in their situation was sparked around 1982 by my colleague Eric St Cyr who responded cryptically to my question about the affordability of the high interest rates being advertised for depositors. The finance company subset of the financial sector expanded enormously during the economic boom. There were few finance companies in existence in the early 1970s but by 1983, fourteen companies were operating. Deposits in finance companies grew from $8 million in 1970 to $980 million in 1983 and assets increased from $17 million to $1058 million in the same period. Depositors were mainly from the household sector with 71 per cent of deposits in 1970-74 and 61 per cent in 1975-1983. The growth of deposits in the finance companies is attributable to the steep rise in household incomes and enhanced interest consciousness. By 1983, the corporate sector had substantially reduced its holdings of deposits in finance companies. Its ownership of deposits decreased from 44 per cent in 1976-78 to 12 per cent in 1983.

Finance companies competed vigorously with commercial banks for loan customers by expanding loans to potential customers on the fringe of the banks' traditional opportunity set. Commercial banks rose to the challenge by expanding loans to previously neglected areas and households. Personal loans by commercial banks rose from 32 per cent of their asset portfolio in 1970-1974 to 43 per cent in 1975-1978. Mortgage loans increased from 1 per cent in 1971 to 5 per cent in 1983. The commercial banks also established "captive" finance companies in five instances.

Despite the benefits of financial innovation conferred by finance companies in terms of broadening the financial structure and reducing financial constraints on investment and production, they introduced serious and ultimately very damaging elements of risk into the financial system. Their assets were highly concentrated in cyclically sensitive sectors, few enterprises, and affiliated companies. Liquidity ratios and solvency ratios were low as was capitalisation. Finally in 1984, two finance companies were suspended by the Central Bank of Trinidad and Tobago and two others had to resort to borrowing from the Central Bank which in its lender of last resort function established a $50 million liquidity support facility in April 1984.

In 1984, I approached the issue of risk and capital adequacy in the financial sector in Trinidad and Tobago at a more conceptual level, accompanied by some empirical data for the commercial banking and finance company segments of the industry. My paper Risk and Capital Adequacy in Depository Financial Institutions in Trinidad and Tobago began by elucidating the concepts of operational risks and capital adequacy as well as the concept of insolvency applied to a depository financial institution. It next outlined and appraised several types of approaches employed in evaluation of risk and capital adequacy, namely, operational rules of thumb applied by regulators and bank inspectors to loan quality, internal operating systems and regulatory compliance; early warning approaches which utilise a cluster of financial ratios to evaluate and predict financial performance; and the risk component approaches which estimate the risk of each financial component separately. The paper then utilised an early warning approach for a preliminary analysis of the commercial banking industry and finance companies.

Considerably more detailed analyses of the commercial banking industry were presented in my paper on "Structure and Performance in Commercial Banking in Trinidad and Tobago" which was presented at the annual conference of the Regional Programme of Monetary Studies in 1984 and was published in 1988 in the Bourne and Ramsaran book, *Money and Finance in Trinidad and Tobago*. It was written during my study leave as a Visiting Professor at the University of British Columbia in July-August

1984. The paper began by underlining the importance of commercial banks in the economy and their possession of countervailing power in relation to the economic authorities. It proceeded to review the history of banking between 1937 and 1965, noting the situation of under-banking before 1946 because of very few banks and almost no bank branches, the predominance of foreign assets in bank portfolios, the minimal share of time deposits in bank liabilities, and the substantial growth of bank assets between 1946 and 1965. It then dealt with growth of the industry, changes in bank structure, and bank performance in the 1965-1982 period. In that period the number of bank offices increased from 46 to 112, bank credit to the personal sector expanded greatly as did foreign exchange transactions. Deposit liabilities increased 22 per cent on average annually and time deposits grew faster than demand deposits and savings deposits as individuals, households and businesses changed their deposit preferences.

The structure of bank asset portfolios changed remarkably after 1965. Foreign assets diminished in importance, government securities, real estate loans and other loans became the main components of bank assets. The study examined the operational efficiency of the banks, examining the trends and structure of operating costs and trends and structure of operating revenues, noting particularly that operating revenues increased faster than operating costs. It was observed that the banks were highly profitable but also had quite high ratios of risk assets to total assets.

I followed up the discussion of commercial banks with a paper "Structure, Costs and Efficiency of the Financial Sector" which highlighted several major issues pertaining to operating costs and efficiency raised by the contemporary financial structure. A distinction was made between productive efficiency which was determined by enterprise-specific internal technical efficiency in resource use and price efficiency and allocative efficiency which were judged by the extent to which financial resource allocation contributed to economic growth or other objectives external to the enterprise. Noting the existence of substantial inter industry cost differentials, the paper explored the potential determinants and influences of economies of scale and economies of scope within the financial sector.

Another component of the Trinidad and Tobago financial system which I examined was the stock market. My paper "Economic Aspects of the Trinidad and Tobago Stock Market" in the Bourne-Ramsaran book was the first paper published on the subject. It described the market as being narrow and thin, where the degree of thinness is measured by the volume of transactions, number of market participants and degree of price volatility.

The market was also adjudged to be not efficient in that it did not afford all market participants equal prospects of gain.

Performance weaknesses in the financial system of Caribbean economies cast doubt on its overall contribution to long-run economic growth. Two papers I published in 1988 dealing with financial deepening, resource mobilisation and economic growth in Trinidad and Tobago and in Jamaica respectively tried to shed some empirical light on the matter. The concept of financial deepening pertains to the increasing prominence of financial institutions and instruments in the economy and expansion of the range of institutions and instruments. The paper on the Jamaican experience 1955-1982 concluded that the financial sector functioned passively with respect to resource mobilisation and was not strongly linked to investment. The one on the Trinidad and Tobago experience 1953-1981 also showed that the financial sector was not a strong mobiliser of domestic savings and that the major increases were linked to government revenues from the petroleum industry. In both countries, the contribution to economic growth was vitiated by investment inefficiencies.

FOREIGN DEBT

Starting in 1980, I had begun to analyse empirically the foreign debt problem in the Caribbean. At that time, I was part of the Institutes of Economic and Social Research in the Caribbean Basin (IESCARIBE) which I co-founded in 1978. It was a Latin American and Caribbean network of economists working on debt, foreign trade, industrialisation and economic growth. The network was centred at Florida International University (FIU) where the initiator and principal organiser of the network, Jorge Salazar-Carillo, Professor of Economics and Department Chair was located.

The network members changed from time to time, but at one point or another included Jorge Antonio from FIU, Juan Jose Echevarria from Fedesarrolo in Colombia, Enrique Delgado from SIECA, Paul Latortue from University of Puerto Rico, Leslie Delatour, Governor of the Central Bank of Haiti, Juan Manuel Villasuso, Rafael Trejos and Marvin Taylor from the University of Costa Rica, Richard Bernal from UWI, Felipe Pazos from the Central Bank of Venezuela, Henry Samper-Gomez and Pedro Palma from IESA, Venezuela, Manuel Gollas from El Collegio de Mexico and Andre Dauhajre from Universidad Catolica Madre y Maestra in the Dominican Republic. The group held several conferences at FIU, in Washington, D.C., and other locations, and one occasion met for a few days in the salubrious atmosphere of a mountainous Costa Rican monastery where the floor and walls were made of stone, there was no hot water, and there was no room heating.

I began my exploration of the foreign debt-economic growth nexus with a paper titled "Government Foreign Borrowing and Economic Growth: The Case of Jamaica" presented at a Regional Monetary Studies conference and published in Social and Economic Studies in 1981. The paper showed that Jamaica moved from a position of relatively comfortable economic growth and foreign debt in the 1960s to a situation of economic crisis and acute financial dependence by the end of the 1970s. The surge in foreign debt was attributed to the rapid growth in government expenditures relative to fiscal revenues. Although theoretical predictions would be that foreign debt would assist economic growth by closing savings and foreign exchange gaps, the empirical analysis of Jamaica showed that government debt-financed expenditures negatively affected domestic savings and distorted resource allocation.

I followed the Jamaica paper with one on "External Debt and Economic Growth in the Commonwealth Caribbean" which was presented at a conference on Latin American External Debt and Economic Growth in February 1982 at FIU and published by Salazar et al in Foreign Debt and Latin American Economic Development in 1982. That paper observed that in situations where domestic savings are inadequate to finance accelerated development, external debt can make positive contributions. Whether it did so or not would depend on the efficiency with which debt proceeds are used, relative allocation to productive and non-productive uses, and the terms and conditionalities attached to the debt.

I presented a paper "Small Countries in a World of Big Finance" to the 12th Annual Conference of the Caribbean Studies Association in Belize in May 1987 in which I provided a comparative analysis of foreign debt in Latin American and Caribbean countries utilising country economic size as the distinguishing variable. The paper attempted to assess the extent to which differences in financial dependence, access to debt, and debt terms are related to differences in economic size and to assess whether current trends in the international financial system posed special difficulties for small Caribbean countries. Twenty-four Latin American and Caribbean countries were examined. The excluded countries were the seven member countries of the Organisation of East Caribbean States, Belize and those countries organically linked to the US, France or the Netherlands. There were several findings. First, the degree of dependence on foreign savings was inversely related to economic size. Second, small, less developed

Caribbean countries accessed private finance from the international system less than large less developed Caribbean countries and the grant elements were smaller. Third, small Caribbean countries had less strong debt-bearing capacity than the larger countries. Fourth, securitisation of international financial flows worked more to the benefit of large Caribbean countries than for small ones. Fifth, the smaller Caribbean countries were in weaker negotiating positions than the larger countries with respect to debt renegotiations and debt rescheduling.

I continued to write on the debt problem until 1990. In 1984, I published a paper on "The International Debt Crisis and Development Strategies in the Caribbean" which noted that the foreign debt of Caribbean countries is predominantly public debt and that debt conditions had tightened as evidenced by increasing interest rates and shorter term to maturity. Debt service ratios were increasing and much of foreign exchange earnings were being absorbed by consumption expenditures. The countries therefore needed to develop export capacity, diversify the commodity composition and geographical destinations of exports, raise domestic savings rates, encourage foreign direct investment, and rebalance the government-private sector shares in the economy.

I authored a report on "The Foreign Debt Situation of Caribbean Countries" for the Latin American Economic System Permanent Secretariat (SELA) in 1988. I also published a paper on "External Debt and Adjustment in Caribbean Countries" jointly authored with Roopnarine Oumade Singh. The latter paper depicted the extent of the debt problem and the short-term outlook. It noted that debt had increased between 1975 and 1985 on the basis of easier and more accessible international bank credit as a result of OPEC oil surpluses, and improved access to funds from multilateral financial institutions. However, debt inflows in the Caribbean had slowed towards the end of the period because of factors such as integration of OECD financial markets, risk-reducing financial innovations and fiscal stringency which caused growth in demand for bank credit within the OECD, and changes in accounting rule and regulatory standards and practices which raised the risk profile of loans to less developed countries. The paper also noted that the foreign debt of Caribbean countries had become more expensive because of the greater use of floating interest rates, shortening of maturities, and reduction of the concessional element in funds obtained from MFIs and bilateral agencies.

The burden of debt repayment indicated by the share of debt service in export earnings and fiscal revenues was shown to be increasing and there was bunching of repayment obligations. The paper appraised several approaches to gauging a country's debt sustainability and adopted a scenario approach to the Caribbean. The analyses led to doubts about the countries' debt sustainability. The doubts were reinforced by analysis of fiscal constraints which indicated that fiscal ability to adjust to severe external debt was limited. Furthermore, adjustment through switching to domestic borrowing was limited by the possible consequences of monetary expansion and crowding out of credit to businesses and the personal sector. Additionally, adjustment through export expansion would be difficult in the situation of geographical and commodity concentration of exports, weak economic growth in industrial countries, and increase in non-tariff barriers.

Real debt servicing capacity in Trinidad and Tobago was the topic of a second report I wrote for SELA in 1989. Shelton Nicholls and I later extended the analysis of foreign debt service capacity to Barbados in a 1990 publication "The Real Debt Service Capacity of Barbados and Trinidad and Tobago". Because debt service capacity in small, intensively specialised, open Caribbean economies is very limited, the essential problem was the capacity of countries to honour debt service obligations without substantially reducing public sector investment, depressing national economic growth, reducing employment in situations of already high unemployment rates, and creating other serious macroeconomic and social problems. Debt relief was seen as the means to assist the resuscitation of investment and economic growth.

Recognising that the multilateral financial institutions were being called upon by debtor countries, bilateral lenders and commercial lenders to help solve the international debt problem that threatened national and global financial systems and global economic stability, I wrote a paper in January 1990 for SELA which dealt with the policies of multilateral financial institutions with respect to debt restructuring. Caribbean countries were heavily indebted to the World Bank and the IMF. Debt service created a negative transfer problem in that debt service to MFIs exceeded their gross disbursements.

The elements of the policy approaches then in vogue were debt relief through reductions in amortisation of principal, reductions in interest payments, rescheduling, provision of IMF resources for reduction of principal payments to private creditors, and structural adjustment, or a menu comprised of some or all of the individual elements. The MFIs limited their policies to facilitating relief by private creditors and bilateral creditors and providing debtor countries with resources to remain current with repayments to the MFIs. They rejected proposals that they should write off any portion of debt owing to them and excluded interest payments from debt relief. These MFI policies significantly reduced the policy options available for Caribbean countries in dealing with their foreign debt problems, especially when the quantum of resources actually provided by the MFIs was small and debt service to them displaced resources which might have been utilised for promotion of economic growth.

CENTRAL BANKING AND MONETARY POLICY

By the close of the decade, I had begun to ponder again the role of monetary policy. In that connection, in 1989 I wrote a paper "Some Fundamentals of Monetary Policy in the Caribbean" and another one on "The Role of the Central Bank in Promoting Economic Development". The first paper stressed the importance of the balance of payments to sustainable economic growth and emphasised that monetary policy has a role in the pursuit of balance of payments objectives. It insisted that the monetary base is the primary source of money supply changes and that central bank credit to government and the balance of payments are its main determinants. The policy burden therefore falls on the central bank to control its credit to the government. The second paper which was presented at the Central Bank of Trinidad and Tobago 25th Anniversary Symposium covered a larger terrain. It sketched the fundamental roles of finance in economic development irrespective of type of economic system. I posited that the role of the financial system is to induce higher levels of savings in financial forms, transform them into capital investment, and distribute them consistent with the dispersion of economic rates of return on investment.

There was also a role in facilitating innovation. The essential role of the central bank in an economic development context therefore has four facets. The first is ensuring stability of the financial system which requires attention not only to macro-dimensions but also to attention to micro-economic dimensions of asset soundness. The second is interest rate policy. Liberalisation of interest rates should be gradual and cushioned by anti-inflation policy and recognition of non-interest intermediation costs. The third is allocative efficiency and the fourth is the promotion of financial innovation.

Interest rate policy is a very important part of monetary and financial policy. It should therefore not be surprising that it occupied a central place in my research on the financial system. Distilling from my work on Jamaica and Trinidad and Tobago, I attempted a general theoretical treatment of Caribbean interest rate policy in a presentation at the 13th Annual Regional Programme of Monetary Studies Conference in Trinidad and Tobago in November 1981. It began with some stylised facts about Caribbean economic reality. Reference was made to differences in profit opportunity, technology, and efficiency in the non-financial sector and to the varying characteristics of credit clienteles. It was noted that the formal financial sector was perfectively competitive, that nominal interest rates were low relative to inflation rates and real rates of return on physical capital, that interest rate spreads were wide, and that interest rates varied among different types of institution and also varied among deposit and credit clienteles. The paper showed that real interest rates were negative and that disequilibria therefore exist in savings and investment markets with consequential dynamic efficiency and static economic efficiency losses in the economy. It also showed that the distribution of income and wealth is affected by interest rate policy and that the distributional effects of disequilibrium interest rate policies could be perverse in the sense of making the distributions of income and wealth less equal.

My work on these subjects was partly stimulated by my membership of the Board of Directors of the Central Bank of Trinidad and Tobago to which I had been appointed in 1987. In August 1987, I agreed to serve on a Cabinet-appointed Committee on Monetary Policy. The Committee's membership in addition to me was Victor B. Mouttet (Managing Director's Assistant, Republic Bank), Terrence Farrell (Director of Research, Central Bank of Trinidad and Tobago), David Abdullah (Education Officer and Treasurer, Oilfield Workers Trade Union), Joseph Pierre (Manager, Recoveries and Support Centre, National Commercial Bank), Leo Pujadas (Director, Central Statistical Office), and Leslie Scotland (Corporate Manager, Marketing Economics, Royal Bank).

The Committee was mandated to examine and recommend on existing limits to Central Bank lending to Government; review the extant Central bank policies on legal reserve requirements on commercial banks and non-bank financial intermediaries; explore "the feasibility of innovative monetary reforms"; study and recommend mechanisms for funding of high priority development activities; make recommendations on selective controls on commercial banks and other financial institutions consistent with national development needs; examine the existing mechanisms for monitoring local private sector activities in external markets, especially those with foreign incorporated entities; and examine the impact of external and retained accounts on the accumulation, regulation and management of foreign exchange.

The Committee was provided with specially written documents by its members and the National Planning Commission. It was also provided with an address that John Humphrey, Minister of Works, Settlements and Infrastructure gave to the Association of Professional Engineers of Trinidad and Tobago on 3 October 1987. Minister Humphrey proposed that the problem of under-utilisation of domestic financial resources for developmental activities could be solved by creating "a second currency" called the Trinity Dollar to be used for purchase of foreign exchange. He envisaged that the Trinity Dollar would be an "insulator" between the domestic currency and foreign exchange. The domestic currency would continue to be used for internal transactions but would only be convertible into foreign currency through purchasing Trinity Dollars which could then be converted to foreign exchange under Central Bank guidelines. The value of the Trinity Dollar would float relative to the domestic currency. Minister Humphrey met with the Committee three times to discuss his innovative proposal but failed to convince the Committee of its technical merits. Specifically, it was thought that the introduction of the Trinity Dollar as a parallel currency would be inflationary, undermine confidence in the domestic currency, create risks in the country's external financial relationships and add to the burdens of public administration.

The Committee made a total of forty-three recommendations on the issues it was mandated to address. Only a few of them are listed here. It recommended against raising the limits on government borrowing from the Central Bank; it recommended that statutory reserve requirements should be maintained and that the new regime for inspection and control of financial institutions should continue; and there should be thorough evaluation of loan quality standards to ensure safety of shareholders capital. The Committee recommended separate assessment and action plans for the efficient operation of the financial system. Its recommendations on various credit matters included discontinuation of the system of overdraft lending and introduction of short-term notes and a menu of actions to improve the operational, economic and social efficiency of the financial system, and commercial bank lending to development banks.

One year later, I accepted an invitation by the government to chair a Committee on Technical Aspects of the Relationship between the International Monetary Fund and Trinidad and Tobago. I had previously been engaged in a Group of Experts to the Group of Twenty-Four in the

United Nations to prepare a report on "Low Income Countries and the International Monetary System". The report was published in 1983 and it is conceivable that the Trinidad and Tobago government was aware of it. The other members of the Committee were Ramesh Ramsaran, Leo Pujadas, the Director of the Central Statistical Organisation (CSO) and Joseph Esau (a leading businessman). The Committee was assisted by Professor Kari Levitt from McGill University in Canada, and by Dave Clement and David Thomas from the CSO. The issue before the Committee was whether Fund officials had done justice to Trinidad and Tobago in their analysis of its economic management and the macroeconomic situation.

This was a politically charged assignment because Davison Budhoo, an IMF staffer, at the time of resigning from the IMF had accused the authors of the Fund report of deliberately misleading the Fund's management and the Trinidad and Tobago government. The Committee pointed to serious statistical flaws and technical deficiencies in the Fund's report which caused unwarranted adverse judgements about the economy and the government's management of the economy. It suggested that they might have been easily identified and corrective action taken if the preliminary version of the report had been made more available by the government to technical staff in the Central Bank and the CSO. In particular, the Committee pointed to the lack of coordination in the provision of official data and the absence of any attempt to verify the accuracy of data used by the IMF. The Committee noted that the CSO was not routinely or integrally involved in the country's relationship with the IMF; commented on the absence of a systematic review process for versions of IMF reports; and noted that there were no procedures for Trinidad and Tobago government representation to the IMF on statistical and corollary flaws in its reports. It concluded that the onus was on the official agencies of the Trinidad and Tobago government to manage the technical relationship with the IMF properly to ensure accurate assessment and reports on the country's economic policies and situation. I took note that Prime Minister Robinson subsequently ensured adequate public dissemination of official reports.

FOREIGN TRADE

The role of foreign trade in Caribbean economic growth was not ignored in my research on Caribbean economies. Together with Wallace Joefield-Napier, I published in 1984 a paper on "Export Performance and Prospects for the Commonwealth Caribbean". It contained an assessment of the prospects for exports of goods and services in the context of the current structure of exports and the importance of exports to the balance of payments and analysed the balance of payments experience of eight Caribbean countries between 1977 and 1981. It noted that a few commodities were predominant in total trade. Inclusion of tourism did not significantly lessen the degree of concentration in trade in goods and services because tourism itself was the predominant part of the exports of countries like The Bahamas, St Vincent and the Grenadines and St Lucia. The paper also noted that there was little geographical diversification of exports. Furthermore, while there were demand-side difficulties in expanding exports, there were also serious supply-side obstacles such as weak production performance, domestic dis-incentives to production, and failure to cultivate new markets. The paper also noted the stagnation of intra-regional trade. Recognising that prospects were adversely affected by declining international commodity prices, the paper concluded by stressing the need to improve production and marketing.

I returned to the topic of foreign trade in a study of "Industrialisation and Foreign Trade in the Caribbean Basin: The Case of CARICOM Countries" done for the Inter-American Development Bank in 1987. My co-authors were Eric St Cyr, Michael Howard (from the Cave Hill campus) and Christopher Clarke. There were nine main findings. One, industrial development had expanded substantially. Two, compositional changes in output were greater in Trinidad and Tobago. Three, foreign trade grew significantly except in Jamaica. Four, manufactured goods were a large proportion of total imports. Five, the Caribbean Basin had only a small share in foreign trade. Six, the US, UK and Canada were the main trading partners. Seven, there was high concentration of commodity exports in Trinidad and Tobago but not in Jamaica. Eight, foreign trade had been influenced by structural factors such as trends in industrial production, foreign exchange scarcities, the inward-looking market orientation of manufacturers, and weak international price competitiveness. Ninth, export performance for manufactured goods was significantly influenced by relative prices and growth of real incomes.

LABOUR AND INCOME DISTRIBUTION

During the 1970s, I had developed an interest in labour market issues and had published on the topics of "structure, power and wage price policy" and "trends and issues in wage determination" in the Caribbean. During the 1980s, I explored the quite different issue of inequality of labour incomes. In the mid-eighties, I authored a paper on "Sectoral Inequality of

Labour Incomes in Less Developed Countries" which analysed data for twelve LDCs and ten developed countries (DCs) for the 1971-1982 period. The LDC set of countries consisted of Bolivia, Chile, Colombia, Jamaica, Peru, Venezuela, Egypt, Kenya, Zimbabwe, India, South Korea, and Thailand. The DC set of countries was comprised of Australia, Denmark, Finland, West Germany, Japan, New Zealand, Norway, Sweden, UK and USA. It concluded that considerably more inequality of labour incomes existed in less developed countries than in developed countries and that there was no discernible tendency for substantial lessening of it over the decade. Labour income inequality was greatest in India and not very pronounced in Africa, Latin America and the Caribbean. The extent of labour income inequality was explainable by sectoral differences in labour productivity, profitability and product market conditions.

A second paper written in the same year examined the effects of economic recession on labour income inequality in LDCs utilising Jamaican data for the 1973-1981 period. It noted the contraction of the economy, the considerable rise in the unemployment rate, and the income ameliorative redistributive policies of the government. The main findings were that labour income distribution worsened during the recession; the lowest paid workers and the lower middle class were the worst affected; and the highest paid group of workers gained relative to the other groups.

ECONOMIC DEVELOPMENT POLICY AND STRATEGY

W. Arthur Lewis in his seminal paper "Unlimited Development with Unlimited Supplies of Labour" published in 1954 had posited that the "central problem in the theory of economic development is to understand the process by which a community" substantially increases its savings rate. He argued that "practically all savings is done by people who receive profits or rents" and therefore the share of profits in national income becomes the major policy variable for influencing national savings rates. Nicholas Kaldor and Luigi Pasinetti separately developed neo Keynesian models in which the distribution of factor incomes between profits and wages had the same role in determination of the aggregate savings rate. In a paper "The Propensities to Consume Labour and Property Incomes in the Commonwealth Caribbean" which I published in the Journal of Development Studies in 1986, I tested the validity of the Lewis-Kaldor-Pasinetti thesis in the Caribbean context with data for Guyana and Jamaica. The main findings were that the corporate sector has high savings propensities and that savings rates out of profits greatly exceeded those out of labour incomes in both countries. The policy conclusion supported by those findings is that changing the share of profits vis-a-vis wages and salaries in national income would substantially influence the national savings rate.

Economic development strategies were addressed more broadly in my later writings. I gave an address on "Development Strategies for the Caribbean" at the Partners of the Americas International Development Seminar in Port of Spain in March 1989. The countries covered in my presentation were the member countries of the Commonwealth Caribbean, Costa Rica, Dominican Republic, Nicaragua, Panama, Venezuela, Suriname and Haiti. I outlined the Caribbean's development problems in terms of lagging economic growth, high unemployment rates and weak production structures. The economic objectives of the 1960-1980 period, were identified as economic self-reliance and equitable economic growth. These objectives were pursued through maintenance and growth of traditional industries and exports, regional integration, public sector economic activity (including State enterprises), and institutional developments in foreign trade and in the finance and education sectors. Notably, there was no development strategy evident with respect to production technology, commodity innovation and market orientation. The common policies which resulted were domestic market protection through tariffs, taxes and quantitative import restrictions; subsidised credit; and public sector employment and expenditures.

In the address, I noted trends in the international economy, including ways in which technological change was eroding demand for some exported raw materials, changes in international consumption patterns, changes in production technology, the imminent graduation of some Caribbean countries from concessional financial resources from MFIs and bilateral aid agencies, and the intensification of protectionism in some traditional developed country markets. Several elements of an appropriate development strategy were recommended: One, sustained efforts to achieve international competitiveness; two, conscious development of new products; three, improvement of production technology through acquisition and adaptation of foreign technology; four, improvement of export marketing and export financing; five, establishment of new export markets; and six, investment in research and development (R&D), human resource development and local materials production. An address on "Imperatives for Caribbean Development for the 21st Century" to the Canadian Association for Latin America and Caribbean Studies Conference at Carleton University in Ottawa on 7 October 1989 basically covered the same ground.

My most complete analysis of development issues and policies is contained in a 1988 publication, *Caribbean Development to the Year 2000: Challenges, Prospects and Policies*, of which I was the main author with assistance from an advisory group of eminent Caribbean economists and public officials. The book is based on a more technical version of the study commissioned by the Caribbean Community Secretariat in 1986. I took one year's leave from UWI to conduct the study with the help of short-term consultants particularly Basia Zaba on demographic projections and Earle Baccus on technology matters. The document contains detailed analyses of economic development and performance from 1960 to mid-1980s, world economic trends, demographic and human resource trends, financial performance requirements and prospects, foreign trade, and production performance and prospects. It ends with policy conclusions and identification of requisite actions by the Caribbean countries. The study served as the basis for a Regional Economic Conference convened by Trinidad and Tobago's Prime Minister A.N.R. Robinson on behalf of CARICOM Heads of Government in 1991. A fuller statement on the contents of the book and the response of Caribbean governments is deferred to a separate chapter on the Caribbean Community. However, in 1992, with the assistance of Cleopatra Crawford, I drew on the study to prepare a paper on economic performance and prospects in the Commonwealth Caribbean for the Canadian International Development Agency.

The more I reflected on approaches to economic policy in the Caribbean, the more I felt that there were serious problems not only in policy design but also in policy management. An invitation to lecture to the Guyana Management Institute headed by my former St Augustine colleague, Lewis Bobb, gave me the incentive to address the subject. I began my paper "Some Fundamentals of Economic Management in the Commonwealth Caribbean" by noting that governments accept responsibility for achievement of broad socio-economic objectives which can be translated into specific targets and goals such as economic growth, price level stability, acceptable or appropriate structures of relative prices, income and wealth distribution, health, nutrition, and education.

I noted frequent and sometimes persistent policy failures and advanced several kinds of explanations which might be termed policy conflicts and policy inconsistency. Policy conflict was defined as the implementation of mutually offsetting policies and policy inconsistency was defined as pursuit of competitive policy goals, i.e., goals which cannot be simultaneously or sometimes even sequentially achieved. Policy conflicts may arise from fragmentation of decision-making and information flows; antagonistic or adversarial tendencies within the political and bureaucratic decision structures which present obstacles to coordination, harmonisation and information flows; and inadequate knowledge about the economic system. Policy inconsistency implies the possibility of policy trade-offs, but these might be difficult to identify because government preferences might not be revealed. Misperceptions also engender policy inconsistency.

The paper also dealt with economic regulations. It observed the conjuncture of proliferation of regulations and their avoidance or evasion by the population. Economic regulations are often motivated by public interest considerations in situations of market failure and economic crises but sometimes are the outcome of self-interested lobbying by one or another group. They can be exploited to yield corrupt outcomes as Gunnar Myrdal stresses in his discussion of the "soft State" or simply discriminatory outcomes in reflection of differential costs and benefits to demanders and suppliers of regulations.

I had dealt with economic regulations in a broader context of the relationship between State and People which was the subject of my Caribbean Studies Association Presidential Address in 1986. The stimulus to my decision to deal with this subject was my observation that the relationship between State and the People was rarely felicitous. My take-off point was Carl Stone's political typology of State-People relationships. His three types were Democratic-Pluralist States typified by widespread political participation, strong civil rights representation, and centrist and reformist economic policies; Authoritarian States characterised by prohibition of mass political participation, restriction of civil rights, and conservative economic policies; and Populist-Statist States characterised by restrictions on people participation in policy formulation and transformative economic policies. I placed Commonwealth Caribbean countries, except Guyana, in the Democratic-Pluralist category. Populist-Statist countries were Nicaragua, Cuba, and Guyana. The countries in the Authoritarian States group were Guatemala, Honduras, Haiti, Suriname and Panama.

I discussed two main economic aspects of democratic pluralism as practiced in the Caribbean. One aspect is the role of the State as economic patron in its acceptance of responsibility for raising levels of living through economic welfare policies. Welfare policies, however, were not notably successful because of defects in policy design, policy inconsistencies, financial constraints and intervening factors such as interest group lobbying against them. Another motive for economic patronage is pursuit and retention of political power but this is not a failsafe strategy as handouts do not always convert into electoral ballots. The second aspect discussed was economic regulation where, following Richard Posner (1974), economic regulation is defined as "taxes and subsidies of all sorts, as well as explicit legislative and administrative controls over rates, entry and other facets of economic activity". I noted that many Caribbean intellectuals are regulatory minded irrespective of their ideological orientation. Common reasons for regulatory actions can be summed up as market failure such as those resulting from natural and created monopolies, positive and negative externalities, provision of public goods, and economic crises which usually induce political pressure for ameliorative action by the State. Regulations may also be due to the State seeking to confer benefits of protection to specific business interests and enterprises. Edward Kane's regulatory dialectics (Kane 1977, 1981) perhaps best describes the fate of regulations in democratic-pluralist States: regulation, avoidance, and re-regulation.

The Address also dealt with the lure of the Authoritarian State. The context for consideration of this matter was a view widely expressed in US academic and multilateral financial institutions circles that given the pressing development imperatives, developing countries should go the Latin American Southern Cone route of political dictatorships as in Chile, Argentina and Brazil in order to accelerate their economic growth and development. They found historical justification in the rapid economic growth of Eastern European countries under totalitarian political and social systems. In these quasi-historical and contemporary analyses, political democracy is expendable in favour of economic growth. Contrary to their claims, there was no sound empirical basis for that policy strategy. International studies in fact showed that there is no relationship between type of political regime and country economic performance.

BUILDING NATIONAL CONSENSUS ON SOCIAL POLICY IN TRINIDAD AND TOBAGO

The Inter-American Development Bank engaged Sir Alister McIntyre in 1993 to examine and make recommendations on the prospects for national consensus in social policy in Trinidad and Tobago. He convened a study team, headed by him, which included Sir George Alleyne (Health), Ms Margueritte Berger (Micro Enterprises, Gender), Professor Compton Bourne (Employment, Finance), Hon William Demas (Resource Person), Dr Neville Duncan (Community Governance and Communications), Mr

Richard Fletcher (Macroeconomics), Dr Errol Furlonge (Education), Ms Camille Gaskin-Reyes (Micro Enterprises, Gender), Mr Bertus Meins (Macroeconomics), Mr Frank Rampersad (Urban/Rural Balance, Finance), Dr Karl Theodore (Housing, Public Utilities, Social Assistance). We assembled in Port of Spain on 11 July and worked together for four weeks. Our report was completed in October 1993.

The Report consisted of two volumes. Volume I provided an Overview and Action Plan. It outlined the guiding principles of the study and its recommendations, namely, (1) Effective interlinkages between policy actions in the economic and social fields; (2) Every programme and project should be subjected to an employment test, given the centrality of the employment issue; (3) A shift from open-ended to targeted programmes; (4) Change in the perception of public and private outlays on social services from one of expenditure on people to one of investment in people; (5) Greater efficiency in social services delivery, associated with improved cost effectiveness and accountability; (6) Greater transparency in delivery of social services; (7) Major changes in the balance of responsibilities between government, private sector and voluntary sector for delivery of social services.

The Volume identifies the principal categories of actors in the social services system. In one chapter, it provides general observations on the situation in the social sectors including poverty and income distribution, the labour market and unemployment, urban/rural imbalances, education and training, health and nutrition, housing, public utilities, social security and safety nets, crime, community governance and communication, and the special problems of women and youth. A chapter focussed on the macroeconomic context for socioeconomic reform. The volume then specifies an Immediate Action Plan which is comprised of an Employment Stimulus Package; Creation of a Community Development and Enterprise Fund; Promotion of export of tourism and other services, and manufactured goods; and Institutional Strengthening within the social services sector. It was proposed that the cost of the Immediate Action Plan be shared between the Trinidad and Tobago government and official international and bilateral agencies. The last chapter in Volume I contained recommendations for longer term reforms in the several major sub-sectors itemised in the Report.

The second volume of the Report (Volume II) which contained the Working Papers, Notes and Reviews on the Social Sectors and Selected Statistics, included two reports prepared by me. One on the contemporary employment and unemployment situation dealt with aggregate employment and unemployment, labour participation rates, duration of unemployment, underemployment, labour incomes, the special issues in relation to youths and women in the labour force and the labour market, and employment possibilities linked to employment targeting and small-scale enterprises. The other was a note on public social expenditures.

UNAUTHORISED MIGRATION AND ECONOMIC DEVELOPMENT

In 1989, Anthony P. Maingot, a Professor at Florida International University, and I organised a study of Caribbean migration to the US and economic development. Our focus was on the economic factors which impelled emigration from the Caribbean to the US. Our study was intended to be an input into the work of the US Congressional Commission for the Study of International Migration and Cooperative Economic Development.

The United States, concerned about the magnitude of unauthorised emigration from Mexico and other Western Hemisphere countries, had enacted the Immigration Reform and Control Act in 1988. Under the provisions of the Act, it established a US Congressional Commission for the Study of International Migration and Cooperative Development. The mandate of the Commission was to examine the conditions of Mexico and other sending countries in the hemisphere which contributed to unauthorised immigration into the US and to consider mutually beneficial reciprocal trade and investment programmes to relieve economic pressures in the sending countries.

As part of our assignment, Professor Maingot and I interviewed the Chairman and other members of the Commission and State Department officials. We also visited one of the US coastguard vessels in Miami, Florida to interview its officers about the nature and scope of their operations.

I prepared the conceptual research plan which sought to focus the study on the economic conditions which influence emigration from the Caribbean. It identified as the point of departure the trends in migration, the relationship with economic cycles, the influence of political conditions in sending countries, the effects of transportation costs, host country policies and socio-cultural settlement systems, and the extent to which intra-Caribbean migration was substitutable for migration from the Caribbean. It then outlined several thematic matters pertinent to understanding emigration and designing emigration policies. One issue was the development of small enterprises. A second issue was the economic structure and the labour market, especially the record of growth and development and prospects for the future. The third issue was the nature and size of the pool of skilled labour in the Caribbean and the options for employment in sending countries. The fourth issue was the link between foreign trade and employment generation and the influence of bilateral and multilateral trade arrangements. Remittances and development were the sixth issue. The seventh issue identified was the employment effects of capital and labour legislation in the Caribbean. Two economic sectors were identified for separate attention, namely, tourism and agriculture. It was envisaged that two country studies would be done and that the study would conclude with discussions of the principal policy implications for the Caribbean and the US.

A total of eleven papers were written for the project, edited by Anthony Maingot, and published by Westview Press in 1991 with the title Small Country Development and International Labour Flows: Experiences in the Caribbean. The authors included Courtney Blackman on tourism and other services, Frank Alleyne on agriculture, Ralph Henry on labour services, and Anthony Gonsalves on foreign trade, bilateralism and multilateralism. The volume also included three papers on Haiti and three on the Dominican Republic.

UNIVERSITY ECONOMICS AND MANAGEMENT

I entered voluntarily into university management when I offered myself for election to the University Academic Committee (UAC) in 1982. I won a place on the UAC, which was the academic decision-making body, second only to the governing Council of the university. I was elected repeatedly and served until 1986. In 1982 also, I was appointed as Chairman of another academic committee, namely, the St Augustine campus Faculty of Social Sciences Sub-Committee of the Board for Higher Degrees which had responsibility for academic administration of postgraduate admissions and graduation processes. I chaired the sub-committee from 1982-1987.

In 1984, I was "volunteered Army style" into the Deanship of the Faculty of Social Sciences at St Augustine. I had returned from a few weeks leave to find a letter dated 19 July 1984 from Vice Chancellor Preston on my desk. He wrote:

> Dear Professor Bourne,
>
> As you are aware the revised Statutes and Ordinances which are scheduled to come into effect on 1st October 1984 will require the appointment at each campus of a Dean for any Faculty that is not a

> single-campus Faculty. The responsibility for appointing the first Dean of the new Faculty rests with the Vice Chancellor. After consultation with the Pro-Vice-Chancellors, Principals of the campuses and current Deans, where appropriate, I have decided – subject to your willingness to serve – to appoint you the first Dean of the Faculty of Social Sciences, St Augustine for the period 1st October 1984 to 31st July 1985.
>
> I would wish you to know that I have given much careful thought to this appointment and in so doing have borne in mind inter alia the need to have as the first Dean in this critical year of the University's history: -
>
> (a) Someone who is likely to command the respect of his peers; and
>
> (b) Someone who has either proven his capability as either a Dean or Vice-Dean in the present system, or someone who by virtue of his status and the way he has conducted himself in his department is likely to be able to cope without difficulty with the delicate task of representing the interests of the various departments in his Faculty.
>
> Because of this, I hope that whatever your circumstances you will regard this appointment to the first Deanship of a new Faculty as a way of giving further service to your University – and important service, since the first year's operation may well determine the future direction of the Faculty.

Even if I was otherwise inclined, which I was not, I really could not refuse Vice Chancellor Preston whom I held in high regard. This appointment was followed up with a letter from the Acting University Registrar dated 15 October 1985 informing me that the University Academic Committee had on 8 July,1985 on the nomination of my Faculty had designated me University Dean of the Faculty of Social Sciences for the period 1 August 1985 to 31 July 1986.

My involvement in university administration and management ceased temporarily in 1986-1987 when I was granted leave to prepare a study on Caribbean long-term development prospects for the Commonwealth Secretariat and the Caribbean Community Secretariat. I resumed administrative duties as soon as my leave ended. I became Head of the Department of Economics from August 1987 to July 1990 and Head of the Department of Management Studies from August 1989 to July 1991. It was unusual for one person to head two academic departments simultaneously, but the Department of Management Studies had been suddenly denuded of senior and experienced staff, therefore I was asked by Acting Vice Chancellor Leslie Robinson to accept the additional responsibility.

One of the activities I undertook as University Dean was to lend support to efforts to establish the Consortium Graduate School of the Social Sciences. The driving force in its conceptualisation and implementation was Professor Edward Greene who spearheaded mobilisation of an endowment of US$1.1 million and financial support from the Ford Foundation, UNESCO, the International Development Research Council of Canada, the Commonwealth Secretariat, and several foreign governments. Stalwart support in his fundraising efforts was provided by Marion O'Callaghan and Hugh Cholmondeley from UNESCO and Betty Sedoc-Dahlberg, Vice Chancellor of the University of Suriname. Charles Maynard, Dominica's Minister of Education, was instrumental in securing the approval of the CARICOM ministerial body in 1982. I, myself, made a presentation as University Dean to the Ministers of Education. It was the intention to locate the Consortium at the Cave Hill campus but because of the absence on vacation of the French government official who had committed financial resources, the funds to close a financial gap of US$50,000 could not be confirmed at the critical decision meeting in 1984 at the Cave Hill campus. The Cave Hill Bursar, Mr Victor Cooke, exerted an inordinate risk-averse influence on the Campus Principal, Sir Keith Hunte, who decided it was too great a risk to take. On Vice Chancellor Preston's initiative, the decision was made to locate the Consortium on the Mona campus. It started operations in 1985.

During the period of my Deanship, the British monarch, Her Majesty Queen Elizabeth the Second, visited the St Augustine campus. I was among the group of university officers accompanying the royal party on the tour of the campus and lunching with them on 1 November 1985. Deans and senior campus officials were presented to Her Majesty. I was assigned to escort The Honourable Lady Morrison, Her Majesty's Lady-in-Waiting, to lunch which was hosted by Vice Chancellor Preston. Attendees included Sir Ellis Clarke, President of Trinidad and Tobago, Mr Errol Mahabir and Mrs Marilyn Gordon, two Ministers of Government, members of the Campus Council, Deans, the University Librarian, and senior campus administration officials. I found Her Majesty to be down-to-earth, humorous and politically knowledgeable and astute.

INSTITUTIONAL REVIEW OF UWI

Between April and December 1987, I engaged in a major study of the University. It was financed by the Canadian International Development Agency. The objectives of the study were: assess the usefulness of international development assistance to UWI; determine how further support would help strengthen UWI; and suggest appropriate forms and mechanisms for institutional support. My co-reviewers were Ronald Hughes from CIDA, Jan Loubser a consultant to CIDA, and Zaffar Ali, who was then Senior Planning Officer at St Augustine. We submitted a report titled "Report on Institutional Review of the University of the West Indies" in February 1988. One of the appendices was a short paper on "Socio-economic Development Needs and Human Resources Supply at the Tertiary Level" written specially by me for preparation of the Report.

In the conduct of the study, we met with UWI personnel and many outside stakeholders, Canadian universities which had links with UWI, the IDB, World Bank, and USAID. More than 350 people were interviewed. The team visited Antigua and Barbuda, The Bahamas, Barbados, Belize, British Virgin Islands, Cayman Islands, Canada, Dominica, Grenada, Guyana, Jamaica, Montserrat, St Lucia, St Vincent and the Grenadines, and Trinidad and Tobago. For some of the visits I teamed up with Jan Loubser, with whom I developed a lasting friendship, and for the other visits Ronald Hughes teamed up with Zaffar Ali.

There were seven sets of findings and conclusions. One, the main means by which UWI had sought to discharge its obligations as a regional institution was delivery of academic programmes which it did well, despite some reservations and criticisms from member countries with respect to unsatisfied human resource demands, increasingly competitive and limited access, too many sub-degree level programmes among the offerings, and inadequacy of information flows about UWI. Two, the effects of the university on regional development are pervasive through its graduates. Restructuring had strengthened relations with Campus Countries, but Non-Campus Countries felt left out. The challenges to UWI were finance, its academic and administrative structures and loss of academic personnel from the Mona campus. Third, UWI was recognised by other tertiary level institutions in the region as the senior institution and was expected to play a leadership role. There were strong ties with national tertiary institutions, UWI provided leadership in teacher education and training, and generally fostered complementarity of programmes and counselled against duplication. Four, the effects of UWI on other institutions could be strengthened through formal representation, functional cooperation and leadership in institution building and systems development. Five, UWI's development priorities were capital development, staff development, outreach, library automation and data base, and institutional cooperation and linkages. Six, unit costs of education service delivery varied widely across campuses as did costs borne by students. NCCs sought to limit their contributions to UWI by limiting enrolment of their nationals but this policy was in contradiction to their human resources needs and the regional character of the University. UWI did not have a general fundraising strategy and was inadequately funded by governments. Seven, UWI was assisted considerably by international development associations and academic linkages.

The Report made many recommendations, some of which influenced the University's policies in later years. In relation to the University's regional mandate, recommendations included: assessing the effectiveness of the current communications mechanisms, public relations and marketing; annual visits to NCCs and Council meetings in NCC countries; expansion of off-campus programme offerings; assistance in capacity building of national colleges and adoption of policies to facilitate transfer into UWI degree programmes; establishment of consultancy mechanisms for governments and governmental agencies; and closer relations with the private sector to maximise mutual benefit. With respect to the University's effects on development, the recommendations included: rationalisation and integration of programmes for NCCs; developing the University Centres into genuine centres for delivery of university services; expansion of UWIDITE; revitalisation of the Guild of Graduates and involvement of alumni in fund raising.

On the matter of relations with other institutions, the Report recommended that UWI concentrate on degree level programmes and increase the proportion of postgraduate students; provide leadership and help to national tertiary level institutions; take the initiative in encouraging participatory process among them; expand cooperation with other universities in the region and with regional organisations, and seek formal representation of the University on key regional forums; and develop an institutional consultancy capacity. With respect to UWI's development priorities, the recommendations were that the University improve its long-term planning process, establish more specific priorities, and develop a systematic approach to ascertaining the development priority needs of the region. Finally with respect to the financial situation, the Report recommended:

re-examination of the economic cost formula; exploration of ways to reduce costs; consideration of a uniform tuition fee structure; consideration of a fund-raising campaign; and re-examination of the University's tax status with a view to attracting donations within the Caribbean.

I sent a copy of the Report to Sir Alister McIntyre who had been appointed Vice Chancellor but not yet taken up office. From the initiatives he took early in his tenure, especially those with respect to the NCCs, the university's financial situation, fund raising, and international cooperation, I am convinced that he studied the Report carefully and endorsed many of its recommendations.

UNIVERSITY COSTS AND PRICING

Having started to focus on university finances, I undertook a study of trends and patterns of costs and of tuition pricing. With research assistance from Anand Dass, I prepared a paper "University Costs and Pricing in the West Indies" in January 1989. It really was a study of the St Augustine experience. Cost and student enrolment data for the 1964-1986 period were analysed statistically. It was concluded that for the campus as a whole real expenditures per student did not increase between 1964 and 1986 but instead tended to decrease. This was an important finding which contradicted the view frequently articulated by governments at budget times that there was cost inflation at the university. The study, however, found significant differences between unit costs of the various faculties. Unit costs in the Faculty of Engineering were higher than in the other Faculties and tended to rise.

Another finding was that the Faculty of Arts and General Studies, Engineering and Social Sciences operated at unit costs and enrolment levels above their optimal levels. The paper after completing the cost analyses turned to tuition pricing, examining the implications of the level of costs for tuition pricing. It found that tuition pricing based on full cost-recovery would mean tuition fees greatly in excess of current levels of fees. It noted, nonetheless, that because graduates received substantial net pecuniary benefits from their university education, there was scope for upward revision of tuition fees.

THE 1987 FUNDING CRISIS AT ST AUGUSTINE

Around the middle of the 1980s, I was invited by Vice Chancellor Preston to participate in a university planning meeting convened at the Mona campus. At that meeting, I voiced the opinion that governments might not be able to provide the accustomed levels of financial support to the University and that consideration should be given to additional ways of mobilising funds to augment government subventions. My opinion was greeted with disbelief. As it turned out, I was right. The Trinidad and Tobago government in December 1987 announced that it was reducing its contribution to the University's budget by $20milion which was equivalent to a 20 per cent cut and that it would introduce a cess on students from 1988. The Trinidad and Tobago cess which required students to pay 10 per cent of the economic costs lasted until 1993. Minister Lenny Saith in Parliament in 1992 justified the cess in terms of relative budget expenditures per student at the different levels of the education system. He noted that total government expenditure on primary, secondary and tertiary education was $873 million and there 190,000 primary students, 98,000 secondary students and 3800 tertiary students at UWI. Given the size of the budgetary allocation to UWI, Government was spending 14 per cent of the education budget on 1.5 per cent of the student population. The Jamaican government in the 1987/1988 academic year also instituted a cess on its students at UWI and used the proceeds to finance part of its contributions to the university budget.

The St Augustine Planning and Estimates Committee responded to the actions of the Trinidad and Tobago government by establishing a Task Force under my Chairmanship. Its members were Professors Wilfred Chan and Keith Laurence, Bursar Byron Williams, and Zaffar Ali. The Task Force was mandated to consult with departments and faculties and review current programmes and services for the purpose of "articulating guidelines and objectives in relation to academic programming and operational arrangements" and "identifying areas where savings could be effected, including estimates of such savings and of any adjustment cost that might be allowed." The Task Force was appointed in July 1988 and started work that month. The "Report of the STAPEC Task Force on the Budgetary Reductions for the 1987/90 Triennium" was submitted in March 1989.

The procedure adopted by the Task Force consisted of detailed interviews with heads of all departments, analysis of documentary evidence on student enrolment, staffing, expenditures, organisational structures and practices; formulation of preliminary conclusions and recommendations; and receipt of submissions on the preliminary findings and recommendations of the Task Force prior to a second round of interviews with Deans, Campus Librarian and Estate Manager.

The central issues and conclusions in the Report are as follows: One, the inescapable corollary of the huge contraction in the budget is a substantial reduction in levels of staffing, given that 70 per cent of recurrent budgetary outlays are staff costs. The critical decision problem was how to reduce staff without deleterious effects on quality of education and training and future development of the campus. Optimal adjustment had to be determined from a campus-wide perspective which would imply non-proportionality of budget reductions at departmental levels. Two, the Task Force found that Agriculture and Engineering were not growth areas measured by student enrolment and that enrolment in Arts and General Studies had been stationary since 1981. Enrolment growth was only strong in Natural Sciences and Social Sciences. It was concluded that resources were sub-optimally allocated to Agriculture and Engineering and to some programmes in Arts and General Studies. Three, the Task Force suggested that persistently low student enrolment could be addressed by introduction of more appealing courses and that efforts had to made to achieve cost efficiency in programme delivery through measures such as more intensive use of academic staff and rotation of low enrolment courses. It was concluded as well that some sub-degree level programmes should cease; that some programmes could be offered on a self-financing basis; and that consideration should be given to programme rationalisation, avoidance of course duplication, and reduction of unit overhead costs. Four, the Task Force proposed merger of academic departments, rationalisation of support staff and services, use of improved technology in data and information services and library services and contracting out of some estate maintenance services. Five, a far-reaching recommendation was that there should be examination of the rationale for the equivalence or identity of salary structures for academic staff and senior administrative staff given functional differences and market differences.

Many of issues and recommendations have remained on the University's agenda for change well into present times.

GOVERNMENT SERVICE

In addition to my service to the Trinidad and Tobago Government on the committee dealing with its technical relationship with the IMF, I participated as a member on several other economic committees and boards.

One of the more unusual was the Port Authority of Trinidad and Tobago of which I was a Commissioner, i.e., a member of its governing body charged constitutionally with responsibility for management of all ports in Trinidad and Tobago. I served from 1981 to 1983 when I resigned to have time for other professional activities. The period during which I was a Commissioner was a time when the Port of Spain had huge bills for overtime payment of port workers, when ships nonetheless paid port workers to allow their own crews to offload cargo expeditiously, when ships spent multiples of the days in port than one would expect if cargo was offloaded efficiently, and a time when the queue of cargo ships awaiting berth at the Port stretched past Chaguaramas.

There are several observations or happenings that stayed in my memory. One is how whenever the local shipping body objected to a proposed action by the Port Authority, a letter would arrive from the international shipping conference threatening sanctions against the Trinidad and Tobago ports. Another is the exasperation with which the Board Chairman, former Commissioner of Police Mr Eustace Bernard, informed the Board that a dismissed worker was still in receipt of salary, years after his dismissal. The worker had appealed the High Court's judgement that his dismissal was legal and for some strange reason the management of the Port assumed that they had to await the outcome of the appeal before terminating payments. I convinced the Board to cease payments unless the courts directed otherwise. The ex-worker wrote a letter of complaint to Prime Minister George Chambers which produced no intervention by him.

A third interesting episode concerned a captain of the inter-island ferry who for several years would not take vacation leave even though advised to do so by his immediate supervisor. It was surmised that his reluctance to take vacation leave was due to his interest in the revenues of the ship's bar. The maritime laws of Trinidad and Tobago gave ship captains the sole right to the revenues generated by operation of bars on the coastal vessels. The Board Chairman was very concerned that the captain might run the ship aground and blame such an occurrence on overwork and fatigue. The Board therefore summoned the captain and instructed him to proceed on vacation leave immediately. After a period of leave, he resumed duties and not long after the ship ran aground near Tobago. It was reported that the captain was not on the bridge at the time but was in the interior regions of the ship attending to financial matters.

EVENTS IN THE CARIBBEAN

TRINIDAD AND TOBAGO

The atmosphere in the building shared by the Faculty of Social Sciences and the Faculty of Arts and General Studies as well as elsewhere on the campus became somewhat intense during the mid-1980s. One factor grabbing the consciousness of everyone was the collapse of world petroleum prices and its adverse implications for Trinidad and Tobago's economy and society given the fact that petroleum production and export was the main driver of national economic activity. The oil price boom covered the period December1973 to May 1980 when prices rose from US$24.91 per barrel to a peak of US$128.97 per barrel. A downward fluctuating trend then ensued but prices still remained well above the December 1973 benchmark for five years. Perhaps for that reason, many Trinidadians had scoffed at Prime Minister George Chambers' declaration soon after his 1981 electoral victory, when prices still hovered around $90.00, that "The Fete Done". A precipitous price decline started in 1986 and prices reached an all-time low of US$25.58 per barrel in March 1986. By then even doubters of an economic recession in Trinidad and Tobago had to acknowledge reality. The country's economic growth rate, which was only 1.5 per cent in 1975, had increased markedly to average 6 per cent between 1976 and 1982. In 1983, it fell drastically and continued to decline by an average 4.4 per cent between 1984 and 1986. Discussions about the quality of economic management by the governing PNM and the possibilities of political alternatives became urgent.

The formation of a coalition by formerly rival political parties to contest the PNM also galvanised the attention of the campus community. The PNM had been the dominant political party, winning all general elections since the 1950s. In 1976, Basdeo Panday's United Labour Front had only managed to obtain 27 per cent of total votes and win ten of the 36 seats under contention compared to the PNM's 24 seats. The Democratic Action Congress led by A.N.R. Robinson, a former PNM Cabinet Minister under Prime Minister Eric Williams obtained 8 per cent of the votes and won two seats. The Tapia House Movement, which was led by the charismatic Lloyd Best, attracted a sizeable liberal intellectual following but failed to garner electoral support, winning no seats and only persuading 4 per cent of the electorate to vote for it.

The opposition to the PNM fared no better in the 1981 elections. The PNM led by George Chambers, who had replaced the deceased Prime Minister Eric Williams, won 26 seats and obtained 53 per cent of the votes. The United Labour Front obtained 15 per cent of votes and won eight seats while the Democratic Action Congress obtained 3.7 per cent of votes and won two seats. The Tapia House Movement failed spectacularly again with only 2.3 per cent of votes and no seat. There was striking evidence that the first-past-the post electoral system could produce anomalous results in that the Organisation for National Reconstruction led by Karl Hudson-Phillips, a former PNM Attorney-General, obtained 22 per cent of the votes but did not win even a single seat.

In 1986, the United Labour Front, the Organisation for National Reconstruction, the Democratic Action Congress and the Tapia House Movement formed a coalition political party, the National Alliance for Reconstruction (NAR) to contest the general elections in that year. It gave hope to some people at the university who had long sought a credible alternative to the PNM. The coalition defeated the PNM by a seat ratio of 33 to three and garnered 66 per cent of total votes cast compared to the PNM's 32 per cent. A few St Augustine academics, namely Carlson Charles from the Faculty of Engineering, Bhoendradatt Tewarie and Brinsley Samaroo from Arts and General Studies took up Ministerial positions in the new government headed by A.N.R. Robinson as Prime Minister and Basdeo Panday as his Deputy. Trevor Farrell from Social Sciences was appointed Executive Chairman of TRINTOPEC, a major energy sector state enterprise. The coalition did not last long even though the government itself remained in office until elections in 1991. Basdeo Panday was expelled from the government in 1989 and formed his own party, the United National Congress, which having been allocated six seats became the new parliamentary opposition. This might have been foreshadowed by one ULF supporting colleague from the Faculty of Arts and General Studies who, surprisingly discomforted by the margin of electoral victory, declared on the morning after the election that the ULF would have to become the opposition in the government.

The national economic decline which started in 1983 continued unabated. Economic recession took its toll on employment, wage and salary rates, profits, import capacity, and living standards, and deflated national confidence in the country's economic future. The NAR government found it necessary to implement an International Monetary Fund structural adjustment programme with onerous conditions, including a ten per cent wages and salaries cut that further displeased many residents. The golden era of the petroleum boom was definitely over.

In 1985, I had done a conference presentation entitled "The Open Petroleum Economy in Crisis: Trinidad and Tobago at the End of the Boom Decade" which foreshadowed the economic decline. The paper began with a quotation from Dudley Seers in 1978 which stated that, "Petroleum economies are ... unlikely to achieve the necessary transformation and to escape their doom". A 1980 publication by me and Wilberne Persaud had warned that, "A dependent underdeveloped oil-resource economy such as

Trinidad and Tobago should not be sanguine about its long-run balance of payments." It pointed to the prospect of a major economic collapse manifested in falling economic growth rates, rise in unemployment, fiscal crisis of the State, further fall in petroleum prices, deteriorating terms of international trade, stagnation in the manufacturing sector, unsustainable increases in aggregate consumption expenditures, incomplete investment projects and the down phase of the credit cycle which would amplify the economic contraction already in train. The policy problematic was posed in terms of minimising the disruptive consequences of the economic downturn, establishing new bases for economic growth especially export-led growth, and restoring factor -price equilibrium which meant letting productivity-adjusted wage rates fall rather than be indexed to price level changes. It was also suggested that the government should seek structural adjustment loans from the multilateral financial institutions and devalue the foreign exchange rate.

GRENADA

The implosion of the People's Revolutionary Government in Grenada in 1983 caused great angst among St Augustine academics, many of whom were sympathisers of the New Jewel Movement and had colleagues who had joined the PRG in various capacities. The immediate source of the problem within the government was a negative assessment of Bishop's leadership by Bernard Coard and his supporters within the government. There were also signs of public disaffection with the Party. Jay Mandle's important book, *Big Revolution, Small Country: The Rise and Fall of the Grenada Revolution*, published in 1985, refers to a survey by Trevor Munroe in which respondents indicated resentment of the heavy demands the Party placed on personal time.

Among Coard's supporters were Leon Cornwall, Ewart Layne and Liam James. Cornwall and Layne were two military officers who I had met at Elvin McDavid's home in Guyana when they had just arrived for military training. Jay Mandle documented Liam James leading the charge with a statement that Bishop lacked, "a Leninist level of organisation and discipline, great depth in ideological clarity, brilliance in strategy and policy."

The Coard faction proposed a joint leadership in which Coard would effectively have control of the Party and Government by having functional responsibility for party organisation, including party organisational development and formation of comrades, and strategy and tactics. Bishop would handle production and propaganda, relations with the working class and youths, military mobilisation and international relations. Bishop agreed on 25 September but subsequently changed his mind. On returning to Grenada from an overseas trip on 13 October 1983, he was immediately placed under house arrest, removed from all official positions and expelled from the Party.

I was lunching with a highly placed political person at a Barbados restaurant when he was informed of Bishop's house arrest. The conversation reminded me of what I had been hearing about imprisonment in Grenada of political dissidents, some of whom were former supporters of the New Jewel Movement. According to Reynold Burrowes' very informative book, *Revolution and Rescue in Grenada: An Account of the US-Caribbean Invasion*, published in 1988, Barbadian Prime Minister Tom Adams discussed with Organisation of Eastern Caribbean States Prime Ministers possible plans for Bishop's rescue a few days after he was placed under house arrest. Burrowes quotes Adams as stating in a public address in Barbados: "I considered that the house arrest of a Prime Minister was so extreme as to imply some measure of imminent violence and disorder."

St Vincent and the Grenadines Prime Minister Milton Cato is reported to have questioned the morality of rescuing Maurice Bishop while there were many people detained by his government for longer than four years. Maurice Bishop had become authoritarian for what other inference can be drawn from the following excerpt from a June 1981 public address (reproduced in Mandle's book), even making allowance for excesses of rhetoric in political speeches: "When the revolution speaks, it must be heard, listened to. Whatever the revolution decrees, it must be obeyed; when the revolution commands, it must be carried out; when the revolution talks, no parasite must bark in their corner ... When the revolution orders, it must be obeyed."

It is reported that on 19 October 1983, a large crowd released Bishop from house arrest and with them, he proceeded to Fort Rupert which sits at the top of a hill reached on a narrow, winding road. I knew the location and knew that the fort housed the armoury when I was last there and probably still did. Therefore, when I heard the radio broadcast of where Bishop and his supporters were heading, I wondered about their purpose and how it might all end. Matters ended very tragically.

Troops loyal to Bernard Coard travelled to the fort, arrested Bishop and five of his key supporters and executed them. General Hudson Austin, a Coard ally, took command of the situation and announced a state of emergency and a 24-hour curfew extending over for four days. I recall the chilling effect of his radio broadcast that anyone on the street will be shot on sight. I thought there and then that Grenada was on the verge of embarking on a regime of military government with the prospect of repeated political destabilisation and overthrow of governments. I thought that that should not be allowed to happen.

Similar sentiments were held by the political leaders of the OECS countries, Barbados and Jamaica. Reynold Burrowes' book records St Lucian Prime Minister John Compton expressing the view that Coard was "a hard line Marxist in the Stalinist mode" who would engineer the demise of Hudson Austin, assume the stance of saviour of democracy and remain intact as leader of Grenada regardless of what other Caribbean Community leaders thought. Compton concluded that, "We could not sit with Coard. We had to clean him out before he cleaned us out."

On 22 October 1983, Prime Minister Adams chaired a meeting of OECS government leaders which decided to invoke Article 8 of the OECs treaty and ask friendly countries for help in stabilising the situation and establishing a peace keeping force. Prime Minister Adams, Dominica's Prime Minister Eugenia Charles and Jamaica's Prime Minister Edward Seaga subsequently formally invited the United States to participate in a military mission which turned out to be an American military intervention which commenced on 25 October during early morning hours. I was awake around 4am listening to Radio Free Grenada when I heard frantic shouts that the island was being invaded and appeals for blood. The invasion had obviously started before the time stated in subsequent news releases by the US government.

Prime Minister George Chambers had decided to stand aside from the CARICOM efforts. He had sought to have the 22 October meeting suggested by Prime Minister Adams held in Port of Spain but that was not convenient to Adams and the other leaders. On the day after the US invasion, Prime Minister Chambers addressed the Trinidad and Tobago Parliament and announced the following decisions: 1. The Trinidad and Tobago Government will not participate in any meeting in which Grenada is not represented. (This was typical Chambers not batting out of his crease, to use his own cricketing metaphor); 2. No Grenadian citizens or nationals would be allowed to enter Trinidad and Tobago without a visa; 3. An embargo would be placed on Grenadian exports to Trinidad and Tobago and on Grenadian registered ships. It is extremely difficult to discern any sensible rationale for the latter two sets of stipulations.

A somewhat different perspective on the military operation was expressed by the American literary figure, Alice Walker who, in her journal,

Living by the Word, wrote on 30 October 1983 how disgusted she was by the invasion of Grenada, describing President Reagan as a "phantom of death". One can infer that Alice Walker was troubled not only by events in Grenada, possibly thinking that the US invasion was responsible for the death of Bishop and the others, but also had a much more pervasive concern about US military adventurism in the world and its effects on the American psyche.

GUYANA

In the late 1970s, Guyana began a prolonged economic decline. In nine of the fourteen years between 1977 and 1990, aggregate economic activity measured by real gross domestic product contracted. Inflation doubled in the 1985-1989 period. Bauxite sector exports, the principal foreign exchange earner in the preceding years, decreased by 60 per cent between 1981 and 1989. International foreign reserves plummeted from US$100 million in 1975 to US$7 million in 1981 and averaged only US$8 million during the 1982 to 1989 period. With the contraction in import capacity, imports of consumer goods and intermediate goods decreased substantially. Government external debt increased from 150 per cent of gross national income in 1980 to 648 per cent in 1989. Total external debt on 31 December 1990 was US$1960 million. Most of it, US$1042 million, was bilateral with US$414 million owed to Trinidad and Tobago, US$138 million to the UK and US$126 million to the US. Operating losses in GUYMINE and BIDCO reached as high as G$584 million in 1989. Employment in GUYSTAC, the umbrella state enterprise body, contracted from 17,132 people in 1981 to 10,947 people in 1989. Guyana had become "one of the poorest countries in the Southern Hemisphere" according to a World Bank Country Study published in 1993.

Given these circumstances of dismal national economic performance and an extremely troubling political environment, it was unsurprising that many Guyanese voted with their feet, opting to emigrate than remain in Guyana. Between 1975 and 1978, the emigration rate had averaged 14,100 people annually. For the 1979 to 1981 period, it had increased to an average of 18,276 people annually and increased still more to an annual average of 25,539 people between 1982 and 1989. The government tried to stop this loss of population by creating many barriers, such as obstacles in obtaining income tax clearance certificates, restrictions on access to foreign exchange, and political intimidation. In one infamous incident there was an unsuccessful attempt to forcibly remove Hugh Saul, a former senior public official who had fallen foul of Forbes Burnham, from a British West Indian Airways aircraft about to depart Georgetown. The pilot foiled the attempt by invoking Trinidad and Tobago territorial law for the aircraft. Despite the obstacles and barriers to emigration, people did succeed in leaving in large numbers, sometimes without much financial resources, sometimes with smuggled jewellery.

President Burnham's government had sought economic assistance from the International Monetary Fund and the World Bank. There was a Structural Adjustment Programme agreed with the World Bank which ended in 1984. There was also an Extended Fund Facility agreement with the IMF in 1980 which ended prematurely in 1982. President Burnham, who had become critical of the IMF in his public statements, declined the terms of a new agreement with the IMF. There was not to be another engagement with the World Bank and the IMF until after Burnham's death in 1984.

President Burnham died unexpectedly on 5 August 1984 while undergoing throat surgery. A few days later, I received a phone call from Vice Chancellor Aston Preston for assistance in contacting Professor Lloyd Braithwaite who had retired as St Augustine Principal and occupied a staff office in the Faculty of Social Sciences. Preston had been trying unsuccessfully to phone him. I informed the Vice Chancellor that I saw Professor Braithwaite almost every day in the building and would let him know that he was trying to reach him. I walked down the corridor, found Professor Braithwaite in his office as usual, and delivered the message. Professor Braithwaite said that he was aware of Vice Chancellor Preston's attempted phone calls, thought that the Vice Chancellor wanted him to represent the University at Burnham's funeral and that he had no intention of going. He sat me down to explain why not. Professor Braithwaite told me that he and Burnham were fellow students at the London School of Economics and members of the West Indian Students Union during the same period. He, Braithwaite, knew of serious ethical concerns about Burnham's stewardship of the Students Union finances during his term as its President.

At a farewell function for Burnham in 1948, Braithwaite had given a speech in which he praised Burnham's intelligence, expressed confidence in his future achievements but concluded by saying that he worried about his morals. Professor Braithwaite felt that his critical remark about Burnham's moral qualities cost him his friendship from childhood with Bernice Lataste, Burnham's girlfriend at the time. She married Burnham in 1951 but never again spoke to Lloyd Braithwaite. Eventually, Lewis Bobb from the Department of Government in the Faculty of Social Sciences, who was Burnham's friend from childhood and an executive member of Burnham's political party in the 1950s, represented the University of the West Indies at the funeral.

Desmond Hoyte, Prime Minister at the time of Burnham's death, automatically succeeded him as President of Guyana and in 1986 started negotiations with the IMF and the World Bank. Carl Greenidge, as Minister of Finance, led the negotiations with the IMF for a new Policy Framework which was agreed after two years of negotiations and a Monitoring Agreement finalised in April 1989. In 1988, the government also agreed an Economic Recovery Programme (ERP) with the World Bank. The ERP constituted a comprehensive dismantling of Burnham's economic policy. Its measures included elimination of price controls, removal of import prohibitions, restructuring of trade tariffs, introduction of a free market for foreign exchange, reduction in the number of government ministries, and reductions in fiscal deficits and money supply growth.

Desmond Hoyte, no doubt informed by technical analyses provided by Greenidge, was known to have become critical of Burnham's management of the economy. Elvin McDavid and Malcolm Parris, both of whom were Government Ministers when Burnham died, told me that they authored a memorandum for President Burnham's attention in which they criticised Hoyte for working against the economic policy of the government and recommended his dismissal. McDavid said that he tried to retrieve the document from Burnham's desk immediately after he died but was too late. Burnham's secretary who disliked him, got there first and gave the document to Desmond Hoyte. Hoyte in his new capacity as President sent McDavid and Parris into temporary exile, McDavid as Ambassador to Moscow, USSR and Parris as Ambassador to Lusaka, Zambia.

McDavid and Parris told me of these events one evening in Guyana upon their return from their overseas posts. They took me to Burnham's by then unoccupied private rural residence and showed me without a trace of regret but rather with humour where they would sit with Burnham on weekend nights and determine who would be dismissed from public sector employment or otherwise punished for alleged disloyalties or disobedience. I had known of this aspect of President Burnham's egocentric, despotic behaviour from the experience of my maternal uncle, Whitney Hutson. He was a structural engineer who had returned from England to work with the Burnham government which he fully supported. One of his last assignments was the construction of a small structure on the compound of the President's residence. Burnham had decreed that only clay bricks should be used as construction materials. My uncle as the project engineer decided to use concrete blocks instead of clay bricks on some part of the building for structural engineering reasons. Burnham observed this in passing one day and reprimanded him, in response to which my uncle replied that clay bricks did not have sufficient strength for the particular purpose. In response to the President's further insistence, my uncle said: "President, I am the structural engineer trained in these matters, not you." He was instantly dismissed and denied opportunity for work any other place in Guyana. He had to migrate to Trinidad where he subsisted on income from sub-contracts provided by colleagues in the construction sector and occasional monetary grants from me. It was a deeply sad situation for a very proud man. He did not return to Guyana until after Burnham's death.

Another informative story was told to me by Malcolm Parris in the company of Elvin McDavid. Parris, while a Minister of Government, underwent compulsory military training in Tanzania. He claimed that he did not take it seriously and on one occasion found it somewhat ludicrous to be asked to dismantle and reassemble high-powered rifles. The Tanzanian government reported him to President Burnham who sent him a stern warning. I had learnt from an earlier experience with Elvin McDavid that there was militarisation of government members, in addition to the quasi-militarisation within the framework of the Guyana People's Militia which was created to augment the personnel strength of the Guyana Defence Force. When I was Elvin's house guest a few years earlier, he asked me to accompany him one morning to some farmland he owned on the East Bank Demerara. We encountered a heavily-ladened pickup truck as we neared the site. McDavid stopped it and enquired about the source of the roof thatching plant material which the occupants were transporting. He evidently thought they were stolen from his property and summoned by phone the head of an army outpost located a couple of miles away. The army officer saluted McDavid on arrival and was deferential, all of which surprised me. Soon after the matter was resolved and we departed the area, I remarked on the behaviour of the army officer to McDavid who informed me that he (McDavid) held superior rank in the military.

DOMINICA

Dominica's politics was turbulent in the 1970s and the start of the 1980s. The country became constitutionally independent of Britain on 3 November 1978. Patrick John, whose political party, the Dominica Labour Party, had won the elections in 1975, was installed as Prime Minister. In less than eight months, there were violent street protests against the government, a general strike was organised by a political coalition entity named the Committee for National Salvation, and there were calls for the resignation of the Prime Minister. The President of the House of Assembly fled to Britain on 11 June 1979 and the House of Assembly on 20 June voted to remove Patrick John from office. He was replaced by Oliver Seraphin, a former member of his government.

On a visit to Dominica later that year, I paid a social visit to a former UWI St Augustine colleague, Bill "Para" Riviere at his home in Portsmouth. He had been among those detained by the Trinidad and Tobago government in the aftermath of the Black Power protests early in the 1970s. He had even idiosyncratically demonstrated his Black Power convictions by repainting his university allocated house and his white Volkswagen motor car entirely black. On returning to Dominica, he had formed one of the several new political parties in Dominica. The new parties were preparing for elections in 1980 and Riviere had his sights set on becoming Prime Minister in some coalition arrangement. I was sceptical about their electoral prospects and of any lasting political coalition because in my conversations with Oliver Seraphin and some of the other leaders there was open criticism of those who were not present.

The elections duly held on 21 July 1980, were handsomely won by the Dominica Freedom Party led by Eugenia Charles. It was the only party that was not subject to splintering, mergers and other permutations during the 1970-1980 period. The result was not a surprise to me. I had predicted it to a group of American businessmen with whom I lunched in Tallahassee, Florida, early in 1980 as the guest of my friend Ivor Mitchell who was a Professor at Florida State University. I was astonished and considerably disturbed by the response of one of the businessmen who, to the visible dismay of his colleagues, asserted that a Freedom Party victory would be most unwelcome to them since their group had expended much financial resources on the Dominica Labour Party headed by Oliver Seraphin.

On 13 February 1981, the government declared a state of emergency and dissolved the Dominica Defence Force in response to the murder of a prominent citizen by some radicals and fears of a coup attempt. In April 1981, there was a plot called Operation Red Dog to overthrow the Eugenia Charles government and restore Patrick John to government. The principal organisers were American right wing and racist extremists led by Mike Perdue, some of whom were later convicted and imprisoned by the US authorities who foiled the plot. Perdue implicated ex-Governor John

Connally and US Senator Ron Paul. Another main conspirator was UK-based Barbadian weapons smuggler, Sydney Burnett-Alleyne. He was convicted and imprisoned in Dominica. Burnett-Alleyne later said in an interview by the *Barbados Nation* that his real intention was to annex Dominica to Barbados in pursuit of personal economic gains and that he was disappointed in Patrick John because he was giving away much land to American businessmen.

There is some credence to Burnett-Alleyne's peeve. On a visit to Dominica during Patrick John's Prime Ministership, I had seen a document where he was offering to commit extensive surface and underground land rights and air rights to a named American corporation owned by a media mogul who was contemplating investments in recreational resorts and who was well connected to the US President. On 18 December 1981, there was yet another attempt to overthrow the government. Major Frederick Newton, the dismissed former Commander of the Dominica Defence Force, attacked the police headquarters in Roseau to free Patrick John. A State of Emergency was again declared and extended to 1984. Newton was tried, convicted and executed. This brought an end to the turbulence with the Dominica Freedom Party winning the elections in 1985 by a wide margin.

ECONOMIC WORK IN AFRICA

UGANDA IN A TIME OF WAR

In January 1983, I received an invitation from the World Bank to be part of a team to prepare a Ugandan Agricultural Rehabilitation Project. There were three World Bank staff members (including a Zambian) and four consultants whose specialities were finance, marketing, and agriculture on the team. We spent four continuous weeks in Uganda. My specific remit as the financial sector specialist was to review the financial institutions and recommend which institutions could be entrusted with the responsibility of administering a US$70 million credit assistance loan from the World Bank.

It was my first time in Africa. Raised in Guyana where most of its population of 750,000 lived on its 459 kilometres coastline and having been resident in the so-called big countries of the Caribbean, i.e., Jamaica with a population of 2.27 million and geographical size of 10,991 square kilometres, and Trinidad and Tobago whose population size was 1.14 million and geographical size is 5,131 square kilometres, my immediate impression of East Africa was one of large population and territorial vastness. Uganda had a population of 13.64 million on a land area of 241,037 square kilometres in 1989.

The team assembled and overnighted in Nairobi, Kenya where we were informed by the team leader that the Ugandan official arrangement for our accommodation at the government-owned multi-purpose Nile Mansions was declined and that instead we would stay at a small hotel owned by an Englishman. The reasons were a combination of security apprehension and moral discomfort. Apparently, the Nile Mansions which were used by General Idi Amin as torture chambers during his Presidency were currently being similarly used by President Milton Obote's security establishment. Furthermore, across the street from the Nile Mansions was the Social Research Centre established by Idi Amin not for the purposes one would associate with such a title but as a detention facility for political enemies who would be executed at his whim and fancy. The World Bank members of the team thought that if the guerrillas then fighting against President Obote attacked the city, the Nile Mansions and the Social Research centre would be prime targets. President Amin's use of the Social Research Centre was confirmed to me by a Ugandan owner of a tea plantation with whom I lunched one day during my stay. He told me that he was snatched on the streets, imprisoned for two weeks fearing death, until his family got word of his whereabouts and bribed the guards to release him. He was taken to the market square in Kampala and ejected from the vehicle by soldiers who immediately snatched a pedestrian as a replacement for him.

Conditions on the ground in Uganda were much more difficult than I could have imagined. On the first night in Kampala, staying in a hotel guarded by armed Tanzanian security, hearing sounds of volleys of gunfire from about 9pm and throughout the night, and hearing running steps and human noises followed by gunfire and then absolute silence in the hotel compound, was an entirely novel experience. I was informed by the leader of the team (whose background before joining the World Bank included military service in Vietnam) that there was an ongoing civil war between President Obote's Uganda National Liberation Army and four guerrilla armies, the most powerful of which was the National Resistance Army led by Yoweri Museveni. Milton Obote had been Uganda's Prime Minister from 1962-1966 and its President from 1996-1971 when he was overthrown by General Idi Amin. After General Amin was himself overthrown, Obote returned as President in 1980 but his rule was soon contested by various informal armies organised along ethnic lines. Obote was finally deposed in July 1985 by army leaders Brigadier Bazilllo Olara-Okello and General

Tito Okello. A Military Council governed briefly but Yoweri Museveni seized control in September and installed himself as President. Ironically, President Museveni is now embroiled in a fierce guerrilla war with the Lord's Resistance Army, a breakaway group from his former National Resistance Army.

In effect, the Ugandan Agricultural Rehabilitation Project mission was being conducted in the middle of a civil war in which ultimately an estimated 100,000-500,000 people died. The economy was in tatters. Food was very scarce because trucks delivering agricultural produce from rural areas were frequently looted by the army and by guerrillas. One ate whatever was available in minute quantities. Potable water in the villages was such a rarity that on one occasion I had to use my Harveys Bristol Cream sherry as my morning mouthwash. Roadblocks by young soldiers in varying states of inebriation were ubiquitous. It was extremely hazardous to be outdoors at night. I grew accustomed to grenade launchers jamming my cheek at many roadblocks and to hearing sounds of gunfire throughout the night. What I found abhorrent were the body counts in the mornings and the almost gratuitous or revengeful violence of the army. I still shudder at the memory of soldiers shooting up a school where children were writing exams in retaliation for a guerrilla attack a few days previously.

There were some scary times personally. For instance, the team was in the Bank of Uganda one night for the press conference at the end of an IMF Mission which paralleled ours when there was shooting in the streets below. This caused some anxiety on the part of our hosts who had to arrange safe passage for us. Another more serious occasion was near Jinga, Uganda's second city and home of the 1st Battalion of the Army. We were travelling in two cars, each with four people, when we stopped at roadblocks. The lead car was stopped by police officers about 100 metres ahead of my vehicle which was stopped by young soldiers. During the search of our belongings, Van Hiltzen, a quite irascible Dutch member of my party, refused to put his freshly laundered, white shirts on the red dirt road. A clash of wills developed between him and the soldiers. Rifles were trained on us, and I heard cartridges entering the firing chamber. I thought I was going to die because of Hiltzen's white shirts. Fortunately, the other group, wondering about our delay in joining them, turned back to check on us in the nick of time.

Despite our self-imposed restrictions on movement in Uganda, we combined some sightseeing with our weekly fieldtrips to districts such as Masindi and Hima which were bordered by the Democratic Republic of the Congo and Kibale, Kasese, Soroti, Lowereo and Mubende which are inland districts. We ventured up a crooked mountain trail early one morning only to be impeded by a huge elephant trumpeting and stamping the ground to force our reversal. We visited a small power station located on the bank of a river and journeyed down the river despite the prevalence of huge green crocodiles. We had a quick swim in a lake with hippopotamuses observing us from a safe distance. We travelled through lion country and saw a pride of lions relaxing under a tree and a few of us even had the somewhat fearful experience of hearing a lion's footfalls near our lodge cabin in the dead of night. We travelled through the Bwindi Forest where on a rainy morning I was able to see a huge male gorilla on the bank of the road. With his muscular stature, luxurious blue velvet coat of hair and imperial stare, he made an indelible impression on me. On my own, I ventured into a village near Kampala where I purchased some batik paintings from an artist whose son I recognised many years later in South Africa solely by the similarity of batik painting which he had on display. The son told me that he had migrated to South Africa as an adult.

One trip was to the tomb of Mutesa II, the Kabaka of Buganda (King Freddie) who had been exiled from Uganda in 1966 when Obote first installed himself as President. King Freddie who was from the Buganda royal family died in England, but his remains were entombed in a huge tent in the Buganda region. The practice was that the widows of the King would spend the rest of their lives in the tent, denied any movement elsewhere and limited in human contact to only the people who served them meals. We saw three widows of questionable sanity residing in the daytime gloom of the tomb. The fourth widow, a much younger woman with whom King Freddie had gone into exile, wisely did not return to Uganda. Women were accorded very low status by Buganda men. As an example, they had to kneel if they were being addressed by a man as I discovered when I sought directions from a young woman in a village on one occasion.

The project focussed primarily on rebuilding Uganda's coffee export capacity. Agriculture which contributed 95 per cent of exports and provided livelihood for 93 per cent of the population was dominated by coffee production and exports, with cultivation of tea, livestock production, and food crops being of much lesser economic significance. My report provided an overview of the banking sector which noted that the Ugandan financial system consisted of the Bank of Uganda as the Central Bank, seven commercial banks, and two development banks. Five of the commercial banks were foreign owned. The locally owned banks were the Uganda Commercial Bank (UCB) and the Cooperative Bank, both of which were owned by the government. The UCB was the largest bank in Uganda. It accounted for 65 per cent of credit and 47 per cent of deposits. It had 54 branches and 2570 employees. The Chairman of its Board of nine members was also the Managing Director. He was appointed by the President, while the other Board members were appointed by the Minister of Finance. Foreign owned banks were declining and had closed their branches outside of the capital city, Kampala. The report discussed interest rates and statutory liquidity which were set by the Bank of Uganda, and credit ceilings which were established by the President in budget speeches. The report then discussed the features of the agricultural credit market, including the narrowness of the formal market, the variety of acceptable loan security instruments, selective direction of credit allocation by the government, and government influence on agricultural product prices, marketing and foreign exchange.

It stated that three fundamental criteria should guide the choice of financial institution for administering the credit project, namely, capacity to efficiently appraise credit applications, capacity to deliver, monitor and recover loans, and degree of flexibility in lending policy. The UCB was adjudged to have the strongest loan appraisal capacity, the strongest network of branches to efficiently deliver, monitor and recover loans, and was flexible with respect to forms of loan security. My report did not support an authorisation role for the Bank of Uganda because of difficulties experienced with previous Reconstruction Credit Programs and the higher implementation costs that would ensue from inserting another entity in the arrangements. It also did not support the proposal by the Bank of Uganda that the UCB should be required to maintain compensating deposits against loans made under the Agricultural Rehabilitation Project. The report also made specific recommendations with respect to interest rates and grace periods applicable to the World Bank loan to the UCB and the UCB's on-lending rate of interest and grace period.

I left Uganda marvelling at its physical beauty, troubled by the civil war, and greatly impressed by the diligence, competence and civility of its public officials who performed their duties without complaint in the most difficult of times for them and their families.

ZAMBIA IN THE TIME OF KENNETH KAUNDA

In May 1983, I made my second trip to Africa, this time to the Southern Africa country, Zambia. Zambia at the time had a population of 6.48 million on a land area of 743,390 square kilometres. I stayed there from 16 May to

11 June. I had been recruited by USAID to lead a team to study and report on Zambian agricultural financial markets as technical assistance to the Ministry of Agriculture and Water Development, Zambia. The other member of the team was Michael Boehlje, a middle-aged Professor of Economics at Iowa State University. I was selected to lead the team because unlike Boehlje who had left the US mainland only once before on a honeymoon trip to San Juan, Puerto Rico, I had extensive field experience in developing countries. We were assisted in Zambia by personnel from the USAID/Zambia office and from the Ministry of Agriculture and Water Development.

Lusaka, the capital city, was in a state of heightened tension, because Zambia was positioned as a frontline country in the anti-colonial and anti-apartheid struggles in Southern Africa. The country had a history of providing operational bases for the Zimbabwe People's Revolutionary Army of the Zimbabwe African People's Union led by Joshua Nkomo and for the African National Congress (ANC) of South Africa. Both the Rhodesian military and the South African Defence Force had conducted military incursions and bombing raids in or near Lusaka. I think that ANC activities were ongoing during my time in Zambia. One evening I stumbled upon a meeting in the bar of my hotel between a group of African (presumably South African) activists and Reginald Green, an American professor with whom I was a member of a Group of Experts co-authoring a report for UNCTAD on low-income countries and the international monetary system. He had worked in Tanzania and was known to be a strong supporter of anti-colonial movements in Africa. I also ran into Adelbert Tucker, a former graduate student from the UWI Mona campus, who said he was working with the new independent government in Zimbabwe and also rendering assistance to the ANC. The Zambian authorities were suspicious of photography and other media for disseminating information on its building infrastructure and encouraged citizens to report any suspicious behaviour or attempts at information gathering by foreigners.

Although security conditions were not extreme, one had to be cautious about travel at night which caused Boehlje and me to spend an inordinate number of nights dining in one of the hotel's two restaurants. The ensuing boredom was relieved by the hospitality of Mike Warren and his wife, George Veitch, Lee Ann McGranahan, Dale Grovesnor and Chris Mupimpila, and the pleasure of hearing a very good South African jazz band one evening.

It was in Zambia that I got my first inkling of how countries evaded the international fall out from dealing with the apartheid regime in South Africa. I learnt that American officials travelling to and from Zambia would choose the very convenient route through Johannesburg but would have two passports, one which would be stamped by South African immigration but not shown to Zambian immigration, and another which would be shown to Zambian immigration. In Swaziland years later, I would witness attempts at sanctions-busting involving UK companies.

The Zambian economy was underperforming in 1982. Real domestic product had declined by 7 per cent and real per capita GDP by 22 per cent since 1976. Inflation was about 14 per cent to 20 per cent according to official and unofficial estimates. The balance payments kept deteriorating and the foreign debt to GDP ratio had increased from 30 per cent to 45 per cent which contributed to a situation in which foreign debt payments comprised 48 per cent of earnings from exports of goods and services. The predominant economic sector was mining (mainly copper) which accounted for 26 per cent of total GDP and 16 per cent of employment and was a major source of government revenue. The agriculture, forestry and fisheries sector accounted for 13 per cent of GDP and 11 per cent of formal employment. The main agricultural commodity was predominantly maize. Of the 613,800 agricultural producers in 1980, 75 per cent were subsistence or traditional farmers, 21 per cent small scale commercial, 3 per cent medium scale commercial, and only 1 per cent large scale commercial. Parastatal enterprises were a significant part of the economic system. They had monopoly marketing power for the major food staples and for agricultural inputs. They were a major part of the commercial banking industry, in insurance services, and in the agricultural credit system. Parastatals were also dominant in mining and manufacturing. The country's central bank, the Bank of Zambia, was at the apex of a financial system which included five commercial banks (four foreign-owned and a newly established parastatal), the Development Bank of Zambia and the Agricultural Finance Company Limited.

The objectives of the study undertaken were an appraisal of the operations of the financial system in relation to agriculture, recommendation of improvements, and advice on additional studies to improve decision-making. The approach taken was to conceptualise the agricultural finance system as an integrated whole, in which there were production, marketing and distribution activities, a variety of financial mechanisms, and varying degrees of self-financing by operators. There were detailed consultations with institutions and individuals from the commercial banking sector, the two development banks, the Agricultural Finance Company Ltd, cooperative banks, the Bank of Zambia, Ministry of Agriculture and Water Development,

World Bank, USAID, and commercial and small farmers near Lusaka and in Magoye.

There were twenty-one main findings. One: agricultural financing requirements were very large, even at existing levels of capitalisation. Two: there was substantial scope for self-financing of current production, probably in the order of 43 per cent. Three: rural savings were quantitatively significant, contrary to popular belief, so that it would be worthwhile to channel such savings into the formal financial system. Four: the agricultural sector had been constrained by limited access to foreign exchange. Five: weaknesses in pricing policies and payments practices inflated the demand for credit by creating financing gaps. Six: the commercial banks and the Agricultural Finance Company Ltd (AFC) were the main sources of agricultural credit, supplying 46 per cent and 45 per cent respectively. The commercial banks serviced large commercial farmers mainly, while the AFC serviced mainly small and medium scale commercial farmers. Seven: fisheries and livestock producers were under-served by the credit system. Eight: considerable difficulties in obtaining credit without government guarantees were experienced by input supply and commodity marketing parastatals as well as by cooperative unions. Nine: interest policies of the central bank resulted in low and rigid rates on deposits and loans which were disincentives to savers and lenders. Ten: interest rate spreads did not cover operating costs and risk costs in credit parastatals and cooperative unions with resultant high operating losses and dependence on fiscal subventions. Eleven: given that interest costs were a small proportion of production costs, there was room for raising nominal loan rates of interest. Twelve: credit parastatals have high loan transactions costs which add considerably to overall lending costs. Thirteen: loan delinquency was a critical problem for the agricultural credit system. Fourteen: the reasons for loan delinquency included inadequate producer margins, high borrower transactions costs, and poor weather. Fifteen: deficient credit appraisal, loan monitoring and loan recovery systems and practices within the credit parastatals were important contributory factors to loan delinquency. Sixteen: a weakness in the loan monitoring system was the absence of post-loan monitoring of the use of loan proceeds and changes in the production and financial situation of debtors. Delegation of loan recovery responsibilities to other agencies was also a weakness. Seventeen: borrowers tended to believe that loan contracts were unenforceable, especially because collateral in the form of land was not readily monetised because of Zambian land law and policy. Eighteen: potential political interference in credit decisions and contract enforcement was a serious problem perceived by credit administrators in parastatals. Nineteen: a grants syndrome permeated the public sector component of the credit system. Twenty: Crop insurance could be required by lenders to reduce credit risks, increase scope for portfolio diversification across crops, and reduce transactions costs. Twenty-one: the heavy dependence of credit parastatals on funds from the government and foreign sources was a potential source of problems such as irregularity of resource inflows, restrictions on portfolio choice and interest rate policies, foregoing of information on deposit activities of credit customers, and foreign exchange risks.

The report recommended the closure of the AFC and cessation of the direct agricultural credit activities of several transient or partial agricultural lenders. It further recommended that the structure of the agricultural credit system should have three components: 1. A Cooperative Credit Scheme funded by rural savings' credit unions, and block loans from the Zambian Agricultural Development Bank (ZADB) and ZCF Financial Services Limited; 2. Commercial Banks, which in addition to savings mobilised from the entire country, would accept loans from the ZADB. The commercial banks would be responsible for servicing large scale commercial farmers and most small and medium scale commercial farmers; 3. The ZABD which would not lend directly to farmers but could lend to input suppliers and marketing agencies. The structure recommended was intended to confer benefits of reduced transactions costs for both lenders and borrowers and reduction of loan delinquency. A second-best recommendation allowed the ZADB to lend directly to farmers in addition to providing block loans to the other credit institutions and agencies. The report concluded with recommendations for three studies, namely Efficiency in Credit Utilisation and Impact of Interest rates on Credit Use and Output; Farm Liquidity, Internal Financing Potential and Demand for Credit; and Estimation of Borrowing Costs and Lending Costs.

The report was accepted by the Zambian government and published as Ministry of Agriculture and Water Development Planning Division Special Studies No. 2 in June 1983. It led to some reforms of the country's rural financial markets.

NIGERIA

My next assignment in Africa was in the West African nation of Nigeria. At the invitation of the World Bank, I participated in a seminar on agricultural credit organised by the Central Bank of Nigeria for its economics staff. It was held on 26-31 October 1988 in Illorin, the main city of Kwara State. I made two presentations, one on Developing a Viable Financial Market for Agriculture, and the other on Exchange Rate Reforms and their Impact on Agriculture.

It was not an enjoyable visit because of endemic corruption and requests for unofficial payments or levies at the Lagos airport on arrival and departure, the non-existence of my connecting flight to Illorin, the resultant necessity of a 4am drive next morning to reach Illorin by 8am, and soldiers who extorted payment at roadblocks. I was greatly relieved to depart Nigeria.

BOTSWANA, LESOTHO AND SWAZILAND

Early in 1989, I was contracted by the United Nations Conference on Trade and Development (UNCTAD) to assist Botswana, Lesotho and Swaziland (the BLS countries) in preparations for renegotiation of the Southern African Customs Union in which they were members along with the Republic of South Africa (RSA). The work was conducted in two phases. The first phase consisted of briefings and familiarisation visits to Geneva and the BLS countries. I spent March 30-April 2 in Geneva for briefing and document review at UNCTAD, April 3-7 in Swaziland for meetings with government ministers and officials, Central Bank of Swaziland, and United Nations Development Programme (UNDP) officials in Swaziland, April 10-13 in Lesotho meeting with government ministers and officials and Central Bank of Lesotho, and April17-19 in Botswana meeting with government ministers and officials, Central Bank of Botswana, and UNDP/ Botswana. The second phase began with a visit to UNCTAD, Geneva on July 1-4 for briefing and an extended stay in Swaziland from July 5 to September 4. A West Indian professional, George Williams from Dominica, who was Interregional Adviser at UNCTAD, was my project manager.

Apart from the specifics of the work undertaken to prepare the report on Fiscal Aspects of the Southern African Customs Union, the mission provided opportunities to know and understand features of the BLS countries, their relationship to South Africa, and the centrality of South Africa in the whole of Southern Africa.

Botswana whose capital is Gaborone was a sparsely populated country of 581,730 square kilometres and 1.24 million people in 1989. It is landlocked by South Africa to the south, Zimbabwe to the northeast, and Namibia to the west and north. Its principal income source is diamond mining. Agricultural conditions are demanding because much of Botswana is the Kalahari Desert. A significant proportion of its labour force work in

South African mines. While in Botswana, I was entertained to a "brie" (a backyard roasted meat event) by Charlie Stayers, a former Guyanese fast bowler who played for the West Indies in 1972 alongside Lance Gibbs, Wes Hall, Chester Watson and Garry Sobers. I also was hosted by Kofi Tetteh, a Ghanian friend of my St Augustine colleague and friend Marion Fraser, who was serving as Attorney-General in Botswana. It turned out that Kofi Tetteh was also a good friend of my Guyanese friend, Horace Nurse, who had until soon before my visit worked as a town planner in Botswana for several years. Kofi Tetteh was also a friend and former legal colleague of Trinidadian, Ulric Cross, in Ghana and the Cameroons and regaled me with stories about him.

Lesotho whose capital is Maseru is also landlocked. It is a small mountainous country situated entirely within the South African landmass. With a population of 1.67 million in 1989 and total land area of 30,000 square kilometres, it is densely populated compared to its BLS neighbouring countries. A large proportion of its landed area is arid even though its rivers contain abundant water which is exported to South Africa. Its male labour force is heavily engaged in work in the South African mines. From my room in the Maseru Hotel, I could see them departing and returning through the nearby border crossing. Lesotho was greatly dependent on remittances from its migrant workers and experienced correlated problems of alcohol and gambling addiction by female recipients of remittances. During the period of my work in the BLS countries, there were only two international flights weekly to and from Lesotho.

Lesotho experienced a military coup in 1986 which installed a Transitional Military Council but retained King Moshoeshoe as executive head of the government. He was exiled in 1987 and replaced by his son, King Letsie III who was himself deposed in 1990. The military strongman was Major-General Justin Lekhanya, Chairman of the Military Junta which overthrew the Prime Minister Leabua Jonathan in 1988. Major-General Lekhanya was himself overthrown in 1991. It is reasonable to conclude that Lesotho was politically unstable during the period of my stay in Southern Africa and that visitors could be easily stranded there because of paucity of international flight options and the hazards of land journeys through apartheid South Africa.

Swaziland (renamed Eswatini in 2018) is also landlocked by South Africa to the north, west and south, and by Mozambique to the east. Its population in 1989 was 798,507 people and land area is 17,364 square kilometres. Its capital city is Mbabane but there is another large important city, Manzini, in the mining district. Its economy is based on agriculture, mining and forestry. Swaziland at the time of the study was a constitutional monarchy of sorts. There was a bicameral legislature consisting of a House of Assembly of 65 members, 55 of whom were elected by an electoral college chosen in a peculiar non-secret process by non-registered voters, and ten of whom were appointed by the Monarch. There was also a Senate of 30 members, ten of whom were appointed by the House of Assembly and twenty by the Monarch. The Monarch dissolves Parliament every five years for new elections. Mswati III was crowned King on 25 April 1986 when he was eighteen years old.

The power of the King was absolute. I attended a function where this was evident. The King summoned the nation for a meeting in the Royal Kraal (an active cattle pasture, as I soon discovered). Everyone has untrammelled right to respond positively to the royal summons and they came from all parts of the country, even walking days to get there. Not knowing what to expect, I had gone straight from the Ministry of Finance attired in a business suit tailored by Yves Saint Laurent. The Royal Kraal was crowded when I arrived. My liaison officer, being female, was denied entry through the same gate as me and earned the vocal disapproval of elderly males when she addressed me in a standing position rather than kneeling in customary tribal fashion. Since no one is allowed to stand in the presence of the King, I duly found a dry spot of dirt on which to sit before he arrived. King Mswati made a rambling speech about environmental protection, then complained about rumours that the new palace under construction for him was insultingly being named after the women's regiment, complained metaphorically about second officers not following instructions of the ship's captain, and then announced the immediate summary dismissal of Prime Minister Sotsa Dlamini who was instantly deprived of all perks and privileges including government transportation from the Royal Kraal. Coming from a tradition of West Indian parliamentary democracy, I was astonished to say the least.

The King's indignation about the naming of his castle reflected the general attitude and policy of Swazi men towards women. Basically, women were treated as subservient, had no voice in family decision-making, could not expect to be asked their wishes or preferences in restaurants, and could only eat at home and at functions after their menfolk had eaten (as I witnessed at a birthday function at the home of the Cabinet Secretary).

A Swazi widow had all rights of custody of her children surrendered during the period of mourning to her mother-in-law who determined the length of the mourning period. Her head was shaved, and she had to wear mourning garb closely akin to a nun's habit and could not be seen in the company of men outside of work environments during that period. She could be assigned to her late husband's eldest brother who would then effectively become her husband.

I learnt about the restrictions on widows from the secretary to the Minister of Finance in whose office I was a consultant. During my first week in the building, I would occasionally see a woman dressed like a nun exiting the elevator. I asked my liaison officer who was the nun and what was her purpose. The answer puzzled me: "She is not a nun; she is a widow." She was always referred to as "the Widow". I started conversing a lot with her as I awaited the Minister and sought her assistance in arranging appointments with high officials. During the work week, I would walk to a small nearby mall to have lunch. One day, the Widow told me that she was going at the same time. I asked her for a lift. She refused outright and responded to my surprise by saying that she could not be seen in the company of men during the prescribed mourning period. This point was reinforced by a chance encounter I had with her one Saturday morning in a supermarket. I must have smiled on approaching her in the aisle and said good morning as I got close. Her response was a blank, unknowing stare. The following Monday in office, I asked her to explain her behaviour. She replied that she was in the company of her sister-in-law who would report her to her mother-in-law, with the possible consequence of suspension of visiting rights to her children. Widows lived in perpetual fear of this power held by their mothers-in-law. About two years later, I received a letter from the Widow in which she told me that her prescribed mourning period had just ended, that she had full custody of her children, that she was now fat and attractive, and that I should return to Swaziland to visit her.

The Umhlanga Festival (Reed Dance) which is held annually in August/September typifies the cultural attitudes. Virginal young women dance in totally revealing costumes before members of the royal family and the nation's men to enable commercial selection of them as brides, with the King having the first choice. I attended the Umhlanga Festival in 1989 and was constantly being offered two brides by female brokers at the festival and even a few days before.

In Swaziland, I caught up with a former Guyanese colleague, Donald Augustine, who was attached to UNDP. I also saw my former PhD student Laurence Clarke who was on a short World Bank mission. After a week in a hotel, I shared a house with Byron Tarr, a Liberian economist working as a consultant with USAID in Swaziland. Byron Tarr had an interesting background in various ministerial capacities in the democratic government of President William Tolbert and in the military government of Master-Sergeant Samuel Doe who overthrew President Talbot on 12 April 1980. He was subsequently imprisoned by Samuel Doe in 1985 and, upon being released, migrated to the US where he worked on contracts for UNDP, USAID and the World Bank. Byron asked me when I was leaving Swaziland to mail letters to two media outlets in London and to phone the US Ambassador in London to inform him that Byron had sent him a letter via me. I duly phoned the ambassador who instructed me to place the letter in a specific mailbox in central London. The instruction aroused my curiosity about modes of communication employed by foreign missions, but I complied without question. Soon after my departure from Swaziland in 1989, President Doe was overthrown, and Byron Tarr returned to Liberia as Minister of Finance in the Interim Government led by Amos Sawyer in 1990.

In addition to Byron Tarr, my new close friends in Swaziland were Gerty Carmichael, a travel agent who Byron and I convinced to set up her own successful travel agency, and Sally Mulalu, a Zambian economist with UNDP in Swaziland. Gerty familiarised me with much of Swazi customs and history, introduced me to the social circles of senior public officials, including the Cabinet Secretary, and army personnel, and briefed me about the South African connections. At her home, I met one of Nelson Mandela's grandsons who she had sheltered from the South African police. Nelson Mandela was still imprisoned on Robben Island in South Africa. A few years later, I met his grand-daughter, Thandi, at the United Nations in New York. In July 1991, President Nelson Mandela visited Jamaica and I was able to have a brief conversation with him prior to the ceremony in which UWI conferred an honorary doctorate on him. He was pleased to learn that I had met his grandson in Swaziland. With Gerty Carmichael, I attended a concert of the South African reggae singer Lucky Dube in Manzini and the annual music festival in Mbanane which featured Eric Clapton and learnt to appreciate the music of Sipho Mabuse and Ladysmith Black Mambazo. Not to be left out, Sally Mulalu ensured that I was exposed to Zambian popular music. I was impressed by the art of South African tribes reproduced in Gavin Younge's Art of the South African Townships and in Peter Magubane's Vanishing Cultures of South Africa.

Gerty Carmichael told me her moving personal story of racial classification in South Africa. I had asked her on one occasion how many mothers she really had because it had become obvious that she was not always speaking of the same person. Her birth mother was impregnated by a white South African whose housekeeper she was in South Africa. She gave birth to Gerty and fearing that her child would be taken away from her in keeping with the apartheid practice of separating light-skinned infants from their mothers, she fled to Swaziland with the infant whom she left in care of her Swazi sister with strict instructions never to disclose to Gerty that she was not her birth mother. Gerty found out the truth and already with a family of her own, found her birth mother sick in a South African village after a search conducted on weekends over many months. She told me that her birth mother's initial statement on seeing her was: "Why did they tell you? I told them not to tell you." Gerty's response was that she had not been told by her "adopted mother" but she just knew and had gone to great trouble to find her birth mother despite being loved and well cared by her "adopted mother". It was a happy reunion.

I did not fully appreciate the scale of the human displacement associated with this mixed-race geographical classification system until in 2000 when I visited the Western Cape of South Africa and saw the massive townships inhabited by people designated by the apartheid regime as "Coloured-Cape" and "Cape-Coloured" peoples.

Swaziland was very dependent on South Africa for food and other consumer goods, equipment, and materials. It was also critically dependent on South Africa for road transportation links to the rest of Southern Africa, and for links to the rest of the world through South African seaports and the Johannesburg Airport. The only other accessible seaport was in Mozambique. South Africa was the economic and transportation hub of much of Southern Africa. Television and newspaper services available daily originated mainly from South Africa. From the newspapers and television, I gained knowledge about the broad contours of the apartheid system as well as about the specific operation of colour classification, reclassifications and geographical resettlement of indigenous South Africans. From the physical maps and other information, I learnt that the re settlements or Bantu states were on land denuded of agricultural quality, having been degraded by mining and that white farmers occupied practically all the good arable land in South Africa. I also learnt that while Black African participation in rugby and cricket were governed by apartheid rules, football was not and indeed was facilitatory of imports of players from neighbouring countries.

South Africa attempted to evade economic sanctions by establishing companies in Swaziland as conduits for South African made goods, as I witnessed in one meeting which I attended in the Swaziland Ministry of Industry and Commerce. The meeting was held with representatives of a South African company that wished to surreptitiously export iron and steel under the guise of scrap iron to Swaziland for re-export as Swazi products to Europe. The main spokesman for the company was an Englishman but when I asked his hitherto silent colleague to speak it was instantly clear that he was Afrikaner. As far as I know, the deal did not materialise.

The Southern African Customs Union (SACU) which I had been contracted to study had been criticised by the BLS countries who had problems with the design of the revenue sharing formula for allocating total revenues from customs and excise duties, questioned the validity and adequacy of the inclusion of fiscal compensatory measures beneficial to them, were unhappy with the time lags in revenue disbursement, and questioned the stabilisation of revenue around a "normal" rate of 28 per cent. My remit was to analyse each individual component of the revenue sharing formula, analyse the import statistics of SACU members, review the revenue sharing formula, estimate import duties and excise taxes levied by South Africa on imported goods destined for Lesotho and Swaziland, estimate the burden of South African excise taxes on those two countries, and estimate the losses due to tariff preferences which favoured South African products. In addition, the study was required to provide estimates of other economic effects resulting from imbalanced SACU arrangements and to propose a simple revenue sharing formula for more favourable estimates for transfer payments and shorter revenue disbursement lags.

The report identified several features of BLS foreign trade. First, a high proportion of imports by BLS countries originate in the customs union, primarily from South Africa. Second, exports to South Africa are small proportions of total exports, except in the case of Lesotho which exported 53 per cent of its exports to South Africa. Third, BLS trade is heavily imbalanced in favour of South Africa. Fourth, South Africa did not import more than 2 per cent of its imports from BLS and did not send more than 9 per cent of its exports to BLS. The report noted that the degree of BLS import dependence on South Africa was unparalleled in any other customs union but was not the result of product characteristics or international market conditions.

The revenue pool increased by 9 per cent annually between 1981 and 1986 but whereas the accruals to Lesotho doubled, those to Swaziland decreased. Nonetheless, customs union receipts comprised considerable proportions of the total tax revenues of both countries. In contrast, customs union receipts comprised a small proportion of South Africa's total tax revenues. The study estimated that 4 per cent of Lesotho's Gross National Product and 5 per cent of Swaziland's Gross National Product accrued to South Africa through the revenue sharing formula, and that there were considerable revenue losses absolutely and relative to GNP from trade preferences which favoured South Africa. The study also investigated the extent of shifting of South African taxes and tariffs to the BLS countries via domestic prices in those countries and measured the implicit income losses in Lesotho and Swaziland. The growth of trade within SACU contributed to growth in output, employment and incomes but did so unevenly in terms of its distribution among the countries. The report recommended that BLS countries seek to increase their share of SACU revenues by strengthening their national tax systems and incorporating into the customs union agreement an enhancement or compensation factor which more fully reflects the income and fiscal losses associated with sales taxes, excise taxes, tariffs, and inflation in South Africa.

The re-negotiations anticipated by the report were overtaken by events. Nelson Mandela was released from prison on 11 February 1990 and all discussions were deferred until the ANC came into office in 1991.

FAMILY AND SOCIAL LIFE

Our sons were doing well at school. Clairmonte (Monty) excelled in his final exams at Fatima College and was initially awarded a Trinidad national scholarship for university until it was realised that as a non-national, he was ineligible. I was a bit concerned about his performance in mathematics in his final year and sought the assistance of my colleague and friend Freddie Campagne who after working with him for two weeks reported that his mathematical ability was fine. The problem was boredom and carelessness because he did not find the work challenging. Meanwhile, Compton (Tunji) was progressing smoothly in preparation for CXC, his first major high school examinations.

In the summer of 1977, Monty and I travelled to England to finalise his entry to an English law faculty. He had offers of places at two University of London colleges, University College and Queen Mary College, and from the University of Birmingham but as late as August had received no reply from the University of West Indies at Cave Hill despite my enquiries to the Registrar, a colleague with whom I had worked closely on many occasions. We therefore had to make the decision to accept one of the English offers and after visiting University College London decided to accept a place in its law faculty. It was a sad revelation to me of how unresponsive and inefficient the UWI student admission process was and how it caused potential students to go elsewhere. It is even sadder to acknowledge that in 2021 not much had changed for the better and that the outward trickle of first-rate potential students had become a stream.

We spent much family time with my Aunt Ivy and Uncle Dan at their home in Arima and at our home in Maracas Valley and St Augustine. We took them to the beach and to calypso tents during the Carnival season. On one occasion, we invited Aunt Ivy to accompany us on a short vacation to Tobago where she had a wonderful time. She and I repeated that visit on another weekend when my mother was visiting from Canada.

My family and I socialised with campus friends and off-campus friends. Much time was spent with Henry and Bernice Jeffers and with Murchie and Nancy Swanston with whom lunches and dinners were regular pastimes combined with Carnival activities. Henry Jeffers introduced us to playing Mas', first with Edmund Hart, then with Poison, Woodbrook Playboys, and Starlift Steel Orchestra. With Merle King we played night mas and enjoyed the street fetes put on by her and her neighbours in Santa Margarita. We went to the calypso tents during Carnival. Spektakula and Kitchener's Revue on Henry Street in Port of Spain were our favourites. In those days, the campus would also be a venue for visiting calypso tents where I remember performances by Shadow and Young Designer.

I also had a cluster of non-university friends. The regular group included two sisters, Marcelle and Jennifer Gairy, Betty Friday, Ann Bramble, Dave Didier, Heathcliff Miller, Neal and Carol Alleyne, and the Bynoe brothers, Roland and Michael. Marcelle, Jennifer and Betty were Grenadians. I was particularly close to Marcelle and Jennifer but have rarely seen them since they migrated to the US in the 1990s. On a visit by Marcelle to Trinidad, I saw both she and Betty Friday at Betty's home in Petit Valley. Marcelle and Jennifer hosted me to dinner at their home in Atlanta during a visit in 2003. It was a pleasure to see Marcelle in 2010 in Shanghai, China, where she was Grenada's Ambassador. Ann Bramble left Trinidad to join the staff of the Caribbean Development Bank, so we were able to revitalise our friendship when I became President of the Bank in 2001. I have encountered Neal Alleyne at University of Trinidad and Tobago activities in recent years. Heathcliff Miller and his wife, Phyllis, a university colleague in the Faculty of Medical Sciences, became good friends of both me and my wife.

One could enjoy various genres of musical entertainment in Port of Spain provided by visiting artistes. Pamela and I saw performances by

Don Cherry and by young rising star trumpet player Wynton Marsalis. We also enjoyed performances by the Lydian Singers and the Marionettes Chorale.

As a family unit, we spent vacation time visiting cultural and nature sites in Trinidad and Tobago and travelling to other Caribbean islands, Mexico, Venezuela, Vancouver, the US and the UK. Our younger son, Tunji, was always the highly organised one on those trips, researching what sites and restaurants to visit and how to travel to them, and also checking out the bookshops to add to his own reading collection and his stock of books to rent to his school friends. In contrast, our older son, Monty, was a dresser whose attention was naturally drawn to stores for elegant men's clothing. During Monty's first Christmas away from home in December 1987, the reduced family unit decided to spend Christmas in New Orleans. We thoroughly enjoyed our time visiting and sightseeing with our friends from the Mona days, Wendel and Joy Wilson and their three daughters, Wendy, Judy and Ann, who had migrated to the US where Wendel had become a Professor of Medicine at the University of New Orleans. New Year's Eve downtown in New Orleans was a joyous street party combined with the festive atmosphere of restaurants and the sounds of live music seemingly emanating from everywhere. Because I stayed for the annual meeting of the American Economic Association meeting early in January 1988, we journeyed to Baton Rouge to spend a few days with Patricia McClean and her husband, Joseph Meyinese. She was a former colleague and friend from the Department of Economics at Mona, who upon completion of her PhD at Ohio State University had joined the academic ranks at Louisiana State University.

I also spent some father and son time with Monty and Tunji separately as did their mother. We would attend football matches at Fatima College and at the National Stadium. I surprised them on one occasion with tickets for us to attend the Gloria Estefan concert in Port of Spain. I visited Monty in England a few times. Once on my way to Copenhagen with Gordon Draper for some discussions with the Copenhagen Business School, I invited Monty to join me for the weekend before the start of my business. We had a wonderful time visiting Tivoli Gardens, the Carlsberg Brewery, the Frederiksberg Palace and the Viking Ship Museum in Roskilde. Tunji accompanied me on a business trip to Barbados where we did some sightseeing in the late afternoons and he visited Harrison's Cave one day.

And there was cricket at the Queen's Park Oval where Pamela and I watched the West Indies playing against the usual cast of Test playing countries. The stand-out performers among the batsmen in the West Indies team were Gordon Greenidge, Desmond Haynes, Viv Richards, Clive Lloyd, Gus Logie, Jeffrey Dujon and Larry Gomes. The outstanding bowlers were Michael Holding, Malcolm Marshall, Andy Roberts and Joel Garner. Ritchie Richardson who had announced himself with consecutive centuries against Australia in Barbados and Antigua in 1984 became a fixture in the team. His powerful square drive is my favourite cricket stroke, formerly played immaculately by Roy Fredericks in his prime.

With South Africa's Nelson Mandela at UWI Mona Campus on 24 July 1991.

The Nuclear Family in London,1992. L-R: Pamela, Monty, Tunji and Me.

CHAPTER SEVEN

UNIVERSITY OF THE WEST INDIES, TRINIDAD, 1990-2001

POLITICAL EVENTS

TRINIDAD AND TOBAGO

A traumatic political event occurred in Trinidad and Tobago on 27 July 1990. The Jamaat al Muslimeen, a radical Muslim group, attempted to overthrow the government by invading Parliament while it was in session. They captured most of the parliamentarians who were present. They also took command of the only television station and one of the radio stations and bombed the police headquarters.

I had not planned to be in Trinidad on that day but had delayed travel to the UK in order to attend Shelton Nicholls' wedding scheduled in Port of Spain on 28 July. My family had travelled ahead of me. Fortune favoured me, for had it not been for a late cancellation of a meeting at the Central Bank, I would have been caught in the middle of the action around the police headquarters which was across the street from my assigned parking lot. As it turned out, I was at home when a telephone call from a friend broke the news to me. I turned on my television set to see the news anchor Jones P. Maderia surrounded by Yasin Abu Bakr, the Muslimeen leader, and several of his forces who were all armed with rifles.

Abu Bakr announced to the nation the assault on the government. He went on to say the Muslimeen had done its part and that it was up to others to do theirs. The latter statement has been widely interpreted as a general call to the population for participation in the revolt, but I think it might have been a call specifically to co-conspirators, possibly located within the Summit of Peoples Organisation, to act in accordance with an agreed plan.

Looting of many business places occurred before a State of Emergency was announced and security forces asserted control over the streets. During the next two or three days, from my veranda I could see night traffic at the airport and concluded that some military assistance whether of a technical nature or boots on the ground was being provided by one or more friendly country. The army engaged the Muslimeen forces with superior power which led to their surrender on 1 August in exchange for an amnesty. Two members of the parliamentary opposition were alleged to have advised the Muslimeen on the drafting of the amnesty document. Canon Knolly Clarke, an Anglican priest who was prominent in the Summit of Peoples Organisation, acted as intermediary between the government and the Muslimeen. The amnesty, although given under duress, was validated by the Trinidad and Tobago Court of Appeal. That decision was overturned by the UK Privy Council which is Trinidad and Tobago's Court of Final Appeal, but the insurrectionists were not re-arrested and prosecuted.

One fatal occurrence during the attempted coup especially saddened me. Accounts about the circumstances vary. Some claim that that there was a shootout between law enforcement officers and Muslimeen members in the home of the mother of Anisa Abu Bakr (the senior wife of Yasin Abu Bakr) on Mendez Drive in Champ Fleurs. Others claim that the law enforcement officers were assailants against law-abiding people. One of the casualties was the only son of my Guyanese friend and former University of Guyana colleague, Omawale (formerly Walter Greene) and Anisa Abu Bakr (formerly Shirley Greene) from a previous marriage. Omawale, who was resident in Jamaica at the time, had asked me a few years previously to take his teenage son's clothing from Jamaica to his grandmother's home because the youngster had decided not to return to his father in Jamaica but to stay with his mother in the Muslimeen compound in Mucurapo, Trinidad. I remember his grandmother tearfully telling me that she worried about his anticipated involvement in the Muslimeen movement.

General elections were held on 16 December in the following year. The governing political party, the National Alliance for Reconstruction, was soundly defeated, obtaining only the two seats in Tobago and securing only 24 per cent of the national votes. The UNC, the political party founded by Basdeo Panday when he was expelled from the NAR, won thirteen seats and 29 per cent of the national votes. The Peoples National Movement won the elections with 21 seats and 45 per cent of the national votes and became the new government. Two colleagues from the Faculty of Social Sciences, John Eckstein and Gordon Draper from the Department of Management Studies, were appointed as Ministers in the government.

GUYANA

On 5 October 1992, there was a major political change in Guyana. The general elections held that day was widely regarded as the first fair elections since 1968. Eleven political parties contested. The elections resulted in the establishment of a new government headed by Cheddi Jagan, a leading figure in the politics of Guyana since the late 1940s. His party, the People's Progressive Party, won 53.5 per cent of the total votes which gave them 28 seats in the 52-seat Parliament. The People's National Congress was first runner-up with 23 seats based on 42.3 per cent of the total votes. The only other political party to gain a seat was the Working Peoples Alliance formed in 1979 as an alliance of the Working Peoples Vanguard Party, ASCRIA, the Indian Political Revolutionary Association and RATOON. The WPA was allocated one seat based on 2 per cent of total votes. The elections marked the end of political dominance by the PNC in the first three decades of constitutional independence from Great Britain.

President Jagan visited Port of Spain soon after he assumed office to meet with Guyanese residing in Trinidad and Tobago. I attended a reception he hosted at the Trinidad Hilton to congratulate him and to renew acquaintance from encounters when he visited Jamaica in the 1970s and from his participation in the 1980s on a Caribbean Studies Association Conference Panel to present a paper at my invitation. I took the opportunity to express the opinion privately to him that he should be wary of demands for instant rectification of the transgressions of the PNC government and instead should be gradual and balanced in his approach. There were repeated opportunities for informal discussions on a variety of political economy matters in the margins of the Conferences of Caribbean Community Heads of Government and State which I attended regularly.

President Jagan came into office with the handicap that he and his Cabinet colleagues had been in the political wilderness for so long that they faced a steep learning curve about the international economic and political environment, modern business organisation and practice, and even about the management of state enterprises which were a major feature of Guyana's economic landscape. Among the most pressing economic problems were a massive foreign debt burden and critical shortage of foreign exchange. On the positive side, there was considerable goodwill and guidance from Caribbean Community counterparts and the international donor community, especially the United States of America, the United Kingdom and Canada.

It was in President Jagan's official residence in Georgetown one night in July 1995 that I had a brief political discussion with Patrick Manning who was then Trinidad and Tobago's Prime Minister. I commiserated with him on his political difficulties which included recently concluded salary protests by trade unions, a battle with the Speaker of the Parliament, an economy not yet fully recovered from the collapse of world petroleum prices, and Parliamentary Opposition calls for general elections. I suggested to him that he should not heed the calls for early elections because improvements in the economy would become more evident soon and the vexation of public servants would wane. Time would be on his side. I thought he agreed with me but perhaps discomforted by a reduction in his parliamentary majority to one seat, he called the elections in October of the same year. At the elections duly held on 6 November, Manning's Party, the PNM, won seventeen seats and Basdeo Panday's Party, the UNC, won seventeen seats. The NAR won two seats and subsequently formed a coalition with the UNC which made the UNC the governing party.

On the same occasion in Georgetown, I met Bharrat Jagdeo, Guyana's Finance Minister, for the first time. He was in the company of Clement Rohee, the Guyana Foreign Minister. I had met Rohee some years previously in the Piarco Airport where I was able to grant him a small favour. Two other people were in the group, namely Gordon Draper, my erstwhile UWI colleague who had become Foreign Minister in the Manning Cabinet, and Kenneth Valley, who was Minister of Industry and Trade in the same Cabinet. Jagdeo had recently replaced Asgar Ally, a former economist colleague from my UWI, Mona years, as Finance Minister. Jagdeo was newly minted. I remember St Lucia's Prime Minister John Compton making fun of his inexperience during the Heads of Government meeting in Georgetown. However, Jagdeo learnt very quickly and soon demonstrated great acumen and negotiating skills in the renegotiation of Guyana debt with its international creditors. The five of us spent a few pleasant hours in discussion of work-related matters and general West Indian conversation that evening in President Jagan's residence and in one of the popular bars on Sheriff Street to which we transited later in the night. It was the start of friendships ended only by death in the case of Gordon Draper and Kenneth Valley.

UNIVERSITY PERFORMANCE EVALUATION, PLANNING AND DEVELOPMENT

APPOINTMENT AS UWI PRO VICE CHANCELLOR

On 1 August 1990, I was appointed Pro Vice Chancellor for Planning and Programming for the entire UWI and Deputy Principal for the St Augustine campus for three years. I was reappointed Pro Vice Chancellor on 1 August 1993 with the slightly different title of Planning and Development and because I had initially expressed unwillingness to continue as Deputy Principal, I was asked to "soldier on" in that post. Even more so than in the case of Vice Chancellor Preston's offer of appointment as Dean of the Faculty of Social Sciences, I could not refuse Vice Chancellor Alister McIntyre's invitation to be a member of his senior management team. We had a long history of working well together in Jamaica, during his period as Secretary-General of the CARICOM, and during his tenure as Director of the Commodities Division at UNCTAD.

When he assumed duties as Vice Chancellor in 1988, I had met with him in Jamaica and declined his invitation to become Director of the Institute of Social and Economic Research, giving as my reason my reluctance to disrupt my sons' secondary education but nonetheless provided him with my perspective on UWI's financial management.

In 1990, he returned with new offers of Pro Vice Chancellor, Planning and Programming or Deputy Principal and said I could choose either post but could not decline his offer entirely. My response was that while I preferred the Pro Vice Chancellor post, I felt that the holder would not have sufficient leverage in his home campus unless he simultaneously occupied the Deputy Principal post. He agreed with me and left me to settle with PVC Richards, the St Augustine Campus Principal, what my specific responsibilities as Deputy Principal would be. I proposed to PVC Richards that I would take responsibility for monitoring the financial situation of the campus and he asked me to additionally take charge of campus security and student affairs.

The other Pro Vice Chancellor appointments made at the same time were Professor Woodville Marshall who was appointed Pro Vice Chancellor for Academic Affairs and Deputy Principal, Cave Hill campus; Professor Gerald Lalor who was appointed Pro Vice Chancellor for Science and Technology and Deputy Principal of the Mona campus; Professor Rex Nettleford who was appointed Pro Vice Chancellor for Outreach and

Institutional Relations; and Professor Edward Greene who was appointed Pro Vice Chancellor for Development and Alumni Affairs.

The new appointments of Pro Vice Chancellors were the outcome of a restructuring of the regional university. The Council of the University had previously taken a decision to study and review the implications of maintaining a Vice Chancellorship which is separate from Principalship of a campus and appointed a Review Committee chaired by Sir Carlisle Burton, Chairman of the Cave Hill Campus Council. Other members included five government representatives on Council, namely Hon. Paul Adderley from The Bahamas, Hon. Cyril Walker from Barbados, Senator the Hon. Carlisle Duncan from Jamaica, Senator the Hon. Clive Pantin from Trinidad and Tobago, and Hon. Henry George from Dominica.

There were five members of Senate, namely PVC George Maxwell Richards, PVC Sir Keith Hunte, PVC F.R. Augier, Professor R. Carnegie, and me. The Chairmen of the Mona and St Augustine Campus Councils (Hon. L. Seemungal and Hon. G. Arthur Brown) were members of the Committee as was Dame Elsie Payne, Chairperson of the Vice Chancellor Selection Committee. The additional members were Mr Walter Edey, Guild of Graduates Representative, and the President of the Guild of Undergraduates.

The Council followed up with a decision on 3 April 1987 to commission a study by Sir Carlisle Burton and Professor Gladstone Mills and to appoint a Monitoring Committee with the same membership as the previously appointed Review Committee. The Burton-Mills Report submitted to the Vice Chancellor in May 1988 recommended functional separation and the establishment of Vice Chancellorships and a few other senior posts to assist the Vice Chancellor.

Vice Chancellor McIntyre, who had assumed duties in September 1988, reported to the Monitoring Committee in 1990. He identified the challenges he saw confronting the University as maintaining and improving academic standards, promotion of integrated research and development (R&D) activities, outreach, the need for major progress in science and technology, strengthening of the planning and development capacity of the University, ensuring financial stability, and the development of the University's capacity for external fundraising. Vice Chancellor McIntyre announced the restructuring of the Office of the Vice Chancellor as follows: Creation of the Vice Chancellor's Personal Office (with Science and Technology included); establishment of an Office of Planning and Programming; establishment of an Office of Outreach and Institutional Relations (including

School of Continuing Studies, Office of University Services, Summer Schools, Relations with TLIs and Distance Education); establishment of an Office of Development and Alumni Relations; establishment of an Office of Academic Affairs; establishment of an Office of Administration; establishment of an Office of Finance. He proposed for the 1990-1993 triennium the appointment of five Pro Vice Chancellors for the academic areas identified, including science and technology to provide policy support to the Vice Chancellor with their responsibilities being "essentially of a catalytic, advisory, and troubleshooting character" and clearly demarcated from line management functions of any other senior positions the appointees might hold concurrently.

In addressing the mandate of the new Office of Planning and Programming, Vice Chancellor McIntyre stated that it would continue the work previously conducted by the Planning Unit at the Mona campus such as the analysis and review of student statistics, staff-student ratios, and teaching loads and "extend it in the areas of programming, monitoring and evaluation". In his view, "The Office of Planning and Programming will undertake a major departure in setting up, for the first time, systematic arrangements for the monitoring and evaluation of academic programmes, and of the performance of Faculties and Departments."

PLANNING AND PROGRAMMING ACTIVITIES

I got to work immediately. Staff were recruited to establish an Office at the St Augustine campus and an Office at the University Centre on the Mona campus. Anand Dass was the first professional recruit at the St Augustine Office where he was later joined by Reanti Singh and Linda Hewitt. Maureen Allgrove and Lorna Parkins were the first professional recruits as Senior Programming Officers at the Mona Office where they were later joined by Fitzgerald Yaw. I had an able and hardworking cadre of other staff in the persons of Elizabeth McComie, Beverley Camps, Ruthven Alleyne and Sharon Armour at St Augustine and Cheryl McDonald-Sloley and Sharon Hamilton at the Mona office. Sharon Hamilton and Cheryl McDonald-Sloley later pursued academic studies and ultimately were appointed to senior administrative positions in the University.

Consistent with its mandate, the Office of Planning and Programming completed detailed student throughput analyses for each of the three campuses for the period covering the 1981/82 academic year to the 1986/87 academic year. It reported on the time taken to graduate, student dropout rates, and the average costs per graduate measured in student years. For the Cave Hill campus, the average time for graduation of full-time students in three-year undergraduate degree programmes was 3.75 years in Arts and General Studies, 3.27 years in Law, 4.45 years in Natural Sciences, and 4.25 years in Social Sciences. For the four-year degree programme in Natural Sciences at Cave Hill, the average time to graduation was 7.95 years. At the Mona campus, the average time to graduate for full-time students in three-year undergraduate degree programmes was 4.95 years in Arts and General Studies, 4.92 years in Natural Sciences, and 4.25 years in Social Sciences. The Natural Sciences four-year degree programme took on average 6.82 years to complete. For full-time undergraduates at the St Augustine campus, the average time for graduation in three-year undergraduate degree programmes was 3.45 years in Agriculture, 4.35 years in Arts and General Studies, 4.08 years in Engineering, 4.85 years in Natural Sciences and 3.98 years in Social Sciences. The years to graduate from the four-year degree programme in Agriculture averaged 6.22 years. The results allowed for efficiency comparisons across faculties and across campuses.

The Office of Planning and Programming also undertook an academic throughput study of the St Augustine campus for 1987/1988 and 1989/1990. The results were not significantly different than those for the earlier period. Costs per graduate in student years were higher in the four-year degree programmes, with those in Arts and General Studies and Social Sciences being the highest, while costs in three-year programmes were lowest in Agriculture, followed by Social Sciences and Engineering. Dropout rates for new students in four-year programmes were as high as 45.6 per cent in Agriculture, 42.4 per cent in Arts and General Studies, and 39.2 per cent in Social Sciences. The percentage of students graduating on time from three-year programmes was 60 per cent in Agriculture, 55.7 per cent in Arts and General Studies, 46.1 per cent in Engineering, 43.1 per cent in Social Sciences, and 37.4 per cent in Natural Sciences. For the four-year degree programmes, the corresponding percentage graduating on time was 32.9 per cent for Agriculture, 24.2 per cent for Arts and General Studies, and 25.5 per cent for Social Sciences. Dropout rates were lower in three-year programmes but still considerable, ranging between 18 per cent in Engineering and 22.5 per cent in Social Sciences.

Other analysis and monitoring activities carried by Planning and Programming included comparative documentation of the ratios of admitted students to qualified applicants in each academic year from 1979/80 to 1990/91 to allow consideration of the scope for increasing enrolment subject to capacity constraints. The St Augustine faculties examined were Natural Sciences, Engineering and Agriculture. In Natural Sciences the highest admission rate was 72.95 in 1984/1985 and the lowest 50.0 per cent in 1979/1980. In Engineering, the highest was 67.3 per cent in 1989/1990 and the lowest was 55.5 per cent in 1979/1980. In Agriculture, the highest was 57.8 per cent in1989/1990 and the lowest was 40.4 per cent in 1979/1980. In general, the faculties at St Augustine were rejecting 59 per cent of qualified applicants to the undergraduate programmes in the 1979 to 1991 period. The analysis for Natural Sciences at Mona showed a 29 per cent rejection rate and that for Natural Sciences at Cave Hill was 39 per cent.

The Office computed student-staff ratios for each faculty at each campus in 1993/1994 and compared them to the norms set by the University. The results showed that Cave Hill exceeded the norms in Arts and General Studies, Law, Natural Sciences and Social Sciences but was below the norm in Education. At the Mona campus, the norms were exceeded in Arts and General Studies, Medical Sciences, Natural Sciences, and Social Sciences, equalled in Law, and higher than actual student-staff ratios in Education. At the St Augustine campus, the norms were exceeded in Arts and General Studies, Engineering, Medical Sciences, Natural Sciences and Social Sciences, equalled in Law and higher than actual student-staff ratios in Education. The inference drawn from the comparative data was that the University was not over-staffed, but instead tended to be understaffed. That finding might well explain the rejection rates for qualified applicants. Other cross-campus comparative analyses included the structure of departmental expenditures, class and lecture room space utilisation, and higher degree registration and graduation.

The kind of statistical performance analyses undertaken and their potential use in stakeholder assessment of the University was novel and not well appreciated by many academic administrators. Early in the 1990s, I presented a paper "Institutional Evaluation and Performance Accountability in the Management of Change" to an Executive Management Retreat organised by Vice Chancellor McIntyre in Rose Hall, Jamaica. I noted the commitment to institutional change at strategically important offices in UWI and made the point that sensible determination of the direction, process and rate of change was conditional upon good understanding of present circumstances and performance and appreciation of future influences on the academic enterprise. I noted that UWI was unaccustomed to being evaluated.

Evaluation exercises such as academic reviews and triennial budget exercises were spasmodic, fragmented, and methodologically deficient. I argued that the University needed "to establish a system of institutional evaluation and a permanent capacity to generate requisite performance indicators." It needed to "shed its unconcern with the facts of its own situation and to ground its self-perception in knowledge rather than impressions". The presentation then stated that performance evaluation meant assessment of performance using performance indicators and that a systems approach is critical because it requires explicit attention to goals and objectives, outputs and inputs, and the relationship between inputs and outputs, as well as attention to sub-systems and components and their inter-relationships. The paper observed that the University viewed itself as a producer of quality human resources and as a social change agent and did attempt to provide some performance indicators such as number and types of graduates and listing of community involvement and public service by staff members, but that the indicators were often imprecise. It noted furthermore that some critical indicators such as student evaluation of academic programmes and work experiences of graduates were not comprehensively or rigorously generated and utilised. The opinion was expressed that UWI had held its place in the market for students because of protectionism afforded by the restriction of government funding to UWI, brand loyalty of Caribbean citizens, and financial constraints which limited students' access to international universities. The paper ended with the observation that the "prospect of evaluation arouses unexplainable disquiet in the academic community which spends much of its time on the evaluation of others" and stressed that performance evaluation is necessary for institutional validation, financial sustainability and growth.

The Office of Planning and Programming was critically involved in securing approval of the triennial budget for the St Augustine. An example of participation in the triennial budget process at St Augustine is documentary information supplied on request to the Chairman of the Technical Advisory Committee on 7 December 1992. The document included (i) recent examination pass rates for individual academic departments, (ii) weekly average classroom hours by academic staff, (iii) major grants received, (iv) student-staff ratios, (v) average weekly teaching hours per course, and (vi) enrolment rates.

A major activity was the preparation of 1990-2000 development plans for the University Centre and the three campuses. As Pro Vice Chancellor for Planning and Programming, I was involved in the preparation of the

Development Plan for the University as a whole, the University Centre Development Plan, the Cave Hill Campus Development Plan and the Mona Campus Development Plan but much of the work was done by personnel on the two campuses and in the University Centre. I had full responsibility for the preparation of the St Augustine Development Plan in which Zaffar Ali, the Campus Registrar, was my most important collaborator along with personnel from the academic faculties and departments and the administrative departments, notably the Registry and the Bursary.

The broad objectives of the St Augustine Development Plan 1990-2000 were (1) increasing the number of graduates from degree and non-degree programmes with special emphasis on agriculture, science and technology, foreign languages and management; (2) achievement of qualitative improvements in the education and training curricula; (3) expansion of access by off-campus and part-time students; (4) enhancement of research capabilities and performance in policy-oriented priority areas and research in frontier areas with potentially large socio-economic development impact; (5) improvement in efficiency and productivity in the University's operations; (6) establishing and advancing UWI's reputation as an institution for education and research in Caribbean and Latin American studies and study of developing countries in various disciplines; (7) improvement of student and staff amenities, including bookshops, campus residential accommodation, and social services.

Total student enrolment which stood at 4248 students in 1989/90 was planned to increase by 56 per cent to 6600 in 1999/2000. Proportionately larger increases were planned for Engineering (97 per cent) Agriculture (46 per cent) and Natural Sciences (37 per cent) than for Education (36 per cent), Social Sciences (29 per cent) and Arts and General Studies (16 per cent). Because Medical Sciences was still in its start-up phase, it was an outlier with a 271 per cent increase in planned enrolment.

The Plan envisaged new specialist degree options in agriculture and food, new programmes in foreign languages, fine arts and archaeology, computer systems development, software engineering, land surveying and environmental management and education. It recognised increased requirements for capital and equipment and for academic and non-academic staff to facilitate programme expansions.

The main capital investments would be in the establishment of a Centre for Language Learning; construction of a new Engineering Block; construction of a new Chemistry Building; construction of a Faculty of Education Building; extension of the Main Library Building; construction of two new Halls of Residence; expansion of the Bookshop Building; construction of a Students Activity Centre; and construction of a Sports Hall. Full implementation of the Development Plan was estimated to cost US$96.25 million.

IDB/CDB/UWI DEVELOPMENT PROGRAMME

UWI's intensive relationship with the IDB began with a technical cooperation grant of $1.3 million in 1991 to strengthen its management and operations in areas such as information systems, financial planning, management auditing, project management, manpower information systems, human resources information systems, fund raising and alumni relations, education administration curriculum development and archives and records management. Consultants were engaged to conduct the various studies and training activities under the overall supervision of Mr Frank Rampersad in the Office of the Vice Chancellor but based at St Augustine. This project was completed in 1996.

In 1991, UWI started discussions with the Inter-American Development Bank (IDB) and the Caribbean Development Bank (CDB) for capital loans and grants to support its long-term development programme. The talks began between Vice Chancellor McIntyre and Enrique Iglesias, President of the IDB and Sir Neville Nicholls, President of the Caribbean Development Bank. Vice Chancellor McIntyre had an amicable professional relationship with both Presidents extending over many years which facilitated a supportive approach by them and their institutions. I led a cross-campus loan team responsible for preparation and negotiation of the loan. The team was comprised of Maureen Allgrove and Anand Dass from my Office of Planning and Programming, Pro Vice Chancellor Edward Greene (Office of Development and Alumni Affairs), Pro Vice Chancellor Woodville Marshall (Office of Academic Affairs), Andrew Lewis (Campus Registrar, Cave Hill), Maurice Webster (Deputy Bursar, Cave Hill), and Zaffar Ali (Registrar, St Augustine). We were ably supported by many designated UWI staff members in the faculties and administration on all three campuses and by specially recruited consultants. The team leader on the IDB side was Pamela Williams, daughter of Eric Williams, the renowned historian and former Prime Minister of Trinidad and Tobago. Her team consisted of economists, architects, engineers and information technology specialists. Pamela Williams provided invaluable assistance and guidance to the UWI team throughout the preparation, negotiation and implementation stages, demonstrating in the process a genuine regard for

UWI and a commitment to strengthening its role in Caribbean development. She became a true friend of the UWI team.

The University's applications for loans were the first instances of such involvement with development banks, preceded only by small grants for research and technical assistance support. The loan preparation and negotiation experiences were a revelation to the university community in terms of the many aspects of loan appraisal and the detailed economic and statistical data analyses that were required.

I prepared for the IDB Analysis Mission in November 1991 a report on the Socioeconomic Situation of UWI Students. The Report profiled students in terms of socio-economic background, costs incurred for university education, and the means of financing, all of which were pertinent to issues of affordability, financing capacity, access, and social equity. The data sources were surveys of 155 Mona students in 1990, 209 St Augustine students in 1991, a survey of 200 Mona students conducted by Professor Carl Stone in 1987, an ISER, St Augustine survey of 340 students conducted by Professor Selwyn Ryan in 1989, Barbados Student Revolving Loan Fund Register on 136 students, and the Report of a Jamaica Government Task Force on Tertiary Education in 1986.

The Report to the IDB Analysis Mission showed that a considerable percentage of UWI students were situated in middle income and upper income categories or from middle income and upper income households indexed by occupational classification of parents. There were differences among students with respect to educational background of parents. At St Augustine, 15 per cent of students had university educated parents, 20 per cent tertiary, non-university educated parents, and 51 per cent had parents whose highest level of education was secondary schooling. At Mona, 47 per cent of students had university educated parents, 17 per cent tertiary, non-university educated parents, and 37 per cent whose parents had no higher than secondary education. Estimates were provided on the mean incomes of students and their parents. Mean incomes for students as well as parents were higher at St Augustine (US$7,491and US$11,175) than at Mona (US$5,834 and US$5,560). The weighted mean for the family incomes of Barbadian students was US$10,312.

Information was also provided on the occupation of parents of students at St Augustine and Mona. At St Augustine, 32 per cent of parents were in professional occupations, 12 per cent in business, 11 per cent in secretarial and clerical occupations, 5 per cent in technical occupations, 11 per cent in manual occupations and 2 per cent in farming. Twenty-one per cent were classified as "Other" and 6 per cent reported no occupation. At Mona, 34 per cent of parents were in professional occupations, 16 per cent in business, 18 per cent in secretarial and clerical occupations, 4 per cent in technical occupations, and 12 per cent in manual occupations. The Report also presented information on the structure of expenditures of undergraduate students compiled annually by the Registry at each campus.

Much of the work subsequently undertaken by the Office of Planning and Programming went into the preparation of the loan request to the IDB. It included the student throughput analyses done for the 1981/1982 to 1986/1987 period, the analyses of student admissions ratios for Natural Sciences, Agriculture and Engineering, analyses of teaching space utilisation and deficits, and social cost-benefit analysis on new investments in the Faculties of Engineering and Natural Sciences at St Augustine. The IDB required the University to give close and detailed analytical attention to its preliminary programmes in natural sciences which were intended to increase the number of students admitted to the degree programmes. It was difficult to convince the Bank about the academic merits and financial viability of such programmes given their low throughput rates and high staff costs.

The CDB part of the capital development project was not as demanding, partly because its scope was limited to a few much smaller construction projects except in the case of the Continuing Studies building at St Augustine and provision of computer equipment for use in distance education.

In the closing stages of loan preparation, the team spent a week at the IDB headquarters in Washington, D.C. completing the documents that would be attached to the formal application. The work was intense, extending into the night and the weekend. I think I gained the reputation of being a demanding task master, but we got it done. The application was duly submitted to the IDB. Consideration by the Bank's Board of Directors encountered an obstacle when the United States Director objected for reasons unclear to UWI. Vice Chancellor McIntyre, on learning of the snag, informed Prime Minister Michael Manley who was a strong supporter of the University.

The Prime Minister phoned President George H.W. Bush who issued instructions for the US Director to desist. The application was approved on 7 April 1992 for a total project cost of US$70 million, of which US$56 million would be loan disbursements and US$14 million counterpart contributions. Years later, I was told by an Assistant Secretary of State that the US Director was upset and wondered how UWI had got to President

Bush. He became even more disturbed about the "temerity" of Michael Manley phoning the US President. The Assistant Secretary of State told me that he responded to the US Director by telling him that he should understand that it was a case of one patrician talking to another patrician.

Of the US$56 million agreed with the IDB, US$12.992 million was for Cave Hill, US$20.077 million for Mona, and US22.93 million for St Augustine. The governments of the three campus territories agreed to guarantee loan repayment. The agreement with the Caribbean Development Bank for US$9.13 million in loan and grant funds, which would be treated as satisfaction of the IDB *pari passu* conditions, was approved by the Bank's Board of Directors in October 1992. Additional funding from CIDA, the European Commission and UWI enabled a total project cost of US$12.349 million on the CDB part of the overall project. Signing of the agreement with the CDB did not take place until 26 April 1993 because of delays in obtaining loan guarantees from the governments of non-campus countries. Additional problems pertaining to legal title to land on which construction was planned then delayed satisfaction of conditions precedent for first disbursement until 10 June 1994.

The IDB component was planned to support the development of the University's capacity in science and technology. The specific investments to be financed at the Cave Hill campus included construction of an inter-disciplinary programme building, installation of an elevator in the library, and renovations to various buildings. Construction and renovation projects planned for the Mona campus were construction of a chemistry lecture theatre, a bio-chemistry building, a science park building and a computer science building. Savings which arose during project implementation allowed for inclusion of capital works on renovations to the main library and expansions to other buildings in the natural sciences faculty.

At St Augustine, the capital investment programme initially included expansion of the Main Library building, construction of a Food Technology building, extensions and physical upgrades to the Faculties of Agriculture, Natural Sciences and Social Sciences, upgrading of the language laboratory, and construction of a Learning Resource Centre for multi-Faculty use. As in the case of the Mona campus, savings realised during project implementation allowed for additional capital works which included the construction of a Centre for Language Learning, construction of a social science administrative building and a computer laboratory, and the upgrade of the electrical, telephone and sewer systems. In addition, the IDB component would finance acquisition of teaching and research equipment, computers and furniture and the installation of integrated Local Area and Wide Area computer networks on the Cave Hill, Mona and St Augustine campuses which would link the academic and administrative departments on each campus and link the campuses with each other and with the 21 non-campus sites. The total construction and installation budget was US$45.33 million.

The IDB agreement incorporated US$2.6 million in provisions for staff development and training and research and development. Funds were allocated to finance overseas training by 115 academic staff and 35 technicians and to finance 35 visiting professors. A provision of US$5 million was made for a Research and Development Fund which would finance six pure research projects and 22 research projects with commercial potential selected through a competitive process on the basis of quality, economic merit and cost-recovery potential. In terms of student access, the IDB agreement aimed at expanding capacity for student enrolment from 2350 to 3420 students in natural sciences, from 700 to 1320 in engineering and from 350 to 500 students in agriculture.

The CDB component was intended to finance construction and equipping of distance education classrooms and offices in sixteen countries, including campus countries, expand and upgrade distance education telecommunications technology at 27 university distance education centres. Supplementary financial resources at St Augustine permitted co-financing of a few buildings to accommodate activities other than continuing studies and distance education. The European Union identified resources under Lomé IV to facilitate inclusion of the Creative Arts Centre within the scope of the building project for continuing studies on the Savannah Lands in St Augustine. The Central Banks which sponsored the Caribbean Centre for Monetary Studies and the Campus Management approved funds to be pooled with those provided by the CDB to construct a building which included a floor for the University Bookshop, a floor for the Distance Education Centre/ School of Continuing Studies, and a floor for the Caribbean Centre for Monetary Studies. The CDB component also provided for curriculum development and production and supply of learning materials and like the IDB agreement, it provided for staff training in the amount of 480 person months. Project management and logistics costs were included in the CDB agreement.

Because the University did not have the in-house capacity to implement a capital development programme of such a large magnitude, the University decided to establish a University Project Implementation Unit staffed with full-time specially contracted staff with capabilities in engineering, computer technology, financial accounting and project management and to establish counterpart Campus Project Implementation Units at Cave Hill, Mona and St Augustine. I was entrusted with the responsibility of overseeing the implementation across the entire University, including the distance education sites in non-campus countries. Gerard Johnson was appointed Director of the UPIU. He was later succeeded by Carlos Hee Houng. Other recruits were Martin Riley who was appointed Director of the St Augustine Campus Project Implementation Unit, Alfred Reid, George Stephenson, Sheryl Whitehall, Joycelyn Opadeyi, Walter Burke, Ian Bennett (IT consultant) and David Geer. The services of Walter Burke were critical in the implementation of the Mona and Cave Hill projects when personnel problems and other issues in the operating environment threatened to seriously delay project implementation on those two campuses. Martin Riley not only did a magnificent job in supervising the design and construction of the Learning Resources Centre at St Augustine in addition to his other duties but also readily agreed to my request that he render assistance to the Mona campus. Pamela Williams continued to be the point person at the IDB and Ancilla Armstrong and Rudy Ameerally the point persons at the CDB.

During the implementation stage of the projects, Pamela Williams was appointed IDB Resident Representative in Barbados. In that capacity, she exercised supervisory responsibilities for the IDB component of the overall capital development programme. Meetings, working dinners and receptions she hosted for IDB President Enrique Iglesias and his Washington-based senior staff, CDB President Neville Nicholls and his senior staff, government Ministers and officials, and the UWI leadership provided valuable opportunities for clarification of implementation issues and maintaining the support of the two development banks for the University.

The project completion report adjudged the implementation of the IDB component of the capital development programme to be satisfactory, stating that, "generally all of the goals and components relating to physical/construction works were fully attained" but noted that some aspects relating to institutional and operational objectives were not fully attained. Particular matters of concern were the assessment that many of the R&D projects were not effectively screened for their commercial potential and were more akin to pure research projects, the shortfalls in overseas training awards because staff were not released, and the absence of maintenance plans at the campuses although one was in an advanced state of readiness at the St Augustine campus.

I thought it necessary to write Vice Chancellor Rex Nettleford, who had succeeded Sir Alister McIntyre, on 28 February 2001 to alert him to the danger to future funding efforts for capital investment and research activity if the IDB final report were to contain those negative assessments and urged four specific actions to prevent such an eventuality. First, formal adoption of systems for maintenance of both buildings and equipment at all three campuses which was a proposal I had made several times in the preceding eighteen months. Second, simultaneous formulation of annual maintenance plans. Third, preparation of an up-to-date comprehensive report on the Research and Development Fund accompanied by a detailed statement on how the University intended to deal with unsuccessful projects, the University's intention to establish a system for revenue sharing in order to replenish the Fund, and the timetable for the formal establishment of the Research and Development Fund. Fourth, communication of the University's response to the issues to the IDB within two or three weeks. I have no recollection or record of any action in response to my letter.

The CDB component also had implementation challenges. Some of them related to the difficulties experienced in getting many governments to complete legal formalities precedent to first disbursement of CDB funds and securing legal titles or leases on lands on which the University had erected its existing distance education centres or planned to construct new ones. Another challenge resulted from innovations in electronic information and communications technology which were rendering obsolete the University's investment in UWIDITE, a problem that had been foreseen years previously by a Canadian consultant on the Canada-UWI Institutional Strengthening Project. His recommendations for transition to internet-based technology were rejected by influential senior UWI administrators with paternal interest in the satellite-based UWIDITE. The CDB agreed to the recruitment of a telecommunications consultant to review the design of the technology upgrade, but recruitment of the consultant and the appointment of a telecommunications network manager were inordinately delayed. The difficulties with respect to curriculum design were described by the CDB review mission in March 1995 as, "limited commitment and indifference on the part of a large number of Faculty members, who view distance teaching as an extra burden", and the under-estimation of the time required to develop course materials.

CANADA-UWI INSTITUTIONAL STRENGTHENING PROJECT

UWI entered into an agreement with Canada (through CIDA) on 20 September 1990 for an Institutional Strengthening Project costed at C$9.253 million. It was intended to be implemented over five years, 1990-1996 but was extended by two years. Many institutional strengthening projects were undertaken, including support for the establishment of the Graduate School; assistance with infrastructure and equipment for distance education; design and implementation of a LAN for the University Centre; technical assistance for consultancy operations, contract research, and business office development; assistance to the Capital Campaign and Alumni Relations; and support for the establishment of the University of the West Indies Centre for Environment and Development which was initially headed by Professor Bishnodat Persaud.

A smaller component of the project provided resources for academic collaboration with Canadian universities primarily through programming of conferences and workshops on a variety of topics including statistical data development and management, financing of education, economic privatisation, and other public policy issues such as role of small businesses, job creation, exports of services, trade and the environment, job creation, and multiculturism and national unity. The Canadian universities initially involved were the University of Toronto, the University of Saskatchewan and the Ottawa/Carleton Research Institute. Caribbean participants were drawn from UWI and from the Caribbean public sector.

The Office for Planning and Programming was assigned responsibility for the ISP in its final year. My main staff support was Mrs Maureen Allgrove who accompanied me on visits to Ottawa and Montreal for discussions with CIDA officials and Concordia University.

REFORM OF UNIVERSITY TUITION FEES

Concerns about the overall financial situation of the University and about the very low, almost negligible, cost-recovery of tuition costs surfaced in discussions with the IDB and the CDB and ultimately led to a decision by the University to reconsider its tuition fee policy when the loans were approved.

The University had begun to review its tuition fee policies since 1991 in the context of low enrolment of students from non-campus countries, the imposition of a cess by both the Jamaican and Trinidad and Tobago governments in 1989, and the special financing arrangements for the Faculty of Medical Sciences at Mount Hope, Trinidad. It established a Committee on Tuition Fees chaired by Frank Rampersad and comprised of me, in my capacity as Pro Vice Chancellor, Daisy Coke (a Jamaican Actuary), K. Dwight Venner (Governor of the Eastern Caribbean Central Bank)), and Stephen Emptage (Vice President, Life of Barbados). The Committee submitted its Report on 8 June 1991.

The Report began by providing details on tuition fees for 1956/1957, 1961/1962, 1962/1963, 1979/1980, and 1989/1990 to show 'low and static' fees which were minimal proportions of economic costs (2.9 per cent in the 1960s and 3.9 per cent in 1989). It detailed the actions taken by governments to mitigate the impact of university costs on their national budgets. It proceeded to outline governmental initiatives to provide loan financing facilities for students, such as the Students Loan Facility in Jamaica and a Trinidad and Tobago scheme in which the government collaborated with commercial banks to offer concessionary interest rate loans guaranteed by government and with repayments deferred to one year after graduation.

The Committee recommended that for Faculties, other than Medical Sciences at Mount Hope, tuition fees should be set on a Faculty basis but should be university-wide in application with the intention of emphasising the unified, regional character of the University and encouraging cross-campus mobility of students. It recommended the inclusion of capital costs in the computation of economic costs and also recommended that students should finance a larger percentage of economic costs than was the policy. The Committee then proposed a structure of tuition fees in which (i) full-time undergraduate students from contributing countries would pay 10 per cent of economic costs in 1992/1993 and 15 per cent in 1993-1996; (ii) part-time students would pay 50 per cent of the normal undergraduate fee; (iii) postgraduate students would be given a 50 per cent discount on fees as an encouragement to increase enrolment; (iv) students from non-contributing countries would pay 100 per cent of economic costs: and (v) non-sponsored students from contributing non-campus countries would pay one-third of economic costs to encourage enrolment from those countries.

The Faculty of Medical Sciences because of its special financing arrangements was treated differently by the Committee. The Committee noted the elements of the financing plan agreed between UWI and the Trinidad and Tobago Government, namely, (i) government payment of $10.685 million to UWI in respect of 1989/1990, $15.563 million in 1990/1991 and $19.498 million in 1991/1992. It recommended that (i) all new sponsored Trinidad and Tobago students, other than national scholars, should pay a tuition fee of 10 per cent of the economic costs averaged over the 1992/1993 -1995/1996 period; (ii) all non-sponsored Trinidad and Tobago students should pay the same fees as the sponsored students; (iii) students sponsored by other countries which contributed to the finances of the Faculty should pay the same tuition fees as sponsored Trinidad and Tobago students; and (iv) students from non-contributing countries should pay the higher scale of fees that had been prescribed. The Committee in making its recommendations took account of the failure of actual student enrolment to match projections that had been made prior to the start of operations as well as the projected operating costs which would have entailed substantial financial deficits and an insupportable fiscal burden on the government of Trinidad and Tobago. It recommended that no upper limit should be placed on enrolment of non-regional students and that special efforts be made to recruit non-regional students. It recommended finally that the fee structure and financing of the Medical Faculty should be reviewed when enrolment had reached its steady state in 1993/1994.

Subsequent to completion of the preparation of the IDB/CDB loan applications, I began work on proposals for a new tuition fee policy for the University. This involved analysis of social and private net benefits from university education, assembling and analysing the survey data on economic circumstances of students and relating them to the issue of affordability, assessing the current situation with student loan facilities, and devising with Frank Rampersad a new student loan scheme for Trinidad and Tobago. Anand Dass in the Office of Planning and Programming provided invaluable assistance with these exercises.

In May 1992, I authored a paper "Educational Cost Recovery Through Higher Tuition Fees" which began with the observations that the University planned a 50 per cent growth in student enrolment by 2000, that the fiscal situation of contributing governments was weak, and that the challenge to the University was how to adjust to the fiscal situation without sacrificing the quality of university education. I noted that the University's response was to diversify its sources of funds, that students should share the costs of their education through payment of tuition fees, and that students seemed to be concerned about the University's cost efficiency and the availability of financial support for them. The paper argued that economic pricing of tuition is complex because of difficult issues pertaining to measurement of the costs of tuition and other learning services, assessment of private and social benefits of university education, and assessment of ability to pay.

Adding to the complexity were philosophical principles of equity and fairness and uncertainties of access to student loans and grants. It was acknowledged that the private costs of a university degree to students includes direct outlays on tuition fees and other university charges, living expenses, educational materials, and transportation expenses. An important implicit cost component is income foregone during the period of study. The paper provided empirical examples of the considerable margins by which the starting salaries of university graduates exceeded those of secondary school graduates and of high social returns of university education, most of which accrued to the graduates. It expressed the view based on the income surveys of students done in 1989 and 1991 and the data from the Barbados Student Revolving Loan Fund that fees set at 10 per cent of economic costs would be affordable to most students, while recognising that a significant proportion of students might experience financial difficulties if they had no access to student loans. The paper stressed that free university education was a privilege obtained at the expense of those who have less access to good quality primary and secondary education, especially in situations where as much as 40 per cent of the secondary school age cohort might not gain entrance to secondary schools and less than 10 per cent of secondary school students progress to tertiary education.

Council Paper 2 of 1992/93 which presented Proposals for Revised Tuition Fees for 1993/94 – 1995/96 Triennium was authored by me and drew on the points made in my paper on Educational Cost Recovery Through Higher Tuition Fees. It stated explicitly that considering the critical financial juncture at which the University was situated and the un-wisdom of relying extensively on government fiscal contributions, "New financing arrangements must be set in place, and a new partnership established, involving the University, the national communities including the students and their parents, Governments and the international community." It described the University's efforts at diversifying its funding sources through contributions from donors and alumni, and through loans and grants from the IDB and the CDB. It also noted the efforts at reducing operating expenditures through staff reductions and utilisation of distance technology for university meetings.

Four reasons were advanced to justify increases in tuition fees: (1) current fees were low; (2) current fees represented a high level of subsidy to UWI students at the expense of the primary and secondary education systems; (3) student loan facilities existed but were not much used by students, e.g., the Jamaican scheme had a less than 40 per cent take up rate and the Trinidad and Tobago scheme a 25 per cent take up rate; (4) higher tuition fees could be serviced from higher incomes. The Council Paper proposed that undergraduate fees be set at 15 per cent of economic cost per full-time equivalent student for sponsored students from contributing countries, at one-third of economic costs for non-sponsored students from the non-campus countries, and at 100 per cent for students from non-contributing countries. Council accepted the proposals, and a new tuition fee regime was put into effect.

I recapitulated many of the issues in a feature address to the 2nd Biennial Cross-Campus Conference on Education on 22 April 1994. Addressing the topic "Education for Development: The Challenge of the 21st Century", I stated that the ultimate resource of a society is its people and identified four components of the required knowledge base for the 21st century, namely, foreign languages, world society (history, culture, politics and economy), science and technology, and technical and vocational education. Noting that less than 5 per cent of the labour force in ten UWI countries were university educated and trained and that surveys of employers reported only 7 per cent of employees were graduates, I advocated an expansion of higher education but pointed out that an appropriate balance had to be struck between the several components or levels of the education sector, noting particularly, the disproportionality of shares in total public expenditures on education. The address then dealt with issues of cost-sharing in higher education, private and social benefits, ability to pay, and entitlement and fairness.

A DIFFERENT BASIS FOR BILLING STUDENTS AND GOVERNMENTS

A parallel activity undertaken by me was development of a rigorous economics approach to estimating costs of the University's operations as a basis for determining tuition fees and government contributions. Governments had long expressed frustration at the opaqueness of the University's basis for billing them. A special committee of Council chaired by Eugenia Charles, the Prime Minister of Dominica, had been appointed late in the 1980s to consider ways of improving the presentation of the University's financial reports. A group headed by Keith Panton, the Managing Director of Alcan, Jamaica, was given the task of reviewing the current accounting methods and presentation formats and making recommendations for improvement. I was a member of the group.

Recommendations were duly made but no substantial change was made by the University.

As Pro Vice Chancellor, I decided to try and bring some clarity and rigour to the costing of the University operations. With the cooperation of the campus bursars and the somewhat sceptical approval of the University Bursar, L.B. Smith, I devised a method for computing economic costs per full-time equivalent student in the University as a whole, on the individual campuses, and in the individual faculties. The method which was adopted by the University took as its starting point the accounting estimates of expenditures in faculties, departments providing non-teaching services on campuses such as library and information services and security, the campus administration, and the University Centre. It allocated them into categories of Direct Faculty Costs, Campus (common services) Costs and University Centre Costs. A Faculty's per capita student cost was then estimated as the sum of its direct cost per student enrolled in that Faculty *plus* its share of campus costs estimated by multiplying total campus costs by the Faculty's proportion of student enrolment on the campus *plus* the Faculty's share of University Centre Costs calculated by multiplying total University Centre Costs by the Faculty's proportion of student enrolment in the entire University. Faculty per capita costs could then be used to compute tuition fees and government fiscal contributions based on the agreed percentages for tuition fees and government contributions. Significantly, this would be the first time that capital depreciation was included in the University's computation of economic costs. Initially, governments objected to its inclusion, but I convinced Prime Minister Owen Arthur, who was himself an economist and Chairman of the University Grants Committee, that it was methodologically correct to do so. This is the approach which the University used from 1993/1994 until sometime after 2001 when there was a tacit departure from common policy with respect to cost sharing between students and governments.

STUDENT LOAN SCHEMES FOR TRINIDAD AND TOBAGO UWI STUDENTS

When the Cess on students was announced by the Trinidad and Tobago government in December 1987, there existed a Student Loan Revolving Fund administered by the government. However, crippled by high loan delinquency, it had become dormant. The government felt the need to introduce a new loan facility to cushion the effects of the cess on students. In 1988, it operationalised a cess loan facility in which six commercial banks provided loans to students utilising their own funds, the government paid them a management fee of 0.5 per cent on loans outstanding, and government also provided an unqualified guarantee on principal and accrued interest. Students could borrow up to 90 per cent of the cess due and payable by them. The loan conditions were one year grace period after graduation, repayment maturity equivalent to the length of the study period, and interest rate set at 3 percentage points below commercial banks' prime rate during the disbursement period and at prime rate during the repayment period. Eligible borrowers were limited to students whose nuclear family income did not exceed $100,000. The take-up rate by students over the period 1988-1992 was very low. Only 25 per cent of the student body accessed the loan facility. The low take-up rate was not because the banks rejected applicants, according to Minister Saith who reported to Parliament on 4 September 1992 that he had posed the question to the banks who responded that no application was turned down. The cess loan facility, like its predecessor Student Revolving Loan Fund experienced high loan delinquency.

At the Council meeting in 1992 at which the decision was taken by the University to raise tuition fees for the 1993/1994 to 1995/1996 triennium, the Trinidad and Tobago government gave the assurance that it would put in place a new loan scheme for its national students at UWI. The Trinidad and Tobago government subsequently in 1992 appointed a committee to examine and make proposals for a revised student loan scheme for Trinidad and Tobago nationals studying at the University of the West Indies. Frank Rampersad was appointed Chairman. I was a member of the Committee. Frank Rampersad and I worked closely in preparation of the background documents which entailed reviewing the cess loan facility, surveying student loan schemes in operation internationally, and drafting the report of the Committee. The Office of Planning and Programming in August 1992, mainly through the efforts of Anand Dass, generated detailed statistical scenarios on student loan models for all three UWI campuses, examining projected time series estimates of loan disbursements, graduate disposable incomes, monthly amortisation of loans, and repayment burden measured by amortisation as a percent of disposable incomes. Information was collected and analysed on student loan schemes in the OECS non-campus countries, the Barbados Student Revolving Loan Fund and the Jamaica Students Loan Bureau.

The Committee held discussions with commercial banks, the National Insurance Board, the Executive of the St Augustine Guild of Students, and the Chairman took the opportunity provided by visits to Barbados and

Jamaica to meet with Trinidad and Tobago students at Cave Hill and Mona. The banks' initial response was reluctance to participate in a student loan scheme. Their stated reasons were the reports of many unsuccessful schemes worldwide, newness of the cess programme and the corresponding absence of sufficient data on loan performance trends, the lengthy term to maturity contemplated, and their presumption that student loans would be high risk-low returns assets. They indicated that they would want government guarantees on the loans. Nonetheless, the banks expressed recognition of the justification for tuition fee increases and the need for financial assistance to students and agreed to give serious consideration to any proposal for their involvement in a student loan scheme. Parallel discussions were held between Professor Gerald Lalor who was then the Mona Campus Principal, Winston Bayley, University Bursar and Director of Finance, and representatives of the Bankers Association of Jamaica on 15 January 1993. They discussed the declared willingness of the National Insurance Scheme to place funds in the commercial banks for on-lending to students, possible interest rates that the banks might charge on student loans, and the role of government guarantees and tax incentives to the banks.

The Report of the Committee on a student loan scheme for Trinidad and Tobago was submitted in April 1993. Given the limitations on the possible amount of government financial support for a student loan scheme, the Committee concluded that more, rather than fewer, students would be facilitated by granting loans only for tuition fee expenses even though in some international jurisdictions student loan schemes also covered maintenance expenses. It further recommended that eligibility would be limited to students whose nuclear family incomes did not exceed $150,000. The reasoning which underlay this eligibility criterion was that given the limitations on the possible size of the loan fund, the family income limit of $150,000 would "maximise the quantum of support which a government sponsored scheme could give to students from low-income families". The Committee took as a guiding principle the need to have arrangements which ensured that access to loans would not be denied because of the absence of bankable securities normally required by commercial banks. Nonetheless, borrowers should be required to provide security because it is normal financial practice and to inculcate appreciation of the financial realities of life after graduation. In discussions with the Committee, the banks committed to accepting loan guarantees from "guarantors of standing".

The recommended size of loans was 90 per cent of the applicable tuition fee for the prescribed period of the degree programme but could be extended by one year. Loans would be repayable with one year's grace over five years or seven years depending on the normal length of the degree programme. Noting the loan delinquency experience of the cess loan facility, the Committee stated that loan delinquency should be dealt with sternly not only because non-payment would weaken the loan scheme, thereby prejudicing access by future students, but also because such behaviour conveyed a mistaken sense of entitlement to public financial resources.

The Committee ascertained that the National Insurance Board was agreeable to making bank deposits to supplement the funds which the banks would commit from their own resources. With such a blended approach to funding of the student loan scheme, the banks would charge 10 per cent. If not, the banks would charge less than their prime rate of interest during disbursement if the government tax-exempted interest accruals during that period, and then charge their prime rate during loan repayment.

The Committee recommended that the government undertake to reimburse the commercial banks for loans in default once the banks have exhausted their loan collection procedures. The institutional mechanism proposed for effecting this recommendation was the establishment of a Guarantee Fund managed by an independent private financial institution. The Guarantee Fund would maintain financial reserves equivalent to 30 per cent of loan balances outstanding. It could be funded through public issue of tuition bonds by the government.

The recommendations were accepted by the government and a student loan scheme was introduced in 1993. The take-up by Trinidad and Tobago students across all three UWI campuses in the 1993/4-1995/6 triennium was low. Only 2,310 students (17 per cent) accessed the scheme for $20.346 million. However, as tuition fees increased between 1996/97 and 2000/2001 and student enrolment also increased, the demand for student loans expanded. By 1999/2000, the cumulative number of loans was 7,259 and the proportion of students borrowing was 34 per cent.

An issue that surfaced towards the end of the period was the affordability of the much higher levels of debt that students had begun to carry. A review of this issue by the Office of Planning and Development in June 2000 revealed that average loan sizes in 1999/2000 were $14, 080 for students in Agriculture and Natural Sciences, $14,279 in Engineering, $9,418 in Humanities and Education, $12,291 in Law, $31,158 in Medical Sciences, and $8,745 in Social Sciences. Monthly loan amortisation could be as much as one-third of gross monthly earnings of new graduates. The options put on the table for consideration were (1) extension of loan maturities; (2)

more concessional interest rates: (3) income tax relief on student interest rate payments: and (4) establishment of a minimum debt service to income ratio. Longer maturities on student loans than those in Trinidad and Tobago were typical of loan schemes in many industrially advanced countries. The advantage of longer maturities is that they reduce the size of monthly outlays relative to graduate incomes and make them even smaller as incomes rise towards the end of the loan repayment period. Reduction of loans rates of interest could be disadvantageous if it reduced the profitability of student loans and made them less attractive to the banks which might then require additional fiscal concessions. Tax reliefs on interest payments by loan recipients identified as an option are not uncommon internationally. Moreover, similar reliefs were provided on residential mortgage payments under Trinidad and Tobago income tax laws. The last option of setting a minimum ratio of debt service to graduate income would have the effect of relieving current debt payment burden for graduates with relatively low incomes and stretching out the maturities of their loans. If interest rates are compounded by the banks, they might perceive a profitability benefit to this option.

THE UWI CAPITAL CAMPAIGN

Vice Chancellor McIntyre began a major international campaign to raise capital for the University's development. He established a Friends of the University organisation in the United Kingdom and persuaded Her Royal Highness Princess Anne to be its patron. In that capacity, she visited the St Augustine campus in 1995. Around the same time, he arranged for the establishment of the American Foundation for The University of the West Indies which had Former First Lady Eleanor Roosevelt and Her Royal Highness, Princess Alice, among its patrons. Its Board was comprised of US corporate leaders and public figures and the famous Harry Belafonte as Chairman.

With respect to the US capital campaign which focussed on corporate donations, I advised the Vice Chancellor that he should have a portfolio of projects sufficiently clearly written and attractive to potential donors and offered the services of my Office of Planning and Development to produce them on the basis of submissions from the faculties and other units within the university. He readily accepted and I engaged Mrs Cleopatra Crawford, one of my former graduate students, to work with me in producing a portfolio of projects which the Vice Chancellor was then able to present at various fundraising forums in the US. I accompanied Vice Chancellor

McIntyre on one such visit to the Exxon headquarters in Houston, Texas where a Senior Vice President committed his company to financing a programme of development fellowships for St Augustine academics. I followed up on contractual matters with the Exxon office in Port of Spain. Several leading American corporations, especially in the electronic communication technology field, provided their support in the form of UWI staff development fellowship opportunities and student fellowships in their companies.

An annual highlight of the American Foundation activities was a fundraising gala in January/February in New York City on the margins of which the University would have fundraising meetings with various groups of potential donors in the boardroom of the Rockefeller Group Corporate Headquarters on the Avenue of the Americas or at some other venue in the city. The University's senior management, i.e., Campus Principals, Pro Vice Chancellors, Director of Finance and Director of Administration usually attended. On one occasion, Mr Terrence Walker, Trinidad and Tobago's Counsel General in New York hosted a reception. There, I met Paula Bowen with whom I developed a close friendship, sharing on many subsequent occasions our mutual love for jazz, Afro-American dance theatre and other Afro-American cultural expressions.

The legendary entertainer and civil rights activist, Harry Belafonte, presided over the Galas which were well attended by both luminaries and supporters of the University. Awards were made to distinguished people in a variety of fields. One of the Luminaries at the Gala in 2000 was Sydney Poitier who had long been estranged from his closest friend Harry Belafonte for some reason no one seems to know. I was told that they had not spoken to each other for years. I was curious to see how they would handle the meeting. As Poitier strode to the stage, Belafonte stepped down and they embraced wordlessly for what seemed an eternity before mounting the stage and engaging in animated conversation like two long lost friends. It was very moving to me as an onlooker. Years later, in 2005 to be precise, when I was no longer a UWI staff member, I, myself, was honoured by the Foundation's Award for Distinguished Contribution to the Caribbean.

OTHER ACTIVITIES

Vice Chancellor McIntyre called on my services in many other spheres of activity related to the University's development. One activity of note was accompanying him to the Conference and Inter-Sessional Meetings of Heads of Government and State of the Caribbean Community held in the various

Member States. Participation in those events presented opportunities for the University to update Heads on its operations and enhance the stature of the University as a contributor to Caribbean development. Vice Chancellor McIntyre was highly regarded by the Heads of Government for his advice on international economic relations and was often invited into the caucuses. We also used the opportunity to lobby governments who were not current in their fiscal contributions to the University to make special efforts to make their payments. We were usually successful in those lobbying activities but there were governments which did not keep their promises.

APPOINTMENT AS CAMPUS PRINCIPAL

In June 1996, I was appointed Principal of the St Augustine campus. I had applied on 12 December 1995 to fill the vacancy created by the resignation of Professor Maxwell Richards and had gone through the normal process of competition for the post which was advertised regionally and internationally. The appointment was warmly received within the University and the wider national and regional community, if I can judge on the basis of congratulatory letters received from academic and administrative colleagues on all three campuses, eminent leaders of the business sector like Anthony N. Sabga, Chairman of ANSA McAL in Trinidad and Tobago, and senior public sector and central banking officials like Ainsworth Harewood (Central Bank of Trinidad and Tobago), Marion Williams and DeLisle Worrell (Central Bank of Barbados), George DePeana (International Labour Office), and Jagdish Siewrattan (Senior Adviser to the Trinidad and Tobago Minister of Planning and Development). I was especially touched by a congratulatory letter from Jamaica's Prime Minister P.J. Patterson who wrote:

> "You have no idea how much importance I attach to the role of the University of the West Indies in the process of Regional Integration and the development of the Human Resources so vital to our very survival and, more so, our progress in the years ahead.
>
> I have quietly watched your own sterling support to the efforts over the years and hope that the overwhelming demands of administration will still leave you in a position to engage in penetrative analyses and incisive contributions as we chart our course."

In my application, I had outlined an ambitious agenda which included (i) dynamic academic programme development to establish new areas which address human resource needs created by structural socio-economic changes and new policy orientations; (ii) commercialisation of non-tuition services to take advantage of income potential created by the need for consultancy services and R&D services; (iii) the positioning of UWI at the forefront of the international relations of CARICOM; (iv) improvement of student services; (v) internationalisation of student enrolment through strengthening of graduate programmes and organised use of specialist library collections, and the targeting of particular source regions and institutions for students; and (vi) improvement of the relationship between UWI and campus and non-campus communities by innovative actions to widen the basis of support.

In the interview by the Selection Board on 13 April 1996, I elaborated on my intended approach to the development of the University, starting with the statement that the principal objective of UWI must be stability and growth in the service of Caribbean development and then spelling out five elements of my vision for the University, namely, (i) being at the centre of Caribbean development; (ii) being academically innovative in teaching and research; (iii) being internationalist; (iv) having high international repute; and (v) being financially strong. I stressed that there were several requirements for success which UWI should not ignore. They included having well-knit, efficient organisational structures for decision-making, service delivery, and reporting; institutional flexibility; international repute; institutional arrangements for multi-level interface with markets for research and consultancy services; and ability to communicate in major international languages. Satisfaction of those requirements would significantly change UWI, but it was the direction in which like other universities it must proceed.

I elaborated that being at the centre of Caribbean development entailed having institutional and informal arrangements for interface with various segments of the national and regional communities in order to better understand and more accurately identify human resource development needs, build a sense of common cause, and build a sense of community and community service among students and staff. It also entailed having capacity for change and innovation in academic and research programmes, ability to communicate in the languages of the Caribbean, and articulation with other educational institutions at national, regional and international levels.

I stated that internationalism is not an alternative to national and regional commitment but was instead a strategy for enhancing capacity to contribute to regional development. Operationalisation of an internationalist strategy meant recruitment of international students for financial gain and for intellectual and cultural enhancement; introduction of academic programmes and courses dealing with other geographical areas and countries; international scholarly collaboration; achievement of international excellence in teaching and research; and striving for more universal or less country-specific principles of knowledge while not sacrificing the specific empirical context of its discovery or application.

I was inducted as Principal at a quite impressive ceremony on the evening of 22 February 1997. Members of my immediate family and extended family were present in addition to many representatives of the Trinidad and Tobago government and major governmental institutions, representatives of the business sector, representatives of the diplomatic community and members of the University community from St Augustine and the other campuses. My Induction Address spoke to one of the lessons I had learnt from my study of long-run growth of nations, namely, the inter-relationship between institutional change and the sustainability of institutions which showed that evolution and adaptation to new situations and trends were essential to survival. My message to the UWI was that change and sustainability were its imperatives on the eve of the new millennium. Sustaining the University's contribution to Caribbean development required "profound, objective institutional analysis and commitment to deliberate, organised change" in the areas of academic programming, community interface, dynamic cost efficiency, and financial restructuring in a regional and global university environment characterised by both competition and cooperation.

My wife hosted a party to celebrate my induction after the formal ceremony. My mother, son Clairmonte, siblings Lynda and Brenda, Aunt Ivy, and many friends and university colleagues, including some from Jamaica and Barbados, were there. It was a great end to the day.

ST AUGUSTINE FINANCIAL SITUATION

Despite the moderately successful efforts by the St Augustine campus to better manage its financial affairs, it was in a poor financial situation in 1988. It had difficulty in paying suppliers promptly, struggled to meet its wages and salaries commitments, and had begun to resort to delaying remittance to the income tax and statutory social security agencies of the requisite deductions from staff and its own contributions. The essential source of the financial difficulties of the campus was the failure of the Trinidad and Tobago government to fulfil its agreed obligations to fund the campus. When the triennial estimates for 1987-1990 were being considered, the arrears on agreed contributions were approximately TT$38 million. They increased until around 1996 when a deal was made between the University and the government on a means of eliminating the arrears.

Vice Chancellor McIntyre and Chancellor Sir Shridath Ramphal (the UWI spin twins as some academics and governmental figures affectionately termed them) negotiated a deal with the Trinidad and Tobago government whereby the government would issue negotiable bonds to the value of the outstanding arrears to the University. A version of this deal had been proposed by the University administration during the meeting of the Technical Advisory Committee on the 1987-1990 triennial estimates in February/March 1988. In that meeting, the University proposed that government bonds could be issued to eliminate the arrears and that the bonds would only be encashed with the agreement of the government and that the proceeds would be used for investment in capital assets partly funded by external sources. The arrangement made in 1996 did not have those conditions. As Principal of the St Augustine campus, I arranged for the St Augustine share of the bonds to be monetised by sale to commercial banks and for most of the proceeds to be re-invested in commercial bank time deposits and the retention of a small portion to be used for the current cash expenditures of the campus. This arrangement, which was unlike the approach taken at the Mona campus, forestalled the depletion of the funds through unsustainable wage and salary increases and ensured the accumulation of capital reserves and earnings which could be used to finance capital works on the campus.

To avert the perennial problem of inadequately informed discussions of the St Augustine triennial estimates at the Campus and University Grants Committees, I instituted the practice of detailed advance briefings of senior officials in the Trinidad and Tobago Ministry of Finance on the trajectory and plans of the campus, its performance, and the proposed budgetary submissions. I was accompanied in those discussions by the Campus Bursar, Sooknath Lackhan, and the Campus Registrar, Zaffar Ali. We often reached consensus on the proposals with the Ministry officials who would then brief the Chairman and other Trinidad and Tobago representatives on the Grants Committees. Because of this procedure, the St Augustine financial estimates were usually approved without much debate.

As I remarked at a farewell reception for me in 2001 when I was about to take up an appointment as President of the Caribbean Development Bank, my tenure as Campus Principal began with the campus in a deep financial hole and ended with it in a very healthy net financial assets position.

ACADEMIC DEVELOPMENTS

MEDICAL SCIENCES

By 1996, the pre-clinical and clinical medicine programmes in the Faculty of Medical Sciences were going well in terms of student numbers and academic performance. However, the state of the Dentistry programme was problematic. One critical challenge was expanding student enrolment to reach the target viability number. Another was difficulty in recruitment of a sufficient number of academic staff. A third challenge was the persistent opposition of the Dental Council of Trinidad and Tobago to the dental programme and to the registration of graduates from the programme.

To get a better understanding of the staffing requirements and approaches to resolving the Dental School problems, I consulted with the American Dental Council, the Canadian Dental Council and several leading universities in Canada and the US. They all indicated that because there are so many sub-specialities in dentistry and earnings from professional practice so high, universities were in an uncompetitive position in the market for dentistry professionals. Among the universities visited was the University of Florida in Gainesville. The visit was facilitated by Professor Carlton Davis from the Faculty of Agriculture who also arranged for discussions and a tour of the veterinary medical school facilities. In Canada, I visited the University of Toronto, but discussions were confined to dentistry. Some universities resolved their staffing difficulties by engaging suitable professionals on a half-time basis at salaries equivalent to the salaries of highest paid full-time professors in other disciplines. This was not an option available to UWI.

With respect to the student enrolment deficiency, Professor Melville who had succeeded Professor Butler as Dean of the Faculty had in 1993 proposed an arrangement with the Manipal Academy of Higher Education in India through which the Manipal Academy would place at St Augustine medical students it had sourced in Malaysia but could not fully enrol in India because of government restrictions. Vice Chancellor McIntyre before deciding on the proposal requested me and Professor Woodville Marshall who was Pro Vice Chancellor for Academic Affairs to make an assessment visit to the Manipal Academy. We were accompanied by Dean Melville, Professor Prabhu (Director of the Dental School) and Professor George Nicholson who was Dean of the Cave Hill Faculty of Medical Sciences. We went via Mumbai to Mangalore where the Manipal Academy has its medical training facilities, including hospitals. We had several interviews with Dr Ramdas Madhar Pai, the President of the Academy, and many of his administrative and academic staff, reviewed academic programme materials and student performance information, inspected teaching laboratories and visited hospitals used for clinical training of medical students. We recommended favourably on Dean Melville's proposal. The scheme for student enrolment was implemented with associated benefits for the Dental School.

As Principal, I expanded the scope of the agreement to include provision of visiting lecturers for extended periods of time in dental specialities in which UWI was deficient. This arrangement provided temporary respite to the staffing difficulty. A medium-term solution was devised by the introduction of a scheme for St Augustine sponsored overseas postgraduate education and training of some of the better graduates from the dental programme on condition that on completion of studies they returned for appointment to the Dental School in the Faculty of Medical Sciences. The scheme worked well; several graduates obtained postgraduate qualifications in the UK and the US and subsequently became UWI academic staff members. The Manipal Academy of Higher Education also agreed to provide technical assistance in the form of personnel, equipment and supplies to the UWI Dental School for setting up a dental pathology laboratory.

The third challenge, i.e., the opposition of the Dental Council of Trinidad and Tobago, was resolved only with great difficulty. Under the Dental Professions Act (1980), the Dental Council is the body with statutory responsibility for the registration of dentists for practice in Trinidad and Tobago. Because the UWI was not on the list of countries from which dental graduates would be granted automatic registration, namely the UK, Canada and the US, the Council used its powers to require that graduates from the UWI Dental School pass a registration examination administered by the Dental Council. At the examinations held in November 1995, ten of the thirteen graduates successfully took the registration examination. The Council repeatedly claimed that the UWI students were being inadequately trained, basing their claims on the gaps between overly ambitious written course syllabi and requirements and actual course delivery and their view that academic staff were inadequately qualified.

I invited the Executive of the Dental Council to meet with me, the Dean and the Director of the Dental School, Professor S.R. Prabhu and Senior Assistant Registrar Mr Wilfred Permell, to discuss their concerns. They responded that they were only available for meetings at night to which I agreed. At one of the meetings, I sought to address their concerns about staff quality by asking them to review the curriculum vitae not only of current members of staff but also of applicants for vacant positions. They ultimately stated that they did not consider themselves competent to do so. At other meetings, the university members produced information from other training jurisdictions which showed that what was taught at St Augustine calibrated closely with international syllabuses and that the curriculum gaps were less a matter of substance than one of over-reach. I, myself, had independently verified the information produced by the Dental School. The Dental Council executives were not persuaded by the evidence.

After several meetings and some discreet gathering of information on professional careers, I formed a few conclusions about the stance and credentials of the Executive members of the Dental Council. One, they were not better academically qualified than the UWI graduates and that most of them had not participated in professional upgrading and refresher programmes in the profession since graduation many years ago. Two, the Executive, even by its own response to the opportunity to review curriculum vita of staff, did not have the expertise to make judgements on academic quality. Three, the real cause for their opposition was a concern that the UWI graduates would increase the numbers of trained dentists in the local market to the detriment of future earnings by existing dentists. One member of the Executive inadvertently voiced those fears in one of the meetings. Four, the only realistic approach to overcoming their resistance was the political one of reducing their statutory power.

The government responded to the impasse by amending the Dental Professions Act (1980) in 1998. The amendments added two representatives from the UWI Dental School and two appointees by the Minister of Health to the Dental Council. One of the appointees by the Minister of Health was intended to represent the interests of the general public. Most important, the amendments added the UWI Dental School to the list of approved training institutions and provided for the automatic temporary registration of graduates from the Dental School and for their full registration upon successful completion of a one-year vocational training programme certified by the Dental School. These amendments provided a permanent solution to the difficulties created by the Dental Council. Ironically, the same members of the Executive who had been so intransigent in their opposition sought my intervention on behalf of the Council before the enactment of the amendments. Naturally, I refused their entreaties.

Towards the close of the decade, the Faculty of Medical Sciences and the campus management had become concerned about fissures in the Faculty's relationship with the Eric Williams Medical Complex, especially the Mount Hope Hospital, as well as with other government hospitals used for placement of medical interns. Dr Tim Goopeesingh, an erstwhile member of the Faculty of Medical Sciences, had become Minister of Health and evidently troubled by the somewhat distressed financial state of the Eric Williams Medical Complex had begun to request financial contributions from the University as payment for use of its facilities, contrary to the agreement between the government and the University for the conduct of the medical teaching and research at Mount Hope. I also learnt through the Faculty of Medical Sciences that some consideration, official or otherwise, was being given to providing internship placements to students from an offshore medical school in St Kitts by displacing St Augustine medical graduates. The Minister of Health went public repeatedly with what I considered exorbitant and unreasonable demands for financial contributions. Eventually, I responded strongly in a statement to the media which caused a temporary ruffle in our longstanding cordial relationship but had the desired effect. The matter was subsequently settled amicably by a compromise agreement about the magnitude of a partnership financial contribution by the University to the Eric Williams Medical Complex. The issue of displacement of St Augustine medical graduates by interns from the offshore medical school did not re-surface.

Another development in the Faculty of Medical Sciences was the start of a clinical training programme in The Bahamas. The enterprising Dean Melville had started discussions with Bahamian health authorities and the Manipal Academy about providing clinical training for students under the Manipal-UWI scheme and for students from Caribbean countries to address a shortage of places for clinical training in the public hospitals in Trinidad and Tobago. There was an obvious need for approval at the highest level in The Bahamas government because of requisite financial outlays at the Princess Margaret Hospital which would be the designated training hospital. I was brought into the picture at that stage. I met with The Bahamas Prime Minister Kenneth Ingraham in the margins of a CARICOM Heads of Government meeting in Barbados to advance the discussions to finality.

Prime Minister Ingraham was favourably disposed but wanted assurance that the University would satisfy its commitments to a start-up date. He said to me something to the effect that when he makes an agreement with anyone to do something, his expectation is that they would. I responded by telling him that I operated on precisely those principles and assured him that the University would deliver on time. Operations were proceeding on that understanding when I was informed by Dean Melville that The Bahamas government was not acting on its financial commitments. I promptly phoned Prime Minister Ingraham and reminded him of the understanding reached in Barbados and especially of my statement that, like him, I held people to their undertakings. He took the point and immediately gave his finance officials directives to release the necessary funds. The clinical training programme was able to start in 1997 with 63 students from the St Augustine Faculty of Medical Sciences. Professor Knolly Butler, who had retired from St Augustine, was appointed as the first Director. This instance was just one of the several occasions in which I found that a direct approach to a Caribbean Prime Minister was helpful in resolving difficulties experienced by the St Augustine campus.

I attempted without success to get the Faculty of Medical Sciences to have collaborative arrangements with some medical colleges in London. Dean Melville, Professor Pitt-Miller, Dr Monica Davis and I travelled to London for discussions with Sir Kenneth Stuart, who was on the Board of the Centre for Caribbean Medicine which was a consortium of the London University medical schools, and with senior officials of some of the medical schools. Sir Kenneth Stuart had proposed that the St Augustine Faculty of Medical Sciences join the consortium or agree to some other collaborative arrangement. The St Augustine Faculty of Medical Sciences ultimately declined to participate probably because Sir Kenneth Stuart had a prominent role in the St George's Medical School in Grenada which was viewed as a competitor institution.

MANAGEMENT STUDIES AND TOURISM EDUCATION

During my tenure as Pro Vice-Chancellor for Planning and Development, I sought to find ways to improve and strengthen the University's offerings in management studies. Accompanied by Maureen Allgrove and with the support of Pamela Williams, discussions were held with the University of Wisconsin in Barbados and in Madison, Wisconsin about the innovative structure and flexible programme delivery arrangements for their certificate in business management programme aimed at would-be businesspeople without formal academic backgrounds. We were particularly impressed by the fact that entrants did not have to commit to the entire programme ab initio but had the option of adding courses as their interest and appreciation of their value increased through experience. We interviewed several of the graduates of the programmes who had established successful small businesses in agricultural commodities for US and export markets, provision of clerical services to government departments, and in restaurant, food and beverage industries. A Memorandum of Understanding was signed between UWI and the University of Wisconsin to allow for institutional collaboration in management education.

For several years after the departure of academic staff like Gordon Draper, Ainsley Mark, Vishnu Ramlogan and John Eckstein, the Department of Management Studies suffered from a lack of senior academic staff and from insufficient research capabilities and experience. I sought to remedy these deficiencies in two ways. One was to negotiate with Concordia University in Montreal, Canada an agreement directed towards strengthening the St Augustine Department of Management Studies. I started the discussions in 1992 when I was Pro Vice Chancellor for Planning and Programming, and Professor Max Richards was Campus Principal. Mr Errol Simms, the Head of Department, and I visited Montreal for detailed discussions with Professor Chris Ross, a former Mona campus colleague who had joined Concordia many years ago, and was Dean of the Concordia Business School, Professor Manek Kirpalani, Director of International Affairs, a few other Business School members, and senior executives from Concordia University.

We agreed on an institutional strengthening project with the following components: (1) Concordia Business School would provide Visiting Professors to assist in academic programme delivery at St Augustine; (2) Concordia Business School would enrol academic staff from St Augustine in mutually agreed higher degree programmes and would do likewise for UWI St Augustine graduates sponsored by the Department of Management Studies; (3) collaboration of academics from the Concordia Business School and the UWI Department of Management Studies in research for the purpose of developing the research competencies and experience of the UWI academics; (4) supply of teaching materials and equipment to the Department of Management Studies; and (5) a programme of joint conferences.

A funding request was submitted to the Canadian International Development Agency which approved the project and the requisite funds for its implementation. The project was successfully implemented over the next five years. Three St Augustine academics pursued graduate degrees at Concordia and several others spent extended periods at Concordia for other staff development and training activities. The academic collaboration facilitated the introduction of a BSc Accounting degree programme and an MSc Management Studies programme.

The second measure was to support some members of staff for postgraduate fellowships at overseas universities. Marcelle Annisette went to University of Manchester on a Chevening scholarship, Gwendolyn Williams to University of Warwick on a Commonwealth Universities fellowship, and Barney Pacheco to University of Colorado on a Fulbright fellowship. They all returned to the Department for variable lengths of service.

Efforts to establish endowed Chairs were not as successful. There was strong support from Mrs Judy Chang, the Chairperson of the Unit Trust Corporation, who was my colleague on the Central Bank's Board of Directors, and from Mr Arnold Piggott, Executive Director of First Citizens Bank. Both financial institutions allocated funds for endowed Chairs, as did the Colonial Life Insurance Company (CLICO). However, the University unacceptably delayed the process of recruiting candidates and the funds ultimately had to be de-committed by the donors.

In the field of tourism education, I encouraged the Department of Management Studies to enter into an articulation agreement with the Trinidad and Tobago Hospitality and Tourism Institute (TTHTI). TTHTI was a government entity established to provide sub-degree level tertiary training and para-professional technical training to people who were either already working in the tourism industry or were intending to work in it. The Executive Director of the TTHTI, Dr Patricia Butcher, invited me to discuss her idea of seeking some means by which the better graduates of the institution could enter UWI degree programmes with advanced standing on the basis of credit for some of the courses completed at the TTHTI and exemptions from some courses in the UWI BSc Management Studies degree.

I was receptive to the idea because I was part of a group that proposed a similar arrangement between the UWI Centre for Tourism and Hospitality Management in The Bahamas and Bahamian tertiary institutions previously. In 1988, I had chaired a Special Committee on Tourism Education in The Bahamas on behalf of The Bahamas government. The other members of the committee were Professor Rex Nettleford and Professor Rik Medlik, a former UK academic with expertise in tourism. Our terms of reference included "considering and advising on the range of options that could lead to an integrated, though flexible and suitable structure for tourism education and training, involving the Bahamian tertiary level institutions currently offering tourism education and training (i.e., the College of The Bahamas and The Bahamas Hotel Training College) and the University of the West Indies." After careful study of the range of programmes, institutions and facilities, and the successful experience of articulation arrangements between the College of The Bahamas and US universities, including Columbia University, the Special Committee recommended, "an institutional framework of collaboration and cooperation, including vertical or hierarchical linkage of programmes, i.e., a situation or mechanism whereby a qualification obtained at one level can be used as a bridge for entry into a higher-level programme." The University of the West Indies Faculty of Social Sciences at Mona which administered the UWI programme in The Bahamas was uninterested.

Subsequent to my discussion with Dr Butcher, I raised the matter with Mr Errol Simms, the Head of the Management Studies Department. His response was positive. He then engaged directly in discussions with Dr Butcher and his departmental colleagues to develop an undergraduate degree option in tourism management and an agreement which permitted TTHTI graduates to enter the UWI programme, subject to satisfying conditions pertaining to their examination success at the TTHTI.

FOREIGN LANGUAGE EDUCATION AND TRAINING

I had long advocated the broadening of access to foreign language education as well as widening of the range of foreign languages taught at UWI. I viewed competence in foreign languages as an important element in building international economic competitiveness of the Caribbean Community and of its people in their personal capacities as well as being an important facilitator of knowledge and understanding of the wider world. I tried to encourage academic leaders at St Augustine to provide optional spaces in their programme structure to allow students opportunities to study and learn foreign languages. Generally, they were not receptive to this suggestion, preferring to fill every possible hour of students' study time with courses within their own disciplines. This meant that there was little demand for foreign language education and training in faculties other than the humanities.

The construction of a Centre for Language Learning was one of the proposals originating from the Faculty of Arts and General Studies in the St Augustine Development Plan for 1990-2000. It was envisaged that the Centre would provide courses in foreign languages as well as courses in English as a foreign language to non-English speakers. The Centre was not one of the projects originally earmarked for funding under the IDB-UWI capital development programme. However, when savings were achieved on other components of the programme, I persuaded the IDB to agree to a re-programming of funds for construction of the Centre which was completed and handed over in 2000. The Centre started operations in 1998 under the leadership of Sylvia Moodie-Kublallsingh who had independently started to offer non-degree courses in Spanish to people outside of her faculty. Over time, the Centre was able to offer training in ten languages including Portuguese, Italian, Mandarin, German and Japanese, in addition to the former staples of Spanish and French. Participants have not been restricted to UWI undergraduates and postgraduates and include corporate clients. Many people have benefited from the courses offered by the Centre for Language Learning.

SPORTS EDUCATION

The arrival of Dr Iva Gloudon as Director of Sports at the St Augustine campus opened an entirely new window in the academic offerings at the campus. Dr Gloudon was an accomplished, experienced and dynamic professional. She developed and lobbied strongly for introduction of para-professional certificate courses in fields such as coaching and training and physical education. I, myself, had attached considerable importance to sporting facilities for students and staff in the development plans for the campus which I articulated on various occasions. I supported Dr Gloudon's efforts fully and drawing upon accumulated financial reserves was able to allocate funds for an impressive Sports and Physical Education Centre which served the dual purpose of a sports hall and an auditorium for university graduation ceremonies. The National Gas Company and the Royal Bank of Trinidad and Tobago were the main corporate donors providing support for construction. Construction began in 2000 but was not fully completed until 2002.

Another of my initiatives drew upon the resources of the Canada-UWI Institutional Strengthening Project to finance technical assistance from the University of Newfoundland, a leader in sports education, in designing and developing programmes for the St Augustine campus. Dawn-Marie DeFour, the Business Development and Marketing Officer in my Office, accompanied me to Frederickton, Canada for discussions with the pertinent senior officials and academics at the University of New Brunswick. Proposals were developed but nothing was implemented until many years later when the Department of Management Studies introduced an undergraduate degree option in sports management led by Roy McCree, a staff member who had completed his doctoral studies in the UK on the economics, sociology and management of sports.

CORPORATE FUNDING

As Campus Principal, I decided to foster close relations with the Trinidad and Tobago business community to obtain their financial support for academic development at St Augustine. This entailed spending many hours at social functions and other events hosted by companies, but it was worthwhile in terms of goodwill gained for the university and grants of funds for equipment and materials and for establishment of Chairs in some academic departments.

Commitments were made by energy sector companies. Ferostaal provided a grant for the Duprey Chair in Reservoir Engineering and BP Trinidad funded a Chair in Planning and Development. Repsol also agreed to provide financial assistance to the Faculty of Engineering. Petrotrin provided software for a geographical information system, and Southern Electric International and Powergen made monetary grants. The ANSA McAL Group donated computer hardware and Informix software. Guardian Life financed a very important programme for recognising and awarding excellence in teaching. The Guardian Life Premium Teaching Award, a MOU for which was signed in 1998, must be credited to Mrs Betty-Ann Rohlehr (Head of the Instructional Development Unit) who coordinated the programme.

SCHOOL OF EDUCATION

Developments in distance education (already described in connection with the CDB programme) were central to the activities of the School of Education. They were overseen by Dr Carol Keller, Deputy Dean for Distance Education, whose role in project development and implementation was invaluable. A novel development was conceptualisation and partial implement of an early childhood care and learning centre. This was the initiative of Dr Carol Logie who discussed with me my interest in providing an after-school care facility for members of staff. She proposed the establishment of a Homework and Day Care Centre on a project basis as a start but envisaged it transitioning to a fully-fledged Early Childhood Care and Education Centre. By November 2000, client specifications for a Child Care centre had been prepared and architects invited to tender for the design of the facility. The Homework and Day Care aspect of the project was implemented in 2001 in the existing premises of the School of Education.

The Early Childhood Care and Education Centre was established a few years later.

As Campus Principal, I made a commitment to approve the construction of a School of Education building to provide additional and improved space for faculty offices, lecture rooms, an auditorium, science and computer laboratories, and a library. I acted on this commitment by allocating funds from financial reserves and ensuring the award of a construction contract in the 2000/2001 academic year. On 24 November 2000, I convened a meeting with the Deputy Principal, Campus Registrar, Dean of the Faculty of Humanities and Education, Director of the School of Education, Director of the Campus Project Implementation Unit, Director Information Technology, Estate Manager, Campus Bursar, and other administrative and technical staff to obtain updates on the status of the architectural design. In 2001, the designs had been completed and a construction firm engaged through a process of competitive tender. Construction was completed in 2004 after I had left the University and I did not see the new facilities until 2013 when I attended a biennial conference in honour of Carol Keller.

INSTRUCTIONAL DEVELOPMENT UNIT

There was a need to address recurring complaints by students about lecture room performance by staff and quality of course materials as well as need to rectify problems of low pass rates in some courses across all academic disciplines. It seemed possible to address these issues by directly seeking to improve the pedagogical skills of academic staff. The decision was made to establish an Instructional Development Unit (IDU) in 1996 and entrust its leadership to Mrs Betty-Ann Rohlehr, a very experienced and well-regarded education professional who served as Director of the IDU from 1996 to 2004. The IDU focussed on the improvement of pedagogical skills through many workshops, lectures and one-on-one sessions with academic staff. It earned the confidence of academic staff who now see it as an essential asset in the system for assuring quality education at the St Augustine campus.

CAMPUS INTERCHANGE OF STUDENTS AND POSTGRADUATE FELLOWSHIPS

Pro Vice Chancellor Marlene Hamilton proposed that the University actively promote interchange of students among the campuses to give some practical meaning to the idea of a regional university. Her proposal for effecting this was that each campus should fund ten semester length student placements at the other two campuses. In 2000, the St Augustine campus allocated funds for the prescribed number of student placements in medical sciences, humanities, education and natural sciences.

The St Augustine campus also allocated funds for postgraduate fellowships in keeping with collaboration agreements or memoranda of understanding reached with foreign universities. An instance that comes to mind are two student fellowships for study of genetically modified agriculture and foods at Guelph University in Canada and at the University of Florida in the United States.

CARIFORUM-UNIVERSITY LEVEL PROGRAMME

In 1996, UWI joined with the University of Technology in Jamaica and with universities in the Dominican Republic and Haiti to start a multi-university programme for graduate studies in selected disciplinary fields. It was one of the projects included in the submissions by CARIFORUM for funding by the European Union under the Lomé IV Programme. I represented UWI at the negotiations which were conducted in Santo Domingo, Dominican Republic. CARICOM countries seemed not attuned to the new political realities in the management of Lomé IV, especially the role of a Spaniard as the director of programmes. They tried to diminish the proposals from the Dominican Republic and allocate an unreasonable proportion of the funds to themselves. This led to a more direct involvement of the Lomé IV Secretariat in the negotiations and a delay in reaching agreement. However, the project submission by UWI was approved.

Apart from UWI, the universities in the programme were the University of Technology in Jamaica, Quisqueya University in Haiti, and in the Dominican Republic Pontificia Universidad Catolica Madre y Maetra (PUCMM), Universidad National Pedro Henriquez Urena (UNPHU), and Universidad Catolica Santo Domingo (UCSD). The Master's degree level postgraduate programmes were intended to be bilingual, with some being conducted in the Dominican Republic and some at the UWI campuses. The specific programmes were agricultural diversification, natural resource management, economic development and reform, international business, public sector management, and architecture (tropical architecture and preservation and conservation of historical monuments). The universities were to decide on the institutional location of the specific academic programmes. The project also provided for infrastructure support, especially in distance education, information technology, and language training. The life of the programme was five years.

It was at the meeting in Santo Domingo that I met Monsignor Agripino Nunez Collado, the head of the Catholic church in the Dominican Republic and Rector of PUCMM. He invited a few of us to lunch at his home to discuss how we would handle the Quisqueya University portion of the university level programme resources if the political situation in Haiti presented insuperable implementation problems. No final decision was made. I again met Monsignor Agripino about a year later at a CARIFORM meeting in Kingston, Jamaica. He asked me to drive him from the Mona campus where he had gone to visit his old friend, Sir Philip Sherlock. During the drive he indicated awareness of an impasse that had arisen between the head of the Dominican Republic ministerial team and Edwin Carrington, the CARICOM Secretary-General, at the meeting during his absence the day before and told me that he would get the Minister to apologise for his conduct. I was sceptical because I had formed the impression that the Minister was arrogant and uncompromising. Monsignor assured me that he would arrange the apology. The Minister appeared at the session next morning, duly made an apology and was not seen again for the rest of the negotiations. I later learnt that Monsignor Agripino was one of President Balaguer's closest advisors. Presumably that was his leverage on the Minister or perhaps he telephoned the President who then spoke to the Minister.

LINKS WITH SOUTH AFRICAN UNIVERSITIES

In 2000, I led a team of Deans from the Faculties of Agriculture, Engineering and Medical Sciences and the Business Officer on a twelve-day visit to South Africa to explore academic cooperation in the fields of agriculture, engineering, and medical sciences. I was cognisant of the challenges South Africa had in soil rehabilitation and conservation and thought that UWI's expertise in soil science could be utilised. There were also several possibilities in the engineering field. With respect to medical sciences, UWI's interests were scientific cooperation and recruitment of students from South Africa.

We met with the academic and executive leadership of the University of Cape Town, the University of Stellenbosch, the University of the Western Cape, the University of Pretoria, Durban-Westerville University, and the University of Johannesburg. The Vice Chancellor of the University of the Western Cape was a former visiting historian at UWI Mona, and his brother was a well-known journalist in Jamaica. By happy coincidence, the Vice Chancellor of the University of Pretoria (a former World Bank economist) had like myself worked in the field of rural financial markets and had been a research collaborator with Douglas Graham (my Ohio State University colleague) with whom I had jointly published several articles on rural financial markets. We were able to agree on areas for collaboration with the South African universities and prepared memoranda of understanding to guide future academic cooperation.

LIBRARY SPECIAL COLLECTIONS

I thought that the Special Collections at the campus library could be a powerful drawing card for international research scholars and postgraduate students of the Caribbean. Towards that effort, I encouraged the Campus Librarian, Mrs Yvonne Stephenson, and Dr Margaret Rouse-Jones, the Deputy Campus Librarian, to add to the Collections which already included the papers and manuscripts of the world-famous Trinidadian author V.S. Naipaul and the less famous but accomplished Trinidadian novelist Sam Selvon. I persuaded photographer Garnet Ifill to sell his photographic chronicles of the Eric Williams and PNM years to the Main Library. I tried unsuccessfully to get Professor Robert Hill, the executor of C.L.R. James estate, to donate or sell the C.L.R. James papers to the St Augustine Main Library but he preferred an American university.

I also had discussions with Lady Dorothy Pitt, the widow of Baron (David) Pitt, and her daughters Phyllis Pitt-Miller and Amanda Pitt to donate Baron Pitt's papers to the St Augustine Library. Baron Pitt was not only an influential figure in Trinidad and Tobago politics of the 1950s. He became a prominent figure in British Labour Party politics and had been an important father figure to Kwame Nkrumah and Julius Nyerere who led Ghana and Tanzania respectively to political independence from Britain and had become their countries' first Presidents. I recall Lady Pitt graciously offering tea in her home and recounting how the two leaders would visit Lord Pitt in London to seek his approval of their leadership in the early days of their presidencies. From her, I also learnt of the bombing of Lord Pitt's London clinic by the apartheid regime in South Africa. Lord Pitt's contribution to the anti-apartheid struggle was so well appreciated that at almost every meeting I held with South African universities in 2000, someone in the audience would rise in special acknowledgement of Professor Phyllis Pitt-Miller who was part of my UWI group and speak of her father's contribution to their liberation struggle. I was greatly disappointed not to secure his papers for the St Augustine Special Collections.

The special jewel in the crown is the Eric Williams Memorial Collection. Dr Williams' books, papers and memorabilia were deposited in the Main Library in 1989. According to the library which inventoried and catalogued the material, there are more than 7000 books and journals and many papers consisting mainly of correspondence, manuscripts, drafts of historical writings, research notes, conference papers and reports. The Main Library also installed a permanent exhibition which depicts aspects of Dr Williams' life. The Main Library has stated that the exhibition's thematic depiction covers early years, family life, scholarship, international statesmanship, education, housing, a vision for the future, social contact and the end of an era. The Garnet Ifill photographic collection is an important complement to the material and artefacts donated by Mrs Erica Williams-Connell, Dr Williams' second daughter, whose vision, abundant energy and persistence, charm and persuasiveness were indispensable to a collection of such comprehensiveness.

I tried to persuade my dear friend Pamela Williams, Dr Williams' first daughter from an earlier marriage to Elsie Riberio, to donate to the Eric Williams Memorial Collection her cache of letters he had written to her mother during their courtship and some other documents and photographs from his secondary school education at Queen's Royal College and his education at the University of Oxford. Having had the opportunity to read the letters and see the other material, I thought they would provide additional insights into a relatively unknown period of his life. She agreed to make the donation but later changed her mind for reasons she did not fully disclose. In retrospect, I thought that she could not bear parting with any of her late mother's prized possessions. Now that Pamela is deceased, I hope that the material can be retrieved by her brother, Alistair, who is the administrator of her estate and that he will donate them to the UWI.

The Eric Williams Memorial Collection was formally declared open at a splendid ceremony on 22 March 1998. General Colin Powell, former Chairman of the US Joint Chiefs of Staff, was the featured Guest Speaker. I had previously been introduced to General Powell in Jamaica in 1995 when the University had conferred an honorary doctorate on him. In Jamaica, he had spoken of his love for the calypsoes of the Mighty Sparrow, Appleton rum and Jamaican popular foods but immediately transited to a restatement of American foreign policy and the role of its military in world affairs. One could understand clearly that in Jamaica he spoke as an American military leader and not as a Caribbean person.

Prime Minister Basdeo Panday also gave an Address at the Opening Ceremony for the Collection. I gave the Opening Address after an invocation by Fr Gerard Pantin. Professor Rex Nettleford gave an Address in his capacity as Deputy Vice Chancellor. Dr Rouse-Jones, who had become the Campus Librarian, provided an Overview of the Collection and Mrs Erica Williams-Connell gave An Appreciation which was a fascinating five-page statement entitled "Dr Eric Eustace Williams: Scholar and Statesmen: A Legacy for the Twentieth Century". Professor Bridget Brereton gave the Vote of Thanks. As Campus Principal, together with Mrs Erica Williams-Connell, I signed the agreement for the Eric Williams Memorial Collection

STUDENT AMENITIES

There were two major developments in student amenities during my tenure as Campus Principal. One was the construction of a hall of residence for students in the Faculty of Medical Sciences at Mount Hope and the re-organisation of the management of the three halls of residence on the main campus and the new one at Mount Hope. With respect to the construction of the new hall of residence, as Acting Principal I had represented the campus in the final selection stage of an architectural design competition for construction of new halls of residence at Cave Hill, Mona and St Augustine. The construction projects were to be financed by the European Union from Lomé III resources. The new hall at Mount Hope which was completed in 1997 was later named the Joyce Gibson-Innis Hall of Residence as a tribute to her services to student welfare over many decades.

Dr Cheryl Bennett, a lecturer in physiology in the medical school was appointed Warden of the Hall. Her appointment was part of a restructuring process I had initiated for the halls of residence. The pre-existing arrangements had outlived their usefulness. Many problems of maintenance and student indiscipline in the halls were being experienced. I therefore changed the remit of the Wardens, giving them more management authority and appointed a new set of Wardens who reported directly to the Campus Principal.

Mr Jerry Medford, an engineer who was a former student resident of Canada Hall and was active in alumni affairs, was appointed Warden of the all-male Canada Hall. Dr Jacob Opadeyi, an academic staff member in the Faculty of Engineering was appointed Warden of Milner Hall (a mixed sex hall), and Dr Cassandra Rogers, also an academic in the Faculty of

Engineering was appointed Warden of the all-female Trinity Hall. The new arrangements worked well.

The second major development was the provision of facilities principally for the commuting student body to have meals, engage in leisure activities and socialise. Other students would be free to avail themselves of the facilities. A Student Activity Centre (SAC) was constructed to provide those facilities. It was funded by the European Union with Lomé IV financial resources. Additional facilities provided in the building were offices for the Guild of Students. The project engineer was Mr Winston Riley, the older brother of Martin Riley who had done such a splendid job supervising the construction of the Learning Resource Centre. Zaffar Ali, the Campus Registrar, and I had a special interest in the completion of the Student Activity Centre and closely monitored its progress to ensure that there was not undue delay. The SAC was formally opened in September 1999 with a ceremonial cutting of the ribbon by Vice Chancellor Nettleford and the European Union Representative.

CAMPUS SECURITY

There were repeated troubling breaches of campus security resulting in loss of staff property, especially motor vehicles, and assaults on students on campus and off campus. My reading of Michael Clay Smith and Richard Fossey's book, *Crime on Campus* provided me with useful perspectives on potential liabilities, the importance of the duty to warn of risks on campus and off campus, the duty to provide adequate security, the duty to screen students and employees, and the duty to control student conduct. They provided a very useful campus security checklist which included perimeter control, lighting and visibility at entrances and on grounds, the adequacy of campus security in terms of numbers and training, student housing regulations, and parking arrangements and regulations. It seemed to me that there were deficiencies in the security apparatus of the campus. Its organisation and management were amateurish, its staff were not well trained, the security headquarters were not centrally located on the campus, and campus lighting was poor. I was particularly concerned that the university was not adequately meeting its duty of care obligations for the personal security of students.

The Campus Registrar, Zaffar Ali, and I invited a team of senior UK police officers (Chief Constables) who were on an advisory mission to the Trinidad and Tobago government to lunch to get some insights into what changes we should consider for improvement of security at St Augustine.

Having weighed the various ideas and recommendations, I thought it was necessary to restructure security operations (including perimeter control), employ an experienced security professional, Mr Wayne Richardson, a former police officer and law graduate, to head the department, arrange for staff training, relocate the security headquarters to a central place on the campus, and insist that adequate lighting be installed in areas and footpaths frequented by students.

An interesting aside to the luncheon discussions with the Chief Constables was their views on the Trinidad and Tobago police service. Three observations made an impression. One: the police force under-utilised its trained resources by allocating clerical duties to officers instead of recruiting civilians for those functions. Two: the practice of providing sleeping quarters in police stations was dysfunctional and had been abandoned in the UK where officers were now required to leave the police stations at the end of their duty shifts. Three: fundamental reform of the police service was unlikely except there was wholesale change in the top tier because of the club ethos that pervaded the service.

STAFF AMENITIES

During my tenure, the campus management executive had begun to discuss improvements needed at the Senior Common Room for academic and other professional staff and the idea of integrating that facility with a conference centre. I was favourably disposed but wanted to give priority to proving a campus-based recreational facility for the administrative and technical support staff for whom there were no facilities. I proposed to convert the former residence of the Estate Manger on the northern edge of the campus into a Junior Common Room. Arrangements were made for design specifications in November 2000 and preparations ensued for the necessary modifications to the building which was ultimately commissioned in 2002 or thereabouts.

In 2000, an Employee Assistance Programme proposed by Will Iton was launched. It was the first in the University. Seminars were held on Health and Wellness, Stress Management, Domestic Violence, and Violence in the Workplace.

ADMINISTRATIVE FACILITIES

I instituted the practice of weekly executive management meetings attended by the Deputy Principal (Professor Baldwin Mootoo), Campus Bursar (Mr Sooknath Lackhan), Campus Registrar (Mr Zaffar Ali) and other line managers depending on the specific agenda. Those meetings constituted a forum at which we could discuss not only policies and various activities but also review the state of the infrastructure for efficient delivery of myriad administrative services. We soon concluded that the main administration building was cramped and inappropriately configured.

It was decided that the official residence of the Campus Principal last occupied by Professor Max Richards would be converted into the Office of the Campus Principal. Our discussion also led to the idea of constructing a new three-storey administration building which would house the administrative services provided in the existing building as well as office space for a planning and development unit, and the newly created Business Office. This idea was overtaken sometime after 2001 by decisions to construct a separate building for student services, to leave the planning and development office in its current location, to convert one of the former campus residences into office facilities for marketing, business development and communications, and to renovate and modernise the Main Administration building to service the bursary and campus registry.

Two other major initiatives were the construction of an administration building for the Faculty of Social Sciences and the establishment of a Campus Projects Office. The Faculty of Social Sciences Administration Building which was handed over in 2000 provided more appropriate office and meeting room space for administrators and provided space for a faculty lounge which could also be used for symposia and similar events. The establishment of a Campus Projects Office in 2000 was intended to facilitate completion of major capital and infrastructure projects on the campus.

BUSINESS INCOME GENERATION

In 1996, I recruited Dawn-Marie DeFour as Business Officer in the Office of the Campus Principal. A few years previously having employed her for a short while as a Research Assistant, I had sponsored her for a Chevening scholarship for postgraduate studies in marketing at City University in London. She re-joined my staff as Business Officer. The purpose of the Business Office was to identify and generate income earning opportunities from teaching and non-teaching services which the University could provide to corporate clients. The Business Office produced a promotional brochure, *Open for Business* which was widely distributed locally and internationally. Ms DeFour also heard my rather negative comments on the St Augustine Campus Annual Reports which I considered to be dull, inward-looking, and uninformative for external readers. She took those comments as stimuli to develop an entirely innovative format and image for the Annual Report. She accompanied me on visits to several institutions in Washington, D.C., including the IMF Institute, the World Bank's Economic Development Institute and the Pan American Health Organisation where we made presentations based on the 'Open for Business' brochure and the new-look Annual Report.

Several income-earning activities resulted from the work of the Business Office in guiding and supporting academic entities. The Real Time Systems Group headed by Professor St Clair King in the Faculty of Engineering contracted with companies in the energy sector for provision of design systems and electronic production controls which were used in Trinidad and in their overseas operations. The Analytical Service Laboratory headed by Professor Frank Gumbs secured a contract for testing the quality of potable water supplied to offshore oil rigs.

Some business possibilities did not materialise. I recall particularly a proposal that Professor Gumbs and his colleague Dr Selwyn Griffith developed for improvement of cricket pitches used for test matches in the Caribbean. There had been an embarrassing and costly abandonment of a test match between the West Indies and India at Sabina Park in Jamaica in 1996 because the pitch was dangerously sub-standard. The next match played by the visiting Indian team was against the Vice Chancellor's Invitational Eleven at Queen's Park Oval in Trinidad. I attended that match and observed poor pitch conditions.

The Test match which started on 24 April attracted negative comments because of poor pitch quality which contributed to a dull draw between the teams. After listening to a television discussion by Professor Gumbs and Dr Griffith on the scientific technicalities of preparing pitches adequately, I contacted the President of the West Indian Cricket Board, Mr Alloy Lequay, and pointed out to him the potential revenue losses that could result from poor pitches and enquired about his interest in the University doing a technical advisory report at economical cost. He expressed interest and I proceeded to convince Professor Gumbs and Dr Griffith to do a detailed study which involved soil tests at the various test venues in the Caribbean, design of bounce tests, use of bowling machines, recommendations for pitch preparation, and training of curators who prepare and maintain pitches. The proposal was submitted to Mr Lequay. After several weeks passed without a response, I phoned him. Mr Lequay expressed regret that he failed to obtain the support of his Board for the project.

RELATIONS WITH TRINIDAD AND TOBAGO GOVERNMENT

It is a given that St Augustine campus principals will interact at least periodically and with varying degrees of formality and success with the government of Trinidad and Tobago. As Campus Principal, I interacted with the Minister of Finance, Selby Wilson, and the Attorney-General Anthony Smart, in the NAR Government of Prime Minister A.N.R. Robinson. With the successor government of Prime Minister Patrick Manning, my interactions were with Minister of Finance, Wendell Mottley, and Minister of Planning and Development, Lenny Saith. I had particularly good relations with the next government of Trinidad and Tobago, especially with Prime Minister Basdeo Panday. There were many interactions with Ministers of Education and Planning and occasional interactions with other Ministers in the government.

Prime Minister Panday and I had interacted socially, but my first formal communication with the Prime Minister was on the matter of work permits by the government to academic staff from other Caribbean countries. Staff had begun to experience unaccustomed difficulty in having their work permits renewed and new recruits were having similar difficulty in obtaining work permits which were essential for assumption of duties in Trinidad and Tobago. To try and resolve the problem, I appeared before the Works Permits Committee comprised of senior public servants. It was an evening meeting in a small, cramped room with a small, uncomfortable foyer where I met Mr Ken Gordon, the Managing Director of a major company, also waiting to appear before the Committee. My meeting with the Committee did not cause me to believe that there were any good reasons for the difficulties being experienced but rather that they were a manifestation of bureaucratic muscle flexing. I decided to write the Prime Minister on the matter. I pointed out that the St Augustine campus, like other UWI campuses, depended upon academic and other professional staff who were nationals of CARICOM countries and that most of the countries contributed financially to the University. I stated that Trinidad and Tobago nationals worked at the campuses in Barbados and Jamaica and that it would be unfortunate if those countries felt the need to engage in tit-for-tat work permit policies. My letter had the intended effect. The difficulties evaporated.

A few years later, Prime Minister Panday invited me to be a member of a government delegation he was leading to Washington, D.C. I accepted his invitation. I attended all the meetings and visits to governmental agencies, George Mason University which had developed an impressive information technology park, and the IBM Center for Electronic Governance. Prime Minister Panday was very enthusiastic about possibilities for collaboration between UWI, St Augustine and George Mason University in establishing a technological park in an eastern region in Trinidad. His enthusiasm was not shared by the UWI Engineering Faculty and discussions in Trinidad upon our return led nowhere. During the visit, I mentioned to the Prime Minister that students were unhappy about tuition fee increases which were scheduled for the coming academic year and were likely to stage public protests. His instinctive response was belligerent, not atypical of the Basdeo Panday who declared that if he and a lion were in a struggle, one should fear for the lion. I explained to him that although there had been a prior agreement at governmental level, economic circumstances had changed adversely, the student unease was understandable and that it would be reasonable to defer the tuition fee increases by one year. He agreed with me and said that if I wrote him formally with my recommendation, he would secure approval by his Cabinet. I wrote him immediately after we returned to Trinidad and Tobago, and he did as promised.

In 2000, there was another formal interaction. I had led a UWI St Augustine academic mission to South Africa to seek opportunities for collaboration with South African universities. We visited the University of Cape Town, Pretoria University, University of the Western Cape, Durban-Westerville University and University of Johannesburg. The UWI team was comprised of Professor Guru Kochhar (Dean, Faculty of Engineering), Professor Phyllis Pitt-Miller (Dean, Faculty of Medical Sciences), Professor Charles McDavid (Dean, Faculty of Agriculture), and Dawn-Marie DeFour (Business Officer). Two spouses (mine and Dean McDavid's) accompanied the mission at the personal expenses of their husbands. The UWI team was well received and many possibilities for institutional collaboration were identified. Prime Minister Panday wrote me soon after we returned to Trinidad to say that he had received complaints from people not identified about the composition and cost of the mission. I promptly replied to him, informing him that it was a low budget exercise, especially because the entire team travelled economy class and that the academic composition of the team reflected the faculties of particular strength and strategic importance at the St Augustine campus. The Prime Minister did not pursue the matter further.

I found Basdeo Panday to be a very jovial and likeable man. I was pleased to host him and his wife, Oma, in the Campus Principal's Reception area at the Annual UWI Carnival Fete. We encountered each other at many social events in subsequent years, including at a 75th birthday party for our mutual friend, Selwyn Ryan. I would sometimes say to him, "You looking good, Bas" to which he would reply, "You not looking too bad, yourself."

I also had good relations with Basdeo Panday's predecessor, Prime Minister Patrick Manning who invited me and my spouse to official functions, including notably the "petit potpourri" he staged on 19 January 1995 in honour of Canadian Prime Minister Jean Cretien who was on a State Visit to Trinidad and Tobago. Our relationship deepened during my tenure as President of the Caribbean Development Bank from 2001-2011.

My relationship with President A.N.R. Robinson started quite formally at the Queen's Park Oval at a Vice Chancellor's Invitational XI match when I sat with him making conversation in the absence of the Vice Chancellor. In time, the relationship developed well. My wife and I attended his inauguration as President of the Republic of Trinidad and Tobago on 19 March 1997. At his invitation, we attended a Command Cultural Performance on 5 August and a State Banquet on 6 August 1997, both of which were held in honour of Flt-Lt Jerry John Rawlings, President of the Republic of Ghana who was on a State Visit to Trinidad and Tobago.

On 30 October 1998, as Campus Principal I hosted the then customary Graduation Dinner for Honorary Graduates. President Robinson was the honorary recipient of an Honorary Doctor of Laws on that occasion. As was my custom, I proposed a toast to President Robinson, lauding his contribution to the Caribbean Community, the UWI and West Indian nationhood. I departed from the tradition by also paying fulsome tribute to Her Excellency Mrs Patricia Robinson for her own role in the development and stability of the Trinidad and Tobago financial system, and her nurturing and support of economists not only from her country but also from across the Caribbean. My remarks about Mrs Robinson endeared me to the President and to his children so much so that I was invited to speak at her 70th birthday anniversary function in March 2000 and to deliver the eulogy at her funeral on 16 September 2009.

RELATIONS WITH THE DIPLOMATIC COMMUNITY AND INTERNATIONAL ORGANISATIONS

Efforts were made to foster closer relationships with the diplomatic community in Trinidad and Tobago. I had particularly good relationships with US Ambassador Mr Edward Shumaker III and his staff, China's Ambassador Mme Zhang Songxian, French Ambassador Alain Girma, and Japanese Ambassador Mr Yasuhiko Tanaka.

My wife and I were invited to many diplomatic receptions as well as to private dinners at the homes of the Japanese Ambassador, the French Ambassador and the US Ambassador. Canada, China, France, Japan, the UK and the US became more active in the interactions with the campus. I also reached out to the Commonwealth Secretariat and the Ford Foundation. These interactions yielded benefits in terms of their assistance in programme delivery in the Centre for Language Learning, provision of expanded opportunities for staff development and postgraduate studentships, donations of learning materials, and funding of research and outreach activities. For instance, the Commonwealth Secretariat financed a workshop in 1996 on Issues in Education Financing attended by officials from ministries of Finance and Education. Ambassador Shumaker and Ms Mosina Jordan USAID Director for the Caribbean in December 2000 signed a cooperation agreement for public information, awareness, and education programmes to mitigate geologic hazards in the Lesser Antilles, and in the same month, France's Ambassador Alain Girma signed an MOU between UWI and the Institute National de la Recherche Agronomique of Guadeloupe for agricultural science and technology.

The Japanese embassy sponsored a Japanese cultural exhibition in October 1999, the Chinese Embassy sponsored a Meet China 2000 competition, and the Colombian Embassy donated to the Main Library 200 books by classic and contemporary Colombian authors. The British Council also donated books to the Main Library, the presentation of 100 books being made by Baroness Scotland, Parliamentary Under-Secretary in the UK Foreign and Commonwealth Office. The Ford Foundation provided a grant of $350,000 for the UWI and St Lawrence University to collaborate on a project dealing with the influence of Africa, Asia, Europe and indigenous peoples within the US, Canada and the Caribbean.

During this period, I also networked with the Inter-American Development Bank (IDB) and UNESCO. I began to attend the annual meetings of the IDB in various countries and regions, including Paris, France and Latin America. At one of those meetings in Latin America, I participated in a special forum on the business of sport at which I made the acquaintance of the great Brazilian footballer Pele with whom I lunched privately and received an autographed photograph of him. I attended several UNESCO meetings in the Caribbean, Latin America, Paris, and Torino, Italy, and served as Vice-Chair of the UNESCO Institute for Higher Education in Latin America and the Caribbean from 2000-2002.

INDUSTRIAL RELATIONS

Late in 1996, WIGUT, the representative trade union for academic and senior administrative staff submitted a claim for a new salary agreement. After delays in obtaining a remit from the government, negotiations finally began in 1997. They soon came to a sticking point which resulted in the union threatening to withhold examination marks to force the University's hand. However, goodwill on both sides, especially between myself and my friend Dr Fitzroy Baptiste who was President of WIGUT, and appreciation of the financial realities created conditions for an agreement without any work disruptions. The agreement signed in February1998 provided for 0 per cent salary increase in 1996/1997, 3 per cent in 1997/1998 and 4 per cent for 1998/1999 as well as for a regional allowance to restore some comparability with salaries at the Cave Hill and Mona campuses.

The next major industrial relations problem was a highly contentious labour strike called by the Oilfield Workers Trade Union (OWTU) which represented non-academic employees of the campus. The Union had requested wage increases of 10 per cent for the 1996-1999 bargaining period. The University's offer in keeping with the remit given to it by government and from which it could not independently depart was 6 per cent over the same period. It was the first time that the OWTU was involved in industrial representation of this group of employees at St Augustine. It had recently become the recognised trade union for them. The OWTU was known for its militancy and many of its labour strikes had violent and intimidatory incidents against management personnel and workers suspected of breaking the picket line and working.

In my capacity as Campus Principal, I had a private meeting with the OWTU President-General Errol McLeod and General Secretary David Abdullah at their request in my Office. I informed them that UWI does not have a free hand in wage and salary negotiations for any category of staff because it had to operate with a remit given by the government. I also told them that the provision of a remit was often long delayed and that revisions were not readily obtained. We discussed what conditions of service the University might be able to improve within salary boundaries. The meeting ended without any indication of what would happen next.

The OWTU proceeded to register a labour dispute with the Ministry of Labour consistent with established industrial relations procedures. A conciliation meeting between the UWI and the union was scheduled by the Ministry in accordance with normal practice. The Campus Registrar

(Zaffar Ali), Campus Bursar (Sooknath Lackhan), Senior Assistant Registrar, Industrial Relations (Will Iton) and I left campus early on 1 April 1998 to attend the conciliation meeting. We noticed on exiting the southern gates of the campus that what seemed to be union picket materials were stocked within the campus perimeter. I immediately suspected that strike preparations were being made and telephoned instructions to the head of the campus security to have them removed. The University team arrived at the Ministry, waited a while for the appearance of the OWTU representatives, and were finally informed that although they were in the building all along, they had decided not to proceed with the conciliation process and had informed the Ministry of Labour that they would be proceeding on a labour strike with effect from that day. As the University team exited the Ministry of Labour, we were confronted by OWTU members who wore union uniforms and displayed strike action placards. Later in the same day, the OWTU President-General participated in unsuccessful attempts to erect strike camps on the campus and led a march within the campus to announce the start of the strike.

Despite my disappointment with the union's strike decision, I remained sympathetic to its cause. However, an event on 14 April fundamentally altered my stance. At about 9.45pm, Molotov cocktails were thrown at my house, fortunately not injuring anyone or causing serious damage. I regarded the act as a declaration of war against me, a war that I determined I would not lose. My public response was: "The job goes on. Classes will keep going and we are determined to have the exams on schedule without disruption". The union leadership denied responsibility and expressed doubt that the incident happened. David Abdullah, writing in his 'David vs Goliath' column in the *Newsday* newspaper on 19 April, said: "The hysteria about some alleged act of Molotov cocktails being thrown at Professor Bourne's house is part of the strategy of diversion." There were also intimidatory acts like wilful damage to motor vehicles and threats against staff unsupportive of the strike and against the President of the Students Guild.

From media statements by the OWTU, other trade unions and their sympathisers, I concluded that the strike was being portrayed, if not conceived, as the embodiment of a larger battle against the government and its economic policies. For instance, the National Trade Union Council in one of its newspaper columns asserted that the UWI strike "signals new stirrings of working people who have been forced into submission by the policies of structural adjustment". Dean Knolly Clarke speaking at an inter-religious service at the OWTU strike camp injected his version of radical

Christianity with the claim that the strike was "a struggle for justice, a struggle against disrespect" while criticising the Students Union for adopting a neutral position. There was no shortage of public commentary on the strike and there were calls for early resolution and suggestions for achieving it, including mediation and going to the Industrial Court made by the Inter-Religious Organisation, Catholic Archbishop Pantin, and Sat Maharaj, Head of the Maha Saba.

The University in a news release on 14 April stated its position on the pay dispute. First, it refuted the union's statement that the University had provided for a 15 per cent salary increase for monthly-paid non-academic staff in its budgetary estimates for the 1996-1999 period. Second, it refuted the union's statement which had been widely publicised that academic staff had been granted a 27 per cent salary increase by pointing out that the agreed salary increases were 0 per cent for 1996/97, 3 per cent for 1997/1998 and 4 per cent for 1998/1999. Third, the Industrial Court had in 1993 declared that the relevant pay comparator for determination of non-academic staff was the Trinidad and Tobago public service and not the UWI academic staff. Fourth, the UWI counter offer was fair and reasonable for several reasons: (a) the lump-sum offer of $1000 for 1996 was equivalent to percentage increases ranging from 2.5 per cent to 5.0 per cent of salary, with the percentage increases being larger for the lower paid employees; (b) the salary increases offered for 1997 and 1998 were 2 per cent and 4 per cent respectively; (c) monthly paid staff received total salary increases of 7 per cent for 1993-1996; (d) UWI non-academic staff compared favourably with public servants who received $4000 in bonds for 1990-1995 and obtained a 5 per cent salary increase for 1996-1998. Fifth, it pointed out that UWI non-academic staff received benefits not available elsewhere in the economy, such as tuition-free access to university education for them and an unlimited number of their dependents. Sixth, the University was willing to subject its case to independent arbitration.

The OWTU adamantly refused to go arbitration or to the Industrial Court. Its Consultant, Joe Young, said that they had gone down that road before with little to show for it: only a 2 per cent salary increase for 1985-1994 and a 7 per cent increase in 1996. The Clerical and Commercial Workers Union also came out against the proposals for mediation.

I drew on my knowledge of the dynamics of strikes and disruptions of labour services based on my academic research and participation in union activities early in my career to fashion a strategic response to the strike. I knew that the balance of power shifts in favour of the employer if income losses by the employer are minimised. I also knew that the balance of power shifts against the union the longer is the duration of the strike because of the adverse effects on worker incomes and their increasing doubts about the likelihood of success. I factored in my knowledge that while union leaders were typically well remunerated, union members were usually unable to obtain strike relief subventions to compensate for loss of earned income because Strike Funds rarely existed. Furthermore, workers on strike usually had to meet the costs of food, union jerseys and other picket line expenses out of their own pockets. The strategy therefore was a straightforward one: maintain academic services and conclude the examination cycle so that the implicit "income losses" from student dis-satisfaction were minimised.

With the cooperation of the Students Guild which stoutly resisted entreaties, condemnations and threats from the union and its sympathisers, evening classes which would normally be held on campus were transferred to off-campus locations, namely the Hugh Wooding Law School and the St Augustine Senior Comprehensive School. Opening hours of the library were adjusted. The Students Guild also initiated arrangements for students to attend laboratory and computer sessions. Attempts to disrupt those services through bomb scares in relation to the library and examination centres were effectively countered by obtaining and implementing advice from the Trinidad and Tobago Defence Force on precautionary security measures that would not only prevent occurrences but would serve to reassure students and staff. In that regard, I was able to draw upon my relationship with Colonel Norris Baden-Semper, who on retirement from the army had become head of security at the Central Bank of Trinidad and Tobago. An attempt was made to disrupt electricity supply to the campus by sabotage of the University's electricity sub-station which was located outside the southern perimeter. This was quickly negated by arranging with the government to provide alternative electricity distribution services to the campus. The good relations I had cultivated between the campus and the government was of inestimable value in securing favourable responses to our request for assistance.

I convened daily meetings with my senior management colleagues and the head of security to monitor the situation and make warranted adjustments in operations. Will Iton, with his expert knowledge of industrial relations law and labour union practice, provided much valuable advice and support to the management team. On one occasion, I widened the attendance to include heads of academic departments but learnt subsequently that a participant had revealed our plans to the OWTU and had begun to spread rumours that the campus was being militarised. That information led me to restrict attendance at the meetings to the original participants. There is no doubt that some academic colleagues were on the side of the OWTU. I heard from none of them during the early period of the strike, not even a word of concern when my house was fire-bombed. However, when it was becoming apparent that the dynamics of the strike had shifted decisively against the union, one of them tried to reach me by phone, presumably to broker a compromise or a face-saving deal for the union. Other people connected to the regional trade union movement were also inveigled to communicate with me. An attempt was made to get Vice Chancellor McIntyre who I had kept fully informed to come to St Augustine to intercede in the strike, but I dissuaded him from coming.

The academic year ended on time with students completing their examinations as scheduled. As anticipated, the OWTU lost its leverage on the university community and was impelled to return to the negotiating table at the Ministry of Labour. The negotiations ended with an agreement between the university and the OWTU for salary increases consistent with the University's offer. The strike should not have happened. I surmise that the OWTU chose the University as a proxy combatant in its offensive against the government on the mistaken assumption that the University was a soft target. The University members of the union were the collateral damage of the three-month-long strike, the "Mother of all Strikes" as Will Iton labelled it.

POLITICAL AND ROYAL VISITORS

Jean Bertrand Aristide visited the St Augustine campus one Sunday morning in 1992. He was at the time an exiled President of Haiti. Aristide was popularly elected in 1990 in the first democratic election held in Haiti since the dictatorships of the Francois Duvalier and Jean-Claude Duvalier. However, he was overthrown by the military in September 1991 and Haiti was ruled by a military junta headed by General Raoul Cedras and a titular President Émile Jonassaint.

In the absence of Professor Max Richards, the Campus Principal, I met with President Aristide and his advisers in the Board Room of the Institute of International Relations. Our discussions were about his intentions of returning to Haiti and the support he was seeking from CARICOM. As it turned out, mass emigration of Haitians to the US and reports of human hardships in Haiti, created international pressure for the removal of the military junta and the resumption of Aristide's presidency.

The United Nations in 1994 approved the use of force and US President Bill Clinton authorised an American invasion scheduled to begin on 19 September 1994. Clinton mandated former US President Jimmy Carter, Senator Sam Nunn and General Colin Powell to meet with the Haitian junta to negotiate terms of its relinquishment of power. Negotiations held between 17-19 September concluded with the acceptance of the US proposals for the unopposed arrival of American military forces and the junta's surrender of power by 15 October 1994. Aristide returned to office and served until 1996 when he was succeeded by Rene Preval.

I met President Aristide again at the annual meeting of CARICOM heads of government in The Bahamas. We had a leisurely stroll during one of the refreshment breaks, reminisced about our meeting at St Augustine and talked about some of the major items on the CARICOM agenda, especially the matter of crime and security linked to the international trade in narcotics on which discussions had stalled. I also met with him in CARICOM forums during his second Presidency from 2001-2004 when he was once more overthrown by the military.

Shortly after Aristide's visit to St Augustine, I received a visit from a young Cuban Minister of Government. I think he was the Minister of Foreign Trade. We had a long discussion, but I did not discern the purpose of his visit other than to secure the goodwill of people in the rest of the Caribbean. I was curious about a gap in his account of his post-university life and asked the question. With some reluctance, he told me that he had served with Cuban forces in the liberation war in Angola.

The last visit of note during my tenure as Campus Principal was that of His Royal Highness the Prince of Wales, Prince Charles, on 22 February 2000. Official welcome remarks were given by Vice Chancellor Rex Nettleford. The Prince delivered an address on the links between British universities and UWI, the Commonwealth and Youth, and Young Business in Trinidad and Tobago. He collaborated with the local business community to launch the Youth Business Trust which is intended to improve access of young people to business loans and provide them with mentorship. I made closing remarks at the Welcome Ceremony. Prince Charles toured the campus, met members of the staff and the student body, and planted a commemorative tree. I sensed that he was especially delighted to interact with the students. A few years later when I was President of the Caribbean Development Bank, and we were both attending a Commonwealth Day function at Marlborough House in London, we exchanged pleasant reminiscences about his visit to St Augustine.

GRADUATION DINNER SPEECHES

The St Augustine campus tradition of speeches by the Campus Principal as host of the annual graduation dinners held in honour of the Honorary Graduates provided me with the opportunity to pay tribute to the Chancellor and Vice Chancellor in addition to the Honorary Graduates. I was pleased to say the following:

30 OCTOBER1998

My wife and I are greatly honoured by your presence and do hope that you are having an enjoyable time.

This is the 50th anniversary year of the University. During more than 40 years of graduation ceremonies, tens of thousands of graduates have marked the fulfilment of their educational aspirations and have embarked on a variety of careers with much expectancy and hope. From the very beginning to now, UWI graduates may have justifiable pride in the international worth of their achievements.

For the last seven years, I have watched graduates processing to receive their diplomas from the Chancellor. I have observed the dawning of their smiles, especially the ladies, as they are greeted by Sir Shridath. Chancellor, I have begun to wonder whether the prospect of your handshake, your congratulatory words and your own radiant smile is not a motivating factor. It is evident that you make their graduation memorable. You make their day.

Ladies and Gentlemen, a Toast to the Chancellor.

As a teenager in 1962, I helped to start a coffee house called Itabo in Georgetown, Guyana. It was a place for intellectual discourse and artistic endeavours. In 1963, a slim, elegant young man paid us a visit and talked about culture and politics. That man was and still is a trade union educator. He is a scholar. A political scientist. A philosopher. A bit of a historian. A man of inward stretch and outward reach. A creative man. An artistic man. A choreographer. A dancer. King Kumina. A Renaissance man. Ladies and gentlemen, there is only one Renaissance man in the West Indies. He is to be found at UWI in the Office of the Vice Chancellor.

I ask you to raise your glasses in a toast to Vice Chancellor Rex Nettleford.

Excellencies, Ladies and Gentlemen, permit me to depart from convention in my next toast. It is to a lady of importance to the development of Caribbean economics. Mrs Patricia Robinson in her capacity as Director of Research at the Central Bank of Trinidad and Tobago in the 1960s and early 1970s by her own writings and lively, very lively, participation in regional conferences helped to shape our knowledge of the financial sector. More than that, she was a source of advice, encouragement, incisive and constructive criticism, and support to many who have since advanced in their professions. Among them are Professor Clive Thomas, Dr Maurice Odle, Jerry Hospedales, Henry Jeffers and me. It was always pleasant and productive to conduct research at the Central Bank. We could depend upon Mrs Robinson's technical help, her good humoured graciousness, and her invitations to lunch at Gaylords. Mrs Robinson, may I take this opportunity to thank you for nurturing our profession during those critical early years. A Toast to Her Excellency.

Chancellor, our 50th anniversary convocation last week was very special, not least for the pride and joy reflected through so many generations of alumni. As I watched the greetings and celebrations on campus, in hotel lobbies, and at Prime Minister Patterson's splendid reception, it dawned on me that I was not witnessing a mere university re-union. *It was a homecoming*. I realised that for all those 50 years, UWI was building the West Indian family. A West Indian community. People with shared values, common purpose, and abiding affinity for each other. His Excellency President Robinson has been fully engaged in the construction of the West Indian community for a good portion of those 50 years. His immense efforts have been primarily at the political level and in political forums but through his involvement in the governance of the University and by his writings and lectures, he has also contributed to the intellectual infrastructure of West Indian nationhood. It is with deep humility that I ask you to raise your glasses in a toast to President Robinson, Doctor of Laws, *Honoris Causa*.

31 OCTOBER 1998

My wife, Pamela, and I are gratified by your presence this evening. We do hope that you are enjoying yourselves.

The graduation ceremonies are of more than usual importance this year. As signified by the remarkable cake on display earlier, the University is celebrating its 50th birthday. Graduates of this year are golden jubilee graduates. The high quality of their performance perhaps suggests that they were cognisant of this fact.

We in the University always eagerly anticipate the infectious goodwill, joy and energy with which our Chancellor imbues graduation ceremonies. Sir Shridath is our energiser.

Many of you may also know of his tremendous leadership contributions to Caribbean unity and development, to the enviable place which the Caribbean occupies in world affairs, and to the global quest for socio-economic justice and sustainable development. I need make reference only to his own strong, determined leadership of the Commonwealth and the world in ending apartheid in South Africa. Strong and determined even in the face of the famous handbag once wielded mightily from No. 10 Downing Street, London.

But there is a side to Sir Shridath which I only saw a few weeks ago. At the first meeting of the College of Caribbean Negotiators, Sir Shridath sat quietly for two days, almost silent by his standards, intervening purposely only to advise, guide and encourage the cadre of negotiators being readied for what may well turn out to be the most decisive set of economic negotiations for 21st century Caribbean. He was the embodiment of the leader expressing confidence and instilling confidence. A Caribbean leader of this generation preparing those of the future. Ladies and Gentlemen, I offer a toast to Sir Shridath Ramphal, Chancellor, Statesman and Leader.

Last night I spoke of the West Indian Renaissance man who is now our Vice Chancellor, Professor the Honourable R.M. Nettleford. Formal title. Formal Respect. But Chancellor, Professor the Honourable Nettleford is also a man of the people and to the people of the Caribbean, he is Rex. In Jamaica, he is Mr Nettleford. "Rex" and "Mr" applied to Vice Chancellor Nettleford by Caribbean people convey much more than any formal titles will ever convey. They convey infinite respect, endless regard and affection, pride and hope.

There is a story which speaks eloquently of these sentiments. Rex Nettleford having surrendered his wallet to a robber in downtown Kingston, indignantly refused to surrender his watch. "He who steals my purse, steals trash but not my watch." As Nettleford protested, there was instant voice recognition by the robber who apologised profusely, returned the wallet and offered safe passage out of the area. "Mr Nettleford, Sah, Ah din know was you." Vice

Chancellor Rex, we at St Augustine do not need to offer you safe passage. Instead, we offer our unqualified commitment to support you in your leadership of the regional university. Ladies and Gentlemen, a Toast to Vice Chancellor Nettleford.

Emerson said: "An Institution is the lengthened shadow of a man." Anthony Sabga, master entrepreneur, indeed casts a long shadow. The institution is ANSA McAL. Here is a man whose business prowess is legendary and evident in the growth of corporate enterprise in Trinidad and Tobago and in other West Indian countries. A man whose life of hard work and responsibility began long before he attained manhood. A man who built a business empire from scratch. I sometimes read biographies of business titans such as Henry Ford and Pierpont Morgan. They all seem to have the following characteristics: acute intelligence, insight, decisiveness, determination, a sense of mission, and later, recognition that their work and actions matter to their country. Ladies and Gentlemen, these characteristics are present in the man we honoured today with the degree of Doctor of Laws, Honoris Causa. A Toast to Mr Anthony Sabga.

Chancellor, the University awarded the degree of Doctor of Letters, Honoris Causa to a long-distinguished man of letters at whose feet the young Nettleford once sat. "Life is a stage, and we all have a part to play", so said the calypsonian, Maestro. Whether as writer, director, actor, professor, Dr Errol Hill with his jaunty stride must have been a compelling figure on whatever stage of life he chose to play. No words of mine can do justice to a career of such enormous value to the spirit of man. Chancellor, I simply move a Toast to the great Errol Hill.

CHANGES IN THE EXECUTIVE MANAGEMENT TEAM

The membership of the Executive Management Team began to change in 1999. Zaffar Ali retired from his post as Campus Registrar in 1999 and was succeeded by Will Iton. Professor Baldwin Mootoo, having been appointed Pro Vice Chancellor for Graduate Studies and Research in 2000, relinquished the post of Deputy Principal. Professor Bridget Brereton was appointed Deputy Principal. Sooknath Lackhan in a letter dated 24 January 2000 resigned from the post of Campus Bursar for personal reasons, which he explained to me centred on serious health challenges he had begun to experience. Mrs Lylla Bada was subsequently appointed as Campus Bursar.

ECONOMIC RESEARCH AND ADVICE

EDUCATION ECONOMICS AND POLICY

Perhaps unsurprisingly, I began to write on the economics of education in a wider context than the University of the West Indies. In 1995, I was commissioned by the World Bank to do a study of Costs and Financing of Education in St Vincent and the Grenadines. The Report submitted in June 1995 began by noting the student enrolment shares of government institutions in the education system, specifically 97 per cent of primary school pupils, 48 per cent of secondary school pupils, and 100 per cent of post-secondary students. The government assisted private schools financially through monetary grants, payment of salaries and wages for a limited number of teachers in "assisted" schools, and payment of tuition fees for students in those schools. Expenditures on education were an increasing percentage of gross domestic product between 1988 and 1993. Atypically for the Caribbean, primary education received the largest share in the total public expenditure budget for education. The Report identified several issues pertaining to resource efficiency. They included rising levels of administrative and general expenditures relative to total recurrent expenditures, rising real unit costs, sparse spatial distribution of the school age population and its correlates of teacher-pupil ratios in excess of prescribed norms and under-sized classes.

In "Educating West Indian Society: Education for All" written in October 1998 in honour of Alister McIntyre, I approached the topic of education more generally. The first cluster of points dealt with the under-provisioning of education services in the Caribbean evidenced by minimal access to pre-schooling, low transition rates from primary schooling to secondary schooling, low secondary enrolment rates, low transition rates from secondary to tertiary level education, and limited facilities for adult education. A substantial part of the paper dealt with the question of what kind of education for all. The answer posits that the question is about minimum education requirements taking account of the context, relevance and quality of education. The paper points to several important contextual factors, notably the closer integration of the Caribbean in the global economy, the homogeneity of political value systems, global integration of production of goods and services, the dominance of science and scientific products in investment, production and consumption, and the openness of Caribbean domestic and export markets to competition. Within that context, the minimum requirements for coping well in the global environment were international communication ability, scientific and technological literacy, and environmental understanding and awareness. The paper suggested that Caribbean countries should aim at achieving educational expenditures equivalent to 23 per cent of gross national product. Because private suppliers are "a market-driven important means of making education for all affordable", governments should encourage, assist, guide and regulate private providers of educational services.

The relevance of the global environment on education policy was pursued specifically in relation to banking industry professionals in an address to the 14th World Conference of Banking Institutes in April 2001. The global features that I identified for that audience were the extraordinary growth in world trade between 1981 and 2000; unprecedented voluntary geographical movement of people for work and recreation; trans-border capital movements, openness of financial markets, and multiplicity of financial transactions; rapid international transference and adoption of institutional design and policies; and the emergence of international regulatory standards and regulatory organisation. Several explanations were offered for those developments in the world economy. First, world economic growth was sustained over the medium term. Second, limits to growth of firms in national markets made firms outward-looking. Third, many countries became committed to the removal of border controls on movement of capital, goods and services and people. Fourth, innovations in production technology facilitated global sourcing of inputs and geographical dispersion of production within firms. Fifth, information and communications technology had a pervasive influence on knowledge and on transmission and communication costs, and also minimised the significance of time zone differences. I suggested that globalisation should be seen as a continuing process.

From this perspective of the global environment, I proposed that the training for bankers should include six elements. One element is knowledge of the variety of corporate organisational structures and production structures. The second is familiarity with a variety of financial instruments. Third is knowledge of financial markets worldwide. Fourth is knowledge and understanding of the cultures of at least the major trading and financial countries. Fifth is acquisition of foreign language skills. My recommendations included resource pooling among training institutions, closer articulation between them and universities, and networking with economic policy authorities.

In a graduation address at the National Institute of Higher Education, Research, Science and Technology in October 1997, I stressed the desirability of striking an appropriate balance between educational provisions at university level and provisions at other levels in the tertiary system. While a cadre of people with the highest levels of education was important, properly functioning societies required a cadre of people in the middle segment of the education and training system and the middle of the educational hierarchy. This was a matter on which I had written extensively in my CARICOM publication Caribbean Development to the Year 2000 to the effect that there would be serious gaps in the range of education and skills were there to be sole reliance on the university sector. It also made sense from a cost-effectiveness perspective to expand educational opportunities through community colleges and to facilitate the entry of their graduates to universities.

In a Feature Address to the International Congress on Challenges to Education: Balancing Unity and Diversity in a Changing World in Aruba in July 1996, I had turned my attention to the subject of international cooperation and competition in higher education. I observed that higher education has always manifested elements of both international cooperation and international competition. I then referred to the elements and concepts of internationalisation identified by modern writers on the subject, one of which is the corporate model which posits that institutions seek to enhance their competitive position and status, another being the liberal model which emphasises cooperation for enhancing global consciousness and competence. I pointed to four influences on internationalisation in higher education: expansion of education providers within countries; financial pressures and income growth objectives; globalisation; and the development and spread of electronic technology.

Turning to competition and cooperation for academic faculty, I observed that developing counties are primarily buyers rather than suppliers in international academic labour markets where they are at a competitive disadvantage because of gaps in remuneration between their institutions and the institutions in developed countries. They could address this disadvantage by cooperative arrangements for staff development and recruitment. With respect to competition and cooperation for students, universities in developed countries are the most active, competing through recruitment missions, alumni networks, tuition fees discounts and other financial aid, introduction of programmes and courses tailored to international students, use of distance education technology, and public advertisements. Lastly, I dealt with contract research and consultancies in which international cooperation could expand opportunities and generate demand for students, staff exposure, market entry, and contract negotiation skills in universities in developing countries.

MONETARY POLICY

CENTRAL BANK OF TRINIDAD AND TOBAGO

I was a member of the Board of Directors of the Central Bank of Trinidad and Tobago from 1987-2000, which spanned periods of government by the PNM, NAR, and UNC. The Central Bank was ably led by its various Governors Dr Euric Bobb, Mr William Demas, Mr Ainsworth Harewood and Dr Winston Dookeran, all of whom were accomplished economists with sound understanding of the national, regional and international economic environment. There was also an excellent cadre of senior management personnel, particularly Dr Terrence Farrell, Mr Jerry Hospedales, and Ms Amoy Chang Fong who served as Deputy Governors, Mr Henry Jeffers as Inspector of Banks, and Mrs Lucille Mair as Bank Secretary and Head of the Legal Department. On the Board of Directors were Mr Carlyle Greaves and Mr John Andrews representing the Ministry of Finance, and Mrs Judy Chang, a senior and well-regarded member of the accountancy profession. I chaired the Audit Committee of the Bank. It was a tumultuous time for management of the financial sector. The Central Bank had to deal with ongoing matters from the collapse of finance companies in the 1980s and solvency questions involving the National Commercial Bank, Workers Bank, and the People's Cooperative Bank which were ultimately resolved by a process of amalgamation and consolidation and establishment of a new commercial banking entity named First Citizens Bank which initially received financial support and close supervision from the Central Bank. It also had to regularise critical asset transfers resulting from the sale in London of Barclays Bank shares to CL Financial Holdings.

CUBA

Throughout the 1990-2001 period, I continued to work on financial sector issues. Remarkably, I was a member of a three-person team which visited Cuba in November 1997. The Cuban government wanted the help of central banks in friendly Caribbean countries. The other members were Colin

Bullock from the Bank of Jamaica and the Governor of the Central Bank of Venezuela. I was assigned by the Central Bank of Trinidad and Tobago where I was a member of the Board of Directors. Because the Central Bank of Trinidad and Tobago certainly had experienced and expert staff who could have been assigned, I assumed it desired to establish some distance from the actual mission.

The context of our advisory mission was the intention of the Cuban government to liberalise its economic system by introducing several market elements into its otherwise centrally managed economic system. At the time, the Cuban tourist industry had not been developed. Its airport facilities were rudimentary. Its fleet of motorised vehicles was very old. There were visible shortages of consumer goods. The foreign exchange rate pegs were idiosyncratic: a US dollar exchanged for one Cuban peso, but a Canadian dollar exchanged for 1.25 Cuban pesos. But there was a strong commitment to selective opening of the economy evidenced a few years later when I revisited Havana. There was a large impressively constructed new international airport. Tourism resorts had been developed, and there was successful marketing of Cuba's tourism in Europe and Canada. The fleet of motor vehicles had been modernised. Realistic foreign exchange rate pegs had been introduced.

Our task was to advise on the implications for the operations of the central bank and to recommend the policy and regulatory changes that would be warranted. We had intensive discussions with various economic agencies and with senior personnel at the Central Bank. During our engagement with the technical and administrative institutions, I observed that many young Afro-Cubans occupied senior positions in the Central Bank and Foreign Ministry.

On the last evening of the meeting, we had a working dinner with President Fidel Castro at his official residence, the Palace of the Revolution. We were greeted by him on entry to the Palace. President Castro was a jovial and charming host. After an hour of conversation with him in a reception room, he remarked that he had invited us to dinner not conversation and that we should all proceed to the dining room. President Castro listened attentively to our findings and recommendations and asked sharp questions. We had been forewarned by scientists at a biotechnology research centre about his acute intelligence, grasp of issues and factual details, and impressive memory. In addition to discussions about our observations and findings on the banking sector, there were wide-ranging commentaries by President Castro on foreign trade and foreign finance during the Nixon and Kennedy Presidencies, on Cuban wage rates, on quality of service and tipping practices in Cuban hotels, on Western movies, and on Cuba-Caribbean history. We were duly offered Cuban cigars after dinner and there I discovered that Fidel Castro had given up the habit. The evening was a marathon one from 9pm to about 1am, at the end of which the only person who did not seem exhausted was President Fidel Castro.

I visited Cuba several times subsequently for conferences and meetings. A few years after the initial visit, I attended a meeting of the European Union and the Caribbean. After I became President of the Caribbean Development Bank in 2001, I visited the Central Bank to discuss with its leadership possible cooperation between Cuba and the Caribbean Development Bank and attended a conference of the Association of Caribbean Economists in Havana. In terms of social activities, I particularly enjoyed spending time in Old Havana, immersing myself in the music and dancing which are hallmarks of Cuba and visiting the museum where I first became aware of the immense contributions of West Indians to the Cuban independence war against Spain and of the Afro-Cuban leadership presence in the first governments and parliamentary assemblies after the war ended.

COMMONWEALTH CARIBBEAN

More in the mainstream, I continued to write on central banking and monetary policy in the Caribbean. In 1995, I authored a paper "Performance Evaluation and Accountability of Central Banks" which began with the observation that central banks are powerful, influential and prestigious agents of the State. It advanced the view that the concept of performance accountability pertains to achievement or non-achievement of economic goals assigned to central banks and that the underlying elements in any accountability framework are goal identification, performance indicators, attribution, and system and rules for accountability. Governments in the enabling legislation for central banks often state broad objectives including currency stability, foreign exchange rate stability, stability of the financial system, and economic growth or development. However, weights are not usually explicitly assigned to the broad objectives.

The paper drew on theories of bureaucracy to argue that a central bank may have a preference function which differs from that of the government in the sense that its implicit assignment of weights to the broad objectives differs from that of the government. However, identification of a central bank's preference function might be difficult because of information gaps and possibly because of deliberate obfuscation by the central banks as a strategy for institutional protection and interest promotion. A revealed preference approach has sometimes been used to circumvent the problem of direct identification of central banks preference functions. However, the revealed preference approach encounters problems such as policy externalities, imprecision, non-uniqueness and multiplicity of performance indicators. There is the additional difficulty of attributing outcomes to central banks, given information asymmetries, non-exclusive diffusion of responsibilities for specific objectives to central banks, i.e., inclusion of other agents of government, and the complexity of macro-economic mechanisms.

The paper discussed provisions for performance accountability in the Caribbean, noting that they are merely formalistic, and contrasted them with the congressional provisions in the United States which too have been considered ineffective because of information asymmetries and inadequate technical background of congressional committee members.

The final section of the paper commented on the then current issue of central bank independence from government. It noted that while there was much international and regional opinion in support of independent central banks, expert opinion on Britain and the US had not always been supportive. It agreed with the position articulated by Bryant (1980) that, "virtually all those who advocate independence, do so because they want the central bank to pursue, or at least to be able to pursue, fundamentally different objectives from those pursued by the rest of the government." The paper concluded that this would result in the preferences of the central bank (as agent) prevailing over those of the government (its principal). "The central bank, not the government, would be the source of monetary and financial policy, shaping the entire framework of national economic policy. It would be difficult to reconcile such an eventuality with the principles of modern democracy."

In a paper "Monetary Theory and Policy: Ruminations" written in 1999, I sought to elucidate some of the problems experienced in conducting monetary policy. I defined monetary policy as policy actions directed to achieve targets or directional change in money stock, aggregate interest rates, or both, to effect changes in the volume and price of credit and in aggregate expenditures. The ultimate targets and goals of monetary policy are general price stability, foreign exchange rate stability, economic growth, and rates of employment and unemployment. There is often irresolution or lack of clarity with respect to the choice of target variables, partly because there may be no clearly understood model of financial market linkages, there are considerations of distributional and welfare impacts, and because knowledge of macroeconomic fundamentals is uncertain. A further complication is that monetary policy is not unidimensional. Contrary to the Friedman-Meiselman unidimensional approach which identified the money stock as the sole target variable, the Tinbergen rule which states that the number of instruments can exceed the number of targets admits the possibility that a single target can have multiple impacts and diffusion effects. Discretionary judgement rather than automaticity becomes the sine qua non of monetary policy.

CENTRAL BANKING IN THE PHILIPPINES

On 7 February 1986, after a snap election called by President Ferdinand Marcos, Corazon Aquino was elected President of the Philippines. When her term ended on 11 May 1992, she was succeeded by Retired General Fidel Ramos. Corazon Aquino was the widow of Benigno Aquino who had been assassinated in August 1983. Her government inherited an economy with serious weaknesses. Gross domestic product had decreased consecutively in 1984 and 1985, foreign debt had reached the troubling level of 93 per cent of Gross National Product in 1986, the commercial banking sector was afflicted by bad debt, energy prices had risen greatly, and the peso was under pressure.

The new government engaged in an economic reform programme which focussed on economic stabilisation and growth and trade reforms. Various reform measures included de-regulation of commodity prices in agriculture and energy, de-monopolisation of the coconut industry, and institutional changes in the commercial banking and development banking industries. Political conditions were not entirely facilitatory. Several reforms were delayed because of the efforts of lobbies within the government and outside of the government while some segments of society were impatient with the rate of progress. On January 22, 1989, a peasant protest outside the Presidential Palace resulted in the death of fourteen protesters, the so-called Mendiola Massacre. A military coup which was attempted in December 1989 damaged the centre of the financial district. Extremist bombings of buildings and infrastructure occurred in the 1990s in Northern Luzon and metropolitan Manila. This was the background to my economic involvement in the Philippines in 1992.

The Aquino government in 1991 began an extensive liberalisation of its foreign exchange market which had until then been completely administered by the Central Bank of the Philippines. The liberalisation process had major implications for the concurrent programmes of macro-economic stabilisation and foreign trade liberalisation as well as for the future operations of the Central Bank. I was a member of a team engaged by IMCC to prepare a report for USAID on the foreign exchange liberalisation programme. The IMMC is a US consultancy firm headed by Robert Vogel, my Rural Financial Markets Group colleague. Other members of the team were Trent Bertrand, a senior economist at IMCC, Juan Carlos Protasi, former Governor of the Central Bank of Uruguay, Eli Remolona, Federal Reserve Bank of New York, and Ponciana Intal and Mario Lamberte who were both from the Philippines Institute for Development Studies. I was in Manila from 22 March to 10 April 1992.

We conducted interviews with many segments of the business community, especially the banking and finance industries, the Central Bank of the Philippines, government ministries, the Manila Stock Exchange, and representatives of the coconut industry, which was the second largest in the world, accounting for 25 per cent of cultivated land in the Philippines, and owning the United Coconut Planters Bank which in 1990 was one of the three main commercial banks in the country. It was common on entering the various buildings to see signs requesting visitors to lodge their firearms at the security desk, evidently a reflection of continuing concerns about the upheavals in 1990 and 1991. I did notice that no one surrendered weapons even though I was told that many visitors were armed.

The draft report submitted in May 1992 had four substantive sections which dealt sequentially with the deregulation of the foreign exchange market, implications for macro stabilisation, implications for international competitiveness and trade liberalisation, and implications for the Central Bank. My primary task was to analyse the implications for the Central Bank and to recommend changes in its structure and organisation. I observed that foreign market deregulation meant that the Central Bank was no longer able to administratively determine the foreign exchange rate and needed to rely on monetary policy conducted through open market operations and the rediscount rate. It needed to have an institutional capacity to gather information on behaviour and trends in financial markets, foreign trade and the macro economy and to respond quickly.

The Central Bank would be still entrusted with management of the country's external debt and would still be engaged in the process of coordinating monetary and fiscal policy. I noted that the Central Bank was huge by international standards. Apart from its occupancy of several large buildings, it had a staff of 6600 people, of whom 60 per cent were technical and professional employees. The staff complement was approximately 341 people per billion US dollars compared to 443 in the UK, 79 in Australia and nine in Singapore. There were many departments, each with elaborate structures. I concluded that the Central Bank was horizontally and vertically fragmented which caused serious problems of internal coordination and delays in making decisions and implementing them. There was an urgent need for a comprehensive review of the structure and organisation. There was also need for a substantially improved and expanded staff development programme.

On 14 June 1993, the legislature approved a New Central Bank Act which redefined the Bank's scope and nature of operations in the spheres of monetary policy, open market operations, securities market transactions, lender of last resort functions, credit policy, banking supervision and regulation and government debt transactions.

DEVELOPMENT BANKING

While in the 1980s a significant portion of my research efforts was focussed on rural development banking, my attention shifted in the 1990s to development banking more generally. On invitation to the Caribbean Development Bank's 12th Anniversary Symposium in 1990, I presented a paper on Challenges and Prospects for the CDB in the 1990s. The presentation began with the observation that the 1980s was a lost decade and proceeded to list the major development problems as high unemployment, reductions in fiscal outlays on social services and welfare, lower levels of living, high levels of emigration which signalled loss of confidence in the future of the Caribbean, and extensive pressure on social and political integrity and cohesion. It identified several constraints and opportunities in the international environment: dismantling of trade preferences; rapid technological trade affecting spatial organisation of production, production technology, and commodity baskets; decreases in international bank credit and increases in net transfers to multilateral financial institutions. These constraints and opportunities pointed to the need for new development strategies focussed on upgrading and development of production capacity, creation of new products, establishment of new export markets, and generation of higher national savings.

The finance constraint based on the two-gap approach was analysed with attention to the large financial requirements for recapitalisation of enterprises and investment in new technologies, and for investment in market knowledge and capacity. Another consideration was financial risks attendant on commodity innovation and marketing of non-traditional goods. The implications for development banks were higher volumes of lending per project, increased riskiness of projects, greater demand for loans, higher loan charges to compensate for greater risks, and the need to develop risk appraisal and management systems.

Because the financial system was deeper, broader and more dynamic than in the 1970s, the Caribbean Development Bank had opportunities not available previously. The opportunities included lending to private financial institutions instead of exclusively to government-owned development finance corporations or development banks, co-financing with large commercial banks, and raising loan capital on regional markets. Lending to private financial institutions or co-financing with them would enable the CDB to indirectly finance working capital, contribute to diversification of its portfolio, and enhance the role of private enterprise in national development.

I returned to the role of development banks with two papers published in 1991. One entitled "Role of Development Finance Corporations in the Commonwealth Caribbean" which was presented at a Conference on Financing Development in the Caribbean in Barbados in December 1989 postulated that development finance corporations were an institutional device for ensuring greater convergence between the supply side of domestic finance and the demand for development finance. Subsidiary roles included reducing the interest cost of credit (though it was important not to negate this by imposing other onerous transactions costs on borrowers) and being agents of technical change if the banks provided technical assistance services to credit clients. It was suggested that DFCs could mobilise domestic financial resources through acceptance of deposits, issuance of bonds, and intermediation with other financial institutions. Several operational problems were identified, including high costs of loan administration, interest costs of fund mobilisation, credit default costs which very often were due to problems in the operating environment of debtors, and difficulties of a legal and political nature in enforcing loan contracts.

The second paper "The Role and Functions of DFCs in the Decade of the 1990s" presented at the Conference of Regional Development Finance Corporations in Ocho Rios, Jamaica, in November 1991 was nuanced differently. It started off with the statement that self-financing among Caribbean enterprises was a hindrance to raising the investment ratio to warranted levels and also impaired the quality of investment. There was a tendency towards sub-optimal convergence between the allocation of financial surpluses and the sectoral pattern of investment. The operations of DFCs could rectify this problem by provision of long-term capital to enterprises and sectors characterised by high expected social returns and by private rates of returns consistent with expected capacity to repay loans. The conditioning environment was analysed. The paper noted the development of the financial sector and discussed existing problems in the production and marketing environment, the danger of adverse risk selection presented by financial market liberalisation, and the risks which might emanate from foreign trade liberalisation and foreign exchange market liberalisation. The conclusion was that DFCs were entering a challenging period because of institutional and macroeconomic changes which therefore required greater care and sensitivity in credit appraisal and loan pricing.

The Caribbean Development Bank invited me to make a presentation on "The Future of Development Banking in the Caribbean" at its 25th Anniversary Seminar in Barbados on 10 May 1995. I began by referring to Joseph Stiglitz's summary conceptualisation of the role of financial markets, namely, intermediation between savers and borrowers; agglomeration of capital; selection and monitoring of projects; and risk transference and risk pooling. I argued that Caribbean financial markets are poor on all counts: that commercial banks were long on deposits and short on credit; that they were strongly risk-averse; and that there were significant financial market imperfections. I noted that development banks were created to fill the gaps in the financial structure through operating as investment niche financiers, engaging in international fund mobilisation, facilitating the accrual of positive externalities through influence on private lenders, encouraging entrepreneurship, disseminating improved technology, and widening access to credit, thereby potentially contributing to more egalitarian distribution of income and wealth.

The case for development banking was still strong but adjustments had to be made for changes in the operational context such as economic liberalisation, privatisation, redefinition of the economic role of the State, and regionalism. These changes would have several channels of influence on development banks, including increased risks, greater scale of enterprises, and the greater latitude of private financial institutions in credit operations, The role of the CDB remained that of provision of investment capital, mobilisation of international financial resources, and promotion of economic integration but it also needed to become more active in provision of funds to the private sector.

My last paper on development banking in the period was at the invitation of the Development Finance Limited to its International Banking Seminar in Port of Spain on 1 April 1996. I presented on the topic "Recent Trends in Financial Markets and Development Banking in the Caribbean". I surveyed seven major sets of developments in the domestic financial sector. First and most pervasive was financial liberalisation in keeping with the general policy of market liberalisation upon which the countries had embarked. The second was financial market reform with the enactment of new financial legislation affecting banks, securities markets, supervisory institutions and corporate enterprises and the levelling of the playing field by removal of government assistance and hindrances to targeted financial institutions. Third, there was considerable financial innovation occurring. Fourth was the proliferation of financial institutions, often of the same generic type. Fifth, considerable financial product innovation and diversification was taking place. Sixth, a few major financial enterprises, mainly commercial banks and insurance companies, had established a physical operating presence in other Caribbean countries. Seventh, foreign exchange market liberalisation had taken place in most Caribbean countries.

The presentation identified changes in the regional financial sector, primarily institutional innovations which paralleled the process in domestic markets, liberalisation of cross-border capital flows, improvement and harmonisation of prudential regulations and supervisory systems, and progress towards currency convertibility. With respect to the international financial sector, the main developments identified were the greatly reduced access of Caribbean countries to concessionary international financial resources, the growth in foreign direct investment to a few countries, and the collapse of private equity markets due to the "tequila effect".

Several implications were drawn for development banking in the Caribbean. One is that development banks would be operating in a more competitive financial sector. Second, there were important changes in their risk environment. Third, there were new opportunities for treasury management created by innovations which create short-term, highly marketable financial instruments and facilities for secondary trading. Fourth, access to international funds might be constrained by the reductions in access to concessionary resources thereby forcing development banks to resort to private capital markets. Fifth, new prudential and reporting requirements would increase operating costs. Sixth, there might be greater scope for co-financing with other financial institutions.

STRUCTURAL ADJUSTMENT POLICY

It was appropriate to situate analyses of Caribbean economic development policy in the context of fundamental changes in the global economic and socio-political environment. This I did in a paper "The Changing World Environment with Special Reference to Small States" which I presented to the "Symposium on Small States: Problems and Opportunities in a World of Rapid Change" in St Kitts in March 1991. I began with the assertion that there have been momentous and frequently unpredicted changes in practically every sphere of human endeavour and that their long-run consequences were uncertain. The changes emanated from large States, but small States needed to adapt to them creatively. I then proceeded to identify and elaborate on some of the major ones.

One major set of changes was high population growth rates in less developed countries combined with low or negative rates of economic growth which generated pressures to emigrate. However, receptivity to immigrants from poor countries had weakened in Canada, UK and US. A second cluster of impactful changes was in international trade. Slower and more variable world economic growth was weakening demand for LDC commodity exports, weakening intra-trade among LDCs, and causing reductions in international aid flows. Furthermore, protectionism had increased between 1981 and 1989, especially in the US and the EU. Bilateralism and managed trade were becoming prominent features of trade policies in industrial countries as was the creation of common economic zones such as those in Europe, North America and Southeast Asia.

Trade preferences which favoured small countries were being imperilled by policy initiatives in Europe, the US and the World Trade Organisation. A third set of changes were located in the production environment. There were significant changes in the geographical organisation of business, intensified search for economies of scope, rapid evolution of production technology, globally integrated production, multi-firm alliances and cross-industry alliances. The changes in production technology reduced locational advantages but at the same time facilitated market entry by smaller firms because warranted plant size and required capital investments were smaller. The new production technologies also necessitated fundamental changes in expertise and labour skills. There were also major changes in the global financial environment. Small countries were experiencing net outflows of financial resources, even in their dealings with the multilateral financial institutions, and were attempting without much success to replace commercial bank debt with marketable securities.

New standards of investor protection and capital adequacy were becoming prevalent. Furthermore, bilateral aid flows were being re-directed to Eastern Europe. However, the heightened global concerns about the environment provided opportunities for less developed countries, including those in the Caribbean, to attract new financial resources by development of environmental projects, proposing debt-for-equity swaps, and highlighting environmental aspects of natural hazard events. The paper also touched on political changes such as the changed conceptions of spheres of influence, geographical strategic importance, military adventurism by the US and the UK, and the emergence of narco-states.

In this quite different global environment from that of the preceding two decades, Caribbean countries embarked on programmes of structural adjustment. I was asked by the International Labour Office in Geneva to prepare a background paper on Social Implications of Structural Adjustment in the Caribbean for a Caribbean Roundtable on Structural Adjustment and Employment Issues in May 1991. I couched the issue in terms of levels of living, noting disparities in levels of living, and identifying its different components such as income, consumption, health, recreation and political rights. The paper considered briefly the international economic situation and outlook with special reference to Caribbean trade, foreign capital and international aid, emigration, the emergence of the Pacific Rim as a global economic growth centre, and the ageing of populations in Europe and industrial America. Structural adjustment was defined as changes in the structure of the economies, in production relations, and in the institutional foundations of society with respect to economic affairs. Successful structural adjustment of economies required considerable capital investment, improvement in production technology and human resource development.

The background paper envisaged a prominent role for private sector entrepreneurs. It raised the critical issue of achieving an appropriate balance between profits and labour incomes, noting the connection with domestic savings, capital investment, and price competitiveness of exports. Achieving appropriate fiscal policies was also critical because taxes were a wedge between personal incomes and personal expenditures and between corporate profits and corporate savings and re-investment. Structural adjustment programmes initially implemented in the Caribbean also include substantial reductions in public expenditures which negatively impacted public sector provision of education and health services, the quality of road and transportation infrastructure, and the magnitude and scope of social safety nets.

Questions about fairness of the distribution of the burden of structural adjustment were central to policy decisions. Social acceptance of decreases in real wage rates would depend greatly on its accompaniment by increasing levels of employment, increase in labour incomes and perceptions of relative disparities in resulting levels of living. Deterioration in social conditions were often decisive influences on political acceptability.

In graduation addresses to UWI St Augustine business school students and graduates circa 1998, I emphasised seven elements of the contemporary environment of special relevance to them. The first was the fact that markets for goods and services in the Caribbean had become internationalised or more open. Second, Caribbean markets and industries were less protected against foreign competition because of the dismantling of trade barriers and the trend towards reduction of production subsidies. Third, the retreat from direct state intervention in production, marketing and finance was a feature of the new reality for business even though governments still retained some responsibility for public protection against extreme market behaviour. Fourth, while rates of corporate taxation were being reduced, there was heightened public expectations that business enterprises would be good corporate citizens. Fifth, frequent and substantial technological change was a major feature of the new business environment. Sixth, investments in electronic communication had become important for achievement of competitive advantage. Seventh, labour and capital had become more geographically mobile than previously.

There were several implications for managers of business enterprises. They needed to think regionally and globally, acquire extensive knowledge, and understand the competitive methods and approaches of enterprises outside their national space, regardless of whether they operated nationally or internationally. They needed to recognise that competition extended to the markets from which they sourced their inputs of materials, labour and capital. Managers also needed to recognise that Caribbean governments had less ability within the new global environment to shelter and protect them from foreign competition.

EXPORT OF ENTERTAINMENT SERVICES

Occasionally policy attention in the Caribbean would turn to the topics of economic diversification and export diversification. In May 1995, during the UWI Vice Chancellorship of Sir Alister McIntyre, the University together with the World Bank organised a conference in Montego Bay, Jamaica on Prospects for Service Exports in the Caribbean at which Maureen Allgrove and I presented a paper on "Prospects for Entertainment Services from the Caribbean: The Case of Music" which continues to be frequently cited by scholars. It was the first attempt by anyone to analyse this topic. We engaged in extensive reviews of national economic information, entertainment industry reports and statistics, and interviewed 23 entertainment industry operators and managers in Jamaica and seven in Trinidad and Tobago.

The paper began with observations about the size of the entertainment industry and the music industry component globally. It then argued that the music industry offered Caribbean countries prospects of "significantly widening the range of economic opportunities to individuals and enterprises, for alleviating problems of unemployment (especially youth employment) and expanding foreign exchange earnings on a sustainable basis." It identified the wide range of labour market skills required, including those of performers, promoters, managers, marketers, producers, sound engineers, and lawyers. It noted that in many instances, especially among performers, there were no formal education requirements and that the industry generated employment throughout the year but much more during festivals. As a generalisation, the music industry, while conferring substantial income benefits to some performers, did not seem to be a sizeable contributor to gross domestic product and to the balance of payments.

The paper then discussed entertainment services, music especially, as an export industry which can be categorised into two components, one in which production and sales are in situ, i.e., patrons come to the production and sales venues as in concerts and festivals, and the other component being one in which the product is sold in the foreign export market, either as a physical commodity like a music compact disc or audiotape or a live performance in a concert or at a music festival. (Internet transmissions were not a delivery mode at the time we wrote.) Both types of markets have ethnic or cultural niche characteristics in the return of Caribbean nationals for festivals, purchases of recorded music and the participation of both Caribbean-based nationals and the Caribbean diaspora in periodic festivals in diaspora cities of residence. Indicative evidence was provided of foreign exchange earned from festivals in the Caribbean, performance fees and incomes of well-known artistes, and sales of recorded music and indigenous musical instruments. It was argued that the global market potential is huge, that international demand was growing rapidly and sustained by new variants of music (including cross-over music) and the incorporation of new elements of spectacle.

The paper engaged in a discussion of the influence of cultural authenticity on competitive advantage. We stated that all popular music is competitive in the broadest sense of substitutability but that despite universal themes such as love and sex in popular music, market performance is much influenced by cultural origins of the music. Cultural authenticity in the perception of consumers requires that performers and composers of the particular genre of popular music originate from particular cultural environments. This means that consumers perceive distinctions between products supplied by performers depending on the performers' cultural backgrounds. Cultural authenticity therefore confers market advantages. (As a postscript, we should have noted that as demand for a genre of popular music increases internationally, as in the case of reggae, non-Caribbean performers adopt the cultural manifestations of Caribbean performers to confer cultural authenticity on their performances.) In any case as we noted, the advantage can be converted into economic gains only if other conditions such as product quality, ability to "cross-over", reliability of service delivery, delivery mode and ease of consumer access are favourable.

We next discussed supply-side market conditions, noting the variety of production units and variations in modus operandi. We conducted the discussion within a conceptual framework which distinguished between geographically immobile providers and geographically mobile providers advanced by Jagdish Bhagwati (1978). In the case of geographically immobile providers, successful export performance requires improving the country's transportation and communications infrastructure (especially internet infrastructure), upgrading technological skills, investment in advanced equipment, careful planning and scheduling of performances, and efficient and comprehensive arrangements for sales to potential consumers. In the case of geographically mobile providers, the main issues which required attention were legal rights of establishment, hindrances on outward and inward travel of performers, contract negotiations and management, Caribbean production capacity and quality in respect of exports of recorded music products, marketing, and protection of intellectual property rights.

Maureen Allgrove and I followed up our conference paper by preparing a UWI project proposal for a music industry training programme to address skill and knowledge deficiencies in production and production management, marketing, and contract negotiations, and some other areas which needed improvement. The proposal was submitted to the Caribbean Development Bank which reported to us that it had unsuccessfully sought the permission of the IDB to use its technical assistance resources. It was reported informally that the Japanese Director at the IDB had vetoed the request on the grounds that music was not an export business, an incredible position to be taken by a man from the land of SONY. It would be almost 25 years later when the CDB finally ventured into financing projects for upgrading skills in the Caribbean music entertainment industry. We also sought to interest New York University which had a strong academic department that dealt with entertainment services to collaborate with UWI in establishing a training programme. We met with one of their faculty members with a Caribbean background, but her response was not positive and nothing came out of this effort.

ECONOMIC VULNERABILITY, RESILIENCE AND RISK MANAGEMENT

Late in the 1990s, Barbadian Prime Minister Owen Arthur spearheaded CARICOM/Commonwealth Secretariat discussions on small States in the global environment. CARICOM was particularly concerned with the situation and prospects of small island States, but the Commonwealth Secretariat understandably had a wider geographical remit. A conference was held in London in January 2000 at which the Caribbean Community, Africa and the Pacific were well represented. I was present and to my surprise on one occasion was asked by an African delegation to speak on their behalf.

I was at the conference because I had written two short background papers, one entitled "Economic Vulnerability, Income Volatility and Economic Resilience of Small States" and the other entitled "Risk Management in Small Vulnerable States". In the first paper, I discussed the Composite Vulnerability Index computed for the Commonwealth Secretariat by Atkins, Mazzi, Easter and Ramlogan which had led the Secretariat and the World Bank in a 1999 report to conclude that, "small states are systemically more vulnerable than large countries, regardless of income." Tom Crowards, an economist at the Caribbean Development Bank challenged the Composite Vulnerability Index and proposed a different index based on a more extensive list of economic characteristics, namely, commodity export concentration, geographical or market export concentration, reliance on external finance, susceptibility to natural disasters, institutional fragility, energy dependence, peripherality, and economic openness. Crowards concluded that, "the more vulnerable countries of the Caribbean rank among the most vulnerable countries in the world by whatever method is employed." In my opinion, Crowards' results emphasised the stark differences in economic vulnerability between small states and large states.

I also discussed income volatility. The Commonwealth Secretariat and the World Bank in the same 1999 report had stated that income volatility is greater in small states than in large states. My paper recapped causes of income volatility identified by the IDB in a report in 1995. They included foreign trade volatility, real exchange rate volatility, volatility of foreign capital flows, and macroeconomic policy volatility. Income volatility should be minimised because of its adverse effects on income distribution, poverty, investment and productivity growth and on social cohesion.

I defined economic resilience as the capacity to recover rapidly from economic shocks. It is the capacity to recover from economic harm or damage regardless of the cause of the harm or damage. It was clear that countries showed different degrees of resilience to uniform external shocks. I proposed the construction of an index of economic resilience. Economic resilience is a multi-dimensional concept with at least three dimensions: the magnitude of the external shock; the duration of the recovery period; and ability to dampen the multiplier effects of the initial shock. The multi-dimensionality should guide the choice of a surrogate empirical variable to measure economic resilience. I concluded by identifying several variables which could strengthen or weaken a country's economic resilience. These are: (1) economic diversification which would increase the likelihood that other sectors can compensate for depressions caused by shocks in the trade sector and other sectors; (2) export diversification which would reduce reliance on individual markets; (3) flexibility of production structure and technology which determines how quickly product composition can be changed and the extent to which production inputs can be substituted; (4) availability of domestic financial resources to buffer against temporary income shortfalls and to finance warranted investments; (5) availability of foreign exchange to augment domestic financial resources; (6) the industrial relations climate; (7) the degree of social cohesion which is pertinent to whether the society can act with a common purpose in challenging times.

The second background paper on risk management identified three kinds of risks: income risks which are defined as the probability of future income flows deviating from their expected magnitudes; price risks, where the deviations are caused by variations in transaction prices or from foreign exchange rate changes; and quantity risks which are essentially production risks, i.e., the probability that future output might be less or greater than projected. The paper drew attention to the existence of various instruments for price management, such as commodity swaps, commodity-linked loans, commodity-linked bonds and "put" option contracts. Quantity risks can be managed by insurance policies like those against crop failures or against losses from natural hazard events. Because self-insurance can be prohibitively expensive, governments have found it advisable to develop schemes for joint coverage and financing of insurance premiums. The paper concluded with an examination of the exposure of the tourism sector to exogenous shocks and proposed that a mechanism for compensatory financing of shortfalls in export earnings might be appropriate.

FAMILY AND SOCIAL LIFE

Our older son, Clairmonte Erlin, having completed his undergraduate law degree at University College London, decided that he no longer wanted to be a lawyer and after careful consideration decided to pursue a career in taxation. He registered with the Chartered Institute of Taxation to do their Associate of the Taxation Institute programme and was recruited as an intern by Price Waterhouse. He completed the taxation programme, earning the ATII qualification (now called Chartered Tax Advisor or CTA). In 1995, at age 27, he made history by being the first person who was not a registered lawyer or solicitor to argue a case before the British Inland Revenue Board. As a Senior Partner at Price Waterhouse, he successfully led a team of four others. Their success saved Unigate, a major British dairy enterprise, an estimated 15-20 million pounds sterling in taxation of its cross-border operations. Not long after, the American branch of Price Waterhouse asked for Clairmonte's secondment to their offices in New York and Washington, D.C. to work on similar issues in the US jurisdiction.

Our younger son, Compton Olatunji, after secondary school, enrolled in the dental surgery programme at the UWI St Augustine Faculty of Medical Sciences in 1991 and graduated in July1996. He then proceeded to graduate studies in the United Kingdom, first in Oral Surgery at the Royal London Hospital in east London, England, and then at the University of Glasgow, Scotland, where he obtained a Licentiate Diploma in Dental Surgery from the Royal College of Physicians and Surgeons of Glasgow in February 1998 and a Master's degree in Orthodontics in 2000. Both his mother and I visited him separately in both locations. He returned to Trinidad in 2000 to take up a lectureship in the UWI Dental School. He published several academic papers which gained him an international reputation and invitations to serve on editorial boards and make conference presentations.

Our social life in Trinidad took the usual course. We spent lots of time with our friends and with my aunt and her husband on mutually enjoyable activities. Many new friends were made in the wider community as my range of professional activities extended into the business and political communities. We also developed close friendships with Pamela Williams who was still based in Barbados and Keith Evans who was based at the IDB head office in Washington, D.C. During this period, our good friends Maurice and Valerie Odle resided in Geneva where Maurice worked with UNCTAD. On one occasion, Pamela and I extended our visit to London to spend time as their guests in Geneva, with a short excursion to Paris which we had not visited together since our honeymoon in 1967. The Senior Common Room (SCR) continued to be one of my hangouts. The SCR also began to organise Carnival fetes which we attended. We became personal friends of Ambassador Yasuhiko Tanaka and his wife Hiroko and were delighted to be their guests for a day in Tokyo on our way back from an IDB meeting in Okinawa in April 2005.

While Compton Olatunji was in the UK, Pamela and I made vacation trips to Guyana where we spent time with relatives and did some sightseeing. Particularly memorable was a trip up the Essequibo River one Sunday morning to a resort island called Baganara. We were accompanied by Fritz and Gem Fletcher. Fritz was a farmer somewhere along the east bank of the river and Gem was lecturing at the University of Guyana. To get to our departure point on the bank of the Essequibo River, we first had to cross the Demerara River on the Harbour Bridge, then travel on the West Bank Demerara Main Road and the West Coast Demerara Main Road to Parika Stelling where we boarded a motorised boat along with about twenty other people. On the river trip, we saw mainly Amerindian people who resided on the banks of the river returning from church or from market shopping in their canoes, propelled by either paddles or outboard motor engines. We also saw clusters of boats tied to the landings of homes and concluded that their neighbours were visiting. The Essequibo River for the people who lived on its banks was the equivalent of an urban highway, a connector to relatives, friends and commerce.

On the way to Baganara, we passed the Two Brothers Islands which were owned by a prosperous goldminer but later became the residence of Eddie Grant, the Guyanese singer who became world famous with his song 'Electric Avenue'. The Two Brothers Islands were so named because there were literally two islands connected by a short bridge. We passed Sibley Hall, the prison on the Mazaruni River where political detainees were held in the 1960s. We also passed Bartica, the town at the intersection of the Essequibo River and the Mazuruni River with a reputation of being a "booty trap" for men mining in the Potaro/Mazaruni district. The Baganara island resort was enjoyable. The island had white sand beaches with crystal clear water. The restaurant cuisine was good. There was music and a lively atmosphere. One could also canoe across to the nearby bank of the river and explore the coast, which we did.

In 1998, Pamela and I travelled to British Columbia to vacation with my mother and siblings. While there, we decided to go on a cruise to Alaska. It was our first cruise. The experience on the Holland America ship Rotterdam was wonderful. We did some sightseeing in the various ports of call and purchased a few curios, some of which are still in our possession. The trip made me aware of the economic benefits of cruise tourism to host countries and the short sightedness of some Caribbean governments who yielded to the opposition of hoteliers to the competitive development of cruise tourism in the Caribbean at that time.

During the UWI visit to South African universities in 2000, Pamela and I, along with the rest of the group, squeezed in some leisure activities in a crowded schedule. We visited the Robben Island Prison where Nelson Mandela was imprisoned for 27 years, saw a few cultural events, toured a safari park, and briefly toured Cape Town, Pretoria, Durban and Johannesburg. We also visited the initial Soweto home of Nelson and Winnie Mandela. One evening, we were hosted to dinner by Marcus Balintulo (a former UWI St Augustine colleague who then headed one of the new technical universities in the Cape) and his Trinidadian wife, Gillian, an accomplished pianist and arranger of steelband music in Trinidad.

As might be expected by now, I took the opportunities provided by business trips to the US to indulge my taste for jazz and blues music. I visited Blues Alley in Washington, D.C., and Fat Tuesday, Iridium, Blue Note, Village Vanguard, and B.B. King's Blues Club in New York City. With my sister Dian in Miami, I was also able to take in concerts at various venues, including at Florida Memorial University which had an annual event organised in honour of Grover Washington, Jr which featured aspiring jazz musicians from university music schools in Florida in the company of some leading performers. The roll-call of performers I heard live includes Ray Charles (with the original Raylettes), B.B. King, George Benson, Al Grey, Jon Faddis, Claudio Roditti, Terri Lyne Carrington, Mulgrew Miller and James Moody.

DEPARTURE FROM ST AUGUSTINE

At the start of May 2001, I departed St Augustine to take up an appointment as President of the Caribbean Development Bank. The decision was made public in March. I received congratulations and well-wishes from across the University community on all three campuses. Many individuals thought that CDB's gain was the University's loss. The Council of the University paid tribute to my service, describing me as "an exemplar in the area of project management ... (who) has set a standard which will be a benchmark" and as "a man of vision, who understands the importance of detail, while never losing sight of the larger picture" and credits the University's success in international fund mobilisation to my "special ability as a team leader ... and negotiating skills."

The Dean of the Faculty of Engineering, Professor Clement Sankat, said in his letter dated 25 April 2001: "We are all proud of this campus and much of this must be attributed to your steady leadership in all facets of campus management." Mr Gonzalo R. Gallegos, Public Affairs Officer of the US Embassy, wrote: "My office has enjoyed and benefited from the years of cooperation and fruitful experience with you and your staff. We greatly appreciate your assistance and are proud to be able to refer to you as our friend. I can surely say that without your insight, support, and encouragement, our Fulbright 2000 Scholarship Program would not exist today. This is one of the many ways your commitment to excellence and the development of Trinidad and Tobago's youth will leave an indelible mark on this country."

Professor Barbara Lalla, another of my senior academic colleagues, wrote on 10 April 2001: "You leave us all with a campus physically more comfortable and aesthetically pleasing than we had before your term of office. More importantly, you have established a balance in emphasis between the disciplines, which may well have changed the course of academic welfare of the campus." She continued: "Under your leadership too, equal opportunity has become more than a buzzword." I took pleasure in these assessments of what had been an extraordinarily hectic and demanding period in my professional life.

Vice Chancellor Rex Nettleford invited me and my wife to a Special Performance by the University Singers in my honour at the Mona campus on 27 April 2001. The St Augustine campus arranged a splendid UWI Farewell Reception on 14 May 2001

On 23 May 2002, the University conferred on me the title of Emeritus Professor.

Meeting Cuba's President Fidel Castro, centre, at the Palace of the Revolution, Havana, 14 November 1997.

After the St Augustine Campus Graduation Ceremony, October 1998. L-R: Vice Chancellor Nettleford, Chancellor Sir Shridath Ramphal, Me and Pamela.

Prince Charles planting a tree at St Augustine Campus, 22 February 2000. L-R: Vice Chancellor Nettleford, Yasmin Baksh-Comeau, Pamela, Prince Charles and Me.

Office of St Augustine Campus Principal Staff, 2001.

Former UWI Senior Management Colleagues, 31 August 2002. L-R: Sir Alister McIntyre, Sir Kenneth Hall and Me.

CHAPTER EIGHT

CARIBBEAN DEVELOPMENT BANK YEARS, 2001-2011

APPOINTMENT AS PRESIDENT, CARIBBEAN DEVELOPMENT BANK

On 1 May 2001, I took up an appointment as President of the Caribbean Development Bank (CDB). I replaced Sir Neville Nicholls, who had been President from 1988 to April 2001.

The CDB entered into force on 26 January 1970 in keeping with an agreement signed on 18 October 1969 by representatives of eighteen governments, sixteen of which were Caribbean regional states and territories and two of which were non-regional states. Several of the Caribbean signatories were leaders of governments, namely, Errol W. Barrow, Prime Minister of Barbados, Robert L. Bradshaw, Premier of St Kitts and Nevis, John C. Compton, Premier of St Lucia, Vere C. Bird, Premier of Antigua and Barbuda, and E.O. LeBlanc, Premier of Dominica. Other signatories were Edward Seaga, Jamaica's Minister of Finance, and Ptolomey Reid, Guyana's Deputy Prime Minister. Borrowing rights are limited to Caribbean members. Canada and the United Kingdom were the two initial non-regional member countries, but they were later joined by France in 1984, Germany in 1988, Italy in 1989 and China in 1998.

The Caribbean membership was expanded to include Venezuela in 1973, Anguilla and Colombia in 1974, and Mexico in 1982. The stated purpose of the CDB is "to contribute to the harmonious economic growth and development of the member countries in the Caribbean ... and to promote economic cooperation and integration among the, having special and urgent regard to the needs of the less developed members." The Hispanic Caribbean members are non-borrowing members of the CDB.

The CDB Presidency was an unplanned development. One day, early in 2001, I received a phone call from Mr Arnhim Eustace, the Prime Minister of St Vincent and the Grenadines informing me that he and his OECS colleague Heads of Government wished to nominate me for the presidency and sought to ascertain my willingness to be considered. Upon reflection, I agreed because I saw it as an opportunity to have a more direct role in the development policies and actions in the various Caribbean countries than was open to me as an occasional consultant and author of scholarly papers and research reports. Having accepted the nomination by the OECS, I thought I should seek the support of the Guyana Government for my candidacy. I visited President Jagdeo in Georgetown to let him know of the nomination and ask for his support. Although not discouraging me, he informed me that he had already committed his support to a Jamaican nominee at the request of Prime Minister P.J. Patterson and would not want to renege on that promise. I assured him that I fully understood his position and would not want it to be otherwise. I subsequently learnt that Jamaica's nominee was former CARICOM Secretary-General Ambassador Roderick Rainford, my longstanding colleague and friend in the Caribbean development and economic integration policy arena.

As it turned out, Prime Minister Patterson, on learning of my nomination, graciously withdrew his government's nominee. I was therefore elected unopposed. Roderick Rainford was among the first people to send congratulations and best wishes on 8 March 2001 to which I responded that there was never any doubt in my mind that I could count on his continued friendship and professional support. On the same day, I received a letter from President Jagdeo in which he stated that over the years he had respected my scholarship and contribution to the Caribbean and assured me of the full support of his government and the people of Guyana.

My appointment was well-received within the Caribbean and outside the Caribbean. I received congratulatory letters and other correspondence from colleagues, associates, and friends some of whom I had not been in contact with for several years. They included members of the diplomatic community, leaders in the business community, and heads of regional organisations such as the CARICOM Secretariat, the OECS Secretariat, the Association of Caribbean States and the Caribbean Examinations Council. His Excellency Edwin Carrington, CARICOM Secretary-General wrote that he recalled with great pride my many and varied contributions to the integration movement and Caribbean development and that he considered my appointment "most propitious as we seek to deepen the process of advancing the welfare of the peoples of the Caribbean Community." Trinidad and Tobago President, Arthur N.R. Robinson wrote on 22 March 2001 to say: "I know that with your vast experience and the high regard with which you are held in the region, your suitability for the post is unquestionable."

Two especially significant letters congratulatory letters came from CDB governors representing two non-regional members of the CDB. Hon. Clare Short, United Kingdom Secretary of State for Development wrote on 13 March 2001. Apart from offering congratulations, she pointed to the importance of the CDB "in reducing poverty and promoting socio-economic development in the Caribbean" and to the leadership I was expected to play in implementing the Bank's Strategic Plan and "developing strategic partnerships with other development institutions in the region." The other letter was from Dr Uschi Eid, the Parliamentary Secretary in the Ministry for Development, Germany on 26 March 2001. Dr Eid also highlighted the importance of the CDB's poverty reduction mandate and the need to progress with finalisation of the strategic plan but additionally drew attention to the issues of good governance and private sector development. In each case there were assurances of the continued support of their countries. I replied in writing to both the UK and Germany Governors on 12 April 2001 assuring them that the issues they raised were central to my own conception of development challenges in the Caribbean and promising to visit them in their capitals for discussions early in my first year in office. What I was also tacitly signalling was the importance I planned to give to achieving and maintaining good relationship between the Bank's leadership and its governing body.

CDB CHALLENGES IN 2000

"The Bank has quite a few things going for it" was my statement to journalist Tony Best and reported in the *Weekend Nation* in Barbados on 21 December 2001. I went on to list the CDB's familiarity with economic activities and policies across the region, its considerable experience in financial management in the Caribbean and across the world, and its strength in mobilising funds in international capital markets. However, I was also quite aware of some major challenges before the bank, identifying a stronger presence in regional economic policymaking, relationships with non-borrowing members, and operational efficiency as three critical matters to be addressed quickly.

In my final address to Governors at the Bank's Annual Meeting in Nassau, Bahamas, on 19 May 2010, I recapitulated and expanded on the challenges as they had manifested themselves and were perceived by the Bank's member countries in 1999 and 2000. I spoke about "the tremendous anxiety felt in 2000 about the (Bank's) future." The United Kingdom had made reference to the withdrawal of France from membership in the Bank, the decision of Germany and Italy not to contribute to a general capital increase and urged CDB to respond to the "challenge of ensuring that no other Member Country feels the need to follow the French example."

In 1999, delegates to the Annual Meeting had expressed disquiet about various aspects of operational efficiency, the stance of senior management towards expansion of membership, the breakdown of relationship with the World Bank, and the weakening of cooperation and collaboration. I was present as an Observer at the Annual Meeting in 2000 and compiled the following composite of statements from Governors and Alternates, some of whom were regional members: "CDB will need a dynamic leadership, it will need vision, it will need to be responsive to its members, both Regional and Non-Regional. It will need to listen carefully to the messages from Governors and to those conveyed via the Board of Directors. It should avoid any perception that it should be predominantly part of any Commonwealth Club. It has not made sufficient use of borrowing from MFIs thereby frustrating implementation of World Bank projects and therefore needed to remove institutional or personal barriers to seeking funds from the IDB and the World Bank. The multilateral spirit which informed the participation of non-members seemed to have weakened in the Bank. The Bank should not in its staffing become a repository solely for regional technicians." Member countries were irked by the delay in completing the Operations Audit which the Bank had commissioned in 1998 and by what they thought was an unenthusiastic response by management to recommendations for expanding membership to the non-Anglophone Caribbean. They were also dissatisfied with turnaround time on loan applications, the rise in administrative expenses relative to average loan balances, and the slow growth in the loan portfolio in recent years.

RELATIONS WITH MEMBER COUNTRIES

My immediate predecessor, Sir Neville Nicholls, made efforts to improve relations with member countries in November and December 2000 by visiting the United Kingdom, Germany, and Italy for discussions with CDB governors or their alternates and with other officials. In February 2001, he visited Canada, Mexico, Colombia, and Venezuela for the same purpose. I intensified these efforts with a round of visits to many countries in 2001 in order to have full exchanges with CDB governors and their officials on their assessment of the Bank, their strategic interests, their vision of the

Bank and its future, and in the case of borrowing member countries, the role they expected CDB to play in their social and economic development. I was accompanied by various CDB staff members, more usually the Assistant Bank Secretary, Mr Volville Forsythe, but including on several occasions, Desmond Brunton, Vice-President for Operations and selected members of staff from his division.

On different occasions, I met with Ministers of Finance in Jamaica and Trinidad and Tobago and with the Prime Ministers of Antigua and Barbuda and the Commonwealth of Dominica. I also visited The Bahamas and Grenada. Visits were made to London in July for discussions with Mr Hilary Benn, the new Secretary of State, Tamara Bello, Head of the Regional Development Banks team, and other officials in the UK Department for Foreign and International Development. We also met with officials in the Foreign and Commonwealth Office before heading to Germany for discussions with Dr Uschi Eid, Parliamentary Secretary, Ministry of Development and her officials, and to Rome for discussions with Mr Lorenzo Bini Smaghi, the Alternate Governor for Italy and with Carlo Monticelli, Head of International Financial Relations, and other officials in the Ministry of Economics and Finance. China was visited later in the year.

I continued the practice of visiting member countries for discussions about the Bank throughout my tenure, extending the discussions to my own perspective on development challenges and my plans for the Bank. Between 2002 and 2011, I visited all member countries, some of them annually and others on a slightly less frequent basis. Some visits were more frequent, extensive and varied than others. I would often combine the visits to borrowing member countries with opening ceremonies, inspections, and closing ceremonies of CDB-financed projects. Participation in opening and closing ceremonies, for example in the Second Phase of the Southern Highway Development Project in Trinidad in September 2003, the Bucco Community Development Project in Tobago in September 2003, the National Irrigation Development Pilot Project in St Elizabeth, Jamaica, in January 2005, and the Parika Roads Project in Guyana in October 2007, was intended to emphasise the Bank's commitment to the social and economic development of the countries in myriad ways. There were two primary reasons for my inspection of projects as Bank President. One purpose was to sharpen my own understanding of the challenges on the ground both with respect to project design and implementation. This made me better able to interface with both the governments, ultimate intended beneficiaries and CDB technical staff. The second, no less important reason, was to deepen my own appreciation and that of Bank staff of the urgency of the social and economic development needs seen through the lens of the potential beneficiaries of CDB projects.

A visit to a rural community in Belize for which a water development and supply project was in a nascent stage stands out in my memory. The potential beneficiaries were able to show me the distance they had to walk to obtain water from a stream which was their only source of water for domestic use. The project, apart from raising their level of living, could result in more efficient allocation of time by the residents and their school age children.

I made my first official visit to Guyana, my native country, from 24-28 February 2002. The Minister of Finance, Mr Saisnarine Kowlessar, a former academic colleague in the Regional Programme of Monetary Studies, met us at the airport with much pomp and ceremony. Much to the surprise of my party and myself, there was an honour guard on our arrival and as expected, I inspected them. A hectic schedule awaited us. On 25th, there was a working breakfast with President Jagdeo; I delivered a lecture at the University of Guyana on Caribbean Development at the Start of the New Century; and met with the Secretary-General of CARICOM. The day ended with a ceremony in which I was appointed a Member of the Order of Excellence of Guyana, Guyana's highest national award. The citation states the reasons best: "in recognition of your scholarship and the distinction and eminence achieved by you in the service of the Caribbean region and the wider international community in the areas of academic economics, public policy and institutional management and for your appointment as President of the Caribbean Development Bank." To put it mildly, I was deeply moved by the recognition and the conferment of the Order of Excellence.

It was all work for the next two days. The entire CDB delegation met with representatives of Guyana's political parties, private sector officials, officials from the public sector and statutory corporations, trade unionists, and non-governmental organisations. I toured Banks DIH, a major manufacturing enterprise which produces Banks beer. The brewery brought back memories of working in the Courage and Barclay brewery in London during my undergraduate years. I lectured at the Guyana Foreign Service Institute on Institutional Cooperation and the Restructuring of Caribbean International Economic Relations.

A particularly noteworthy subsequent visit was in March 2007 for the XIX Summit of the Rio Group on 3 March to which I had been invited by its Chairman, Guyana's President, Bharrat Jagdeo. I was invited to make a statement to the Group. In my statement, I noted that the intention of the Rio Group was not limited to engendering close economic, social and political relations among members of the Group but extended to the establishment of a common development agenda within the global framework. The agenda, as I envisaged it, must address widening inequalities in income and wealth and in access to productive resources, access to opportunities for gainful employment, and access to social services, notably health care, education and safe water. I identified several programmes or initiatives for deepening relations. One was intensification of trade relations which needed to be facilitated by improvements in air, maritime, road transportation services, and in electronic communication services. Another was financial networking of markets and institutions which could be further promoted through convergence of regulatory standards and simplification and uniformity of rules and procedures. A third set of programmes or initiatives should aim at strengthening the multi-lingual capabilities of the region's residents and deepening their knowledge of the societies and economies.

It was at the Summit that I first met Brazil's President Luis Inacio Lula da Silva and his Foreign Minister Celso Amorim and publicly welcomed Brazil's declaration that it intended to become a member of the Caribbean Development Bank. This led to more formal discussions during visits by me to Brasilia and less formal discussions between me and President Lula and the Foreign Minister in various forums elsewhere in Latin America, South America and the Caribbean at which we were both present. At the Summit, I also made the acquaintance of Hugo Chavez, President of Venezuela.

Relationships with the UK did not enter a troubled phase and my early visits to London ensured that they did not. In 2002, the Department for Foreign and International development provided a grant to support efficiency reforms at CDB. In 2009, the Bank received a UK Trust Fund grant of five million pounds to assist its work on regional integration and regional economic partnership agreements and in 2010, the UK approved the second tranche amounting to five million pounds for the Caribbean Aid for Trade programme.

Canada was an important feature in my interactions with non-borrowing member countries. While visiting in September/October 2001, I spoke to the Nova Scotia Environmental Industry Association on "The Role of the Caribbean Development Bank in the Future Development of the Caribbean". I provided a light introduction to my address by making reference to some historical similarities and linkages between Halifax and the Caribbean, such as being gateways for "nomads and settlers" from earliest times; strategic geopolitical significance for European rivalries; Governor Captain-General Cornwallis' establishment of a fishery in 1749, possibly laying the foundation for a once booming trade in salted cod fish between Halifax and the Caribbean where, according to the Mighty Sparrow, Canadian cod was still favoured in the 1970s; the links in education pioneered by Dalhousie University in the 19th century; the presence of the Bank of Nova Scotia in the Caribbean; and the unenviable status of Halifax and Port Royal in 17th century Jamaica, as the two most sinful cities in the world. In Halifax, I also had discussions with Dalhousie University on their intentions to collaborate with the University of the West Indies. I did not return to Halifax until the 38th Annual Meeting of the Bank in May 2008. Canada hosted that meeting with Beverly J. Oda, Minister for International Cooperation in the Chair.

In June 2005, I again paid a visit to Ottawa for discussions with government officials, including Mr Jamal Kkokhar, Director-General, Latin America and Caribbean Bureau Department of Foreign Affairs, and was also able to meet with diplomatic representatives of Barbados, Guyana, Venezuela, Cuba, and Panama at a reception graciously hosted by Trinidad and Tobago High Commissioner His Excellency Arnold Piggott at his official residence. In the same month, on invitation from Canada, I attended the Montreal International Conference on Haiti. This was a high-level meeting convened by the Government of Canada under the Prime Ministership of Paul Martin to explore governance and development financing issues following upon the overthrow of President Jean Bertrand Aristide and installation of a Transitional Government headed by Prime Minister Gerard Latortue (the older brother of Paul Latortue, my friend and academic colleague from IESCARIBE. Among the participants were Hon. Aileen Carroll, Canada's Minister of International Cooperation, Hon. Pierre Pettigrew, Canada's Foreign Affairs Minister, the Haitian Minister of Planning, Pamela Cox, World Bank Vice-President for Latin America and the Caribbean, Haruhiko Karuda, President of the Asian Development Bank, and Donald Kaberuka, President of the African Development Bank. In 2006, I returned to Canada to visit Ottawa where in June, I spoke on Poverty Reduction and Economic Integration in the Caribbean to the Round Table, and in Toronto in October where I addressed the Newsmakers Breakfast and the Canadian Foundation for the Americas and delivered a lunchtime lecture at the University of Toronto.

The Government of Canada also facilitated my initial participation in the Conference of Montreal in June 2006. The Conference is held by the International Forum of the Americas. Its founder is Gil Remillard, a former successful Quebec politician and lawyer who creditably occupied several ministerial positions in the government of Quebec. It brings together leaders of Canadian banking and business enterprises such as the Bank of Canada, Toronto Dominion, Business Development Bank of Canada, RBC Financial Group, CIBC, and SNC-Lavalin International, former Prime Ministers, Foreign Ministers, Finance Ministers, and senior governmental and business representatives from Latin America, the Caribbean, Africa and Asia for in-depth policy analyses and discussions on major themes of the global economy. At the Conferences, I was able to interact with senior management personnel from the Asian Development Bank, the Export-Import Bank of Thailand, senior officials from Malaysia, the Ghana Minister of Finance and Economic Planning Mr Kwadwo Baah-Wiredu, senior management personnel from the African Development Bank, and Gabon's Ambassador to Canada, Joseph Obiang Ndoutoume.

Participants in the formal lunch and dinner sessions to which I was always invited included, on different occasions, the Rt Hon. Joe Clark, former Canadian Prime Minister, the Hon. Peter MacKay, Canadian Minister of Foreign Affairs, the Rt Hon. John Major, former UK Prime Minister, Henry Kissinger and Mrs Madeline Albright, former US Secretaries of State, Dr Angel Gurría, OECD Secretary-General, and Mr Bernard Kouchner, French Foreign Minister in the government of President Nicolas Sarkozy. I took the opportunity to raise with Minister Kouchner the possibility of France's re-engagement with the CDB. I attended every year until 2011 and addressed the Conference on "Economic Challenges of the Caribbean Community" in June 2006, "Public Governance, Private Sector Growth and the Public Interest" in June 2007, and "Global Financial Crises: Uncertain Recovery" in June 2009. The International Forum has an affiliated entity called the Toronto Forum for Global Cities which on invitation I addressed on the topic of "Financing Transportation Infrastructure" in December 2008. At the Toronto Forum, from presentations by Colin Anderson, the Chief Executive Officer of Ontario Power Authority, Price M. Pelletier, President and Chief Executive Officer of Port of Montreal, and James C. Cherry, President and Chief Executive Officer of Aeroports de Montreal, I gained insights into privatisation of ownership and management of public utilities and sea and airports well before these kinds of developments were under consideration in Jamaica and other Caribbean countries.

The CDB received reciprocal visits from Canadian officials. Mr Kerry Morash, Nova Scotia Minister for Environment and Labour, accompanied by other officials and parliamentarians, visited in October 2005. Mr Robert Greenhill, President of CIDA, accompanied by Helen Corneau, Director for United Nations and Commonwealth Programmes visited in July 2006. Prime Minister Stephen Harper visited Barbados in July 2007 and while not visiting the CDB, sought my assistance in the local organisation of the Ideas Forum at which he was the featured speaker. I worked closely with Canada's diplomatic representatives to ensure its success, in appreciation of which Prime Minister Harper on a few occasions sent me personal letters of thanks and beautiful Canadian Innuit sculpture.

I accepted an invitation to visit China, the newest member of the Bank, in September 2001. My wife and I travelled from London, UK on 12 September, the day after the Al Qaeda terrorist attacks on the United States of America. Not surprising, there were scarcely any international passengers in Heathrow Airport or on our flight to Beijing. CDB Vice-President Desmond Brunton had travelled from Barbados the previous day. In China, we had discussions with Mr Zhou Xiaochuan, the Governor of the People's Bank of China and CDB Governor, Mr Ma DeLun, Deputy Governor and Alternate CDB Governor, other senior officers of the central bank, some provincial governors and other provincial leaders in the provinces, and chief executives of various state enterprises in finance and construction industries.

The Chinese government was keen on exposing us to their own challenge of combatting poverty in China and took us on a field trip to one of the impoverished districts where an elderly beneficiary insisted that I enter her married son's bedroom to see the bed she was finally able to purchase for him after his three years of marriage. The Chinese were extraordinarily gracious and generous hosts for our entire week in China as we travelled across the country, with Shanghai as our final place of visit before departing for a day trip to Hong Kong en route to the Caribbean. One concrete outcome of the visit to China was an agreement for a Chinese Technical Cooperation Fund valued at US$1 million to finance consultancy services and training activities for the benefit of CDB Borrowing Member Countries. The technical cooperation fund had been proposed by the Chinese government during the visit. The agreement was signed in Barbados on 13 December 2002.

The Caribbean Development Bank received a delegation from the China Development Bank on 7 December 2005. The purpose of their visit was to show support for the Caribbean Development Bank and to learn of the concerns of the Caribbean and the CDB, as well as to explore possibilities for further cooperation with the CDB and indicate opportunities for CDB in China. I indicated my awareness of China's four-point commitment to poverty reduction, namely, obtaining most favourable trade relations; enlargement of development assistance to highly indebted countries; preferential loans for trade and infrastructure investments; and provision of training. China Development Bank expressed its willingness to consider assisting the Caribbean through CDB in natural hazard management and infrastructure. It informed CDB that it was considering involvement in an inter-continental highway system in Latin America. China Development Bank requested the assistance of CDB in obtaining the commitment of Caribbean countries to the One China policy. The visit of China Development Bank was followed by a visit of China Exim Bank on 17 May 2006 to seek ways of cooperation with CDB. China Exim Bank drew attention to cooperative agreements it had with regional development banks and raised the possibility of access to concessional loans in Chinese currency.

From 10-15 September 2006, I led a CDB delegation to China on invitation of Mr Zhou Xiaochun, in his capacities as Governor of the People's Bank of China and Governor of the CDB. The Governor thought that the visit would, "further strengthen the existing friendship and cooperation between China and the Caribbean Development Bank." The other members of the CDB delegation were Assistant Bank Secretary Volville Forsythe, Director of Projects Carlson Gough and Director of Finance and Corporate Planning Warren Smith. Like on the previous visit in September 2001, the activities were intensive.

On 11 September, we met with Mr Li Ruogu, President of China Exim Bank, Mr Chen Yuan, President of China Development Bank, Mme Wu Xiaolung, Deputy Governor, PCB, and Mr Mu Huaipeng, Director-General of PCB Financial Market Department. CDB focussed its presentation on the prospects for a CDB bond issue in China and the possibility of a line of credit from China Development Bank. With respect to a bond issue, we were specifically interested in the type of currency, the process for registration and issuance, the terms and conditions for bond issue, including pricing, minimum size of issue, terms of payment, and restrictions on use of funds. With respect to a line of credit from China Development Bank, we wanted to ascertain terms and conditions for the line of credit, procurement restrictions, if any, and restrictions, if any, on the use of the line of credit.

China Development Bank elaborated on their idea of being a lead manager in raising funds in Asian capital markets, their interest in umbrella financing for projects in agriculture, public utilities and social sectors and their interest in provision of technical assistance and training. China Exim Bank indicated knowledge of economic restructuring in the Caribbean. It elaborated on its interest and/or involvement in the sugar industry in Barbados and Guyana, the co-financing of port infrastructure, geo-thermal energy, regional maritime transportation, and a bridge between Trinidad and Tobago.

During the morning of the following day, we participated in a Seminar on China-CDB Business Opportunities moderated by Mr CAI Jianbo, Deputy Director General of International Development in PCB. Carlson Gough addressed the topic of business opportunities with CDB. During the afternoon we met with Mr Dong Xiaojun, Deputy Director-General of the Latin American Department in the Ministry of Foreign Affairs.

On 13 September, we travelled to the Chinese Academy of Agricultural Sciences outside Beijing. At CAAS, we met with Dr Zhang Lijian, its Vice President, Dr Zhang Lubiao, Director General, Department of International Cooperation, other senior management staff and researchers. The discussions focussed on provision of technical services to the Caribbean through CDB, sharing of China's agricultural development experiences, and services to CDB on its projects, and agreements leading to memoranda of understanding with Caribbean universities. The visit to CAAS led to a subsequent mission by CAAS staff to assess the state of greenhouse technologies in the Bank's Borrowing Member Countries and the preparation of proposals for technological upgrading in the Guyana rice industry and the technology used in greenhouse cultivation.

My last visit to China was in July 2010. The Bank had agreed to participate in the Shanghai World Expo from 1 May to 31 October 2010. CDB joined the CARICOM Secretariat in mounting a Caribbean Community Platform to display and promote the culture and products of the Community. The Platform was staffed by CDB and CARICOM on a rotational basis. I attended on CARICOM Day, 17 July, together with Grenada Prime Minister Tilman Thomas and CARICOM Secretary-General Mr Edwin Carrington.

Germany was visited several times. The CDB delegation was well received in Berlin on each occasion. In 2001, the discussions were primarily aimed at eliciting the views of Germany on the development issues and CDB performance and communicating to the Governor, Dr Uschi Eid, how I intended to address the several challenges identified by Governors. I was also invited to observe a working session of the Bundestag where I was surprised by the informality of dress of German parliamentarians compared with their Caribbean counterparts.

In my visit in 2004, Dr Eid, despite being ill with influenza, met with us, joking that with a critical vote about to be taken in the Bundestag later that day, no member of the government could stay away and that even a pregnant colleague was asked to delay childbirth until after the vote. In our discussions, I focussed on the upcoming negotiations for the Sixth Cycle of the Special Development Fund with the primary intention of getting the German government's agreement to contribute financially. Germany after contributing to earlier cycles had declined to contribute to the Fifth Cycle. Dr Eid indicated that her government was unlikely to contribute to the Sixth Cycle, to which I countered that CDB had addressed the concerns expressed in 2000, that she had expressed satisfaction with the progress made at the Bank's Annual Meeting in 2004, and that refusal of Germany to contribute to the Sixth Cycle of the SDF would be interpreted as continuing German displeasure with the Bank. Dr Eid was convinced by my arguments and committed her government to a contribution.

The negotiations for replenishment of the SDF were completed in December 2005 with members pledging $158.1 million with a sizeable contribution from Germany. Subsequent visits to Germany involved intensive discussions with the new Governor, Ms Karin Kortmann, on CDB matters, the membership of Haiti in the Bank, and on the German interest in climate change, natural disasters and the world environment. This interest accorded closely with my own agenda for new emphases in the Bank's work.

I had previously participated in a global conference on climate change (Make Markets Work for Climate Change) hosted in Amsterdam by the Netherlands government in October 2006 and had addressed various forums in the Caribbean on climate change, natural hazards, and the environment intermittently since 2002. Ms Kortmann facilitated a visit to the Potsdam Institute for Climate Impact Research. Following upon encouraging discussions in Potsdam, I broached with Ms Kortmann the interest of CDB in German technical assistance support to address matters of climate change. This initial endeavour yielded positive results with German programme support years after I had demitted office.

I visited the Non-Borrowing Member Countries in Latin America on more than one occasion, sometimes for discussions with the Governors and their senior officials, sometimes to participate in conferences or international meetings organised by international agencies, multilateral financial institutions or the European Union. In Mexico City in November 2004, in addition to discussions at the Ministry of Finance, I lectured at Ciudad University. I travelled to Guadalajara, Mexico for the Summit of Heads of State and Governments of the European Union and Latin America and the Caribbean in May 2004 and to Medellin, Colombia, in March 2009 for the Inter-American Development Bank Annual Meeting. The two countries were also visited several times for discussions on other matters such as replenishment of the Special Development Funds and the plans for increasing the Bank's authorised capital stock.

In my numerous visits to the Borrowing Member countries, I made sure that not only the constitutionally independent countries were visited but also those countries that were associated states or colonies of the United Kingdom. I visited the Turks and Caicos Islands several times and in November 2006 participated in a conference on development banking co-sponsored by the CDB and TCI government and in November 2007 spoke on "Nature and the Economy: Addressing the Delicate Balance" at a Conference on the Environment at which Al Gore, the unsuccessful US Presidential candidate was the Featured Speaker. In my last visit to the Cayman Islands, I participated in The Cayman Finance Summit which took place on 6 May 2010. Participation in the CARICOM Heads of Government twice yearly meetings provided other opportunities to engage the countries' leadership in discussions about the work of the CDB, their own expectations and requests for Bank support, and the importance of them lending their support to the Bank's mobilisation of funds from international capital markets, official donors and multi-lateral financial institutions as well as the Bank's efforts to secure technical assistance for programmes of strategic importance to the countries.

Another aspect of my efforts at improving and strengthening relations with member countries was engaging the Barbados-based members of the Board of Directors, i.e., those representing Barbados, Canada, China and the UK, in both formal and informal discussions outside Board meetings about the work of the Bank. This allowed for better mutual appreciation of concerns, objectives and constraints of countries and their representatives and those of the Bank and engendered collegiality when matters were raised at Board meetings. Related to this aspect was my practice of ensuring that Bank staff responded to comments, questions and suggestions from Directors fully, accurately and professionally in acknowledgement of the professional capabilities, experience and institutional commitment of Board Directors.

DEVELOPMENT PARTNERS

INTER-AMERICAN DEVELOPMENT BANK

Contrary to the view articulated by some at the CDB's Annual Meeting in 2000, the Bank had a solid relationship with the IDB. It had managed a line of credit from the IDB. The two institutions had in 2000 decided to formulate an Economic Reconstruction Programme and a CARICOM Reconstruction Facility for CDB members. Ms Pamela Williams, a senior IDB staff member, was seconded to the CDB's President Office to organise and manage a Task Force which held meetings in Barbados, Grenada, St Vincent and the Grenadines, St Kitts-Nevis and St Lucia in 2001. The CDB President, Sir Neville Nicholls, led the Task Force. As the successor to Sir Neville Nicholls, I continued the work of the Task Force with meetings in Belize and Trinidad and Tobago in 2001.

The relationship with the IDB became even stronger in subsequent years. There were Task Force meetings in Guyana and Belize in 2002. In the same year, CDB received a second loan of $20 million from the IDB for on-lending to OECS member countries. The IDB President, Dr Enrique Iglesias, who I knew well from the time of the UWI long term capital development programme in the mid-1990s, accepted my invitation to attend the CDB Annual Meeting in the Cayman Islands in May 2002 and deliver the William G. Demas Memorial Lecture on "Financing the Restructuring of Caribbean Economies in the context of Globalisation". In May 2003, President Iglesias and his senior advisors visited the CDB headquarters in Barbados. We agreed on annual meetings of the Presidents of the CDB and the IDB. We focussed our discussions on the OECS, IDB financing of the Caribbean Regional Technical Assistance Centre, and coordination and cooperation in common countries.

In June 2003, IDB and CDB collaborated on an International Symposium on Pension Reforms in the English-Speaking Caribbean at which Dr Euric Bobb from the Office of the IDB President gave Opening Remarks and Dr Marion Williams, Governor of the Central Bank of Barbados, gave the Feature Address. The Symposium was attended by experts from the Caribbean, Latin America, Europe and the US. In that year, the two institutions collaborated with Microfinance Ltd (MICROFIN) on a Microfinance Roundtable. In 2004, IDB agreed that the CDB would administer its technical assistance grant of $650,000 to the Caribbean Regional Technical Assistance Centre. In May 2005, I addressed the IDB

Conference on Meeting the Competitiveness Challenge in Barbados on the topic of Approaches to Sectoral Development Policies. I always attended the IDB's Annual Meetings in various places, including Santiago in Chile, Lima in Peru, Fortaleza in Brazil, Medellin in Colombia, and Calgary in Canada.

The Presidency of the IDB changed in May 2005 with Mr Luis Alberto Moreno succeeding Dr Enrique Iglesias. The relationship between the IDB and the CDB deepened. Mr Moreno visited CDB in June 2006 for the annual meeting of Bank Presidents and for its Workshop on Disaster Risk Management which led to future collaboration on mainstreaming disaster risk management. In May 2007, he attended the CDB Annual Meeting in Caracas in Venezuela. On 14 November 2007 at the invitation of President Moreno, I addressed the Executive Board of the IDB.

In 2009, I addressed the IDB 50th Anniversary Symposium in Port-au-Prince, Haiti, and also made introductory remarks at the IDB Workshop on Long Term Development Challenges and Opportunities for Trinidad and Tobago in Port of Spain, Trinidad. Collaboration of conference-type activities continued with a CDB/IDB seminar on housing affordability and the Civil Society Dialogues in CDB borrowing member countries in 2007 and with a seminar in December 2008 co-sponsored with the IMF and World Bank on Global Financial Crisis and the Caribbean. On the lending side, there was also collaboration between the IDB (and the World Bank) in 2008 on the creation of a $130 million Programme Based Loan Facility in the CDB.

WORLD BANK

Relationship with the World Bank which was a matter of expressed concern in 2000 was speedily repaired. I visited the World Bank Head Office in Washington, D.C. for discussions with Mr David Ferranti, its Vice-President for Latin America and the Caribbean. We discussed World Bank technical assistance to CDB on development of the latter's private sector strategy and policy, joint financing, and joint organising of conferences. The World Bank followed up on the matter of technical assistance on the CDB private sector strategy and policy by providing assistance through the International Financial Corporation (IFC) with the CDB two-day forum on Private Sector Development Strategy.

On 24 January 2002, I spoke at the Opening Session and chaired a panel on the World Bank sponsored Roundtable Discussion on the Eastern Caribbean Currency Union Financial Sector in St Kitts. In June of the same year, I spoke on the International Financial Institutions Panel at the Caribbean Group for Cooperation in Economic Development (CGCED) meeting in Washington, D.C., in the presence of St Kitts-Nevis Prime Minister Dr Denzil Douglas, the IMF Managing Director, and the Presidents of the World Bank and IDB. Later in the month, I spoke on Global Cooperation for Caribbean Development at the 3rd Annual Conference of the World Bank Staff Exchange Programme.

In 2004, a decision was taken to move the CGCED from the World Bank to the CDB, which became its Secretariat. In 2005, it was renamed the Caribbean Forum for Development and in the same year held its inaugural plenary conference on Managing Transformation for Competitiveness in Barbados. In my Opening Address to the Forum, I stressed several key issues, including the less benign and less supportive international economic environment, poverty persistence in the Caribbean, economic growth deceleration, weak macro-economic management, insufficiently strong private sector entrepreneurship, and social disorder.

In May 2009, the new Vice President for Latin America and the Caribbean, Mrs Pamela Cox, addressed the CDB Annual Meeting in the Turks and Caicos Islands. In 2010, the two Banks signed an MOU for a comprehensive long-term approach for effective development through sustainable, equitable economic growth and poverty reduction.

As was the case with the IDB, I attended the joint Annual Meetings of the World Bank and the IMF, one particularly notable meeting being in October 2009 in Istanbul, Turkey, where Mr James Wolfenson, President of the World Bank, re-committed his institution to assist Caribbean Community countries with debt restructuring, problems of access to financial resources from multilateral financial institutions, and the tax haven problem created by the OECD. At the CARICOM Heads of Government meeting in Antigua and Barbuda in July 2008, he had offered a package of assistance comprised of sending a team of experts to devise country -specific debt amelioration strategies; his lobbying the Bank's International Development Agency to exempt highly indebted middle income countries from the per capita income eligibility criteria; encouragement to other international financial institutions to make Caribbean Community countries eligible for concessionary loans on the basis of vulnerability and resilience factors; and mediation of the differences between CARICOM and the OECD on the tax haven problem.

EUROPEAN INVESTMENT BANK AND EUROPEAN UNION

The CDB actively courted the European Investment Bank (EIB) for assistance to provide financial support to the Caribbean and invited it to become a member of the CDB. In 2002, I met with representatives of the European Union and the EIB in Brussels and Luxembourg, notably Mr Philippe Maystadt, the congenial Belgian President of the EIB, on matters of CDB access to resources for development of private enterprises, on-lending for financial institutions and structured investment programmes in the CDB.

In 2004, I again met with Mr Maystadt and his colleagues in Brussels to discuss three main matters. First, joint strategies of the CDB and EIB, focussing on renewal of EIB financing. Second, EIB contribution to CDB share capital, which the EIB President committed to raising with the EIB Board in May 2004. Third, CDB's role in private sector financing and collaboration with EIB. In 2005, EIB visited the CDB, and at the CDB Annual Meeting in Guyana, Director-General Louis Biancarelli announced approval of a Global Line of Credit to CDB for 40 million Euros for private and public sector development.

In 2006, the EIB approved a Loan Guarantee Facility of twenty million Euros for productive projects by the private sector and commercially operated public companies financed by financial intermediaries. At the CDB Annual Meeting in Montego Bay, Jamaica in May 2006, Governors of the CDB agreed to amend the Bank's Charter to permit institutional membership. This was intended to pave the way for EIB membership which seemed a real prospect. However, difficulties were encountered with some EIB shareholders (France in particular, we heard) and the matter was not successfully concluded.

European Union representatives in Barbados collaborated with CDB on several matters, including supporting the Bank's engagement with the EIB. Mr John Calighoru and Mr Amos Tincani interacted closely with me as President of the Bank.

UNECLAC AND OAS

The United Nations Economic Commission for Latin America and the Caribbean (UNECLAC) is a very important organisation for generating economic growth and socio-economic development strategies and policies and for leveraging international financial resources for the benefit of Latin America and the Caribbean. Because of the role and status of UNECLAC, I readily accepted an invitation from its Executive Secretary, Dr Jose

Antonio Campos, a Colombian economist who I had first met during my association with IESCARIBE in the 1980s, to make a presentation on financing sustainable development at a Regional Preparatory Conference of Latin America and the Caribbean in Rio de Janeiro, Brazil, in October 2001. The UNECLAC conference was preparatory for the World Conference on Sustainable Development scheduled to be held in Johannesburg, South Africa in 2002. At the end of the Conference, courtesy of Dr Ocampo, Dr Marlene Attzs and I toured Rio, discussed mutual academic interests and started a close friendship and professional relationship including publication in 2005 of an academic journal paper entitled 'The Role of Economic Institutions in Caribbean Economic Growth and Development'.

I invited Dr Ocampo to attend the CDB Annual Meeting in 2002 and to deliver the William G. Demas Memorial Lecture at the CDB Annual Meeting in St Kitts-Nevis in May 2003. He spoke on the subject of "Small Economies in the Phase of Globalisation". UNECLAC collaborated with the CDB and the Turks and Caicos Islands Investment Agency for a Conference on Development Banking in the Caribbean: Towards a Regional Approach in November 2006. Dr Antonio was succeeded in the post of Executive Secretary of UNECLAC by Ms Alicia Barcena, a Mexican national, in July 2008. The relationship with CDB continued smoothly. From 30 May-1 June, 2010, I attended the 33rd Session of UNECLAC in Brasilia and spoke on the subject "State, Political Action and Social Covenants: An Equation in the Making".

There was also collaboration with other United Nations agencies and the Organisation of American States (OAS). On invitation from the Director-General Jacques Diouf, I attended a Food and Agricultural Organisation Annual Meeting in Rome and visited the Director-General on a subsequent occasion. The leadership of the OAS changed in 2005. As CDB President, I received His Excellency Ricardo Lagos, President of Chile, and a delegation which included Mr Jose Miguel Insulza, Minister of the Interior on 21 February 2005. President Lagos was a distinguished academic economist with whose work I was well acquainted. The discussions covered the Caribbean regional economy, the role of development banks in regional integration, programmes and actions for overcoming poverty, the CDB's priorities for 2005/2006, and joint activities with the OAS.

The visit was clearly intended to garner support for Mr Insulza's candidacy for the post of OAS Secretary-General to which he was duly appointed on 26 May 2005. I had subsequent contacts with several diplomatic representatives and officials at the Organisation of American States, including Ambassador Ellsworth James, Chair of the OAS Permanent Council, Ambassador Gordon Shirley, Chair of the Inter-American Council for Integral Development and OAS Assistant Secretary-General Albert Ramdin. R.L. Ronald Scheman, who I had known from the 1990s when he was the US Director at the IDB and with whom I had a very cordial relationship, was Director-General of the OAS's Inter-American Agency for Cooperation and Development. On 12 April 2006, I addressed the Inter-American Forum which is a joint meeting of the OAS Permanent Council and the Permanent Executive Committee of the Inter-American Council for Integral Development. In 2010, CDB partnered with FAO, World Bank, CARICOM Secretariat, European Union, the Caribbean Agriculture Research Development Institute and the Inter American Institute for Cooperation in Agriculture (an OAS entity) to stage the Caribbean Regional Symposium on Agriculture.

CARICOM SECRETARIAT

The Caribbean Community Secretariat is a highly important development partner of the CDB. The Bank is represented at the twice-yearly meetings of the Caribbean Community Heads of Government and at all the councils of the Community which deal with economic matters. The two institutions work in complementary and reinforcing ways to advance the economic integration of the Bank's borrowing member countries. The Bank used its resources extensively after 2001 to support initiatives for regional economic integration.

In 2003, it co-financed a report titled "CARICOM Single Market and Economy: Assessment of the Regions Support Needs" by Havelock Brewster. In 2004, it designed the method of funding of the Caribbean Court of Justice (CCJ) and mobilised the funds on the international capital markets for on-lending to the governments for financing of their contributions to the CCJ.

In 2005, it provided technical assistance funds for the Regional Negotiating Machinery established by the governments to coordinate and manage the process for the major trade and economic negotiations with the European Union and the Free Trade Area of the Americas proposed by the USA and seconded a staff member to work in the RNM. In 2005, the Bank also contributed financially together with the WHO, PAHO and the CARICOM Secretariat to a Caribbean Commission on Health and Development. The establishment of the Caribbean Commission on Health and Development was a follow-up to the Nassau Declaration of Caribbean Community Heads of Government that the "Health of the Region is the Wealth of the Region". I was a member of the Caribbean Commission which was chaired by Sir George Alleyne, former Director-General of the Pan-American Health Organisation and Chancellor of the University of the West Indies. In 2007, the Bank made a financial contribution to establish the Caribbean Risk Catastrophe Risk Insurance Facility which is an institution for providing insurance coverage to Caribbean Community governments for natural hazard events. In 2008, the Bank co-financed with CARICOM Secretariat a study on Cost of Regional Air Travel and financed a study on Regional Public Goods.

The CDB took the lead in some other initiatives. In 2005, it recommended to Heads of Government the establishment of a CARICOM Development Fund and the following year did much of the preparatory work for the establishment of the Regional Development Fund which was established in 2008. The Bank was given responsibility by Heads of Government for the preparation of report on establishment of a regional stabilisation fund and a proposal on automaticity of funding of the CARICOM Secretariat. In 2009, as CDB President, I was assigned the chairmanship of the Council of Finance and Planning Task Force on Regional Strategies for Mitigating the Global Financial Crisis.

In 2009, the Bank provided a grant to the CARICOM Secretariat to support preparation of a Strategic Plan for Regional Development. Preparation of the Strategic Plan involved technical contributions by Caribbean experts on the full range of economic sectors, some economic infrastructure services such as maritime and air transportation, private sector development policy and capacity building, institutional strengthening, human resource information systems and macro-economic development policy framework. The experts included Professors Norman Girvan, Dennis Pantin, Claremont Kirton and Andrew Downes, Dr Ranjit Singh and Mr Gregory McGuire from the UWI, Dr Ena Harvey from IICA, Mr Fritz Pinnock from the Caribbean Maritime Institute, Ambassador Havelock Brewster, Dr Camella Rhone and Mr Hollis Charles. The principal technical representative from the CARICOM Secretariat was Dr Maurice Odle, Economic Advisor to the Secretary-General. I was appointed Chairman of the Advisory Committee responsible for the preparation of the Strategic Plan for Regional Development.

One initiative which did not work out as planned was the Bank's effort to manage Trinidad and Tobago's Petroleum Fund which was intended to provide relief to CARICOM states affected by rising prices of crude oil. I had been approached by Prime Minister Patrick Manning in the margins of a meeting of CARICOM Heads of Government in Grenada in July 2004 about his desire to provide financial assistance to affected countries through the CDB which he thought would not only manage the Fund effectively but would also insulate his government from direct requests from the countries. CDB in conjunction with the Trinidad and Tobago Ministry of Finance and Planning worked on the Prime Minister's idea between August and November 2004.

At the Heads of Government meeting in Port of Spain on 8-9 November 2004, Prime Minister Manning announced the decision to establish a Petroleum Stabilisation Fund to support poverty reduction initiatives. This was well-received by the Heads of Government. The CDB submitted to the Trinidad and Tobago government a draft document which outlined the background, structure and operational procedures of the Petroleum Fund to be established in the CDB, financed from a percentage of petroleum revenues of Trinidad and Tobago indexed to the monthly average prices of Brent crude oil, and capped at TT$25 million per month. It was proposed that 50 per cent of the allocation would be used for purchases of petroleum from Trinidad and Tobago and that the remaining portion could be used for fiscal and budgetary support, natural disaster mitigation and relief, and technical and vocational training in selected areas, such as small business development, tourism and related services, and ICT.

Not hearing from the Trinidad and Tobago government for several months, Desmond Brunton, CDB Vice President for Operations and I met with Minister of Energy Conrad Enill in Port of Spain to enquire about progress at the Trinidad and Tobago end only to be told that there was a decision not to have CDB manage the Fund but to place it in the CARICOM Secretariat because a few of the potential beneficiaries had expressed their preference for the latter arrangement. At the Inter-Sessional Meeting of Heads of Government on 9-10 February 2006, it was decided that Ministers of Finance would decide on allocations of resources from the Fund which would also make a one-time disbursement of $20 million to the Regional Development Fund which was a separate CARICOM development finance entity initially designed by the CDB and established in 2008. Suffice it say that the arrangement did not work well for the CARICOM Secretariat or for the Trinidad and Tobago government.

UNITED STATES

The United States had not been actively engaged with the CDB for many years since their funding of programmes in the 1970s but had started to re-engage in 2000 with a grant of $3 million for the establishment of a Disaster Mitigation Facility in the Bank. Soon after Haiti became a member of the Bank in 2007, I visited the US State Department to see whether the US would be interested in financing a line of credit or a grant window for Haiti through the CDB. The Assistant Secretary of State and Treasury officials with whom I met indicated that the US government preferred to deal directly with Haiti. There were other contacts with the US. I received an invitation from the Congressional Black Caucus and from the Chairman of the Ways and Means Committee to meet some legislators at a reception held in the House of Congress in 2007. I was able to have informative discussions with Congressman Charles Rangel, Congressman Charles Meeks, and several representatives of other congressional districts across the US.

At the reception, I met Mr Robert Allen Stanford, who had extensive business interests in the Caribbean, including ownership of Caribbean Star and Caribbean Sun airlines, the Bank of Antigua, Stanford Bank of Venezuela, newspapers in Antigua and Barbuda and St Kitts-Nevis, and the Stanford Cricket Ground in Antigua and Barbuda. Stanford, with his right hand on his heart, proclaimed himself to be a Caribbean person, with some justification because he was a dual citizen of the US and Antigua and Barbuda where he currently resided, had resided previously in Montserrat and St Croix, had sponsored the first and second Stanford T20 cricket tournament in the West Indies in 2006 and 2008, had co-sponsored with the England Cricket Board a T20 cricket series between the West Indies and England in 2008, and had been made a Knight Commander of the Most Distinguished Order of the Nation by Antigua and Barbuda in 2006.

Stanford proposed in January 2007 a merger between Caribbean Star Airlines and LIAT (1974) Ltd. The CDB advised Antigua and Barbuda, Barbados, and St Vincent and the Grenadines, the main shareholders of LIAT (1974) Ltd, against purchasing their equity in the merged entity with a loan from Stanford which would give him total ownership of the merged entity if they were delinquent on loan repayment. Instead, the Bank funded the $60 million equity injection by loans to the three governments. Stanford decided not to proceed with the merger and LIAT (1974) Ltd bought out Caribbean Star in June 2007.

In 2008, I was invited to a reception to be held in the House of Congress in honour of Mr Robert Allen Stanford but declined as I had gained information from my diplomatic contacts in Barbados about questionable financial activities of his which were attracting negative attention from both the UK and US governments. He was arrested by US federal authorities in 2009, charged with financial fraud of billions of dollars, and convicted and sentenced to 110 years imprisonment in 2012. Antigua and Barbuda revoked his Knighthood in November 2009, and the Eastern Caribbean Central Bank acquired the local operations of the Bank of Antigua and renamed it the Eastern Caribbean Amalgamated Bank.

On a subsequent occasion, on invitation from the US Overseas Private Investment Corporation (OPIC), I attended an investment conference in El Salvador to speak on the role of CDB in financing the Caribbean private sector.

EXPANSION OF MEMBERSHIP IN THE BANK

Sustained efforts were made to expand the membership of the Bank between 2002 and 2011. With respect to borrowing member countries, an attempt was made to re-engage Suriname on its membership application which had been approved by the Board of Governors sometime in the 1990s. CDB Vice-President Mr Neville Grainger visited Suriname and corresponded with senior government members and officials to ascertain the difficulties preventing Suriname from completing the formalities for accession. Progress was excruciatingly slow, and it was not until September 2013 that Suriname completed the requirements and joined the Bank in December 2013.

Slow progress on finalising Haiti's membership had become the breaking point in France's relationship with the Bank and had also troubled other non-borrowing members of the Bank. My own involvement with Haiti, which began in 1980, combined with my knowledge of shareholders dis-satisfaction caused me to make strenuous efforts to bring Haiti into the Bank as a borrowing member. Mr Faubert Gustave, the Haitian Minister of Finance was invited to the Bank's Annual Meeting in St Kitts-Nevis in May 2003.

By 2005, Haiti had completed the formalities for membership but there was a political setback with the overthrow of President Jean Bertrand Aristide in February 2004 and the installation from 2004-2006 of an Interim Government which was not recognised by all CARICOM member states. Nonetheless, in 2007, in anticipation of Haiti's membership, I organised several presentations to Bank staff on Haitian economy, governance and politics, and culture and history under the President's Discussion Series which I had started to lift the intellectual life of the Bank. Charles Clermont, Vice President of Societe Financiere Haitien de Developpement spoke on the "Business Environment and Prospects in Haiti". He highlighted the long-term decline of rural economy, the necessity of accelerated job creation, and the critical importance of observing the rule of law. Dr Michael Dash, Professor of French at New York University (and a former academic colleague at the UWI Mona campus) spoke on "Culture and Customs in Haiti". Professor Dash argued that Haiti's culture, problems and current difficulties were all explicable without resorting to mythical ideas about the country's extreme uniqueness, and that what is required is a strengthening of the Haitian State and its institutions. Ambassador Colin Granderson from Trinidad and Tobago spoke on politics and governance.

Haiti joined the Bank formally on 19 January 2007. Mr Daniel Dorsainvail, Haitian Minister of Economy and Finance, attended the Annual Meeting in Caracas as Haiti's representative on the Board of Governors. Given the dire economic situation of Haiti and the acuteness of the social and economic problems at the level of households, CDB provided financial assistance through grants for strengthening and capacity building in the public sector and for education of primary school children. Its Education for All project co-financed with other donors was approved in 2007. The project design was influenced by dismal facts such as one-third of the primary school-aged population were not enrolled in school and 20 per cent of those enrolled did not complete the prescribed five years of schooling. The project was designed to finance nutrition, provision of learning materials, learning programmes, and teacher training. In July 2007, \$4 million was granted for an Urban Community Driven Project (PRODEPUR) and an additional \$5 million was granted in 2010. PRODEPUR was intended to improve access to basic social infrastructure services, generate income for vulnerable communities, and additionally to provide social infrastructure for communities disadvantaged by the earthquake in 2010. The CDB also granted \$0.8 million for public sector training in financial management.

Between 2008 and 2009, I visited Haiti several times for discussions with the President Rene Preval, members of his government and other officials. President Preval and I had a very cordial relationship, bolstered by the several opportunities we had for interchanges in the margins of the CARICOM Heads of Government meeting at which I represented the CDB. I regarded him as a good person who was fully committed to the development and good governance of Haiti. I do not have such a high opinion of some of his predecessors and successors. Shortly after my last visit to Haiti as CDB President, Haiti was struck by a disastrous earthquake on 12 January 2010. CDB joined other donors in providing major financial assistance for earthquake relief, recovery and reconstruction.

I did not return to Haiti again until 27 July 2018. I was invited by Dr Paul Latortue (my IESCARIBE friend and colleague from the 1980s) to lecture to students in the Master of Business Administration programme at the Universite Notre-Dame d'Haiti. Apart from the lectures, I met with the leadership of the Banque de la Republic d'Haiti (Haiti's Central Bank) for exploratory discussions on studentships for Haitians at the University of the West Indies, the Haitian desire to have construction companies in CARICOM augment existing capacity in Haiti, and an expanded role for the Caribbean Development Bank in Haiti given the establishment of an office in Port au Prince. Present in the meeting with the Central Bank were Mr Jean Baden Dubois, Governor, Dr Fitz Duroseau and Mr Ronald Gabriel, members of the Board of Directors, Mr Gabriel Verret, Economic Counsel to the President of Haiti, and Mr P.J. Raymond Magloire, a consultant in Economics and Finance who had previously served as Governor of the Central Bank. I had known Dr Duroseau and Mr Magloire previously. I was also interviewed by *Le Nouvelliste*, the most important newspaper in Haiti, on CARICOM and the CDB.

During that visit, on which my wife accompanied me, we were able to do some sightseeing and observe visible signs of improvement in living standards as well as signs of the emergence of organised gang control of segments of some districts, including in Petion-Ville. On our day of departure, which was attended by much drama and chaos at the airport, we observed one instance of the major public demonstrations and breaches of the rule of law that continually constrain Haiti's social and economic development.

Brazil joined the CDB as a regional non-borrowing member on 31 December 2015. This was the culmination of efforts which started formally in 2005. From 27-30 September 2005, I visited Brazilia accompanied by Assistant Bank Secretary Volville Forsythe to start discussions with the Brazilian authorities about membership in CDB and the possibility of contributions to the Bank's Special Development Fund. We met with Dr Jose Carlos Miranda, Secretary for International Affairs, Dr Benvindo Belluco, General Coordinator, International Financial Institutions in the Ministry of Planning, Dr Alexandre Rosa, Deputy Secretary for International

Affairs, and Mr Augusto Cesar Castro from the Ministry of Foreign Affairs. The response was encouraging. I took advantage of meetings on various subsequent occasions in Latin America and the Caribbean to have follow-up discussions with both President Lula and Foreign Minister Amorim in which they reassured me that Brazil would be actively taking steps to join CDB. Brazil's application for membership was duly submitted and approved by the Board of Governors in May 2008. The remaining formalities took years to complete because of legislative delays in the Brazilian Parliament, although President Lula, in fulfilling a commitment made to me personally, ensured that Parliamentary approval was given during his last year in office. There was also a delay in the submission of requisite documents to the United Nations by the government which succeeded President Lula's.

While in Brasilia in September 2005, I was invited by President Lula to the First Meeting of Heads of State of the South American Community Nations from 29-30 September. One of my vivid memories from that meeting is President Lula in the Chair valiantly trying to restrain the loquacious President Hugo Chavez.

Unsuccessful efforts were made to get other countries to join the non-borrowing membership of the Bank. Visits were made to Puerto Rico and to Costa Rica in 2003. The visit to Costa Rica was suggested by Carlos Echevarria, that country's ambassador to Trinidad and Tobago from 1999-2005, with whom I was acquainted. I combined discussions with the Costa Rican government with a visit to the Inter-American Institute for Cooperation in Agriculture (IICA), headquartered in San Jose. At IICA, I met with Dr Chelston Brathwaite, its Director-General, Dr Arlington Chesney, Deputy Director, and other staff including Marvin Taylor and Rafael Trejos, former economics associates in IESCARIBE. The Bank also had an interest in Spain joining the Bank.

The Spanish Prime Minister had attended the CARICOM Heads of Government Meeting in 1999. Spain's Ministry of Economy and Finance officials visited the CDB in 1999, and the Bank made an exploratory visit to Madrid from 27-29 November 2000. Along with Assistant Bank Secretary Volville Forsythe, I visited Madrid on 27-29 January 2003 to follow up the early initiatives for membership and to explore other possibilities of cooperation. We met with the Director General for International Financing, the Deputy Director General for Multilateral Financial Institutions, and Advisor for Sub-Regional Institutions in the Ministry of the Economy. They were updated on developments at CDB, and Spain was invited to the Bank's Annual Meeting in 2003.

The CDB also approached India during the Prime Ministership of Dr Manmohan Singh (2004-2014). The Bank engaged Sir Shridath Ramphal, former Commonwealth Secretary-General, who knew the Prime Minister well to intercede on its behalf in 2006/2007. The feedback was encouraging at first but internal difficulties in the government caused a setback. Those difficulties seemed to have been resolved in 2007 and the Bank was invited by the Minister of External Affairs to visit in 2008. I led a CDB delegation which included Vice-President Grainger and Assistant Bank Secretary Forsythe to New Delhi in February 2008. By the time we arrived there was another political turn for the worse of which we only became aware a few days after our arrival. This delayed the start of any discussions with the Ministry of Finance. Finally, we only met mid-level civil servants and when the discussions started it became clear that the Indian government was no longer interested in a relationship with the CDB and that the entire trip was a waste of the CDB's time. The Bank also started discussions with the Republic of Ireland and visited Dublin in 2004 for meetings with senior government officials.

OPERATIONAL EFFICIENCY

Mindful of the critical remarks at the annual meeting in 2000 about the efficiency of the CDB, I signalled my approach to some aspects of the issue in my address at the Bank's annual meeting in 2003. I noted the Bank's reputation for quality of project appraisals and integrity of its decision-making in which "objectivity, consistency and sensitivity to shareholders' interest are of central importance." I stressed reputation as an influence on ability to mobilise international funds, prefacing this observation with CDB President Sir Arthur Lewis's statement in Grenada in 1972 that the CDB is a bank and that one consequence of being a bank is that it cannot lend to un-creditworthy entities without imperilling its own creditworthiness. I also drew attention to Lewis's address to the CDB annual meeting in Antigua in 1972 which dealt inter alia with procurement policies and procedures for Bank-financed projects. He pointed to the reasonable expectation of providers of funds that "their suppliers, contractors and consultants should have an equal chance to bid for contracts" and to the behavioural implications for the Bank in terms of policies and procedures that ensure open, fair and competitive bidding even at the cost of some delay.

I ensured that the Bank acted urgently and in a sustained manner to implement the recommendations of the Operations Audit which was monitored by a Task Force of Board Directors. A Change Management consultancy contract was awarded to Universalia, a Canadian company, to undertake the requisite process studies in the main operational departments and to oversee consequential departmental restructuring and re-engineering of work processes. The policies and procedures for recruitment of managerial and professional staff were revamped to make all positions open to competition from all member countries and to make room for early career and mid-career applicants. Consultancy contracts were awarded for review of the Bank's procurement policies and procedures with a view to making them more competitive and efficient.

In 2004, lending policies were reviewed, and the Bank began to introduce ways of providing guidance to clients, improving processes for project preparation, appraisal, monitoring and evaluation. There is evidence that the Bank became more efficient because of these changes. Administrative expenses as a percentage of average loans outstanding decreased, the average size of loans and grants increased, and the turnaround time between receipt of loan application and Board consideration was substantially reduced. However as I said in my last address to the Board of Governors in 2010, it was necessary that the Bank strengthen the trend towards greater client responsiveness, that there be continual efforts to regenerate, rejuvenate and enrich its intellectual capital by broadening the geographical origins of its new recruits and by rebalancing the age profile of its staff, ensuring all the while that newer and younger recruits find an environment which adequately values the freshness and currency of their knowledge and accepts the obligation of mentorship in the intricacies of development banking.

NEW DIRECTIONS AND EMPHASES

I sought during my Presidency of the Bank to provide new directions and emphases in both the Bank's work and in the wider public policy domain within the holistic framework of economic growth and socio-economic development strategies and policies. I did so in various ways: by focussing selectively on some development issues during my annual addresses to the Bank's Board of Governors; through speeches and lectures at conferences, seminars and meetings; and through service on specific boards and committees. I suppose that because of my background as an academic researcher, I decided on the topics, did the necessary research and prepared the presentations myself.

PRIVATE SECTOR DEVELOPMENT

My first action to rekindle and strengthen public policy commitment to private sector development was joining forces with the Caribbean Association for Industry and Commerce (CAIC) to convene a Private Sector Summit in Barbados on 4 March 2002. Mr Gary Voss was the President of the CAIC at the time but as I noted in my address to the Summit, the idea was first suggested at the CDB's Annual Meeting in St Lucia, May 2001, by Mrs Charmaine Gardner, who was then President of CAIC. Mrs Gardener challenged the Bank to change the perception that it was a bank for governments only and urged it to respond to the requirements of the private sector. By December 2001, the Bank was well advanced in its preparation of a revised Strategy for Private Sector Development which envisaged a continuation of an emphasis on indirect lending to the private sector through loans to financial intermediaries and technical assistance to small and micro enterprises. The Summit was intended to enable better understanding of private sector needs.

My address on Building Enterprise Capacity in the Caribbean to the Bank's Annual Meeting in Grand Cayman on 15 May 2002 provided an extended statement of my own views on the matter of private sector development. I began by stating that because of globalisation, Caribbean enterprises must compete with foreign enterprises within national and regional markets and within international markets and that their competitiveness will depend upon success in building enterprise capacity defined as the ability or capability to produce and sell goods and services in a competitive environment. Five determinants of enterprise capacity were identified, namely, command over productive inputs, quality and effectiveness of human systems in enterprises, the strength of interest representation in domestic and foreign markets, the capacity of business organisations to advocate effectively and provide support to members, and the enterprise governance framework which includes accountability provisions and the legal system. This perspective underpinned a re-conceptualisation of the role of CDB and financial intermediaries to extend to provision of production credit, support of institutions which can effectively assess credit and other financial risks and reduce the extent of informational asymmetries in financial markets, direct provision of equity capital, and capacity enhancement in the regulatory framework for corporate governance.

One immediate outcome was the Bank's support for the establishment of a capital markets rating institution, Caribbean Information and Credit

Rating Services (CARICRIS), with an equity contribution in 2004 and my membership of the Board of Directors from its inception in 2005 until 2011. The expectation was that the operations of CARICRIS would improve the objectivity and reliability of credit risk assessments of companies and governments and thereby facilitate capital market access by them.

Another outcome was the Bank's equity contribution for the establishment of the Eastern Caribbean Stock Exchange in 2003. I continued to show support for capital market initiatives by accepting an invitation from Ms Judith Mark, the Administrator of Trinidad and Tobago's Venture Capital Incentive Programme to deliver the Feature Address at Venture Point 2003 4th Annual Conference on Fostering Regional Development through Entrepreneurial Activity on 16 January 2003. I attended the Euromoney/Latin Finance Conference in the Dominican Republic in October 2003. Ms Mark also attended which provided further opportunity for capital market discussions started in January and the development of a close friendship. I made a presentation on the Caribbean Investment Climate at the Euromoney/Latin Finance Conference in Jamaica in June 2007. Partly because of these initiatives and also because of my "significant contribution to the development of economies and the capital markets of the Caribbean through research and publications", Caribbean Money Market Brokers made an award to me on 5 September 2006. Barbados Prime Minister Owen Arthur who spoke at the function stressed the importance of building a regional capital market and anticipated positive effects of CARICRIS on the financial discipline and governance of enterprises.

I returned to the importance of the framework for business success in my address on public governance and private interests to the 13th Conference of Montreal in 18-21 June 2007. I drew attention to the need for a sound macro-economic framework and no less important the need for a regulatory framework conducive to business efficiency. I referred to the World Bank's estimates of the high transactions costs of doing business in the Caribbean particularly with respect to transactions such as starting a business, obtaining licenses, registering property, paying taxes, enforcing contracts, and closing a business. I reiterated these cost elements in a subsequent lecture at a business sector function in Georgetown, Guyana that was well-attended by public officials. These transactions costs had also been detailed in my address on "Challenge and Opportunity:

An Investment Overview of Caribbean Community Countries" at the Euromoney/Latin Finance Caribbean Investment Conference in Rose Hall, Jamaica, on 11 June 2007. Other facets of the enterprise development challenge were explored in my address to the CDB Annual Meeting in Halifax, Canada, in May 2008. I spoke on the topic of Enhancing Trade Capacity and Competitiveness. Having restated the requirements for trade capacity, which include capital investments in enterprises, access to working capital and investment capital, investments in improved technology, government investment in economic and social infrastructure, and the macro-economic and regulatory framework, I restated the central problem within the private sector as weakness in supplying goods and services with requisite price and quality competitiveness and supply reliability. The recommendations for achieving trade competitiveness applied to private sector enterprises as well as to governments. They included strengthening business and trade information systems, improving productivity, deriving scale and scope economies in production and sales, adoption of modern production technologies, improvement of the regulatory framework to lower transactions costs of doing business, and investment in the supporting physical infrastructure.

Given the emergence of a private sector driven economic growth paradigm and progress with regional integration, especially with respect to the cross-border movement of business capital, it was to be expected that there would be changes in the approach of development banks. In my keynote address to the Development Banking Conference in the Turks and Caicos Islands in November 2003, I stated that development banks would need to expand the private sector proportion of their asset portfolios, take account of regional complementarities and inter-linkages which may affect assessment of credit risks and benefit-cost analyses, and also consider taking advantage of the opportunities which may arise for financing investment in regional economic infrastructure.

Two industries received attention throughout my tenure. In 2002, the Bank convened an Expert Group meeting on agriculture and one on tourism. At the meeting on tourism, I documented statistically the relatively poor performance of Caribbean Community destinations between 1996 and 2002 in terms of visitor arrivals, volatility, occupancy rates, and loss of market share. The issues which needed to be tackled were quality of service, upgrading of plant and equipment, cost of service, and the need for product differentiation.

With respect to agriculture, I returned to its development challenges occasionally after 2002. In June 2007, I addressed the Agriculture Donor Conference organised by the CARICOM Secretariat in Port of Spain, Trinidad and Tobago. I noted that a dynamic and efficient agriculture sector was critical to rural livelihoods and signalled the CDB's consideration of investments in irrigation systems and other farm infrastructure, marketing capacity, sanitary and phytosanitary capacity strengthening, and technical assistance in production and marketing. I addressed the Caribbean Food Crops Society in Miami in July 2008. There, I noted the importance of the sector in terms of percentage share of gross domestic product and percentage share of export earnings in several countries. However, the sector displayed serious weaknesses such as low productivity; divergence between product composition supplied and product composition demanded; lack of price competitiveness; vulnerability to natural hazards like hurricanes and storms; poor physical infrastructure; praedial larceny; and alienation of agricultural land. All of these pointed to the need for substantial new investments in the sector, technology education and technology diffusion, investments in drainage, irrigation and flood control, land distribution policies, modern marketing and distribution systems and institutions for trade in agricultural commodities, and a supportive regulatory framework which includes curbs on praedial larceny.

NATURAL HAZARD VULNERABILITY AND THE ENVIRONMENT

In 2003, I sought to point to the importance of dealing with disasters caused in the Caribbean by natural hazards events like hurricanes, tropical storms, earthquakes and volcanoes not in a reactive disaster relief and reconstruction way but by adopting policies and taking action to mitigate and prevent natural disasters.

My address to the Annual Meeting of the Caribbean Development Bank in St Kitts in May 2003 was entitled Natural Hazard Vulnerability and Caribbean Economic Development. It pointed to the record of vulnerability to natural hazards in the Caribbean, stretching back even to the destruction of Port Royal, the original capital city of Jamaica, reputedly the most sinful city in the world and destroyed on 7 June 1692, some say by a God despairing of the influence of monarch or Pope. But my focus was on the years since 1960.

I drew attention to the immediate and long run negative effects on economic growth, stressing that, "repetitive episodes of capital stock destruction and replacement can have permanent negative effects on achievable economic growth." I pointed out that vulnerability to natural hazards is not a permanent state but depended not only on the probability of events occurring but also on policies and actions taken to manage the likelihood of damage, and the extent to which physical structures, production arrangements and social arrangements are designed to withstand the effects of natural hazards when they occur. I argued that financing of disaster relief and recovery and disaster insurance, though important, were not adequate policy responses, and that natural hazard mitigation deserves much greater attention. I also pointed out that progress in reducing natural hazard vulnerability will complement policies to manage and mitigate international trade vulnerability and financial vulnerability. I recommended that CDB and its development partners design financial programmes for investments in disaster mitigation targeted at residential property owners, business enterprises and the public sector, and that public policy should provide impetus by ensuring the existence of appropriate regulatory and incentive structures.

On 26 June 2006, I made Opening Remarks at the CDB/IDB Technical Workshop: Management of Disaster Risk Through Fiscal and Budget Planning. Mr Luis Alberto Moreno, IDB President, also made Opening Remarks. It was a high-level workshop attended by 77 participants drawn from relevant Caribbean regional and national public agencies and government departments, donor governments, institutions and organisations, United Nations agencies, and universities. Presenters including Dr Cassandra Rogers, Manager, CDB's Disaster Mitigation Facility for the Caribbean, Dr Len Ishmael, Director General of the Organisation of the Eastern Caribbean States, Prof Gordon Shirley, Jamaica Ambassador to the US, Mr Franklin McDonald, Coordinator, UWI Institute for Sustainable Development, and several international presenters from the International Institute for Applied Systems Analysis, Ministry of Finance and Public Credit in Colombia, University of Maryland, and University of Toulouse.

In my remarks, I signalled the importance of future sea level rise in the Caribbean, noted the strong connection between climate change and the frequency and intensity of natural hazard events, and also drew attention to environmental degradation often linked to survival strategies by the poor. I reiterated the point made in 2003 that disaster relief, disaster rehabilitation, and insurance and contingency financing are not sufficient policy responses to natural hazard vulnerability because they are not risk-reduction measures. I advocated ex ante risk reduction through public policy directed at several vulnerability-increasing practices, namely, unplanned and unregulated residential settlements, especially in vulnerable areas, unregulated business construction, non-observance of building codes, and weakly resourced physical planning agencies.

Late in the following year, I turned my attention more directly to the environment. I had previously dealt with the subject at the UNECLAC Regional Preparatory Conference of Latin American and the Caribbean for the World Conference on Sustainable Development to be held in South Africa in 2002. At the Regional Preparatory Conference of Latin America and the Caribbean, which was held on 23-24 October 2001 in Rio de Janeiro, I made a panel presentation on Financing Sustainable Development in the Caribbean Community. I noted the vulnerability of Caribbean Community countries to people-induced environmental degradation, the sensitivity of governments to environmental risks, the difficulty of precisely quantifying financial allocations for environmental conservation and protection, the paucity of international financial development assistance to the countries, and their reliance on the CDB. I noted that the main environmental challenges were marine pollution, chemical-intensive agricultural technologies, and encroachment on hinterland areas and forest reserves by mining and forestry. I ended by endorsing the recommendations for environmental protection which included greater priority for preventative measures, reconstruction of eco-systems, support for capacity building in relation to marine and coastal resources, international support for training and education, and creation of financial mechanisms based on vulnerability indices.

At the Turks and Caicos Islands Conference on the Environment: Fostering a Green Culture in November 2007, I delivered an address "Nature and the Economy: Addressing the Delicate Balance". I noted several expert opinions that economic growth can adversely affect the environment but counselled that economic growth by relieving poverty can also benefit protection and conservation of the environment. I presented a summary environmental scorecard for the Caribbean which depicted severe loss of forest cover; endangerment of coral reefs by sediment, marine and land-based sources of pollution and over-fishing; serious pollution of coastal waters; depletion of mangrove swamps; beach and coastal erosion, rises in sea level temperatures; a steep trend for sea levels to rise; and considerable deficiency in access to sanitation services among the growing urban populations. I counselled that an appropriate policy orientation would need to give explicit attention to natural capital in the economic growth process in recognition that environmental resources are assets; pay attention to the effects of environmental degradation on public health and human capital; and recognise the economic opportunities that can be created from promotion of environmental goals, for example the link between biodiversity and econ-tourism. I argued that an activist approach to environmental management by both governments and communities is highly desirable and suggested that the agenda for action should include forestry conservation and reforestation, biodiversity conservation and species propagation, management of use of mangrove swamps, solid and liquid waste management, urban and rural planning, and strengthening of environmental governance. Financing of environment actions and capacity is a challenge which requires concerted and collaborative efforts nationally, regionally and globally, and the avoidance of free rider behaviour by communities, private enterprises, national governments, and foreign nations.

URBAN DEVELOPMENT

In my address to the CDB Annual Meeting in Caracas, Venezuela, in May 2005, I brought up a subject which had become a major problem in Caribbean countries but was rarely the focus of explicit policy attention. The subject of my address was Urban Development: Challenges and Approaches. I began by drawing attention to the enormous expansion of the urban population in Caribbean Community countries in the 30 years since 1975 and noted that by 2020 the urban population would comprise 17 per cent of the total population and be located primarily in the main metropolitan areas. I also pointed to the growth of informal settlements which are deficient in sanitary facilities and other infrastructure services such as water, electricity, telephones, roads, and elementary schools, and are often located on steep and unstable slopes with attendant risks of soil erosion and landslides or in flood plains, all of which result in poor quality of life. I also touched on the problems of urban decay and traffic congestion on main arterial roads. I ended with a call for action which identified improvements in the physical environment; recognition that urban communities, even the informal settlements, are places of social cohesion and economic networks so that regeneration and improved access to services are preferable to relocation; the need for substantial improvement in road capacity and quality; properly functioning land allocation and property transactions systems; and preservation of historical and cultural sites.

SOCIAL DIMENSIONS OF DEVELOPMENT

The CDB focussed much of its work on poverty amelioration and poverty reduction, receiving tremendous support from its borrowing and non-borrowing member countries for the main programmes, namely the Special Development Programme (SDF) and the Basic Needs Trust Fund (BNTF) through which it pursued poverty reduction projects and other initiatives. An invitation from the University of the Virgin Islands to deliver the Alfred O. Heath Distinguished Lecture on 14 March 2005 provided an opportunity to elucidate the poverty issue.

My lecture entitled "Poverty and its Alleviation in the Caribbean" began by raising a question about the universality or identity of measures of poverty, noting that some declarative statements like: "Poverty is pronounced deprivation in well-being" (World Development Report 2001) are not as illuminative about the condition of the poor as others. For example, "To be poor is to be hungry, to lack shelter and clothing, to be sick and not cared for, to be illiterate and not schooled." (World Development Report 2001) The income or monetary approach which is used more in developed countries than in developing countries to measure poverty compares the individual's or household's income situation to an arbitrary standard. The capabilities approach is more directly linked to the second declarative statement.

In describing poverty in the Caribbean, I pointed to relatively high levels of income poverty within a spectrum of 20 per cent to 65 per cent depending on the country, progress in reducing poverty in some countries during the 1990s, the phenomenon of "working poor", the extent of poverty among the elderly, the greater incidence of poverty in rural areas, and the limited access of both rural and urban poor to physical and financial resources, education, and social and physical infrastructure services such as sanitation. I identified multiple negative effects of poverty, including inadequate levels and standards of consumption for nutritional health, safe and healthy livelihoods; environmental degradation; social exclusion, low self-esteem and confidence; and social alienation. I identified six causes of poverty in the Caribbean: low-income employment; income and wealth inequality; global inequality of income, access to resources and consumption; Caribbean economic volatility; absence of personal coping mechanisms and inadequate social safety nets; and limited access to services for improving education and skills. I concluded by advocating achievement of economic growth as a fundamental requirement for poverty reduction and alleviation, but also advocated reduction of income and wealth inequalities, better management of economic volatility, greater access to the markets of rich countries in the world and strengthening of social safety nets.

My next major treatment of the poverty issue was my Sir Arthur Lewis Memorial Lecture "Economic Growth, Poverty and Income Inequality" delivered at the Sir Arthur Lewis Memorial Conference at UWI St Augustine in Trinidad on 26 September 2008. I sought to demonstrate the centrality and inter-relatedness of economic growth, poverty and income distribution in the Caribbean. I noted that though the countries had achieved respectable growth between 1985 and 2004, poverty remained a major problem with multiple effects on economic growth itself and that there was a causal connection from economic growth to poverty. Income inequality and consumption inequality had also persisted in that period.

Despite my enduring focus on the problems of poverty and inequality, it became increasingly obvious to me that policy focus on economic progress as a means of improving human welfare was too narrowly conceived as poverty reduction and that attention ought to be paid to other important indicators of human wellbeing and progress. In my first annual address to the Bank's Board of Governors in St Lucia in May 2001, I had signalled an interest in broadening the development perspective by identifying health promotion, illness prevention and health care as critical to maintaining human capital and enhancing its productivity and went further in a short address on Health Issues in the Caribbean at the Mona Academic Conference held 13 August-2 September 2001 with the following statement: "The rationale for a development bank's concern with health is not confined to improving the quality of human capital and its productivity. It must go far beyond that utilitarian conceptualisation to envision investments in health as contributing to a social good which is the quintessence of human society, namely human lives, the lives of men, women and children. After all, physical survival must take precedence over economic growth and development and the quality of human life is itself the central object of economic growth and development."

I elaborated on this perspective in my address to the Bank's Annual Meeting in Georgetown, Guyana in May 2005 with a speech entitled "The Soft Underbelly of Caribbean Economic Progress". I argued that social progress has not matched economic progress and that it has been "insufficient in its distribution across households and districts to cap the wells of discontent which threaten the sustainability of future economic growth." The major social and political problems constituted "the soft underbelly of Caribbean economic progress." I listed several indicators of insufficient social progress: access to health care and hospitalisation; infant, child and maternal mortality rates; undernourishment; access to education services; access to improved water supply; inequality of opportunity and of income; and poverty. Social discontent was reflected in work stoppages, other forms of labour market disruptions, corruption, and crime. The policy conclusion I drew was that Caribbean governments should focus much more on social policy than previously and that development agencies, like CDB, should join the countries in addressing the social agenda.

In a later speech delivered in Grenada as the Annual Everard Dean Memorial Lecture on the topic of Exploring Sustainable Strategies for Promoting Inclusive Growth in Regional Economies, I couched the issues in terms of inclusive growth which was defined by the World Bank as "growth that allows people to contribute to and benefit from economic growth" and by the Commission on Growth and Development which defined inclusiveness as "a concept that encompasses equity, equality of opportunity and protection in market and employment transitions". I argued that to reverse the non-inclusiveness of Caribbean economic growth and make it inclusive several policies and actions could be considered. One was adoption of appropriate policies which narrowed earnings differentials between jobs, industries and sectors without creating disincentives to personal investment in education and training, job and career mobility, and productivity. Another was expanded public provision of education across the entire educational spectrum from early childhood to tertiary education. A third was reduction of the access and quality gaps between urban and rural communities with respect to utility services, transportation infrastructure and health services.

EFFECTS OF GLOBALISATION ON CARIBBEAN ECONOMIES

Several lectures and addresses which I delivered during my tenure dealt with the macro-economic performance of Caribbean countries. They include "Caribbean Development at the Start of the New Century" delivered at the University of Guyana on 22 February 2002; "Regional Economic Performance and Prospects" presented to the 23rd Conference of Caribbean Community Heads of Government and State in Guyana on 3-5 July 2002; "A Perspective on Caribbean Development in Troubled Times" delivered to the Department of Economics, UWI Mona on 8 April 2003; "Caribbean Development in Troubled Times: Trends and Prospects in the Regional and International Economy" delivered at the Clark Atlanta University Centre on 10 April 2003; and "Approaches to Sectoral Development Strategies" presented at the IDB Conference on Meeting the Competitiveness Challenge in Barbados on 4 May 2004.

These lectures and addresses outlined weaknesses in macro-economic performance like slow and volatile economic growth, persistently high unemployment especially among women and youths, fiscal imbalances and public debt, and identified briefly some of the contributory factors such as lack of economic and export diversification, low levels of competitiveness and production inflexibility in key sectors, labour market rigidities, cost-inflating public sector bureaucracies, the decreasing access to overseas bilateral financial aid, and profound structural changes in the global environment.

The global context received extensive treatment, starting in January 2003 with my presentation to the 4th Annual SALISES Conference in Barbados where I spoke on the subject "Small States in the Context of Global Changes". I began by noting that the world in 2000 was fundamentally altered by remarkable shifts in economic and political power, new institutional governance structures affecting corporations and international trade and finance, a strong tendency towards global governance, the globalisation of markets, the rapid rise of global communications, and the emergence of a global culture facilitated by the innovations in communications technology. I stressed that globalisation was not so much a new phenomenon as a situation of denser interactions across national boundaries and greater geographical spread. Its principal features were the extraordinary growth in world trade, unprecedented voluntary cross-border movement of people, more complex and dense trans-border capital movements and greater openness of financial markets, rapid international transference and adoption of institutional design and policies, and the emergence of international regulatory standards and organisations.

In the international political dimensions, the United States and mega-transnational corporations had become two distinct centres of power. Small states were marginalised, their sovereignty having little more than juridical meaning, and they had no more than a lobbying role in the formulations and amendments to international rules of the game to which they are subject.

In "A Perspective on Caribbean Development in Troubled Times", I pointed to the fact that within this new global framework, trade preferences were being replaced by new modalities of trade between the Caribbean Community countries and their traditional trading partners, modalities shaped and administered by the World Trade Organisation as well as those embodied in regional economic partnership agreements. Some consequences of the operation of the new modalities were integration of their domestic markets into the world competitive environment in which they were at a disadvantage, loss of international market share in traditional commodity export markets like sugar and bananas, asymmetrical application of WTO rules on subsidisation of national industries, and reciprocity as a basis for entry into the markets of developed countries.

There were also implicit new modalities of financial engagement with the world evident in the decreasing role of bilateral aid flows, increased reliance on foreign direct investment in the tourism, energy and mining sectors of some countries, and increasing recourse to international private capital markets by those countries able to do so. In my presentation on "National Planning by Small Non-Strategic Developing States in the Face of Declining Overseas Development Assistance" at the Planning Institute of Jamaica's 50th Anniversary Conference on Economic and Social Development Planning in November 2005, I detailed the adverse trends in disbursements of bilateral concessional debt, multilateral concessional debt and private debt to individual Caribbean Community countries between 1982 and 2001 and explored the implications for national planning.

The implications of the various global developments for economic policy and strategy were elaborated in "The Impact of Globalisation on Developing Economies: Are We Ready?" an address on 31 May 2006 to the Barbados Investment and Development Corporation Conference. I pointed out that local producers would have to achieve higher levels of productivity, establish more competitive prices and offer better quality products in order to retain market share in domestic markets in the face of foreign competition.

In export markets, it was necessary to recognise that there was a transition from periodically negotiated product prices and quotas to open market competition in which product prices, product quality and supply reliability were critical determinants of competitive ability. Product innovation and seeking markets among diaspora communities could also be important responses to the changes in the global economy. Furthermore, as recommended in the Caribbean Development in Troubled Times addresses, in the circumstances of intensified global competition, Caribbean Community countries would be well advised to improve intra-Caribbean export market prospects by facilitating intra-regional capital investments, seizing opportunities for regional import-substitution in agriculture and food products, and increasing exports of some manufactures such as rum. The countries should also focus attention on product demand latent in internal markets, for example, by inter-linking agricultural production with the tourism sector.

In general, there needed to be restructuring and modernisation of major economic sectors and the economic and social infrastructure, an active search for economies of scale and scope through increasing firm size and diversifying firm output, and repositioning of the economies in the global system. Many of these points about globalisation and its implications for the Caribbean were restated and sometimes elaborated in Economic Challenges in the Caribbean Community, a panel presentation on 8 June 2006 at the 12th Conference of Montreal. That presentation indicated that fiscal reforms to broaden tax bases and improve tax administration would need to be supplemented by debt restructuring and debt relief. It also identified the partial replacement of fossil fuels by other energy sources such as solar, wind power, ethanol and geothermal as a worthwhile component of the economic transformation strategy.

In April 2009, I attended the Fifth Summit of the Americas hosted by the Government of Trinidad and Tobago under the leadership of Prime Minister Patrick Manning. The Inaugural Session was addressed by the President of Argentina, Cristina Fernandez de Kirchner, the President of Nicaragua, Daniel Ortega, the Prime Minister of Belize, Dean Barrow, the President of the United States, Barack Obama, and the Prime Minister of Trinidad and Tobago, Patrick Manning, in that order of presentation. It was a potentially explosive start with President Ortega making strongly critical remarks about US policy but was calmed by a diplomatically astute speech by President Obama. The following day, President Evo Morales of Bolivia spoke in much the same vein as President Ortega. Contrary to the expectations of the Latin American contingent, President Hugo Chavez of Venezuela took a very conciliatory approach, declaring that many would have expected him to attack Obama, but he wanted friendship. He capped his speech with a present to President Obama.

I made a presentation at the 11th Hemispheric Private Sector Forum at the Summit of the Americas. On 16 April, I spoke on “Economic Stimulus Packages: Returning to Growth”, directly addressing the financial burden of the adjustment programmes Caribbean countries had found it necessary to implement in response to the global economic and financial crisis. The economic stimulus packages had three main elements: increased public expenditures on economic and social infrastructure; direct expenditure subsidies and grants to businesses and households; and tax waivers and other forms of reliefs. The adjustment programmes also included various policies to reduce the cost of credit and increase access in situations of heightened credit risks and the provision of liquidity support to endangered financial institutions. I expressed scepticism about how helpful the financing facilities established by the G20 countries in the World Bank and the International Monetary Fund would be to Caribbean Community countries, most of whom had been graduated from access to concessionary resources from both institutions.

In an address to the 39th Regular Meeting of ALIDE General Assembly in Curacao on 19 May 2009, I indicated that only IDA-eligible countries of which there are nine in Latin America and the Caribbean can have access to the Rapid Social Response Fund and the Global Food Response Programme. The IMF's Flexible Credit Line would also not be very accessible because most countries were unlikely to satisfy pre-set criteria with respect to sound public finance, a record of steady sovereign access to international capital markets on favourable terms, capital accounts dominated by private flows, low and stable inflation, and a comfortable foreign reserve position.

The global crisis had implications for the domestic financial sector, some of which I pointed out in "Challenges for the Financial Sector", an address to the 50th Anniversary Symposium of the IDB in Haiti on 17 July 2009. It led to greater demands for bank sector finance from both governments and the business sector for activities for economic transformation and restructuring. It also intensified problems that business enterprises experienced in accessing finance by decreasing access to trade credit and by depressing business incomes and profits in major sectors and industries. A third consequence was diminished appetite for corporate equity as well as declines in equity prices. Financial institutions were therefore confronted with greater risks and lower returns. Their response tended to be defensive rather than enterprising. They improved risk management systems and policies, increased loan loss provisioning and reduced bank credit. An enterprising approach might have included risk-sharing through co-financing arrangements with other financial institutions.

HIGHER EDUCATION AND ECONOMIC GROWTH AND DEVELOPMENT

The Caribbean Development Bank had an active portfolio of projects in the primary and secondary school systems of its borrowing member countries. I thought that the valuable role of tertiary and higher education and the economics of providing those services could benefit from public discourse. Between 2002 and 2008, I gave addresses on various aspects. In November 2005, I addressed the Annual Conference of the Association of the Caribbean Universities and Research Institutes (UNICA) in Curacao on "The Role and Significance of Higher Education in the Sustainable Development of the Caribbean". I referred to the economics literature which showed that by enhancing the quality of human resources, education contributed to economic growth and to studies which found that in the Caribbean there were sizeable social rates of return to university education even though they are lower than those accruing from expenditures on primary and secondary education. I drew attention to the important role of knowledge creation and diffusion and of technology innovation and transfer in the process of economic growth, and to the potential effects of university education on the quality of governance and the promotion of social cohesion and social responsibility.

In the 12th Rudolph Goodridge Memorial Lecture delivered at the UWI Cave Hill campus on 10 December 2002, I dealt relatively fully with the subject of "Costs and Returns in Caribbean Higher Education". I started with the observation that Caribbean Community countries exhibited substantial private and public expenditures on tertiary education and then presented some empirical results indicative of high rates of private and social returns. Private costs have tended to increase. Labour costs are the major component with wage rate homogeneity being the predominant characteristic among academics. Improvements in product quality, changes in education technology and academic wastage through student drop-out and low completion rates are also important cost drivers.

In an address entitled "Perspectives on the Financing of Tertiary Education in the Caribbean Community" on 21 November 2005, I observed that the Caribbean had begun a transition from elitist tertiary education to mass tertiary education. The stimuli for the shift included substantial positive private returns to investments in tertiary education anticipated by individuals and the expected contribution of tertiary education to economic growth and development. Noting that production costs and consumption costs accruing to institutions and students respectively are high in tertiary education, I identified possible sources of finance such as grants from national governments, philanthropic contributions, grants from foreign governments and agencies, grants from the Caribbean business community, student tuition fees, entrepreneurial activities and debt creation and discussed some of the issues which arise in relation to them.

With respect to business sector donations, recognition by enterprises that they benefit from the social returns to investment might be an important incentive, but it might be negated if a free rider position is adopted by them. In relation to financing by national governments, mass tertiary education placed considerable strains on public finances. On the matter of student tuition fees, the pertinent considerations are how much weight should be given to the beneficiary should pay principle, the fiscal affordability of full or partial fiscal subsidies of tuition expenses, and household income capacity. It was noted that the rise in student demand provided by private tertiary institutions indicates that consumers of tertiary education services are economically rational.

CIVIL SOCIETY AND ECONOMIC GOVERNANCE

Uneasy is how the relationship between civil society organisations and governments in the Caribbean Community might be accurately described. The CDB nonetheless in its Basic Needs Trust Fund programme incorporated community representatives of civil society in the formal structure for making decisions about the community projects to be financed. This approach was not entirely welcomed by some political leaders who were either concerned that in some instances the community representatives were associated with opposition politics or that the decision authority of their governments was being diminished by this mechanism of participatory governance. I obliquely addressed these issues in my address on Perspectives on Economic Governance in the Caribbean to the Bank's Annual Meeting in Tobago on 12 May 2003.

Having discussed economic governance at the macro level, I turned to the role of civil society. I noted that the Westminster model of Caribbean public governance was one of centralised decision authority, but that civil society held the contrary view that communities and beneficiaries should participate meaningfully in public governance. I cited Alexis De Tocqueville (1946) and Anthony Giddens (1998) to show that the gain from civil society participation in public governance has been extensively recognised. I argued that if, as Giddens asserts, there are no permanent boundaries between government and civil society, then there are no permanent rights, configurations and structures for incorporation of civil society organisations in public governance. Caribbean societies would be better guided by the Rex Nettleford concept of government as "a hub in a network of social/power partners engaged in a process of continuing interaction for the purpose of policy formulation and implementation."

I recognised that there are legitimacy questions about many civil society organisations, mainly on matters such as democratic representation internally, transparency of internal decision-making, funding sources and financial accountability. These issues had previously been raised by me in an address to the Forward Conference convened by the CARICOM Secretariat in Guyana in July 2002. I had stated there that non-governmental organisations could be important as development agents because governments could not do all that is required on their own and needed the help of empowered partners. However, many NGOs were ad hoc, unreliable, not adequately rooted in their communities, and dependent on grants especially from international donor agencies with a consequential tendency towards unstable mandates as donor interests and preferences altered. However, as I reminded in the May 2003 Address, while countries seek to ensure the legitimacy of civil society organisations, they must also be mindful that the legitimacy of the State is neither absolute nor exclusive.

I returned to the issue of civil society participation in an address I was invited to give by Prime Minister Patrick Manning at the Opening Ceremony of the Civil Society Forum at the Fifth Summit of the Americas on 14 April 2009. I began with the following quotation from the Johns Hopkins University Center for Civil Society Studies: “Real progress in overcoming poverty, ill health, environmental degradation, and injustice ... requires not only the authority of governments, but also the ingenuity and initiative of the world’s growing civil society sector and the millions of people it can help mobilise for effective social action.”

I noted that Caribbean CSO have been champions of the most disadvantaged members of society, social change and economic justice, which has sometimes led to an adversarial relationship with governments. Nonetheless, it was rational and appropriate to view them as partners in the development process since the partnership could enhance the quality of governance and assist in making social and economic development more inclusive. Purpose, pragmatism and flexibility should guide the interaction between civil society and governments.

STAFF AMENITIES

Concerned by some challenges of the Bank’s working habits to the personal well-being and family life of Bank staff, I ensured that two facilities were provided in the scarcely used Staff Facility Building on Bank premises. One was an after-school facility which school-age children of staff members could occupy and do their homework and studies while awaiting the end of their parents’ workday. This was in a sense a continuation of my interest in this kind of staff support when I was Principal of the UWI St Augustine campus. The After-School Facility was equipped with computers and other information technology supports. The other facility was a fitness centre for use by staff and their families at times convenient to them. Both facilities were appreciated by staff.

RAISING THE BANK'S PROFILE

During the Presidencies of Sir Arthur Lewis and Mr William Demas, CDB had a high profile in intellectual and economic policy circles in the Caribbean and elsewhere in the world. It was not unusual for the Bank President and the Bank's technical staff to attend conferences and make presentations on various aspects of Caribbean economic growth and development. This presence of the Bank diminished during the Presidency of Sir Neville Nicholls who himself maintained a high profile regionally and among the multilateral financial community. Many of the speeches and addresses which I delivered in the 2001-2011 period of my Presidency were intended to continue the tradition of my predecessors but at a heightened and revitalised level of activity. In addition to those already identified, I delivered addresses to many gatherings: the International Labour Office in Geneva on a platform which included UNDP Administrator Helen Clark; the Caribbean Academy of Sciences; the Miami Conference on the Caribbean Basin; the Caribbean and Central American Action Conference; the Institute of Chartered Accountants of the Caribbean; the Planning Institute of Jamaica; the International Meeting of Caribbean University Administrators; the Annual Conference of University Administrators; the Confederation of Caribbean Credit Unions; Sir Arthur Lewis Memorial Conferences organised separately by the Eastern Caribbean Central Bank and the University of the West Indies; various public forums organised by the CARICOM Secretariat and the Commonwealth Secretariat; and the St Lucia Chamber of Commerce.

The range of topics was eclectic. It included Caribbean economic recessions from a historical perspective; varieties of Caribbean economic growth; debt and economic growth; making the best of economic booms; the future Caribbean economy; Caribbean credit unions in an age of competition; the global economic crisis, developing economies and the role of multilateral development banks; the new focus of international organisations and the implications for the Caribbean; national planning by small, non-strategic developing states in the face of declining overseas development assistance; quality education and the Caribbean Single Market and Economy; and Guyanese economic performance, migration and prospects.

I initiated a President's Discussion Series for presentations by Bank staff and outsiders to an audience comprised of both Bank staff and members of the wider community. St Kitts-Nevis Prime Minister Dr Denzil Douglas,

St Vincent and the Grenadines Prime Minister Dr Ralph Gonsalves and Barbados Prime Minister Mr David Thompson were among the invited presenters. The practice of holding a Caribbean Development Bank Roundtable sponsored by Institutional Investor was started in 2006. Craig Leon from Institutional Investor was a very supportive collaborator of the Bank and moderated the Roundtables held in March 2006, April 2007 and April 2009. Participants in the Roundtables included senior personnel from Citicorp, Bear Stearns, Moody's, Standard and Poor's, European Investment Bank, Gravitas Capital, RBTT Jamaica Ltd, Jamaica Bauxite Institute, and Sagicor Jamaica.

Several important conferences were also organised during this period. Vice-President of Operations Desmond Brunton took the lead in organising jointly with the IDB a high-level symposium on pension reforms in the English-Speaking Caribbean in June 2003 which led to an IDB/CDB book entitled, *Workable Pension Systems: Reforms in the Caribbean* and edited by Brunton and Pietro Masci. It contained insightful chapters on Pension Reform Policies and Politics in the Caribbean; Reforming Pension Systems; the Case for Pension Reforms; Needs Assessment of Pensions Systems; Private Pension Regulation and Supervision; Systemic Pension Reform in Latin America; Recent Pension Reforms in Sweden and Italy; Political Economy of Reforms in Brazil's Civil Service Pension Scheme; Public and Private Roles in Pension Reforms; Annuities and Pensions Reforms: Main Issues in Developing Countries; Social Security Schemes and Potential Reforms; Old Age Pensions Reform; and Role of Multilateral Development Banks in Pension Reforms.

A landmark conference was held in September 2009 on Growth and Development Strategies. The Director of the Bank's Economics Department, Dr Denny Lewis-Bynoe took the lead in organising and managing it. There were seventeen contributors from the Caribbean Community.

In 2010, the Bank published the contributions in a book, *Growth and Development Strategies for the Caribbean* edited by UWI Economics Professor Frank W. Alleyne, Dr Denny Lewis-Bynoe and Ms Xiamora Archibald. The contributions included "Growth and Development Strategies for the Caribbean" by Professor Andrew Downes; Recent Developments in Growth and Development Theory and Policy with Special Reference to Small Developing Countries" by Dr Roland Craigwell; Productive Sector Development in the Caribbean: The Agricultural Sector" by Carlisle Pemberton; "Productive Sector Development in the Caribbean:

Manufacturing and Mining" by Dr Jonathan G. Lashley; "Productive Sector Development in the Caribbean: Tourism and Hospitality" by Mr Cecil A. Miller; "Trade and Industry Policy in the Caribbean" by Dr Winston Moore; "Trade Policy in the Caribbean" by Dr Roger Hosein; "Financial Aspects of Growth and Development in the Caribbean" by Mr Anthony Birchwood and Ms Andina A. Bracklin; "Caribbean Community: the Elusive Quest for Economic Integration" by Professor Norman Girvan; "Political Integration in the Caribbean: A Policy Approach" by Professor Vaughan Lewis; "Governance and Economic Development in the Caribbean" by Professor Selwyn Ryan; "Managing the Growth and Development Process: Issues of Planning and Regulation" by Philip Osei, Allison Montgomery and Ricardo Williams; "The Labour Market and Human Resource Development in the Caribbean" by Dr Roy D. Thomas; "Migration and Remittances in the Caribbean" by Professor Claremont Kirton; "Crime and Development: A Review" by Dr Corin Bailey; "Environmental Dimensions of Development in the Caribbean 1960-2009: Recommendations for the Future" by Janice Cumberbatch; and "Conclusion: The Way Forward" by Professor Andrew Downes.

GENERAL CAPITAL INCREASE

In my address to the Bank's Annual Meeting in 2004, I stated that there was need for an increase in the Bank's subscribed capital which placed statutory limits on its ability to borrow in international capital markets. The Bank's subscribed capital had not been increased since 1990. I continued to raise this matter frequently in my meetings with shareholders' representatives.

A Special Governors' meeting was convened on 14 September 2008 on CDB's future financial resource requirements. It was agreed that the Bank's capital resources were inadequate for even modest short to medium term requirements of the borrowing member countries. I therefore assembled a small team of Bank economists consisting of Mr Adrian Debique (Deputy Director of Finance) and Dr Denny Lewis-Bynoe Director of Economics) to work closely with me in preparing submissions for the approval of the Board of Directors and the Board of Governors. We journeyed to the capitals of regional borrowing and non-borrowing member countries to make presentations to leaders of government and their Bank representatives on the merits of the case for a general capital increase and the specific targets for which we sought approval. The preparation and visits were greatly appreciated everywhere. Finally, at the Annual Meeting in May 2010 in

The Bahamas, the Board of Governors approved a 150 per cent increase of the subscribed capital to $1 billion and a new strategic plan which envisaged among other things a doubling of the loan programme for 2010-2019.

FAMILY AND SOCIAL LIFE

We were accommodated in a house built to accommodate the previous Bank President in Fort George Heights close to the Bank's offices. He never occupied it. It was furnished and used for staff gatherings until we arrived. We had to modify furnishings and interior decorations and landscape the spacious grounds to meet our standards. My wife, who had taken a course in landscaping at the Samuel Jackman Prescod Institute in Barbados, created a beautiful landscape populated by decorative plants, shrubs and trees, and fruit trees. We soon discovered after moving into the house that there was a serious termite problem, resolution of which required us to live at a hotel temporarily. Given the location of the premises, security adjustments also needed to be made to the structure of the house and to a small building on the premises which at my request was converted into a personal gym. A night guard service was provided but not always reliable since the guards were sometimes observed sleeping on the job.

Family and social life proceeded in the accustomed manner. My wife and I received visits from overseas relatives and friends and in turn visited them, sometimes at Christmas, sometimes in the summer vacation. We frequently entertained friends in Barbados and were also entertained by them. We cruised the Baltic region with stops in Copenhagen (Denmark), Malmo (Sweden), Helsinki (Finland), Oslo (Norway), Gdansk (Poland), Tallinn (Estonia) and St Petersburg (Russia). On another cruise, we travelled in the Mediterranean region with stops in Rome (Italy), Naples (Sicily), Barcelona (Spain), Monaco, Malta and Tunisia.

Next, we cruised the Caribbean with stops in The Bahamas, Cayman Islands, Virgin Islands, Mexico, Panama, Costa Rica and Colombia. We were delighted to encounter our good friends Richard and Clare Kellman as well as Dunbar McIntyre and his wife Maureen on that cruise. We did a lot of leisure travel by air as well, for example visiting Las Vegas for my wife's birthday and New York City for my birthday.

On the latter occasion, Stephen Forbes (owner of *Forbes Magazine*), with whom I had breakfasted a few years previously in Miami, hosted us along with prominent business, media and political personalities, including former Canadian Prime Minister Brian Mulroney, to dinner and theatre on Broadway and a day's cruise of the Hudson River on his yacht, 'The

Highlander'. My wife accompanied me on trips to attend the IDB Annual Meetings in Santiago, Chile, in Lima, Peru, and in Forteleza, Brazil. In Peru, we took the opportunity to visit Machu Pichu and en route to Forteleza we spent a few days in Sao Paulo.

In Barbados, we were able to enjoy the company of old friends like Jan Loubser and Rosina Wiltshire, Pamela Williams, Clive and Marion Williams who graciously held an Appreciation Function for me when I was awarded the Order of Excellence, Guyana's highest national award in 2002, DeLisle and Monica Worrell, Woodville Marshall, Jean and Norma Holder, Lewis Bobb, Oscar Bayrd, John and Patsy Dow, and Cassandra Rogers. We made new friends, a few from the CDB like Neville Grainger and his wife Erica, Volville Forsythe and his wife Desiree, Rudy and Bibi Ameerally, Ed Cummings, Anthony Maughan and Marjorie Riley, and several others from outside the Bank, including Joanne Goullet, Amos and Hydrun Tincani, and Leroy and Faye Parris.

I also had a group of friends with whom I socialised at the Croton Inn. The group included my old friends John Dow and Horace Nurse, Neville Grainger, Wallace Edinborough, Ed Cummings, Boyd Angoy, Bunny Arno, and Laurajan Obermuller. Many a happy hour was spent in the company of these friends from quite varied walks of life.

Barbados, during those years, hosted a good jazz festival at which my wife and I heard the great Herbie Hancock, Kirk Whalum, Marcus Miller, Roy Hargrove, Dianne Reeves and Roberta Gambarini. One highlight of my time in Barbados was a splendid surprise party which my wife arranged for my 60th birthday. My mother and siblings were all there together with many other relatives, old friends from the Caribbean and farther away, and friends, associates and colleagues who resided in Barbados. Another was the wedding ceremony for our son Compton Olatunji (Tunji) and Lazena which took place at our residence in 2007. My wife's eldest brother, Hilbert Telman, was the officiating pastor. Sara Telman, Tunji's cousin, sang a beautiful solo. The ceremony and the reception which followed were attended by many relatives and close friends from Guyana, Trinidad and Tobago, Canada, the UK and the US.

DEPARTURE FROM THE CDB

An election was held for the post of President nearing the end of my second term in 2011. I was nominated by Guyana and urged by several governments, including The Bahamas and some in the OECS to contest for re-appointment. Against my better judgement, I did so. The successful candidate was Dr Warren Smith, a sitting Vice-President of the Bank, who had been nominated by his country Jamaica and supported by Trinidad and Tobago. Since those two countries held 64 per cent of the regional shares and since the tradition was for the non-regional members to confirm the regional outcome, the result was to be expected.

A splendid farewell function was held for me on 19 April 2011 at which there were many tributes to my years of service by members of the Board of Governors or their representatives, members of CDB staff, the Secretary-General of CARICOM, and several people who could not be present such as the Chancellor and the Vice Chancellor of the University of the West Indies. I had previously received letters of appreciation from several governments and institutions, including Dominica, Germany and the Inter-American Development Bank. The Governor for Germany, Gudrun Kopp, expressed recognition and deep gratitude for my "outstanding leadership in charting the direction of the Bank" and said that my "contribution in promoting CDB's role in social development and poverty reduction has been highly appreciated by Germany."

The Prime Minister of Dominica in his letter highlighted my "contribution to the Commonwealth of Dominica especially during the period of the economic downturn in 2002 to 2004" and assistance with other projects and programmes. Mr Luis Alberto Moreno IDB President expressed appreciation of "the warm and productive relationship we have enjoyed" which he regarded as being "essential to furthering the special relationship" between the two institutions, remembered "our close collaboration in responding to regional emergencies, including the recent food, energy and international financial crises" and "the effectiveness of our collaboration in countries that are members of both banks where development efforts have been challenged by severe fiscal and debt problems and where close coordination among all development partners has been crucial to achieving positive results."

At the farewell function on 19 April, I responded by expressing my appreciation for the efforts by the organisers of the event and lightened proceedings with the following joke: "Rumour has it that there was a Bank President who, at the end of a 20-year stint, had a farewell party at which he expected staff to write memorable cards saying how much they would miss him. Well, some wrote things like 'we will always remember you' and 'without you the bank will never be the same' and so on. The President was not quite satisfied; he wanted something from the heart, so he said to one of them, 'Dave, you have been working with me from the start. I am retiring now. What do you have to say about that?' With elegant economy of words, Dave responded, 'The best news in twenty years.' Ladies and gentlemen, Dave is not here tonight."

I indicated that I considered it an honour and privilege for me to have been able to work and interact with CDB staff at all levels, with government officials of Borrowing Member Countries and Non-Borrowing Member Countries, with regional organisations and institutions and with civil society organisations in the Caribbean. I concluded by extending best wishes to the new leadership of the Bank as they respond to the economic and social challenges ahead.

Not to be outdone by the formal official farewell function, Bank staff held their own farewell function at the Bank on my final day in office. To quote the CDB Extra publication, "The Bank's fourth President heard stirring tributes from a number of people, some of them read in absentia. The tributes not only highlighted Dr Bourne's accomplishments as President, but also showcased other aspects of the man – from his sense of humour to his love of fine cigars. Those giving tributes were Mr Neville Grainger, Mrs Valerie Jones, Mr Mark Taitt, Mrs Sonia Hunte and Dr Denny Lewis-Bynoe. Words were read on behalf of his former secretary (Mrs Lorraine Beckles), and Dr Warren Smith." Mrs Lorraine Beckles was my Personal Secretary for the first few years of my tenure and was succeeded by Mrs Valerie Jones. The excellent service, consideration and good humour they provided together with Mr Randolph O'Neale, my chauffeur, contributed immensely to my productivity and enjoyment of my time at the bank.

With Guyana's President Bharrat Jagdeo (far right) and (L-R) the Hon. Ashton Chase, Guyana's Prime Minister Sam Hinds and me on conferment of the Guyana Order of Excellence in 2002.

Me and Pamela on conferment of the Guyana Order of Excellence in 2002.

Caribbean Development Bank farewell function in 2011.

The family in Trinidad in December 2012: (L-R) Monty, Tunji's wife Lazena and grandson Luke, grandson Jackson, me, Tunji, Pamela and grandson Che, Monty's wife Jo, granddaughter Darcy and adopted granddaughter Diana.

CHAPTER NINE

CARIBBEAN ECONOMIC INTEGRATION

Caribbean economic integration is one of my enduring professional interests. Over the years, I have studied, lectured, and written on several aspects of the integration experience of the Caribbean and have been an active participant in some of the processes leading up to major decisions about furthering and deepening Caribbean integration. My first substantive direct professional participation in the work of the Caribbean Community was when I was contracted in 1986 by the Commonwealth Secretariat to prepare for the CARICOM Secretariat a study entitled Caribbean Development to the Year 2000. My last engagement on economic matters was presentation of a commissioned report in June 2012 on implications of the global economic crisis. From 1990 to 2012, I attended nearly all the Conferences and Inter-Sessional Meetings of the Heads of States and Government of the Caribbean Community where on several occasions I presented reports and advisory memoranda. My focus always was on economic and financial aspects of the integration movement.

RETROPSPECTIVE ON CARIBBEAN INTEGRATION CONCEPTS AND DESIGN

In two speaking engagements sometime between 2007 and 2008, I offered my reflections and assessment of the journey towards integration of the Caribbean. In delivering "Caribbean Integration: A Progress Report" to an audience at the UWI Cave Hill campus in 2007, I noted that 2008 should have been the 50th anniversary of the Federation of the West Indies and further noted that the passage towards integration has been slow and difficult with episodes of reversal and non-fulfilment of agreements to integrate, including the break-up of the West Indian Federation in 1962, the secession of Anguilla from the Associated State of St Christopher-Nevis-Anguilla in 1967, and the still-born political union of the Windward Islands in the early 1990s.

Sir Alister McIntyre and I had attended the announcement and first meeting of the Regional Constituent Assembly of the Windward Islands in St Vincent and the Grenadines. It was chaired by Justice Telford Georges, a distinguished Caribbean legal practitioner and scholar from Dominica. In the speech at Cave Hill, I recounted the historical antecedents, including the Windward Islands Federation 1833-1956, the Leeward Islands Federation 1871-1956, the call by Albert Marryshow and Captain Cipriani in 1932 for a Caribbean Federation, and that of Grantley Adams, Norman Manley, Albert Gomes and John Renwick in 1947 for a closer association between the British West Indian colonies. I also listed the efforts at integration subsequent to the break-up of the Federation, specifically the formation of the Caribbean Free Trade Association (CARIFTA) 1965-1972 and the formation of the Caribbean Community in 1973.

In the second speech, my remit was to explain the failure of the West Indies Federation in 1962. I began with the observation that the Federation was a multi-faceted endeavour which encompassed in its span of objectives political integration, economic integration, socio-cultural integration and self-determination. Focussing on the economic aspects, I stressed the economic situation and aspirations of the colonies and the economic strategies and policies which generated unbearable tensions about the distribution of potential economic benefits from federation and about burden-sharing as well as about loss of the limited quasi-sovereignty which existed at that time.

The leading political architects of the Federation saw it as an instrument of economic development and political independence. Eric Williams who, having proposed a Pan-Caribbean federation in 1942, later proposed a West Indian federation in 1955 and 1959. In his words, "The hope of economic advantage from federation comes first, followed by the desire to be independent of foreign control." Williams thought that a federal government had to have authority for regional economic planning, taxation, foreign borrowing and exchange control, otherwise the federation would be discredited and be divisive. The West Indies Federation was a federation of economic unequals, but not uniquely so as the history of federations in the world show that at their inception federations are always an integration of economic unequals.

Economic inequality among states is not necessarily fatal. It is essential to have a dynamic perspective which sees the generation of income and wealth among the partners as a positive-sum arrangement rather than a zero-sum arrangement. The acid requirement is that each participant must envisage a better future within the federation than outside it. This entails positive economic growth over some reasonable time period. If not, satisfaction of the condition of positive-sum outcomes would require income transfers from growing members to lagging members. Federal discussions were constrained very early by a stress on existing initial differences in economic situations and prospects rather than on the possibilities of greater incremental growth through integration. In the Jamaica Opposition Leader Alexander Bustamante's view, Jamaica was a growing economy ("walking"), Trinidad, Barbados, Antigua and British Guiana were lagging ("creeping"), and the other countries were badly lagging ("not yet creeping"). He asked: "How can the walking and creeping and the babe who has not begun to creep yet, how can they walk on the same avenue?"

The absence of a dynamic perspective also contributed to fears about emigration from some countries to their better off federal partners. The leader of Jamaica's government, Norman Manley, and those in the Leeward and Windward Islands favoured the free movement of people, but Eric Williams was particularly concerned about this since at that time Trinidad and Tobago was receiving 7,500 West Indian immigrants annually. He saw the solution as deliberate policies for generating income and employment in the lagging countries, such as regionally planned economic development and federal fund raising, including debt creation, to finance the capital investment programmes. A regional development strategy could explicitly address the problems presented by economic inequality among members, making the issue one of how to foster and promote balanced economic growth instead of an issue of redistribution, i.e., how to distribute the fruits of economic growth achieved by those countries which were growing to stagnant ones. However, there was no commitment to regional development strategy or policy, nor to regionally coordinated capital mobilisation in the federal arrangements of 1958.

Even though equalisation or disparity-minimisation through regional development is a soundly conceived strategy, the history of successful integrations or federations in the US, Canada and Europe strongly suggest that resource transfers through fiscal grants and loans are an important component at least in the early stages. However, the ability to make resource transfers depended critically upon federal fiscal capacity. In the West Indies Federation, fiscal capacity was minimal and intended to finance the costs of federal administration rather than to supplement the income capacity of member countries.

Given the conceptual deficiencies in the economic approach to the West Indies Federation in 1958, the only features left to buttress the edifice were the political arrangements which turned out to be quite fragile.

The Caribbean restarted its regional integration efforts in a major way with the signing of the Treaty of Chaguaramas in 1973. CARIFTA was a highly important intermediate stage as it fostered intra-regional trade and institutional arrangements for consultations and coordinated decisions by member states on many economic matters. The Treaty of Chaguaramas was modest and conventional in its integration objectives. They included the creation of a common market, coordination and regulation of economic relations and trade relations for accelerated, harmonious and balanced development, equitable distribution of benefits, functional cooperation, and coordination of foreign policies. The Treaty provided for the integration, expansion, and protection of regional markets for goods. It made no commitment to the free movement of capital or to policy harmonisation or policy coordination. On the movement of people, its declaration in Article 38 is stark: "Nothing in THIS Treaty Shall be Construed as Requiring or Imposing any Obligations on a Member State to Grant Freedom of Movement Into Its Territory, Whether or Not Such Persons ARE Nationals of Other Member States."

The Treaty of Chaguaramas was revised in 2001. The revised treaty is far reaching conceptually. The revisions were impelled by awareness of globalisation and market liberalisation and the shift in national economic policies towards private sector led models of economic growth. The Preamble states: "The Commitment to Deepening Regional Economic Integration Through the Establishment of the CSME in ORDER to Achieve Sustained Economic Development Based on International Competitiveness, Coordinated Economic and Foreign Policies, Functional Cooperation and Enhanced Trade and Economic Relations with Third States."

The Treaty emphasises cross border flows of factors of production and capital as facilitators of production efficiency and economies of scale in enterprises but is cautious about the merits of globalisation and private sector led growth. It provides for rights of establishment by firms in countries other than their national domicile, prohibits new restrictions on capital movements, and commits member states to removing those which exist.

Other important provisions were to enable resource transfers through a CARICOM Development Fund and to establish a regime for disadvantaged countries. In sum, the revised Treaty of Chaguaramas makes provisions for integration of markets for goods and services, for coordination of foreign policies, for functional cooperation, and for equitable distribution of the benefits of integration. However, the identification of who are the disadvantaged can become problematic because it is tied to the criterion of per capita income and there may be sufficiently dramatic and sustained changes in relative income status of countries to generate calls for reclassification or abandonment of the disadvantaged country provision.

DEVELOPMENT CHALLENGES AND PERFORMANCE OF CARIBBEAN ECONOMIES

CARIBBEAN DEVELOPMENT TO THE YEAR 2000

The Report entitled Caribbean Development to the Year 2000 comprised of 337 pages of text, tables, figures and a bibliography was published jointly by the Commonwealth Secretariat and the Caribbean Community Secretariat in 1987. I was credited as the main author. It was based on a technical study "Development Performance and Prospects in the Caribbean Community to the Year 2000" which analysed in great detail the medium and long-term economic development performance and prospects for Caribbean Community countries which I had been contracted by the Commonwealth Secretariat in 1986 to prepare for the Caribbean Community Secretariat. I was assisted by commissioned papers by two subject specialists. Basia Zaba submitted two papers, one on the "Labour Force in the Eastern Caribbean: Its Size, Structure and Growth as measured by Recent Censuses" and the other on "The Age and Sex Structure of the Labour Force in the Commonwealth Caribbean: Projections for 1980-2000." Earle Baccus prepared a paper "Production Performance and Potentials in the Caribbean Community".

The Caribbean Community Secretariat established an Advisory Group comprised of nineteen people drawn from the Secretariats of CARICOM and the Commonwealth, the Caribbean Development Bank, the Caribbean Congress of Labour, the Caribbean business community, national government agencies and diplomatic representatives, the University of the West Indies, and the IMF/World Bank Development Committee. I benefitted especially from comments and suggestions from Alister McIntyre (University of West Indies Vice Chancellor), William Demas (Governor, Central Bank of Trinidad and Tobago), Bishnoodat "Vishnu" Persaud (Director and Head, Economic Affairs Division, Commonwealth Secretariat), Byron Blake (Director, Economics and Industry, CARICOM

Secretariat), Marius St Rose (Director, Economics and Programming Department, Caribbean Development Bank), Vaughan Lewis (Director-General, Organisation of Eastern Caribbean States), Marshall Hall (Managing Director, Jamaica Bananas Producers Association Limited), Jack Clarke (Senior Advisor, IMF/World Bank Development Committee) and Anthony Hill (Jamaica Ambassador to Geneva, Switzerland).

It was the view of the Commonwealth Secretariat and the Caribbean Community Secretariat that the main analyses, conclusions and recommendation presented in "Caribbean Development to the Year 2000" would be more directly accessible by governments and that it would place greater emphasis on policy issues than on empirical verification of the underlying economic propositions.

The Report identified several sets of challenges and opportunities. It documented low or negative economic growth in the Caribbean Community member countries between 1980 and 1985 and argued that economic growth rates of at least 6 per cent yearly were required to alleviate the backlog of high unemployment which typified the economies in addition to coping with the labour force growth and employment challenges arising from demographic changes projected to the year 2000. Many challenges were associated with changes in the world economy. The changes included pervasive technological progress, foreign exchange rate volatility, imbalances between major economies which reduce availability of financial surpluses for development finance, falling commodity prices, negative net capital flows to developing countries, premature graduation of Caribbean middle income countries from concessionary financial flows from multilateral financial institutions, slow growth of world trade, and substitution of synthetics for raw materials in production of manufactured goods.

The Report pointed to the need for Caribbean Community countries to improve international competitiveness and export performance; the importance of increasing government and private savings; the necessity of improving production efficiency, production diversification and product development; and the important facilitatory role of capital market development, including equity and venture capital. It drew attention to imbalances in the supply of education and training and the demand for skills and knowledge; to public service inefficiency; and to the need for governments to provide strategic leadership and direction to the economies. The Report suggested that there were economic growth possibilities associated with regional production for domestic and regional markets, investments in alternative energy, market expansion in non-traditional trading partners, direct foreign investment, and the tourism sector.

There were fifteen sets of policy conclusions in the Report. Some of them are summarised here. One: the Caribbean Community should be guided by clear indications that much of the growth in international commodity demand will be for new products, some of which will either be competitive or will displace the region's export staples. The response must therefore be to improve competitiveness, develop new products, strengthen export marketing, and increase financial supports. Two: there was continued potential for growth in the tourism sector, but the Caribbean Community should begin to develop strategies to capitalise on the emerging trend for international trade in knowledge-intensive services, such as higher education, medicine and engineering. Three: exporters in the region should target non-traditional markets like those in the Pacific Rim and Latin America. Four: upgrade production technology and include technology policy as part of overall development plans and programmes. Five: increase investments for human resource development and reconfigure the balance between technical/vocational education and higher education to increase the cadre of technicians and artisans in the labour force, and provide greater support for research and development (R&D). Six: improve financial intermediation through financial instrument innovation to increase risk-bearing and the investment use of financial surpluses; promotion of measures to reduce intermediation costs; development of capital markets; and restoration and maintenance of confidence in reasonable access to foreign exchange. Seven: substantially raise domestic savings and investment rates and improve investment efficiency. Eight: selective and phased dismantling of national market protection systems and ensure competitive pricing in domestic factor and product markets.

The Report dealt with the touchy subject of trade preferences for Caribbean Community exports. It stated that although developing countries have resisted removal of trade preferences, it was likely that they would not survive in the future global trade environment. With respect to export prospects for bananas, there was not much prospect for long-term growth in UK demand, and in the European Economic Community market, production costs, prices and traditional trading patterns were formidable barriers. With respect to sugar exports, there was a poor outlook for long term growth or even constancy of Caribbean Community sugar exports. On the positive side, the Report identified coffee, cocoa and citrus, fruits and cut flowers and foliage as promising export opportunities.

The Report was presented to the Heads of Government at their annual Conference in Antigua and Barbuda on 4-8 July 1988. The Heads of Government noted that the Report assessed the prospects for the Caribbean against the backdrop of the fundamental structural changes in financial, technological, geopolitical and other aspects of the global environment, and the expanding working age population. They recognised the need to adopt policies for greater competitiveness. Heads of Government "reaffirmed their commitment to seeking higher levels of national economic performance, accelerated human resource development and increased employment opportunities and to explore the range, price and quality of regional products. They agreed that intensified regional cooperation and coordination would help."

Heads of Government at their meeting in Grenada in July 1989 accepted a proposal presented by Trinidad and Tobago Prime Minister A.N.R. Robinson for a tripartite conference of Heads of Government, representatives of the private sector and representatives of the labour movement in the third quarter of 1990 to "determine the strategies and policies which should be adopted to meet the challenges of economic development and integration likely to face the Region in the twenty-first century." Preparations for the Regional Economic Conference, as it was termed, included the establishment of a Coordinating and Planning Committee to prepare documentation, hold consultations with regional bodies and institutions, and assist governments in their preparation for the Conference. I was assigned the task of drafting the Working Document which was then "amplified and amended by the Coordinating and Planning Committee and therefore represents the views of that Committee."

The Working Document was entitled 'Guideline for Economic Development Strategy for CARICOM Countries into The Twenty-First Century'. It began by noting that the Report on Caribbean Development to the Year 2000 had "served to impress upon the governments and peoples of the Region the urgency and enormity of the development challenges." It then lists new developments in the global framework since 1987, in particular geopolitical changes like the dismantling of political and economic structures constructed in conformity with socialist ideology, the economic approaches to the West by the Soviet State, the imminent full market integration of Western Europe in 1992, the Enterprise of the Americas Initiative, the redirection of financial flows to Eastern Europe, the re-unification of Germany, and concerns about international narcotics trafficking in the Caribbean. The Working Document urged serious attention to the US-Canada Trade Treaty, the proposed US-Mexico trade agreement and the Enterprise of the Americas Initiative and recommended that the Caribbean Community should be favourably disposed towards membership in the new economic zones while strengthening the cohesion of its own sub-groupings.

Eight policies were identified for economic resuscitation and growth. They are outward-oriented development policies; regional cooperation; strengthening of internal sources of growth; greater self-reliance; equitable growth; social partnership; institutional reform and development; and policy continuity. The Working Document provided several recommendations for action. It recommended rationalisation of regional air and sea transportation and improvement of intra-regional freight service. It recommended exploitation of the Exclusive Economic Zones. It recommended agricultural zoning and planned afforestation; technology acquisition, use and development, including rationalisation of the existing infrastructure for science and technology and strengthening of the links between research and development institutions and industry and commerce. Other recommendations pertained to infrastructure development, health and nutrition, education and training at all levels, and natural resource management. It concludes with a recommendation on the relative roles of the public and private sectors along with NGOs and other social partners in national and regional economic policies.

The Regional Economic Conference was hosted by Trinidad and Tobago in February 1991. The Heads of Government at their meeting in St Kitts-Nevis in July 1992 congratulated Prime Minister Robinson on the Conference and expressed appreciation of the uniqueness of the broad-based participatory approach for preparing the Region to meet the challenges of the 21st century. They committed to the recommendations for human resource development, outward looking development strategies, widening and deepening of regional cooperation, and enhancement of democratic traditions and processes. It was agreed that the conference should become a Triennial Consultative Conference of the Social Partners.

IMPROVING COMPETITIVENESS FOR CARIBBEAN DEVELOPMENT: REPORT OF THE TRADE AND ADJUSTMENT GROUP

The Caribbean Regional Negotiating Machinery led by Sir Shridath Ramphal and the CARICOM Secretariat appointed in November 2000 a Caribbean Trade and Adjustment Group (CTAG) to examine in detail the trade and adjustment issues arising from the major international trade negotiations in which the Caribbean Community was involved. Funding was provided by the Inter-American Development Bank.

CTAG was comprised of ten members with Dr Richard Fletcher (Principal Advisor, IDB) as Chairman. I was Deputy Chairman. The other members were Dr Richard Bernal (Jamaica Ambassador to the USA), Mrs Wendy Craig (Deputy Governor, Central Bank of The Bahamas), Professor Andrew Downes (Director, SALISES, UWI), Dr Alvin Hillaire (Senior Economist, IMF), Mr Alan Slusher (Director, Economics and Programming, CDB), Sir Dwight Venner (Governor, Eastern Caribbean Central Bank), Ms Evelyn Wayne (CARICOM Coordinator) and Dr DeLisle Worrell (Technical Assistance Advisor, IMF). Ambassador Havelock Brewster was Technical Advisor to the Group.

A total of 24 written contributions for consideration by CTAG were made by experts on many economic and social sectors, industries, and other economic matters, including tourism, telecommunications, entertainment services, private sector development, infrastructure, financial sector, exchange rate regimes, human resource development and management, health and health services, and WTO and Cotonou negotiations and agreements. The CTAG Report "Improving Competitiveness for Caribbean Development" was submitted in August 2001.

The recurring theme of the report is attainment of competitiveness in both traditional and emerging industries. CTAG saw this as essential for enabling the Caribbean Community to benefit from potential access to world markets. It recommended seven priorities for attention of the Heads of Government – One: the adoption of a coherent approach to international trade policy; Two: designation of the CDB as the Community's premier development financing institution with substantially greater capitalisation; Three: implementation of a plan for revitalising and improving the competitiveness of traditional agriculture; Four: approval and implementation of a Caribbean Tourism Development Strategy; Five: establishment of a competitiveness programme; Six: organisation of a regular Caribbean Economy Forum; Seven: preparation of a region-wide human resource retention and development programme.

Several analytical conclusions underpinned the recommendations. Trade policy was seen as hampered by inadequate resources, expertise, and experience, and by the absence of a regional development policy. In agriculture, poor prospects for extra-regional exports of traditional products like sugar and bananas were envisaged because of near-zero growth of import demand, unstable commodity prices, loss of trade preferences, and global foreign trade liberalisation. Some industries like rum and services, including tourism and entertainment services, had export growth potential provided there was upgrading of plant and equipment, improvement of product quality and price competitiveness, investment in human resource development, and forging of production and market linkages. Competitiveness also depended on macroeconomic adjustment, capital market development, the efficiency of the monetary and foreign exchange systems, labour market reforms and organisation, public sector modernisation and efficiency, and cooperation between the public sector and the private sector.

REGIONAL ECONOMIC PERFORMANCE AND PROSPECTS

More than ten years after the Regional Economic Conference in response to my Report on Caribbean Development to the Year 2000, economic growth issues were again taken up in my presentation on "Regional Economic Performance and Prospects" to the Conference of Heads of Governments in Guyana on 3-5 July 2002. I recounted the developments which influenced economic performance over ten years. They were reductions in overseas development assistance unmatched by compensating private investment inflows; the recourse to the more expensive private capital markets that governments found necessary; the phasing out of trade preferences; efforts in the global political economy environment to create and operationalise new rules of the game for conduct of international affairs, especially with respect to business transactions; and unravelling of the Community's social fabric. I drew attention to several major instances of performance weaknesses, including the deceleration of economic growth, rise in economic growth volatility, contraction of the banana industry, decline of non-traditional export manufacturing, price and product quality competition in tourism, and limited economic diversification of the economies and their export markets. There were also governance, transparency and accountability issues in the public sector.

I advocated a market-driven approach to production opportunities rather than a resource-driven approach. I recommended that major attention be given to human resource development since there will be reliance on entrepreneurial capacity for identification and pursuit of market opportunities, for design capabilities and production capacity to make the products, for broad-based knowledge to source inputs cost-effectively, and for appropriate marketing capacity to tailor marketing efforts to the markets targeted by enterprises. Other areas for focussed attention by governments included transactions costs of doing business, labour market rigidities, borrowing costs, development of money and capital markets, health related issues, and the social fabric. I also pointed to the need for progress with respect to harmonisation of legislation, rules, procedures and administrative practices, the full realisation of the CSME as a critical requirement for international competitiveness and resuscitation of economic growth, and the need for special financing mechanisms for avoiding economic polarisation in the Caribbean Community.

The Heads of Government discussed the economic situation, declared awareness of the issues and problems, and agreed to establish "a technical committee to develop with urgency, proposals for a regional stabilisation programme, including a Stabilisation Fund."

REGIONAL STABILISATION FUND

There seems to have been some confusion about who should prepare proposals for the establishment of a regional stabilisation fund. Alan Slusher and I understood that CDB was asked to do so, and we duly worked on a document "A Proposal for A Regional Stabilisation Fund" which I presented to a Special Meeting of Heads of Government in St Lucia on 16 August 2002. No communique for that meeting can be found on the CARICOM Secretariat website but I recall that there was another critical, somewhat contentious, item on the agenda, namely the structure of the reporting relationship between the Caribbean Regional Negotiating Machinery, Heads of Government and the CARICOM Secretariat which was resolved in caucus by the Heads of Government.

The Proposal for a Regional Stabilisation Fund presented by me listed basic design issues and considerations which arise, such as appropriate size of the fund, access arrangements, management arrangements, the degree of macroeconomic smoothing intended, policies and measures to ensure that fund resources revolve. Two very important issues would be the role of policy conditionality and the degree to which countries differ with respect to timing, magnitude and duration of external shocks which would influence the warranted size of the fund and its feasibility. The recommendation was for the establishment of a Regional Stabilisation Fund with a medium-term capital target of US$184 million at the end of four years, on assumption that the average GDP loss rate is 1.64 per cent, that only three out of fourteen countries are likely to experience GDP loss in any single year, that the average length of sequence of GDP loss is two years, and that the Regional Stabilisation Fund will provide loans equivalent to 50 per cent of GDP losses.

The immediate capitalisation target was US$75 million, on assumption that the Fund will have to be financed by an interest-bearing loan repayable in six years. It was proposed that the Regional Stabilisation Fund would be normally funded by a fixed percentage of members fiscal revenues, set initially at 0.5 per cent of fiscal revenues, to generate the medium-term capital. The immediate capitalisation requirements could be financed by loans from each Central Bank at rates of interest equivalent to their normal rate of return on investment of foreign currency reserves, and repayable in six years with a three-year grace period on repayments of principal. Draw down limits should be established at the outset, interest should be set at 2 per cent above the Regional Stabilisation Fund borrowing rate, and loans should be repaid in six years, inclusive of three years grace period. It would be advisable to specify macroeconomic performance conditions which would include fiscal balance, tax effort, inflation, foreign debt exposure, and domestic debt exposure. The Regional Stabilisation Fund should be a separate legal entity.

A Committee of Central Bank Governors must have been mandated by Heads of Government separately to prepare proposals for a stabilisation fund because on 16 February 2003, they presented to the Intersessional Meeting of Heads of Government in Trinidad and Tobago a proposal for a Stabilisation Fund capitalised initially with US$50 million and increasing to US$150 million within five years.

The Conference of Heads of Government meeting in Jamaica on 2-5 July 2003 "reaffirmed their decision to establish the Regional Stabilisation Fund with initial capital of US$50 million, rising to US$150 million in five years. Twelve members committed to subscribe capital. The Caribbean Development Bank was requested to manage the Fund. However, at the Inter-Sessional Meeting in St Kitts-Nevis on 25-26 March 2004, the Heads of Government agreed that there was "not sufficient enthusiasm shown for the Regional Stabilisation Fund despite nearly two years of effort to develop the concept and mobilise resources" for it. This marked the end of efforts to establish a Regional Stabilisation Fund. Evidently, the insuperable obstacle, as voiced as early as August 2002 in St Lucia, was the acute difficulty member countries anticipated in making their contributions from their severely constrained fiscal revenues.

REGIONAL STRATEGIES FOR MITIGATING EFFECTS OF THE 2008 GLOBAL FINANCIAL CRISIS

In 2009, I chaired a Task Force established by the Caribbean Community's Council for Finance and Planning to identify the critical challenges facing CARICOM as a result of the global financial crisis and global recession; to identify the areas and sectors for priority attention; outline possible mitigation measures; highlight feasible remedies and emphasise those responses which should be avoided; establish a system for continuous monitoring and tracking of effects of the crises; and identify areas of commonality and areas of collaboration, including support mechanisms and strategies for approaching international financial institutions.

The Task Force was comprised of representatives from the Committee of Central Bank Governors, the Caribbean Centre for Money and Finance, the Caribbean Regional Negotiating Machinery, the Caribbean Development Bank, the University of the West Indies, the Caribbean Association of Industry and Commerce, the Caribbean Congress of Labour, the Ministries of Finance of Suriname and of St Vincent and the Grenadines, the Caribbean Community Secretariat, and the Organisation of Eastern Caribbean States Secretariat, and the Employers' Confederation by invitation from the Chairman of the Task Force.

The Report was submitted on 23 June 2009. It identified the tourism, entertainment, construction, mining and energy, public administration, financial and agriculture sectors as priorities for examining the impact of the global crisis on the Caribbean Community. The tourism sector was severely impacted because most consumers are from North America and Europe, the two regions most affected by the crisis. There were negative effects on the entertainment sector, airline and ground transportation services and the construction sector. Declining global demand and falling international energy prices led to contraction in Trinidad and Tobago's energy sector and in Jamaica's alumina industry. Public revenue shortfalls combined with increased pressure for increases of public expenditures widened fiscal deficits. The financial sector was adversely affected by depreciation in their portfolios of foreign assets, decline in remittances by the Caribbean diaspora, declines in foreign direct investment and reduced access to trade credit and the international capital market.

Indirect effects were felt in the insurance industry where there was a meltdown of the CL Financial Group. Several things contributed to that corporate meltdown. Decreases in world prices of methanol reduced corporate income. Drastic reductions in value of the Group's real estate investments in Florida compromised overall asset quality. Denial of credit from German banks created short-term financial pressures. Moreover, the Group operated a high-risk business model in which there was excessive related-party transactions, a high interest rate fund mobilisation strategy to finance high risk investments, and an exceedingly high leverage of the Group's assets.

Only in the agriculture sector could the impact of the global crisis be viewed positively because of the opportunities it presented for food import substitution.

The Report presented a stylised list of counter-cyclical measures adopted by the Caribbean Community countries, specifically, public expenditure programmes, tax waivers and reliefs, and special credit programmes. It documented the financial assistance provided to countries by the Caribbean Development Bank and noted the Bank's relaxation of its loans policies, including reduction of counterpart requirements, commitment fees and interest rates, to facilitate access by their countries. It suggested that national policy responses could be augmented and strengthened by regional policy actions which could include a regional stimulus strategy focussed on agriculture, food security, tourism, and other regional production initiatives being considered in the Strategic Plan for Regional Development under preparation. Priorities for regional action in the financial sector would be cross-border financial regulation and supervision, a region-wide system of deposit insurance, and the creation of a regional liquidity facility from which countries could obtain short-term financial assistance. In relation to access to international financial resources for crisis relief and adjustment, the Report recommended approaching suppliers of existing debt to relax disbursement conditionalities, removal of impediments within the Caribbean to rapid and efficient implementation of externally funded projects, and approaches to the multilateral financial institutions, notwithstanding the access barriers posed by normal application of per capita income criteria. The Caribbean Centre for Money and Finance was recommended to supplement national efforts in continuous monitoring of the effects of the crises.

Heads of Government at their Conference in July 2009 in Guyana having considered the Report, established a Task Force led by Guyana's President Jagdeo, and comprised additionally of four members of the Conference of Heads, the CARICOM Secretary-General, the President of the Caribbean Development Bank, the OECS Director-General, and the Director of the

Caribbean Centre for Money and Finance to facilitate mobilisation resources and to present a core set of proposals for going forward. I do not recall any meetings of the Task Force.

REGIONAL DISPARITIES AND CHALLENGES TO COMMUNITY INTEGRATION

In three papers written in the 1980s, I probed analytically the influence of disparities in economic growth and inflation on intra-CARICOM trade performance. The first paper "Intra-CARICOM Trade Performance and Problems" was written in 1985 as part of a consultancy report "Exchange Rate Policy within the Caribbean Community" prepared by me, Winston Cox, Felix Solis and DeLisle Worrell for the IDB and the CARICOM Secretariat. It used estimates of price and income sensitivities of import and export demand in Barbados, Jamaica and Trinidad and Tobago generated by Nassau Adams, Wallace Joefield-Napier and Carlos Holder and DeLisle Worrell.

The responsiveness of import demand to changes in incomes and prices strongly suggested that divergent national rates of economic growth and inflation rates will cause divergent trade performance within the Caribbean Community. The second paper "Influence of Inflation and Economic Growth Rates on Intra-Regional Trade" was written in 1987, as was the third paper "Distributional Aspects of Caribbean Economic Integration". The second paper estimated relative price and income elasticities of intra-regional import demand from 1964-1983 in the cases of Barbados, Jamaica, Trinidad and Tobago, and for 1972-1983 in the case of the OECS group of countries and compared the trends of economic growth and price inflation. The main conclusions were that national price level differences influenced trade disparities and that in no case was the income growth condition for balanced growth of intra-regional trade satisfied. The third paper was essentially expositional. It used international trade theory to demonstrate how distributional effects arise naturally from economic integration schemes like the Caribbean Community and introduced proposals by William Demas and Alister McIntyre for mitigating them.

On 25 June 2003, I addressed the issue of disparities and potential polarisation more broadly in a lecture delivered in Grenada as part of the Thirtieth Anniversary Celebration of the Caribbean Community Distinguished Lecture Series. My topic was "A Caribbean Community for All". I began by stating that a Caribbean community should not be regarded as a set of institutional arrangements for trade, commerce, uniform policies and joint or coordinated actions. I conceptualised a community as being essentially constituted of the linkages between people in a multiplicity of ways, at many levels and in varying degrees of intensity. A Caribbean Community comes into being through kinship, cultural affinities, interactions in the common Caribbean space for work and leisure, and in all those dimensions of human life that cause people to feel one and the same.

I noted that, although there was some similarity in economic characteristics, the member countries of the Caribbean Community varied considerably in economic experiences. There were wide differences in per capita gross domestic product. Economic growth rates exhibited considerable intra-CARICOM variation, as did inflation rates. There was also considerable diversity in terms of social indicators of quality of life. Additionally, the homogeneity of linguistic, cultural and governance systems which had previously characterised the Caribbean Community because of the British colonial history of its initial membership had been altered by the entry of Suriname in 1995 with its different linguistic practices, culture, political system, and governance experience, and by the entry of Haiti with its French linguistic, cultural and political and governance traditions. I stated that diversity does not invalidate the concept of community of nations but that persistently large or increasing divergence in economic situations and prospects could create tensions and lead to dis-integrative pressures in any community. Members of the Caribbean Community needed to have a sense of shared benefits and that it was this mutuality of benefits that sustains its community spirit.

I argued that it was important to understand the dynamics of full economic integration. With respect to elimination of trade barriers, an inevitable consequence was that in importing countries, there are gains to consumers through lower prices but losses to producers through substitution of lower priced imports for their relatively more expensive products. Furthermore, if resource endowments are not uniform across the Community, distribution of gains will not be equal. It is not a question of fairness but one of competitive ability. What matters most is whether there is meaningful opportunity for lesser endowed countries to export and whether their export performance is improved by existence of a community market. The Caribbean Community market was important for several countries, many of whom have improved their export performance because of their membership of the Community. It can therefore be concluded that there is a sharing of the gains, although not as equally as might be desirable, and that the extent to which members gain can be influenced by their efforts to develop their own production capacity and improve their competitiveness.

Turning to the controversial subject of labour in the Community, I stated that geographical mobility of labour is a critical equalising force in economic communities, whether those communities are political federations or economic unions. I argued that labour market integration can help to boost the stock of human resources in lesser endowed countries, build production capacity, improve regional and extra-regional trade competitiveness, and relieve production bottlenecks due to unavailability of local labour. I did not give credence to fears about burden on social services in labour-recipient countries in recognition of the fiscal and social security contributions migrant labour would be required to make and because appropriate arrangements for portability of pensions and social security benefits would reduce the dependence of new migrants on the accumulated monetary contributions of resident workers. In my view, the seemingly intractable problem of restrictions on geographical mobility of labour in the Caribbean Community is due primarily to refusal to accept the concept of a common economic space which must be the core of Caribbean Community philosophy.

Capital flows are to be seen as another potentially equalising factor in the Caribbean Community. Recipient countries may be able to build infrastructure capacity, enhance social and physical infrastructure, and finance current economic activity to improve economic performance in the short run and long run. There has been remarkable growth in cross-border corporate investment. Nonetheless, recipient countries have not been fully welcoming. Foreign exchange controls, work permit regulations and the clamour of protective nationalism constituted formidable obstacles to the potential trans-border investor in the Caribbean Community. I also identified potential benefits of more efficient utilisation of excess liquid financial resources in domestic financial markets, more innovative and competitive financial markets, and improvements in quality of service.

Retention of foreign exchange controls has been defended as necessary to insulate domestic interest rates and to avoid capital flight. While it is true that capital mobility will influence domestic interest rates and lead to market convergence that is not a bad outcome if one of the Community's goals is creation of a common financial space. With respect to capital flight, the experience of the countries with foreign exchange controls is that they have been wholly ineffective in stopping overseas portfolio investments by Caribbean residents. The main influences on capital mobility are not foreign exchange controls but investors' economic and political risk management and quests for higher rates of return than are possible in controlled financial environments.

In recognition that market forces are insufficient for building sustainable economic communities, the lecture then dealt with the role of explicit redistributive policies, noting early proposals and analyses by William Demas, Alister McIntyre, and Havelock Brewster and Clive Thomas specifically on the economic strategies that might be employed to avert or remedy economic polarisation within the Caribbean Community. The proposals and strategies included regional industrial planning and complementarity, promotion of agricultural exports from the CARICOM LDCs and their specialisation in domestic food production, and the deliberate creation of poles of economic growth such as tourism. Another set of approaches focussed on financial accommodation. The Caribbean Development Bank from its inception had a Charter obligation to pay special attention to the needs of the CARICOM LDCs and had favoured them in its allocation of soft funds and overall provision of financial resources. The Revised Treaty of Chaguaramas also envisaged a financial mechanism. Protocol II provided for the establishment of a development fund to provide financial capital to countries disadvantaged by accession to the CARICOM Single Market and Economy (CSME).

I had opportunity to make the same kind of assessment and advocacy of the Caribbean Community in a paper "The CARICOM Development Fund for Disadvantaged Countries, Regions and Sectors" which I prepared for publication in The Integrationist in April 2005 and in an address "Sharing the Benefits of Economic Integration" which I gave to the Annual Presentation Awards Dinner of the Guyana Manufacturing and Services Association Ltd in Georgetown, Guyana on 28 October 2005. I stated that the CSME was necessary to provide the economic size and scale of operations for the individually small Caribbean countries and economies to compete in a world increasingly characterised by creation of economic unions, regional trade blocs and geographical unification. The CSME was conceptualised as an economic framework for maximising the efficiency of production, enhancing international competitiveness, achieving food security and structural diversification of economies, and improving standards of living.

I elaborated on the provisions in the Revised Treaty of Chaguaramas with respect to diversity, disadvantage and compensatory policy. The Preamble to the Revised Treaty stated that, "some Member States, particularly the Less Developed Countries (LDCs), are entering the CSME at a disadvantage by reason of the size, structure and vulnerability of their economies", that, "persistence of disadvantage, however arising, may impact adversely on the economic and social cohesion of the Community", and that, "disadvantaged countries, regions and sectors will require a transitional period to facilitate adjustment to competition in the CSME". It commits member countries to "effective measures, programmes and mechanisms to assist disadvantaged countries, regions and sectors of the Community." I pointed out that "disadvantaged" is not a straightforward concept in an operational context. According to the Revised Treaty, it could mean a particular subset of countries or countries, regions and sectors that require special support transitionally or temporarily because of the operations of the CSME or because of some totally unrelated action such as a disastrous natural hazard occurrence or high international indebtedness.

Because the Revised Treaty names a particular subset of countries, namely Antigua and Barbuda, Belize, Dominica, Grenada, Montserrat, St Kitts-Nevis, St Lucia, and St Vincent and the Grenadines, as disadvantaged without reference to any economic criteria, it left unanswered the questions of whether they can cease to be disadvantaged when their economic circumstances change and what would be the empirical measures of sufficient change, or whether their disadvantaged state is a permanent condition. I was mindful of the fact that in 2000, Antigua and Barbuda and St Kitts-Nevis were in the top per capita income group of Caribbean Community countries, that Belize, Dominica, Grenada and St Lucia were in the second tier, and that only St Vincent and the Grenadines was in the bottom tier. The other definitions of disadvantage in terms of natural disasters, economic shocks and HIPIC status are clearly intended to convey that the disadvantage is temporary, not permanent. However, they extended the remit of the compensatory or equalising mechanisms to encompass economic rehabilitation and economic stabilisation.

I ended both presentations with a short discussion on the funding of the CARICOM Regional Development Fund. I stated that adequate funding was critical, that the requisite funding level would be driven by the demands of member states, that it would be challenging to devise mechanisms for dependable, stable funding unless contributions were indexed to some appropriate revenue base in contributing countries, and that consideration had to be given to the primacy of the differential need principle in financial allocations by the Fund while ability to pay should be the primary principle in determining fiscal contributions to it.

THE FUNDING CHALLENGE FOR CARICOM INSTITUTIONS

AUTOMATICITY OF FINANCING

Caribbean Community institutions have been bedevilled by recurrent deficits in member states' payment of their assessed contributions. The CARICOM Secretariat and the Caribbean Agricultural Research and Development Institute are two of the prominent institutions so affected. The governments have not been unmindful of the difficulties created for the institutions but have faced fiscal challenges which occasionally have led to questioning the value and efficiency of the institutions. The Heads of Government and States received at its Intersessional Meeting in Port of Spain on 26 February 1991 the Report of the CARICOM Review Team chaired by UWI Professor Gladstone Mills. In the discussion of the Report, they identified "the need for a thorough examination of the source of financing of the Community's activities, including possible arrangements for obtaining an independent source of such financing for the Secretariat's budget and for the operations of other regional institutions, including the UWI" and agreed that these issues should be examined at the level of officials.

A Working Group of Senior Finance Officials which was subsequently constituted recommended an import tax levied on extra-regional imports as the new method of financing the work programme of the Secretariat. The levy should be set initially at 0.125 per cent for all member states, except The Bahamas for which it should be 0.02 per cent.

The financing issue was placed before the Heads of Government in the Time for Action Report submitted by the West Indian Commission to a Special Meeting in Port of Spain in October 1992. The West Indian Commission had been appointed by them in 1990 with a mandate to formulate proposals for advancing the goals of the Treaty of Chaguaramas. The Commission was comprised of leading intellectual and executive figures in the Caribbean integration movement. Its Chairman, Sir Shridath Ramphal, had been a senior legal official in the West Indies Federation and its Vice-Chairman, Sir Alister McIntyre, had served as CARICOM Secretary-General from 1974-1977. Other members included Mr William Demas who had formerly served as Secretary-General of CARIFTA and CARICOM and as President of the Caribbean Development Bank, Professor Vaughan Lewis, Director-General of the Organisation of the Eastern Caribbean States, and Roderick Rainford, then current Secretary-General of the Caribbean Community.

The Commission proposed, among many other things, that regional governance would be substantially improved by establishment of "a central directorate deriving its authority from the decisions of CARICOM governments taken collectively" and "working within the parameters of policy decisions by Heads." The Directorate, termed the CARICOM Commission, would be comprised initially of a President and two Commissioners appointed by Heads of Government by consensus for a term of five years, renewable once. The CARICOM Secretariat would be the Secretariat of the CARICOM Commission and its Secretary-General would be ex officio member of the Commission. The West Indian Commission proposed that the Directorate be financed by automatic transfers agreed by member governments and further proposed that the transfers be financed by an import tax of 0.15 per cent on extra-regional imports, except for The Bahamas where the tax would be 0.025 per cent. The funding proposal by the West Indian Commission was not essentially different from that of the Working Group of Senior Finance Officials. The proposal for a CARICOM Commission was not accepted by the Heads of Government for reasons not entirely transparent to me and several other participants in the meeting in Port of Spain but clearly had nothing to do with the financing aspect of the proposal. Heads decided instead to establish a Bureau of Heads of Government by 1 January 1993, to strengthen the CARICOM Secretariat, and to establish a Caribbean Community Council of Ministers.

In their July 2003 meeting in Montego Bay in Jamaica, Heads of Government adopted the Rose Hall Declaration which again placed the issues of a CARICOM Commission and the financing of Community institutions on the decision agenda. The Heads of Government, in making the Rose Hall Declaration, were influenced by a major, insightful document tabled by Jamaica's Prime Minister P.J. Patterson entitled 'CARICOM Beyond Thirty: Charting New Directions'. The document contained the "central proposal that the Community should now consider the establishment of a CARICOM Commission, which would have the effect of streamlining and strengthening decision-making and implementation in the Community." On the financing of the CARICOM Secretariat, it stated that, "the first issue is that of introducing a certain degree of automaticity in the financing of the budget." The Heads of Government agreed "in principle" to establishment of a CARICOM Commission or other executive mechanism with full-time responsibility for deepening regional integration, accountable to the Conference of Heads. They also agreed "in principle" to adopt the principle of automatic resource transfers for the financing of Community institutions. It was decided that St Vincent and the Grenadines Prime Minister Ralph Gonsalves would chair a Prime Ministerial Expert Group on Regional Governance.

The Prime Ministerial Expert Group established technical groups, one of which dealt with the automaticity of financing. As President of the CDB, I chaired the Technical Group which had as its other members Ambassador Havelock Brewster, Sir Alister McIntyre, Dr Patrick Kendall (CDB economist, co-opted) and Mr Elmer Harris (Bank of Guyana economist, co-opted). Dr Kendall prepared a very useful background paper for the Technical Group.

The Report submitted to Heads of Government in St Lucia on 14 November 2003 defined automatic financing as financial resource flows based on a fixed set of rules, which nonetheless are subject to change. The merits of automatic financing were specified as effective guarantee and predictability of financial resources to the regional bureaucracy and improved efficiency of resource flows. The Technical Team noted that precise proposals on financing modalities could not be made until guidance was given by Heads of Government on the institutional architecture and the specific institutions to be financed. Nonetheless, it outlined two principles that could be used to determine members' contribution, namely the capacity to pay principle which essentially indexes financial contributions to levels of national income or Gross Domestic Product, and the benefit principle which had been given little prominence in regional discussions because of the problem of identifying and quantifying benefits and in recognition that benefits are already captured in the measurement of national income. The Team was of the view that the benefit principle at best could be an adjunct indicator. It was roughly estimated that given the current institutional configuration, the annual requirement for financing Community institutions was US$30 million. The Team recommended that the resource base for determining automatic financial flows should be Gross National Product or Gross National Disposable Income and that to ensure financing stability it should be averaged over three years.

Consideration was given to several revenue streams, including import duties, consumption or other transactions taxes, "sin" taxes, i.e., taxes on gambling, tobacco, and alcohol, poll taxes, and exit taxes. The recommendation was for application of a percentage of import duties initially to start the process. The recommendations were supported by three appendices, one of which examined in detail consumption taxes, import duties and personal income tax as revenue stream options.

The Heads of Government did not make a decision other than to release the reports of the Technical Sub-groups to "the Community at large." Prime Minister Ralph Gonsalves presented the Report of the Prime Ministerial Expert Group on Regional Governance at the Intersessional Meeting of Heads of Government in Paramaribo, Suriname, on 16-17 February 2005. It was Prime Minister P.J. Patterson's penultimate meeting as Head of Jamaica's Government. It was obviously a great disappointment to him that the Meeting only agreed that Prime Ministerial Expert Group had discharged its obligations and referred the recommendations on establishment of a CARICOM Commission and automaticity of financing to the Bureau of Heads which would make recommendations for consideration at the July 2005 Conference of Heads of Government. There were no recommendations forthcoming at the July 2005 Conference of Heads or at subsequent meetings. The proposals for a CARICOM Commission and automaticity of finance were left in abeyance.

FINANCING THE CARIBBEAN COURT OF JUSTICE

Caribbean Community Heads of Government at their Conference in Georgetown, Guyana, on 3-5 July 2002, after intense discussions and an overnight caucus convened by St Kitts and Nevis Prime Minister Dr Denzil Douglas to convince one of his surprisingly reluctant OECS Prime Ministers, committed to the establishment of a Caribbean Court of Justice (CCJ). Trinidad and Tobago Prime Minister Basdeo Panday offered his country as the site for the CCJ.

Heads of Government stated that they were, "deeply concerned that the Court should be financially sustainable and independent" and correspondingly decided to establish a Trust Fund for its financing based on a one-time contribution of US$100 million by governments. The basic operating principle was that the CCJ Trust Fund would invest the capital and that the earnings from the investments would finance the recurrent budget of the CCJ. The Heads of Government authorised the President of the CDB to raise the funds on the international capital market for lending to governments to finance their contributions to the CCJ Trust Fund and required him to report on progress at the 14th Intersessional Meeting scheduled for February 2003. At that meeting, I reported that the Bank's Board of Directors had approved the Bank's recourse to the international capital market to raise US$96 million to capitalise the CCJ Trust Fund and provide the remaining

US$4 million from the Bank's Special Fund Resources. Reassured by this announcement, Heads of Government decided that the inauguration of the CCJ should occur no later than the second half of 2003.

Getting to the stage of CDB Board approval required some joint strategising and manoeuvres by myself and President Jagdeo, the then Chairman of the Caribbean Community. A few months after the July 2002 meeting, I visited President Jagdeo to express concern about relative inaction on the formalisation of the CCJ Trust Fund and requested that he should table CCJ start-up operational matters for discussion at the next Bureau of Heads meeting in Barbados. He did so but the meeting did not discuss financial matters except to reiterate the general go-ahead to the CDB. In a subsequent phone call to President Jagdeo, I indicated that, especially given the negative association falsely being drawn between the establishment of the CCJ and imposition of death penalties by some media commentators within the Community, non-regional members of the CDB's Board of Directors could possibly vote against the Bank's efforts to assist in the financing of the Court if they were not appropriately guided by the Bank's Governors in Canada, Germany, Italy and the United Kingdom where there was generally official policy and strong public sentiment against the death penalty. Political intervention by him in the form of a letter to the Bank's Governors would forestall that eventuality. President Jagdeo readily agreed and asked me to draft the letters for his signature, which I did promptly. The strategy worked. As Bank President, I received communication from the Governors assuring me of their support for capital market intervention by the Bank and that their representatives would not oppose the project when it was put before the Board of Directors for approval. Incidentally, sometime after the decision, one Director asked me if I had drafted the letter to her Governor because the style seemed like mine. I demurred of course: President Jagdeo's letters were President Jagdeo's letters.

The CDB duly raised the funds required on the international capital market. I was able to report to the 16th Intersessional Meeting of Heads of Government in Paramaribo, Suriname, on 16-17 February 2005 that the conditions precedent to disbursement having been satisfied by the member countries of the Court, the Bank was able to almost immediately release US$100 million to the CCJ Board of Trustees. A decision was made to inaugurate the Court in Port of Spain on 16 April 2006.

I was drawn back into matters of CCJ financing about five years later when the global financial crisis depressed asset values and earnings on government securities and corporate equity thereby creating cash flow problems for the CCJ. The President of the CCJ, Justice Michael de la Bastide, sought the advice of the Bank. I led a CDB team comprised of Mr Adrian Debique and Mrs Faye Hardy for a review of the Court's financial situation and the development of proposals to alleviate the current difficulties.

FINANCING THE CARICOM DEVELOPMENT FUND

The process of establishing the CARICOM Development Fund (as the regional development fund was officially named) was somewhat protracted. The Caribbean Development Bank was much involved in discussions leading up to the final decisions by the Heads of Government in July 2006 to have the CARICOM Development Fund fully operational in July 2007. A Caribbean Development Bank team led by the Bank's Economics Department prepared a Technical Paper "Development Fund: Some Issues for Consideration" for the 10th Special Meeting of CARICOM Heads of Government in Port of Spain in November 2004. The Technical Paper reviewed the European experience with its Structural Fund and several issues for consideration, the most important of which were the size of the Fund, its sustainability, eligibility and allocation criteria, its method of proving financial assistance (i.e., loans or grants), the permissible uses of funds, the adjustment period, and administration. The Technical Paper was referred to a Technical Team commissioned by the Community's Council for Finance and Planning (COFAP). Caribbean Development Bank members included Alan Slusher, Director of Economics, and Douglas Leys, General Counsel. The Technical Team was mandated to examine the issues highlighted in the Bank's Technical Report and make recommendations to COFAP, to consider the scope for consolidation and rationalisation of other specialised funds, and to take account of the other financial contributions member states were required to make to the Community.

At its meeting held on 10 June 2005, the Technical Team made several decisions. It decided against a proposal for earmarking a percentage of Fund resources for the LDCs; it agreed that business enterprises would be eligible for financial support; it decided that the size of the Fund should be based on a needs assessment study but recommended a start-up capital of $45 million; it decided that the choice of financing method should be left to the management of the Fund. The Technical Team also discussed various methods of funding the CARICOM Development Fund, including government fiscal contributions, loans to governments from the Caribbean Development Bank specifically for financing their contributions to the CARICOM

Development Fund, contributions from specialised facilities, contributions from the regional private sector, and public lotteries. This was a virtual smorgasbord of financing options on which no decisions were made.

COFAP at its meeting on 12 December 2005 requested the President of the Caribbean Development Bank to lead a technical team to examine the issues and the proposals and to make recommendations for operationalisation, financing and management of the CARICOM Development Fund for its consideration on 24 January 2006. The Heads of Government seemed to have become concerned about the pace of progress because at their meeting in St Lucia in July 2005, they requested COFAP to meet in September to finalise the recommendations to operationalise the CARICOM Development Fund.

A Caribbean Development Bank technical team was convened by me on 9-10 January 2006. It made seven recommendations. First, it would be necessary for the decision authorities to carefully specify the particular situations, including the duration of time, under which the special and differential arrangements would apply. Second, there must be prioritisation of CARICOM Development Fund activities and operations because of capital funding constraints. Third, some members could decide to defer accessing Fund resources initially. Fourth, members should decide on the maximum affordable level of their contributions. Fifth, international development partners of the Community should be approached for contributions to the CARICOM Development Fund. Sixth, if it was decided that loans rather than grants would be the modality for financial assistance, loan clients should be required to situate their project applications in the framework of national investment programmes. Seventh, the CARICOM Development Fund could instead operate as an interest subsidisation fund, thereby requiring a smaller capital base.

COFAP made a supplementary request to the Caribbean Development Bank at its Third Special Meeting in Jamaica on 18 May 2006. It requested contribution formulae other than the CARICOM budget contribution formula and specified that the formulae should include the relative shares of member countries in Community aggregate GDP, relative shares in per capita GDP, and relative shares in Community aggregate benefits from the Caribbean Single Market and Economy (CSME) and should apply varying weights to each of the three components.

I personally prepared the presentation to COFAP. The document pointed out that the CARICOM formula is based on GDP to represent economic size which is not always a reliable indicator of economic well-being. The use of per capita GDP is also intended to represent economic well-being without regard to internal distribution of incomes. The incorporation of CSME benefits while intuitively appealing has practical and practical limitations given data deficiencies in the national statistical systems, the problem of attributing benefits to the CSME when there are other influences on CARICOM trade outcomes, and the fact that benefits from a trade transaction accrue to both importers and exporters.

I developed the formula in conformity with the guidelines and presented three different percentage contribution scenarios. The derived contribution shares for the individual CSME members were compared with the shares derived from use of the CARICOM formula. The contribution shares generated in the scenarios exceeded the percentage shares generated by the CARICOM formula for member states with relatively high per capita GDP and were lower for those member states with relatively low per capita GDP. The magnitudes of the differences are smaller when more weight is placed on CSME benefits. Most important, application of the COFAP requested formulae would require much larger percentage contributions from the designated LDCs, i.e., Antigua and Barbuda, Belize, Dominica, Grenada, St Kitts-Nevis, St Lucia, and St Vincent and the Grenadines than would be required if the CARICOM budget contribution formula was used.

The CARICOM Heads of Government agreed in February 2006 that the CARICOM Development Fund should aim to be capitalised at US$250 million, with member states contributing at least US$120 million. In July 2006, they further agreed to the contribution formula proposed but it is not evident in the Communique whether it was one of those proposed by me. They mandated that both the CARICOM Development Fund and a companion Regional Development Agency would be fully operational in July 2007. The role of the Regional Development Agency would be to attract investment, assist industries to become efficient and competitive, and promote structural diversification and infrastructure development. The legal agreement for the CARICOM Development Fund was signed by Heads of Government in 2008/2009. Total assessed contributions were $90.34 million of which the MDC portion was $76.28 million and the LDC share $14.06 million.

The purpose of the CDF as declared in the agreement was financial and technical assistance to the disadvantaged countries, regions and sectors. Funds would be allocated to them to address economic dislocation and other adverse economic impact arising from CSME operations, adverse social impacts from the CSME, structural diversification and infrastructure development needs, facilitation of regional investment promotion and mobilisation, and facilitation of business development and enterprise competitiveness.

The CARICOM Development Fund started operations on 24 August 2009. At that time, the assessed contributions from members amounted to $100 million but only $81.2 million was paid up. All members had fulfilled first tranche obligations by January 2009 but only two members met their second tranche obligations by July 2009. Assessed contributions were revised upwards in 2015 to $165.841 million, of which member countries actually paid up $103.608 million. The Fund has experienced repeated shortfalls in receipts of the assessed contributions from member states.

It has benefitted from financial grants from donors such as the Government of Australia, China, Luxembourg and Turkey, from the European Union and from the Caribbean Development Bank.

DEVELOPMENT OF CARICOM CAPITAL MARKETS

Caribbean Community Heads of Government in 1994 established a Working Group on Financing for Caribbean Development led by Sir Alister McIntyre who was then Vice-Chancellor of the University of the West Indies. The specific mandate was to develop recommendations for increasing local private savings, accelerating development of regional capital markets, and increasing access to foreign portfolio investment and direct foreign investment. The Working Group of which I was a member submitted a report on Development of Capital Markets in CARICOM to the 6th Intersessional Meeting of Heads in February 1995.

The Group concluded that urgent development of capital markets was a prerequisite for achievement of those objectives. It thought that effectively functioning capital markets would facilitate resource mobilisation by governments and the private sector and also facilitate privatisation of state enterprises. Six requirements were considered fundamental: an adequate and properly functioning legal and regulatory framework; performance of financial and intermediation functions; capital market awareness; workable systems for dissemination of capital market information; adequate supply and demand for investment instruments; a stable macro-economic environment. The Group recommended that priority attention should be given to establishment of the legal and regulatory frameworks; institutional arrangements for capital market development; development and expansion of secondary markets for securities; removal of discriminatory aliens landholdings laws which affect CARICOM nationals; restoration of currency convertibility; and closer intra-government consultations on macro-economic policies.

Specifically with respect to the legal and regulatory framework, the Group recommended enactment of modern company legislation along lines drafted by the Caribbean Law Institute, enactment of Securities Acts and Financial Institutions Acts, anti-trust and fair competition legislation, laws and regulations for employee share ownership, legislation for the Caribbean Investment Fund, and repeal or modification of alien landholdings laws. The recommendations for development of financial intermediations were that the Central Banks should be mandated to facilitate secondary trading of securities, and that governments should obtain country credit ratings. With respect to public awareness, the Group recommended that national exchanges should make information on market transactions more readily available and more complete, that governments should publish information on their securities more regularly, that companies should make their financial statements available on a timely and regular basis, and that in general there should be international best practice for capital market reporting and standards. The Group recommended that governments should widen the range of their securities issues, actively promote their trades on secondary markets, and arrange for public quotations on shares of state-owned enterprises. They should also encourage company listings by reducing costs of incorporation, promote venture capital funds, and encourage institutional investors to acquire private equities. The Working Group recommended several measures to foster the development of the regional capital market. They included introduction of harmonised legal and regulatory frameworks for management and operations of securities markets and listed companies and for cross-listing, and ratification of the CARICOM Double Taxation Agreement.

Heads of Government at their Conference in July 1995 in Guyana adopted the recommendations and areas for priority action and committed to accelerate the process of capital market development.

APPROACHES TO POLICY COORDINATION AND HARMONISATION

In 1985, the Caribbean Community Secretariat and the Inter-American Development Bank commissioned a study on Exchange Rate Policy within the Caribbean Community. It was authored by a team of economists comprised of me, Felix Solis from the Centre for Latin American Monetary Studies, Winston Cox and DeLisle Worrell from the Central Bank of

Barbados. We were requested to make recommendations on appropriate foreign exchange rate policies and on the place of foreign exchange policy within the Caribbean Community. The study was motivated by the then current situation of different foreign exchange rate systems and policies in operation in the various member countries of the Community and the concern that foreign exchange rate policy could be used by countries to gain a competitive advantage over their Caribbean Community partners.

After a detailed review of the historical evolution of foreign exchange rate arrangements and practices from their common origin in British colonial economic systems in the Caribbean Community to the various systems and institutions established by the newly constitutionally independent countries, the Study concluded that exchange rate policy by any member of the Caribbean Community was not motivated by competitive intent vis-à-vis other countries in the Community and that foreign exchange rate policy should be evaluated in the context of individual countries' international balance of payments. Several options were canvassed for regional adoption: a unified foreign currency exchange rate; a single CARICOM foreign exchange rate applied only to intra-CARICOM trade; multiple foreign exchange rates; individual countries could set their own foreign exchange rates; and Community members would be free to maintain controls on foreign trade and foreign exchange access by private transactors.

The Study also considered a CARICOM unit of account for transactions within the Community but deemed it unsustainable because the pooled demand for foreign exchange to support the payments situation of the countries, especially under conditions of trade and inflation volatility, would be insupportable by the pooled foreign exchange reserves of the countries. The Study recommended that countries consult and exchange information more on economic policies. It recommended that each country should be able to set its own foreign exchange rate and advised that a unified foreign exchange rate was not feasible in present circumstances. It recommended avoidance of trade controls, foreign exchange controls and special tariffs on goods originating in the Community. It recommended that large foreign exchange rate devaluations be accompanied by a phase-in period for intra-CARICOM trade.

The matter of economic coordination and harmonisation was approached more broadly in a report prepared for the Caribbean Community Secretariat in January 1994. The Report "Macroeconomic and Trade Policies and Structural Adjustment in Support of Regional Integration in the Caribbean" was prepared by a team which I led. It consisted of six papers. I wrote the lead paper on Macroeconomic Policy Coordination and Harmonisation and Convergence in CARICOM which drew partially on papers written by the other team members. Arnold McIntyre wrote two papers, one on Regional Trade Policy and the other on Trade Liberalisation in CARICOM. Michael Howard also wrote two papers, one on Structural Adjustment Programmes in CARICOM, and the other on Fiscal Harmonisation in CARICOM. Peter Robson wrote on World Trade and Regionalism.

I began the paper on macroeconomic policy coordination, harmonisation and convergence by defining policy coordination as formal and negotiated coordination in policy making among members of a regional community but noted that it does not entail identical policies among them. Harmonisation is the concerted effort to achieve effective similarity of policies and is better interpreted in relation to sets of policies rather than to any single policy. Both coordination and harmonisation are intended to improve allocative efficiency by reducing policy distortions which can affect trade and factor movements within the Community. Coordination and harmonisation are not easily achieved largely because political costs ensuing from them often precede the political gains. The degree of similarity in macroeconomic outcomes in the Community will influence the scope for coordination and harmonisation.

In the Caribbean Community, macroeconomic performance is highly dissimilar. Structural adjustment policies are also not uniform within the Community. Matters which impinge on efforts to achieve policy coordination and harmonisation are differences in the initial conditions of partner economies, their resilience to external shocks, and the length of the adjustment period for achieving harmonisation. Initial conditions influence governments' assessment of political space for what could be unpopular decisions and the priority that may be given to national objectives over regional ones. Weaker resilience to external shocks means that economic adjustment is more difficult and the costs of policy coordination greater. Changes in the regional business environment such as cross-border operations of companies and larger cross-border capital movements, as well as changes in the global environment such as environmental standards, create pressures for policy harmonisation within the Caribbean Community.

The issues pertaining to coordination and harmonisation of monetary and credit policies and fiscal policies were discussed. On monetary policy, pertinent considerations are possible spill over effects of national monetary policy on intra-regional capital movements, investment, production and the balance of payments. If monetary union and full capital mobility are achieved in the Caribbean Community, capital mobility will become even more sensitive to interest rate differentials. Unrestricted mobility of capital provides a strong incentive for monetary policy coordination. The benefits from coordination will be reinforced by extra-regional capital mobility caused by structural adjustment programmes. The influence of national laws and regulations on capital movements provide another strong reason for harmonisation if financial market integration is one of the Community's objectives. Fiscal effects of national fiscal policies on the economies of partners could be substantial but coordination of aggregate fiscal policy is difficult because public expenditure-revenue policies are on the political frontline with the costs of fiscal restraint being near-term and nationally concentrated while the benefits are medium-term or long-term and are regionally distributed. Tax harmonisation may be easier to achieve. The approaches to tax harmonisation include modifying statutory tax rates, the tax base, and tax administration systems to arrive at equivalent effective tax rates.

The issue of macroeconomic policy coordination and harmonisation became more frontal on the Caribbean integration agenda with the signing of the Revised Treaty of Chaguaramas. Article 14 of the Revised Treaty makes coordination and convergence of national macro-economic policies an explicit responsibility of the Council for Finance and Planning. Article 44 calls for convergence of macroeconomic performance through coordination or harmonisation of monetary and fiscal policies, including policies relating to interest rates, exchange rates, tax structures and national budget deficits. It is an open question how effectively the objectives implicit in Articles 14 and 44 have been pursued and attained.

CARIBBEAN COMMUNITY AND CARIFORUM ECONOMIC NEGOTIATIONS

The Caribbean Community and CARIFORUM, which is the Caribbean Community plus the Dominican Republic, have been involved in major international economic negotiations between 1990 and 2007 which have had fundamental impacts on their economic organisation and performance and on their economic prospects.

I have been involved in the background work on two occasions. The first was in 1998 when I was a member of a team commissioned by the CARICOM Secretariat and the Caribbean Regional Negotiating Machinery to prepare a background study on Competitiveness of Caribbean Financial Services and WTO-Related Negotiating Strategies. The team was led by

Dr Maurice Odle who was at the time CARICOM Technical Adviser. The other members were Mr Trevor Carmichael, a lawyer by profession, and Dr Laurence Clarke, Director of the Caribbean Centre for Monetary Studies. The second was in 1999 when I led a team commissioned by the Caribbean Regional Negotiating Machinery to prepare a background study on a Regional Partnership Agreement Between the European Union and CARIFORUM ACP Countries. The other team members were Dr Shelton Nicholls, a UWI economist and Dr Tyrone Ferguson, a political economist at the UWI Institute of International Relations. The team was assisted by Earl Boodoo, Dorian Noel, Philip Colthrust and Tracy Polius. Carlos Moore, a Cuban scholar at the UWI, contributed substantially to the aspects dealing with Cuba.

The Study on Competitiveness of Caribbean Financial Services and WTO-Related Negotiating Strategies was presented at a meeting of the Caribbean Regional Negotiating Machinery Working Group on Global Trade and Economic Issues in Port of Spain in Trinidad in March 1998 and then to a Special Meeting of Senior Finance Officials and other Technical Experts in Bridgetown, Barbados in April 1998. The main findings and recommendations were presented to a meeting of Finance Officials in Georgetown, Guyana in May and then to the Council for Finance and Planning in Castries, St Lucia, on 29 June 1998.

The purpose of the Study was to provide an analytical framework for guiding discussions by Caribbean governments on the financial services commitments they could make at the WTO if they wished to deepen their participation in global financial services liberalisation. By 1997, many developed countries, developing countries and transitional economies had made significant commitments to financial services liberalisation. The Financial Services Agreement permitted countries to commit to liberalise only those industries, products and instruments they specifically identified. Commitments could be made in relation to abolition of restrictions on right of establishment, increase in equity participation of foreign companies, freedom of residents to use foreign financial services, and facilitation of use of foreign managerial, technical and skilled personnel. Caribbean Community countries had committed marginally in 1997, making commitments only in respect of reinsurance, and in a few instances in life and general insurance, banking, and other financial services.

Part 1 of the Study described the evolving WTO financial services regime. Part 2 provided a detailed discussion of the evolution, structure and performance of the financial services industry within the Caribbean

Community. Part 3 contained an extensive treatment of competitiveness within the industry. Part 4 dealt with legislative and regulatory regimes. Part 5 discussed strategies for offers to the WTO and Part 6 provided a Model Schedule of Commitments. There was an annex containing a preliminary analysis of Electronic Commerce and the Future of Caribbean Financial Services. It was concluded that there was need for a mixed strategy which essentially would require exposing the Caribbean Community financial services sector to a degree of competition while avoiding destructive effects. A nine-point strategy was suggested: 1. Less than status quo; 2. Status quo with grandfathering; 3. Restricting the number of new entrants over time; 4. Increasing market access while modifying National Treatment and Most Favoured Nation status; 5. Pro-active penetration of the international diaspora market; 6. Deepening liberalisation with prudential safeguards; 7. Establishing a negotiating nexus between the offshore industry and the onshore industry; 8. Gradualist vs Harmonised approach; 9. A rational eclectic approach. The Study expressed the view that the negotiations would yield beneficial outcomes if the negotiators combined selected elements of each component of the nine-point strategy as a basis for a meaningful and holistic set of commitments.

The recommendations in the Study took account of regional integration and the CSME. They were formulated with consideration of cross-border supply of financial services, consumption abroad, commercial presence, and movement of natural people. It recommended that there was no need for barriers to foreign entry in commercial banking because the domestic banks were sufficiently strong and competitive but that efforts should be made to strengthen their competitiveness. Liberalisation of services in the insurance industry should be gradual and should be accompanied by improved regional arrangements for re-insurance. The Study concluded that crowding out of regional stocks was a possibility to be carefully factored into the negotiations.

The Study on the Regional Economic Partnership Agreement between the European Union and CARIFORUM ACP Countries was presented in two volumes. Volume 1 dealt with Economic Aspects of a Regional Partnership Agreement. Volume 2 dealt with Special Issues in Relation to CARIFORUM and Cuba. Final versions were provided to the Caribbean Regional Negotiating Machinery in March 1999.

The second chapter in Volume 1 established the quantitative significance of the European Union market for merchandise trade of CARIFORUM countries. The top ten CARIFORUM exports were identified. Most of the exports were subject to low tariffs but tariffs were high on some products with potential for helping economic diversification in the Caribbean. CARIFORUM exports were subject to significant non-tariff barriers within a framework of health and environmental standards. The elimination of CARIFORUM tariffs on imports from the EU would entail considerable losses of fiscal revenues in the short-term because tariff revenues comprise large proportions of total fiscal revenues, because of narrowness of the tax base and because of weak tax administration systems. However, long-term revenue gains could be realised if the regional partnership agreement has substantial positive effects on CARIFORUM economic growth.

The Study examined the situation for import of services into Europe which were very large and increasing with the largest markets being Germany, France and the United Kingdom. The main service exports from CARIFORUM to the European Union were tourism, entertainment and offshore finance. The services imported by the European Union which were of potential interest to CARIFORUM are personal, cultural and recreational services, professional services in the fields of information and communication, market research and advertising, law and accountancy, and medical and health services. There were several restrictive elements in the European Union market, including those on movements of natural people, rights of establishment, licensing and recognition of professional qualifications, discriminatory practices in information and telecommunications industries, and quantitative restrictions on cultural products.

CARIFORUM, in contrast, had committed to liberalisation of trade in services under the General Agreement on Trade in Services. The Study therefore recommended safeguarding or advancing eight positions: One, incorporation of provisions which liberalise entry and temporary stay of people for business purposes; Two, exemption of temporary stay service providers from work permit and labour certificate requirements; Three, waiver of nationality requirements for delivery of professional services; Four, European recognition of educational and professional qualifications; Five, removal of discriminatory laws and regulations with respect to health insurance for travellers from the Caribbean; Six, no erosion of the secrecy and jurisdictional protection advantages of Caribbean offshore financial sectors and no erosion of tax competitiveness; Seven, promotion of open competition regimes in the communications industry, open competition in government procurement of services; Eight, unrestricted access by CARIFORUM consumers to electronic communications networks and software.

Dealing with financial flows, the Study discussed the major financial capital needs of CARIFORUM countries and noted trends in the availability of international financial resources, including decreasing and unstable official development assistance, the growing importance of foreign direct investment, and the heterogeneity of CARIFORUM country reliance on official grant funding and private finance outflows. It suggested that obtaining foreign direct investment should be a major objective. It recommended that facilitation and encouragement could be provided through creating and maintaining conducive conditions with respect to cross-border capital transactions, repatriation of profits and incomes, movement of natural people, non-discriminatory fiscal treatment, and acquisition of land for business purposes. It did not see much short-term prospect for European Union portfolio investment in CARIFORUM countries. It recommended that official development assistance could be targeted on the basis of special and differential treatment.

The Study concluded that a regional economic partnership agreement would not be a good choice for CARIFORUM for several reasons. There was little prospect of significant growth in merchandise exports; manufacturing exports were handicapped by domestic supply problems and non-tariff barriers in the European Union; the potential for exports of services was dependent on removal of supply-side constraints and European non-tariff barriers; domestic industries were vulnerable to import competition; and short-term losses were likely to be large. Instead, the recommendation was for a regional economic cooperation agreement. The essential differences between it and a regional economic partnership agreement would be phasing of the provisions for reciprocity and reduction of trade preferences, and supplementation of the trade agreements with a programme of development assistance intended to raise productive capacity, improve productivity and international competitiveness, and support economic diversification.

The Study advocated special treatment for CARIFORUM Less Developed Countries. It noted that while principles of special and differential treatment were well established, attention has shifted to Least Less Developed Countries (LLDC) and that the more recent international classification of LLDCs was unfavourable to CARIFORUM. Nonetheless, the European Union Green Paper provided a negotiating opening by acknowledging inherent vulnerability of Small Island Developing States, environmental problems, geographical fragmentation, migration flows, narcotics trafficking, and democratic changes as reasons for special consideration of developing countries outside the LLDC category. The Study recommended that CARIFORUM should emphasise its Small Island Developing State status, be actively involved in efforts to construct a vulnerability index; should seek to ensure that specific economic, social and physical vulnerability factors are incorporated in a comprehensive programme; attempt to have financial cooperation programmes structured as tranche or access and disbursement windows; safeguard commodity provisions by embedding transitional adjustment periods; and seek concessions on trade-related environment standards and electronic communications systems.

The Study discussed matters pertinent to the possible inclusion of Cuba in CARIFORUM. It was noted that Cuba had adjusted its development strategy, especially through market liberalisation, tourism industry development and attraction of foreign direct investment, following upon political restructuring in Eastern Europe. The European Union was displaying strong economic interest in Cuba and had increased its foreign trade and financial transactions with Cuba. Inclusion of Cuba in CARIFORUM was of strategic importance to both Cuba and CARIFORUM. The main issues relating to Cuba's incorporation into a CARIFORUM free trade agreement with the European Union were the extent of Cuban leadership commitment to a minimum package of political reforms; the extent of Cuban competition with respect to the protocols for sugar, rum and bananas; resource additionality or resource competition; political conditionality of access to European Union aid; and competition in the tourism industry.

On 16 December 2007, Caribbean ACP members concluded negotiations with the European Community for a reciprocal trade agreement which replaced the Cotonou Agreement between ACP countries and the European Union but had been declared non-compliant with WTO trade liberalisation principles and had to be replaced by 2007. The Information Unit of the Caribbean Regional Negotiating Machinery published in 2008 a document "The EPA at a Glance" which is very informative of the process from the Caribbean side, the objectives and the outcomes of the negotiations. Many of the points parallel those put forward in the Report prepared by the team which I led. CARICOM Heads of Government, according to the document published by the Caribbean Regional Negotiating Machinery, had set nine negotiating guidelines for the negotiators. One was to retain preferential access and minimise erosion of preferences. The second was to minimise any adverse impact of liberalisation, especially as they affect

CARICOM LDCs. The third was to maximise market access of Caribbean merchandise to Europe. The fourth was to increase service exports, especially in products capable of generating short-term benefits. Fifth, there should be encouragement of direct foreign investment. Sixth, CARIFORUM competitiveness and economic diversification should be enhanced through innovation. Seventh, small and medium size enterprises should be protected and fostered. Eighth, conclude a trade agreement which is relevant and appropriate to CARIFORUM development needs. Ninth, seek additional funding for capacity building, integration support, and implementation of the economic partnership agreement.

The Caribbean Regional Negotiating Machinery in its document identified six major objectives of the negotiators: One: expansion and improvement of CARIFORUM industries and economic growth, employment and business opportunities through service exports and exports of a wider range of goods which have comparative advantage. Two: provision of better opportunities for CARIFORUM imports of goods and services from Europe at lower prices. Three: improved access to technology and knowledge. Four: increased competition within CARIFORUM markets from European imports with the objective of improving efficiency. Five: formulation of rules for fair trade and recognition of critical differences in the relative economic situations of European and CARIFORUM countries. Six: ensuring sustainability of CARIFORUM development through commitments to environmental standards, labour standards, labour rights, and human rights.

The Economic Partnership Agreement embodied principles of asymmetry in trade rules, cooperation, financial and non-financial development assistance, reciprocity, adherence to Most Favoured Nation and National Treatment principles, fostering of regional integration, differential treatment of LDCs, and regional preference. The Agreement provided for immediate duty-free and quota-free access for all CARIFORUM goods, except rice and sugar which would be accorded that status in 2010 and 2015 respectively. CARIFORUM was not obliged to start reducing its tariffs on imports before 2011 and would then do so on a phased schedule which extended for twenty-five years. There would be no removal of tariffs on sensitive goods imported by CARIFORUM countries. Non-tariff barriers were ruled out by adoption of National Treatment principles. There was also asymmetry in the provisions on export subsidies on agricultural products, with European Community members being required to remove them while CARIFORUM countries could retain their export subsidies, provided they were not non-compliant with WTO rules.

Regarding trade in services, 29 European countries liberalised entry provisions for CARIFORUM professional service providers not established in Europe, self-employed professionals, and short-term business visitors. There are also provisions in the Agreement for financial and non-financial support for capacity development, sectoral standards and regulatory regimes, human resource development and training, and development and implementation of frameworks for equivalence of skills and mutual recognition of skills within CARIFORUM.

CARICOM ENGAGEMENT WITH THE US BUSINESS COMMUNITY

At the CARICOM Heads of Government meeting in Barbados on 1-4 July 2007, US Congressman Charles Rangel proposed that Caribbean leaders "undertake a dedicated visit to New York City to interact and cement ties" with the Caribbean and Afro-American communities. The Heads recalled the recent meeting with the US House of Representatives Ways and Means Committee chaired by Congressman Rangel and agreed to make a visit. During the visit, meetings were held with the political leadership in Brooklyn, the Mayor of New York, Michael Bloomberg, at Gracie Mansions, former Mayor David Dinkins, and many leaders of major American business enterprises such as Citicorp and JetBlue.

The morning meeting with the business sector took place in the Board Room of Chase Manhattan. Several speeches were made by the CARICOM leaders prior to the breakfast intermission, but they were of a general nature without specifics about the economic issues confronting the Caribbean and the avenues for potential supportive engagement with US business enterprises, so much so that Robert Wright, the President of Citicorp in the final intervention before the adjournment counselled that the Caribbean delegation should indicate what kind of assistance they wished from the US business community. In that context, I was asked by the Prime Minister of Belize, Hon. Dean Barrow, to speak on his behalf on the financial challenges and needs of the Caribbean.

THE STRATEGIC PLAN FOR REGIONAL DEVELOPMENT

In 2009, the CARICOM Secretariat undertook the preparation of a Strategic Plan for Regional Development by assembling a team of Caribbean experts to prepare technical contributions on the full range of economic sectors, some economic infrastructure services such as maritime and air transportation, private sector development policy, capacity building and corporate governance, public-private sector partnership policy, macroeconomic development policy framework, institutional strengthening, and human resource information systems. It was the most comprehensive Caribbean economic planning undertaking under the auspices of the Caribbean Community Secretariat.

The experts were Professors Norman Girvan, Dennis Pantin, Claremont Kirton, Andrew Downes, and Winston Moore, Dr Ranjit Singh and Mr Gregory McGuire from the University of the West Indies, Dr Ena Harvey from the Inter-American Institute for Cooperation in Agriculture, Mr Fritz Pinnock and Ibrahim Ajagunna from the Caribbean Maritime Institute, Ambassador Byron Blake, former CARICOM Assistant Secretary-General, Ambassador Havelock Brewster, Dr Camella Rhone, Mr Ian Bertrand, Principal of El Perial Management Services and former CEO of BWIA, and Dr Hollis Charles, former Director of the Caribbean Industrial Research Institute from 1970-1990. The principal technical representatives from the CARICOM Secretariat were Dr Maurice Odle, Economic Advisor to the Secretary-General, Ms Desiree Field-Ridley, Advisor, Single Markets and Sectoral Programmes, Dr Gem Fletcher, Special Advisor to the Secretary-General on Functional Cooperation, and Ms Evelyn Wayne, Programme Manager, Macroeconomic and Trade Policy Coordination. I was appointed Chairman of the Advisory Committee responsible for the preparation of the Strategic Plan.

The recommendations in the Strategic Plan for Regional Development were based on very detailed and expert analyses of the major economic sectors and the institutional framework and policies which affected their operations and performance. Dealing with shipping, the document written by Fritz Pinnock and Ibrahim Ajagunna pointed out that cost of shipping in the Caribbean exceeded the average for the world and that the focus of customs and excise operations was on generating fiscal revenue instead of the facilitation of trade. It noted the lesser importance given by governments to cargo berthing and handling vs cruise ship docking and port services, the low productivity of ports in CARICOM, and the low ranking obtained by the ports in international rankings of countries on matters like logistics and linear shipping connectivity. It also commented on the old age and small size of vessels servicing the Caribbean, the unreliability and high freight costs of intra-regional maritime transport and questioned the competitiveness and sustainability of Caribbean maritime transportation. It discussed schooner and small vessel operations in the Eastern and Southern Caribbean, noting that there were about 600 vessels in operation, their very small average length of 35 metres, and that they moved about 400,000 tons of cargo annually.

The challenges experienced by the schooner and small vessel sub-sector included lack of International Maritime Organisation certification, the age and maintenance limitations of vessels, lack of on-board cargo refrigeration facilities, difficulties of accessing insurance for cargo and vessels, lack of supporting infrastructure including dry dockage, maintenance and proper mooring facilities. The document identified and discussed other challenges in the Caribbean maritime industry. There were regulatory, legal and environmental challenges associated with the International Maritime Organisation, the International Labour Organisation, the International Convention on Safety of Life at Sea, MARPOL on pollution, and the International Shipping and Port Security Code.

The document stated that overall capacity and number of carriers in the Caribbean was adequate but harmonised regulatory and legal reforms are needed to create incentives to improve management and administrative practices, stimulate investment for modernisation of existing facilities, and efficient pooling of resources. It suggested that government monopoly of port ownership was not conducive to competition. It concluded that coordination of trans-shipment could reduce costs; rationalisation of the regional shipping network and sharing of infrastructure investment costs would be beneficial; maritime labour policies and practices should be modernised, and seafarers trained; customs procedures should be harmonised and rationalised; and Caribbean shipping companies should comply with international laws on maritime safety and the environment. The document recommended a regional approach to port security and safety, standardisation of certificates and adoption of global labour market regulations, harmonised legislation for the maritime transportation industry, and the conduct of economic, social and environmental impact assessment studies to guide port development and infrastructure.

Air transportation was dealt with by Ian Bertrand. The document advocated a strategic vision for a single regional entity and identified several preconditions for success. It stated that it is critical that the regional and national validating elites 'internalise' that profitable, competitive, regionally domiciled airline(s) are in fact in the best interests of CSME and tourism, which is the region's leading industry. Recommendations were made in four main areas. One cluster of recommendations dealt with improving the demand for inter-regional and extra-regional air transport by greater focus on intra-regional and multi-destination tourism, attraction of members of the Caribbean diaspora, and review of the level of intra-regional airfares which were too high in comparison with air fares to the US. A second cluster advocated aggressive diversification of airlift by early adoption of "open skies" air services agreements, amendment of the CARICOM Multilateral Air Service Agreement to one based on the Multilateral Agreement on the Liberalisation of International Air Transportation and lobbying other members of the Association of Caribbean States to adopt 'Open skies' policies. The third cluster recommended strengthening of regional airlines by functional cooperation and integration of schedules aimed at generating economies of scale; alliances with international airlines; maintaining IATA Category 1 status; establishing a Common Air Space; improving relations with countries in hub-spoke structures; maintaining a commercial culture; and adequate capitalisation of the airlines. The fourth set of recommendations was for expansion of airline services internationally.

Agriculture and agro tourism were discussed in two documents. Ranjit Singh dealt with intra-regional agricultural production and trade policy. Several matters were identified for priority regional action. They were science, innovation and technology, development of an efficient regional market intelligence and market facilitation system, harmonisation of sanitary and phyto-sanitary regulations, establishment of a CARICOM food safety and quality assurance system, and the intra-regional transportation and associated infrastructure. The document concluded that the existing CARICOM institutional model for technology support should be replaced by a Regional Agricultural Research System comprised of a Centre for Agriculture Research Policy in CARICOM (CARPC) and a CARICOM Agricultural Research Institute (CARI).

The Centre's role would be to formulate research policy and manage the research system, including funding and allocating research grants on a competitive basis. The role of the Institute would be to execute the research programmes approved by the Centre. Universities in the region would be pro-active in research and assist in activities to improve the quality and effectiveness of agricultural extension services. The document identified the absence of a harmonised sanitary and phyto-sanitary system as a formidable handicap to intra-regional trade in agricultural products. It also recommended adoption of Good Agricultural Practices and Good Manufacturing Practices to alleviate consumer concerns about food safety. Ena Harvey dealt with agro-tourism.

Two major policy initiatives were recommended. One, consolidation of legislative, policy and institutional frameworks for increased production, processing and distribution of agro-products. This would entail improvements in regional transportation, market information systems and infrastructure, adoption and adherence to regional and international requirements for certification and quality assurance, skills training and certification of agro-entrepreneurs. The second major recommendation was for consolidation of services which support investment in agro-tourism. These include those pertaining to production, post-harvest handling and processing, and value chain services such as health and wellness tourism, heritage tourism and culinary tourism.

The document by Claremont Kirton on financial services reviewed financial services integration efforts and policies in the Caribbean, including the defunct CARICOM Multilateral Clearing Facility and CARICOM Travellers Cheques, and the Liliendaal Declaration by CARICOM Heads of Government in July 2009 which committed countries to cross-border financial supervision collaboration in the Committee of Central Bank Governors, the Caribbean Association of Insurance Regulators, the Group of Securities Regulators and the Regional Competition Commission, establishment of a College of Regulators, improvements in standards of disclosure, transparency and corporate governance by private and public companies, financial support for existing development finance institutions, and enhancing regulation of international financial institutions within the Caribbean financial services sector.

The document also reviewed the situation in capital markets; policies and systems for deposit insurance; foreign exchange controls systems, policies and practices; financial sector regulations; e-commerce in the financial sector; and the financial sector implications of the various multilateral trade agreements. It recommended eleven strategic goals for financial integration: 1. Implementation of the CARICOM Financial Services Agreement; 2. Facilitation of information sharing across critical policy-making institutions and the wider public; 3. Facilitation of efficient, effective administration of banking and financial institutions Acts; 4. Implementation of cross-border financial requirements; 5. Development and improvement of systems for e-commerce; 6. Addressing prudential issues in the regional financial sector; 7. Improvement and harmonisation of tax systems; 8. Adoption of a single currency; 9. Addressing issues relating to winding up and liquidation of financial institutions, including the need for coherent legal frameworks; 10. Increased training and human resource development in the sector; 11. Achievement of the most favourable outcomes from multilateral trade negotiations, including those for economic partnership agreements.

Winston Moore wrote the section on niche manufacturing. The document provided an overview of the manufacturing sector which noted significant growth between 1970 and 2000 and significant decline subsequently and attributes the decline principally to loss of competitiveness in the main industries. Nonetheless, there are some products such as beverages, fertiliser, dyes and colouring materials, essential oils and perfumes which are competitive in global markets.

There appeared to be little scope for increasing intra-Caribbean trade and for production integration. The document therefore deals extensively on possibilities for expanding exports to the Caribbean diaspora markets in Canada, the USA and the UK. The strategy advocated is one of niche manufacturing with the Caribbean diaspora markets as the target. The niche manufacturing strategy could be supported by regional actions and policies. There could be investment in knowledge and agreement on shared standards. A regional marketing strategy could be developed, inclusive of fostering and developing distribution networks in the diaspora host countries. Regional institutions could be established to support regional niche marketing or existing institutions like the Caribbean Export Development Agency could include promotion and assistance to niche manufacturing in their programme portfolio. Manufacturing associations and chambers of commerce could be utilised as implementation agencies in the individual CARICOM countries.

The document specified an extensive list of actions and timelines which should be taken to implement the broad strategy recommendations. They include a regional audit of tax incentives legislation, adoption of a common regional package of incentives, conducting a marketing campaign, enactment of laws and provision of incentives to support the development of venture capital funds, provision of assistance to niche manufacturing companies to ensure adoption of quality standards and improvement of their export marketing capabilities, and collaboration with the universities in meeting identified knowledge and skills needs and in research and development of products and production technologies. Byron Blake assisted by Timothy Odle examined the situation with exports of services. It was noted that as many as twelve different kinds of services had been identified by countries as potential exports. The document recommended a strategy of open-ended clustering around some critical attributes of CARICOM countries. The recommended clusters are creativity and the creative industries, sports, education services, health and wellness, professional services, maritime services, and environmental services.

The Strategic Plan for Regional Development also addressed issues such as public sector-private sector partnership, the adequacy of knowledge and data on the labour force and human resources, corporate governance, and the macroeconomic framework for Plan implementation. Havelock Brewster wrote the section on a framework for CARICOM Public-Private Partnership Policy. It noted that PPPs were justified in the context of public sector financial resource constraints relative to social and physical infrastructure investment needs. Three possible modalities for a PPP policy framework were identified, namely, Community legislation, development of harmonised laws and rules, and development of broad Community guidelines. The document proposed a template for the Policy Framework.

Havelock Brewster also drafted a Framework for Corporate Governance based on existing legislative, regulatory and policy instruments in CARICOM. The document by Andrew Downes dealt with the topic of Human Resource Information Systems. Noting that human resources of the Caribbean Community would be critical for achieving the objectives of the Strategic Plan for Regional Development, it recommended the design and adoption of a regional Human Resource Information System (HRIIS) comprised of a Social Accounting Matrix-HRIS (SAM-HRIS) which provides the macro framework for human resource development at national and regional levels, a set of satellite human resources accounts which would emerge from different sectors of the SAM-HRIS, and a corresponding set of transition matrices which could be used for forecasting human resource changes and needs.

The section on macroeconomic development policy was based on a document prepared by Norman Girvan which, having reviewed the issues and recommendations in the specific sectors, listed ten elements which should be contained in the Regional Macro-economic Development Policy Framework: 1. Exchange Rate Stability; 2. Harmonised and Low Inflation Rates; 3. Low Fiscal Deficits; 4. Manageable Debt Burdens; 5. Harmonised, Low and Stable Interest Rates; 6. Harmonised Credit Policies towards Strategic Plan for Regional Development activities; 7. Harmonised Incentives Policies towards Strategic Plan for Regional Development activities; 8. Harmonised Tax Policies towards Strategic Plan or Regional Development Activities; 9. CARICOM Common Investment Policy; 10. CARICOM Common Financial Services Policy. It recommended that the Caribbean Community should adopt a Protocol on Macro-economic Policy for Development and designed a template of the recommended Protocol.

For reasons not known outside of the CARICOM Secretariat, the final draft of the Strategic Plan for Regional Development in 2010 was not placed by the Secretariat on the agenda of any of the CARICOM Ministerial forums or on the agenda for the Conference or Inter-Sessional Meetings of the Caribbean Community Heads of Government.

IMPLICATIONS OF GLOBAL AND REGIONAL DEVELOPMENTS POST, 2009

My last formal engagement with CARICOM on economic matters was presentation of a commissioned report "Implications for CARICOM Economies of Global and Regional Developments" to the Conference of Heads of Government in St Lucia on 5 July 2012.

I began by noting that the global economic crisis was at its worse in 2009, that economic recovery began in 2010 but was faltering and uncertain because of economic decline in some European Union countries; political risks in economic stabilisation, restructuring and fiscal consolidation programmes; and risk of a new episode of financial market collapse connected with potential sovereign debt default in Europe. The following factors in the global situation were of special relevance to CARICOM: persistence of high rates of unemployment in the US and Europe; weak recovery of private consumption expenditures in Europe; reduction of household debt in the US; high government foreign indebtedness in advanced economies; greater risk apprehension and risk avoidance in global financial markets; projected large demands on global financial resources by advanced economies; and strong economic growth of Brazil, Russia, India, China and South Africa: the BRICS countries.

Next, I reviewed economic performance in CARICOM. By 2011, most countries had emerged from the widespread recession of 2009-2010, even though marginally in Barbados and St Lucia. Antigua and Barbuda, St Kitts-Nevis, St Vincent and the Grenadines, and Trinidad and Tobago had continued to decline. Projections by the International Monetary Fund were for positive economic growth in all CARICOM countries in 2012 and 2013. Growth would be slow or moderate in most cases but strong in Haiti, Guyana and Suriname. I highlighted the importance of sustained recovery in the tourism industry and the ability to satisfy or successfully contend regulatory and political demands confronting the international financial services industry and the international business registration industry in CARICOM. The Report emphasised that generation of sustainable employment to relieve currently high levels of unemployment would rest upon recovery and growth of business activity in the main economic sectors, given the limited fiscal capacity of governments.

Three stress points in the regional financial sector were identified: rise in loan delinquency and loan loss provisioning; increase in excess liquidity; and fears about financial sector stability and regulatory and supervisory adequacy following upon the collapse of CLICO, even though regionally coordinated monitoring, regulatory and supervisory actions were being taken. I also drew attention to stresses in CARICOM pertaining to trade imbalances and highly publicised complaints about problems affecting the movement of natural people, while noting steady progress towards integration in the Organisation of Eastern Caribbean States which recognised that small economic size and regionally uncoordinated decisions and actions limit rather than expand the scope for beneficial utilisation of domestic resources and for beneficial engagement with the international community.

The challenge before the CARICOM countries was to raise economic growth rates and sustain them at least for the medium term. I suggested that it was appropriate to start with recognition that the reasons for poor economic performance are primarily domestic and regional and that the global crisis accentuated performance that was already lagging. The warranted approach to revitalisation of Caribbean economies would combine sector development policy, economic diversification, improvements in cost efficiency in the public sector, reform of public tax-expenditure policy, and the completion of the integration agenda, especially in relation to the movement of capital and labour.

Regarding tourism where demand is strongly sensitive to consumer prices, the comparatively high rates of taxation, fees and surcharges on hotel accommodation levied by governments placed the industry in CARICOM at a significant competitive disadvantage with other destinations within the Caribbean and elsewhere in the world. This ultimately depresses both industry earnings and fiscal revenues. I suggested that lower tax rates could increase intra-regional travel and international demand (more tourists, longer stays, greater expenditures in restaurants, etc.) and increase fiscal revenues.

Labour productivity, product quality and product innovation in the CARICOM tourism industry were also matters requiring attention. I advised that the agriculture sector merited special attention because of prospects of early gains in employment and regional import substitution. A four-pronged approach was recommended: 1. Utilisation of idle land in targeted programmes which match production with demand; 2. An investment programme in improved production technology and infrastructural supports; 3. Improvements in the food marketing chain; 4. Facilitation of the growth of the regional market for food crops, fruits, vegetables and livestock products through alleviation of administrative and regulatory barriers and through providing fiscal and credit incentives for expansion and upgrading of inter-CARICOM maritime freight transport.

Regarding the mineral sector, the main challenges in the newly producing countries was to avoid negative spill-overs from the booming sector to the rest of the economy and to manage economic surpluses to ensure adequate investible resources for future economic growth. Concerning public sector efficiency which strongly influences national productivity and international competitiveness, it was suggested that governments focus on process engineering aspects of service delivery, starting with those services identified in the World Bank's Costs of Doing Business Reports. Attention was also drawn to the existence of the Strategic Plan for Regional Development which contains many proposals for accelerating growth in various sectors and industries.

The final section of the Report dealt with issues pertaining to the financing of economic growth. It stated that the countries had to make efforts to raise their investment rates which were currently lower than those which prevailed in 2007, and that fiscal space for government investment expenditures had to be achieved by reducing recurrent expenditures within the overall expenditure budget. It counselled that not much reliance should be placed on foreign aid because international flows to the Caribbean have been decreasing, global aid has contracted, the proportion allocated to poor countries has increased, and resources of the international financial institutions have been diverted to economic rescue and stabilisation of European economies. It advised that recourse to commercial debt by CARICOM governments was not an option with good chances of success in the current international financial environment of increased risk apprehension and greater risk avoidance by financial institutions and capital market investors.

Credit ratings downgrades for several CARICOM countries and widening interest spreads on their bonds had weakened the chances for successful international bond issues. This, however, did not mean that CARICOM countries should not prepare strategically for re-entry into international capital markets by achieving sustainable public finances and credible debt bearing capacity. The Report recommended the encouragement of corporate financing in international capital markets. Even though this was not an easy option because of the family-owned nature of most business enterprises, the underdeveloped state of local capital markets and capital market information services, and the cost disadvantages of small financial requirements, the prospects would be improved by strong domestic and regional capital markets and good corporate governance frameworks. Foreign direct investment was likely to flow increasingly to countries with mineral sectors, strong manufacturing sectors, and strong tourism industries. It noted that the challenge of accessing resources from multilateral financial institutions and regional development banks was satisfaction of portfolio risk criteria and development effectiveness. In that regard, debt sustainability, fiscal sustainability and project implementation capacity are critical. It suggested that greater efforts could be made to attract financial capital from the Caribbean diaspora and to channel the flows into production sectors to a greater extent.

Remittances are large relative to GDP in some countries but flows of portfolio capital have been deterred by policies governing outward capital transactions and repatriation of profits and incomes, and by concerns about the efficiency and effectiveness of the legal and regulatory framework for investor protection. An option for very careful consideration was use of commercial bank excess liquidity which would have to be carefully calibrated with the demands for foreign exchange resources which would ensue from activation of idle funds in the banking sector.

It is evident that the Heads of Government carefully considered the Report. The Communique of the Conference stated that they agreed that the major focus of the Community at that time should be on economic growth and development. They considered the performance of CARICOM economies in the global context and gave attention to developments in financial markets which had implications for CARICOM and its major trading partners. They recognised that the global developments "were merely compounding problems existing in the Region". They agreed on the need to re-examine policy approaches to economic growth and development and to review fiscal policy with reference to the balance between taxation and expenditures in that context. The Heads of Government identified various sectors of the economy, including tourism, agriculture, and construction as ones with prospects for early resuscitation of economic growth. They agreed on the need to develop a Caribbean Investment Programme to support efforts at economic stabilisation, growth and competitive production.

Greeting Guyana's President Cheddi Jagan at UWI St Augustine Campus, circa 1996.

Dining with Jamaica's Prime Minister Percival J. Patterson at UWI 50th Anniversary Dinner in Kingston, Jamaica in July 1998.

In conversation with Trinidad and Tobago's Prime Minister Basdeo Panday, far right, circa 1998.

Making a presentation to Trinidad and Tobago's President A.N.R. Robinson at President's House, 19 July 2001.

With Barbados Prime Minister Mia Motley at the Anthony N. Sabga Caribbean Excellence Awards Ceremony, Barbados, 2019. L-R: Dr Marion Williams, Pamela Bourne, Prime Minister Mottley, Me and Gloria Nelson.

CHAPTER TEN

IN LIEU OF AN EPILOGUE: STILL IN THE CARIBBEAN DEVELOPMENT VINEYARD

PERSPECTIVES AND STRATEGIES FOR ECONOMIC GROWTH AND DEVELOPMENT

Between 2011 and 2019, I was presented with several opportunities to speak and write on Caribbean economic growth and development. One such occasion was when I delivered the Feature Address on "Private Sector Development, Economic Development Perspectives and Strategies for Growth in the Caribbean" to the Strategic Regional Dialogue on Private Sector Development in the Caribbean at the Compete Caribbean Regional Consultative Forum at the Cave Hill School of Business on 8-9 April 2013. Another was a lecture presentation on "Economic Situation, Opportunities and Challenges in the Caribbean Community" to an MBA class at the Universitie of Notre Dame d'Haiti on 28 July 2018.

In Haiti, I noted that total Gross Domestic Product as a measure of economic size was US$74 billion in the Caribbean Community in 2016 but was unevenly distributed among the countries. Trinidad and Tobago's GDP was 33 per cent of the total, Jamaica's 18 per cent, The Bahamas 12 per cent and Haiti's 10 per cent. At the other end of the spectrum were Guyana and Suriname with 5 per cent each. There were considerable differences of purchasing power adjusted per capita gross national income. The top four countries in the group of fourteen countries were Trinidad and Tobago with US$30,520, The Bahamas with US$29,790, St Kitts-Nevis with US$26,300 and Antigua and Barbuda with US$22,980. The bottom four countries consisted of Haiti with per capita income of US$1,830, Belize with US$7,890, Guyana with US$8,120 and Jamaica with US$8,690. Barbados, Dominica, Grenada, St Lucia, St Vincent and the Grenadines, and Suriname were within a middle range of US$10,170 to US$17,830, with Barbados being at the upper end and Dominica at the lower end.

In the Feature Address at Cave Hill in 2013, I provided information on persistent deceleration of economic growth in many of the CARICOM countries between 1990 and 2010. I indicated in Haiti that economic growth performance continued to be unimpressive between 2013 and 2017. The performance since 2017 has not been much better except in Guyana where economic growth rates maintained the upward trend which started in 2016 and changed dramatically to 44 per cent in 2020. All the other countries recorded negative economic growth rates in one or more years. The main inference I drew from the depiction of Caribbean economic growth performance since 1990 is that global economic recovery will bring only limited respite to CARICOM countries unless there is urgent attention to the fundaments of economic development in the region. The fundamentals include structural problems in major economic sectors and industries.

Analysis of the tourism industry would reveal that it is an aging industry in need of modernisation of plant, equipment, product portfolio, managerial practices and attitudes to enable it to regain competitiveness in the Caribbean and wider world. The tourism industry in CARICOM experienced decreasing growth rates of tourist arrivals between 1990 and 2005, substantially so in The Bahamas, Barbados, and St Lucia; its share of the Caribbean market contracted; and most of the growth in room capacity has taken place not in CARICOM but in Cuba, the Dominican Republic and Puerto Rico. Taxes and quasi-taxes on airline transportation, departure taxes on travellers, and taxes and other charges on tourist accommodation substantially raised final prices to consumers in an industry that is sensitive to comparative prices. Development strategies for sustainable growth of the CARICOM tourism industry would need to focus on revision of taxation policies towards the industry, investments in improving the tourism infrastructure such as internal transportation, roads, beaches, historical sites and natural attractions, and combined efforts by government and industry operators to expand geographical markets. Other pivotal sectors like energy, mining, manufacturing, agriculture, and air and maritime transportation require strategic attention.

CARICOM economies have a problem of low and declining productivity. This has been identified in several technical studies and official reports. The problem is reflected in the low ranking of the countries in the Global Competitiveness Report and the Ease of Doing Business Reports. The contributory factors to low productivity and efficiency weaknesses in the private sector are managerial approaches and practices, the institutional framework of laws, regulations and rules which restrict labour market flexibility and raise production costs, and the ethos of trade unionism with a proclivity for work stoppages and other means of reducing the effective supply of labour.

The labour market itself has been adversely affected by poor macroeconomic performance. As I stated in a presentation on "The Economic Performance of the Caribbean and its Impact on the Labour Market" to the Meet the Court Symposium organised by the Industrial Court of Trinidad and Tobago on 17 May 2014, unemployment has increased because of retrenchment of employees in the private sector and in the public sector and cutbacks on transfer payments and subsidies which diminished financial resources available to enterprises and households which then adversely affect their purchases of goods, services and labour. There was also the discouraged worker phenomenon whereby previously employed people and those who have not worked previously withdrew from the labour market because of pessimistic perceptions about their employment prospects. Another aspect is the higher incidence of female and youth unemployment.

Economic recession and stagnation and higher levels of unemployment have weakened the bargaining power of workers and depressed wages which have failed to keep up with inflation. Migration of workers within the Caribbean Community and countries elsewhere in response to poor economic performance in home countries has been another labour market consequence. The labour migrants to Caribbean countries tend to be in less well remunerated segments of the labour markets and tend to be less protected in terms of worker rights and working conditions.

I showed in a report prepared for the International Labour Office in February 2018 that these trends have been contrary to the ILO's Decent Work Agenda to which Caribbean governments committed. The Decent Work Agenda has four strategic priorities. The first is the promotion and establishment of labour standards and fundamental principles of rights of work. The second strategic priority is creation of opportunities for decent employment of men and women. The third strategic priority is enhanced coverage and effectiveness of social protection for all. The fourth strategic priority is strengthening tripartite approaches and social dialogue in the formulation of national policies. Given all these issues of concern in the labour market and business environment, comprehensive labour market reform, preferably on a trilateral basis substantively involving governments, the private sector and labour organisations is warranted.

CARICOM countries rank very low on the Global Competitiveness Index. The lowest ranks are obtained on regulatory and administrative frameworks, infrastructure, macroeconomic policy, education, goods market efficiency, labour market efficiency, market size and technical readiness. Because they have open, foreign trade dependent economies, CARICOM countries cannot develop unless they fix their international competitiveness problems. Careful prioritisation and combining of strategic goals are necessary. The institutional framework should be top of the list. The principal, most pervasive obstacle to development in CARICOM countries is not finance, human resource capacity or other such constraints. It is a highly dysfunctional public institutional environment which imposes tremendous transactions costs on enterprises and individual people, as amply reported in the World Bank's Ease of Doing Business Reports.

International shipping costs should also get priority attention. Shipping costs are higher in CARICOM than in its main international trading partners. Other costly elements of international trading transactions, such as the documentation and transactions time required to complete import and export processes in CARICOM countries compound the negative effects of shipping costs on international competitiveness.

The International Monetary Fund in 2017 provided an encouraging economic outlook for CARICOM countries for the 2018-2023 period. Higher growth rates were forecasted in most countries starting in 2018 and continuing into 2023 but with very few exceptions, economic growth rates would remain below 4 per cent. The main exception was Guyana where a 28 per cent growth rate was forecast. The main reasons for the favourable forecasts for the region are resurgence in commodity markets for gold and energy reflected in rising commodity prices, stable growth in global tourism demand, imminent large-scale production and export of oil in Guyana, and revenues generated by economic citizenship programmes in the OECS countries. At the time of the IMF forecasts, gold was a major export for Guyana and Suriname; oil and gas for Trinidad and Tobago, Suriname and Belize; and tourism in all the countries except Guyana and Suriname. Economic citizenship programmes contributed 5 per cent of the combined GDP of Antigua and Barbuda, Dominica, Grenada and St Kitts-Nevis in 2015.

It seems not to be sufficiently appreciated that population size, demographic structure, and spatial distribution help to define the set of economic opportunities available to individual countries in the region and that there are economies of scale in production, market access and demand for Caribbean exports achievable if countries pool their resources and combine their strategies on a regional basis instead of proceeding on an individual country basis. There are limits to enterprise growth within domestic markets. The estimated total population of the Caribbean Community in 2018 was 18.5 million of which 60 per cent was in Haiti, 16 per cent in Jamaica, 7 per cent in Trinidad and Tobago, 4 per cent in Guyana, and 3 per cent in Suriname. The population of the remaining nine countries constitute 9 per cent of the total. Inevitably the constraint of domestic market size will either impel the more enterprising firms to seek opportunities internationally or cause the unenterprising ones to stagnate or wither.

Fiscal policy has been contractionary and regressive rather than expansionary and progressive. Fiscal consolidation programmes have as their core elements capital expenditure reductions and reductions in subsidies and fiscal transfers which were initially intended to alleviate human vulnerability through improved access to health services, education and training, food, housing, utilities, transportation, and other essential services. The fiscal challenge for CARICOM governments has been posed by the rigidity of fiscal revenues and the large proportion of fiscal revenues unavoidably allocated to servicing public debt.

The presentation in Haiti concluded by discussing the scope for regional investment and trade in food and tourism. I pointed to the substantial reliance on imported food in all CARICOM countries co-existent with agricultural production capacity and potential in several countries. This means that there is considerable scope for agricultural development targeted towards food import substitution. An important element in complementary agricultural development strategy and food import substitution strategy would be investment in distribution and marketing components of the domestic food supply chain. With respect to tourism, the time is right for investment and marketing strategies focussed on expanding demand for intra-regional leisure travel. Critical elements in such strategies would be increases in affordable airlift capacity, reliable air and sea transportation, promotion of heritage, culture and festivals as important facets of the tourism product range, and ability of people at all levels in the supply of tourism services to communicate in more than one regional language.

Compounding the problem of slow, volatile and unsustainable economic growth is the problem that the economic growth which has been achieved is not inclusive, as I argued in a Plenary Address on "The Role of Microfinance in Promoting Inclusive Growth in the Caribbean" to the

Caribbean Microfinance Forum in Miami, 6 July 2015. It has become customary for CARICOM countries to cite with pride their ranks on the United Nations Human Development Index. Comforting as they might be to many people, the Human Development Index does not tell the whole story and provides little insights into people participation in the economic growth process and the distribution of the benefits associated with the modest economic growth achieved.

Fundamental aspects of the development process are human vulnerability and human progress. Public policies in the Caribbean Community have given considerable attention to poverty alleviation but the UNDP Caribbean Human Development Report for 2016, *Multidimensional Progress: Human Resilience Beyond Income*, for which I was a lead author along with Warren Benfield and Kenroy Roach under the coordination of Allison Drayton, advocated a broader multidimensional approach which takes account of several other human vulnerabilities. Adult illiteracy is still a problem in countries with high human development ranking. In several countries, fewer than 50 per cent of the population aged 25 years and older have received secondary education. Infant mortality rates while decreasing remain in excess of 10 per cent in some countries. Adult mortality rates are also high.

Poverty remains an important challenge for public economic policy. The population-weighted poverty rate for the 2001-2015 period was 44 per cent. Many countries were in a range of 22 per cent to 41 per cent; Haiti was as high as 59 per cent. Trinidad and Tobago, Barbados, Dominica and Belize were between 16 per cent and 20 per cent. Only The Bahamas was lower with a 10 per cent poverty rate. The Caribbean poor might be blessed, but they are not waiting to inherit the earth, judging from the rising tide of crimes against property and the seemingly uncontrollable growth of narcotics trafficking in the Caribbean. Not only is the incidence of serious crime a cause for concern, but Caribbean societies should also not in good conscience accept a state of affairs in which 200 to 700 of every 100,000 members of their countries are incarcerated and in which governance of parts of urban and rural districts are effectively under the control of organised gangs.

The Caribbean Human Development Report stated that the chances of being poor were increased by limited access or no access to public water supply, overcrowded dwellings, poor housing quality, large sizes of households, and household unemployment. The chances of sliding back into poverty were reduced by receipt of migrant remittances, health insurance, pensions, better household dwellings, self-employment of household heads, and employment in technical and associated professions.

Public expenditures on health care and social protection in the Caribbean Community compared unfavourably with Latin America and the Caribbean as a group. The most vulnerable groups in the region are women, youths, children, the elderly, people with disabilities, indigenous peoples, and Maroons people in Suriname. Several governments in the Caribbean Community have attempted to lessen these instances of human vulnerability through public expenditure programmes which provide a variety of assistance, including social security and old age pensions, subsidised access to medical care and medication, low-cost public housing, school feeding programmes and grants for education, and subsidised public transportation for adults and school children. However, their ability to make a substantial difference is limited by the poor economic growth performance of the countries, the limited fiscal space they have, and heavy debt burdens which are concomitants of slow and volatile economic growth.

FINANCING CARIBBEAN COMMUNITY DEVELOPMENT

Several matters in the fiscal sector, the financial sector, and the international financial environment featured in my continuing work on the development financing problems of the Caribbean Community. The framework was perhaps set in the Feature Address which I gave to the Tobago House of Assembly's Conference on Financing Development on 12 November 2013. My Address was on "Financing Strategies for Small Island Developing States". It noted that financial capital is an essential requirement for production and delivery of goods and services in market economies and for investments intended to accelerate economic growth and induce social and economic development. Financial mobilisation by governments, private enterprises and households is therefore a central concern of states, whether small or large, island or continental. Because the private sector and the household sector are major players in the socio-economic system, governments cannot confine their attention to their own financial mobilisation situation but must be mindful of the situation of the other two sectors. Their strategies must therefore be all-encompassing in scope, seeking to improve financial access for themselves as well as for their two economic partners.

Increasing pressures to expand current expenditures and the requirements of capital investment programmes will cause fiscal measures to be part of government financing strategies. Taxation is the core element in the fiscal strategy. There may be an inclination to raise effective rates of income taxation of enterprises and households but there is the danger of taxpayers viewing substantial increases as an imposition and an unintended incentive to intensify their efforts at tax avoidance and evasion. Transactions taxes and property taxes are also used in many jurisdictions. The levels of income and asset values in both the business sector and the household sector determine taxable capacity which sets limits on realistic expectations from tax increases. A further consideration is that the ratio of fiscal revenues might absorb too high a proportion of the country's resources measured by Gross Domestic Product and that a greater element of supply-side tax policy should be present in Caribbean fiscal policy.

A full range of debt financing options is not available to all Caribbean Community governments. Some have no Central Bank from which they can borrow, or they might be circumscribed from borrowing because of the special arrangements governing membership of the Central Bank as is the case with OECS countries. Even when governments are legally able to borrow from their Central Banks, the amount of foreign exchange reserves available to the countries limits the extent of their borrowing. Governments have often borrowed from domestic commercial banks, other private financial institutions, and government-operated social security and pension funds. This has entailed activation of unused lending capacity or rearranging asset portfolios to accommodate the government at the expense of other creditors. In the latter instance government debt would crowd out private debt. In the commercial banking industry, the situation has been one of excess liquidity attributable to weak demand for loans by customers deemed by the banks to be creditworthy, increase in loan delinquencies in situations of anaemic economic growth, business closures, and higher than usual levels of unemployment and job redundancies, and increased risk aversion by the banks.

Foreign borrowing has been problematic and is not a feasible option for some countries. The confidence of foreign lenders has been eroded by very high levels of indebtedness, and the recent history of voluntary and involuntary debt restructuring, rescheduling, and default in Latin America and the Caribbean.

Only five CARICOM countries went to the international bond market between 2012 and 2021. Jamaica and Trinidad and Tobago went frequently. Jamaica raised $2.5 billion in 2012, $1.8 billion in 2013 and in 2014, and then substantially decreasing amounts of $850 million in 2017, $600 million in 2020 and $300 million in 2021. Trinidad and Tobago bond issues were smaller than Jamaica's, except in 2016 when$1.6 billion was raised. The amounts raised in 2013, 2018, 2019 and 2020 were between $500 million and $550 million. There was an issue of $816 million in 2021. Barbados went to the market three times: 2014, 2015 and 2021. The first issue was for $2.5 billion, the second for $320 million, and the third for $400 million. By 2015, it had become obvious to international investors that the Barbados economy and government were in serious financial trouble. Suriname went to the bond market for $636 million in 2016 and $125 million in 2019.

Several adverse developments have prevented governments from obtaining favourable terms on their infrequent approaches to the international bond market since 2012. In a report to UNDP in 2015, I noted that they include weaknesses in domestic economic management reflected in large debt overhangs, challenges in achieving fiscal consolidation, weak and ineffective budgetary planning and control, and lack of success in developing resilient economies. Another source of difficulty was deterioration in international capital market ratings by influential credit rating agencies like Standard and Poor's and the increase in risk premiums which resulted. Nonetheless, CARICOM countries should endeavour to return to the international capital market. International support for fiscal reforms, debt restructuring and relief, bond guarantees and indemnities should be helpful in restoring creditworthiness and improving market perception of risks. Improvements in public sector management would have similar effects.

Caribbean Community countries benefitted a great deal in the past from overseas development assistance (ODA) in the form of grants and loans from developed countries and from multilateral financial institutions and regional development banks. Inflows of funds from official donors decreased significantly by the end of the 1990s. The UNDP's Regional Bureau for Latin America and the Caribbean engaged me in 2015 to prepare a report to which I alluded previously on "Financing for Development Challenges in Caribbean SIDS: A Case for Review of Eligibility Criteria for Access to Concessional Financing". I was required to analyse trends and the current situation of development financing in the Caribbean with special attention to concessional finance and make recommendations for improvements. I was assisted by Megan Alexander, Daren Conrad and Julia Jhinkoo, three young economists from the St Augustine campus of the University of the West Indies.

For ten Caribbean countries in receipt of Overseas Development Assistance (ODA), the data showed that ODA varied between 0.1 per cent and 5 per cent of their Gross National Income but that there was a precipitate decrease in flows after a spike around 2008-2010. The traditional official donors are the UK, the US, Canada and Japan, but they have been joined by new bilateral donors like Australia, China, Israel, Korea, Kuwait, Taiwan and the United Arab Emirates. Cumulatively over the 2000-2013 period, the largest traditional official donors were the UK, the US and Canada. Bilateral flows have been on the decline as aid preferences shifted towards low-income countries and countries in post-conflict situations, and in response to other changes in aid eligibility criteria such as political and social fragility in potential beneficiary countries, and geopolitical interests of donors.

The income eligibility criteria for concessional funds from both bilateral donors and multilateral financial institutions have become formidable access barriers for Caribbean Community countries because of their status as middle-income and high-income developing countries. In the report to UNDP in 2015, I recommended a development needs approach which recognised that development needs are not unidimensional or fully captured by the per capita income of a country. The concept would include factors such as poverty, sustainable livelihoods, and equitable access to essential services, including health care and education. I also recommended consideration of the need to foster and maintain social cohesion, citizen security and national stability even in countries unaffected by internal wars and which therefore would not be deemed post-conflict countries. I recommended that per capita national income should be abandoned as an eligibility criterion for access to concessional and non-concessional development finance assistance and that economic vulnerability should be adopted as an eligibility criterion. The application could distinguish categories of countries and their access based on the measures of vulnerability and reflect the principle of gradual transition in access to development financial assistance instead of abrupt ineligibility or graduation when countries reach an income threshold. The case has been made for including criteria which take account of the extreme vulnerability of Caribbean economies to external economic shocks and natural hazard events. Various vulnerability indices have been constructed for possible use by official donors and the multilateral financial institutions.

The Commonwealth Secretariat has been a leading advocate for their use. In addition to sponsoring some of the work on vulnerability indices, they collaborated with the Center for Global Development to convene a consultation on "The World Bank's Income Classification Systems: Is It

Time for Change?" on 23 June 2016 in Washington, D.C. In the session "Perspectives on a Unified World Bank Income Classification System", I made a presentation on "Intra-Regional and Extra-Regional Challenges" in which I outlined the major challenges of sustained economic growth, poverty and inequality, unemployment, exposure to economic shocks, natural hazard vulnerability, and mobilising adequate finance for economic growth and development. I stated that it was erroneous to ignore the heterogeneity of the Caribbean and adopt a "one size fits all" approach in evaluating aid applications and designing programmes. I recommended that the World Bank country classification system should be modified to reflect use of multiple criteria instead of a single criterion, take account of poverty, take account of cost of access to private international capital, and take account of vulnerability to external shocks. Six years later, these matters are still being advocated by CARICOM's political leadership and are still on the international agenda for consideration and change.

Foreign direct investment is important. It has substantially augmented domestic investment, especially in countries with minerals, oil, and gas production resources and those with large international tourism sectors. Net foreign direct investment in CARICOM totalled US$36.7 billion between 2010 and 2020. The main recipients during that period were The Bahamas with 35 per cent, Jamaica with 18 per cent, Guyana with 15 per cent, and Barbados with 10 per cent. Inflows decreased considerably in most countries after 2015. Guyana, which in 2015 had only 8 per cent of FDI inflows, has become a very substantial FDI recipient because of investments in its vast offshore oil and gas resources. Foreign direct investment inflows are quite substantial relative to the economic sizes of the individual CARICOM countries. In Guyana and Grenada, FDI inflows comprised as much as 22 per cent and 14 per cent of GDP. The range was 4 per cent to 6 per cent in St Vincent and the Grenadines, The Bahamas, Dominica, Belize, and Barbados.

In the Report to UNDP in 2015 and in the presentation in Haiti in 2018, I discussed the role of financial transfers and capital investments by the Caribbean diaspora in financing Caribbean development. Personal remittances are substantial when measured against an aggregate measure of the size of the economies. In 2020, they are estimated to be as large as 22 per cent of Gross Domestic Product in Jamaica, 21 per cent in Haiti, and 14 per cent in Dominica. The range is 7 per cent to 8 per cent for Guyana, Belize, Grenada, and St Vincent and the Grenadines, and 2 per cent to 4 per cent for Barbados, Antigua and Barbuda, St Kitts-Nevis, St

Lucia St Vincent and the Grenadines, and Suriname. In some instances, they exceed earnings from exports of goods and services.

Migrant remittances have financed higher levels of household consumption on durable goods and non-durable goods, expenditures on education and health services, and expenditures on construction and maintenance of homes. In those ways, they have contributed to alleviating some of the development challenges of Caribbean Community countries. Investment in bonds by diaspora residents have been mooted in various quarters, including Caribbean Heads of Governments forums, as another mechanism by which the diaspora can assist in financing Caribbean economic growth and development.

The financial advantages for the potential recipient countries apart from the flow of funds could be interest costs that are lower than those in the international capital markets and possibly more favourable risk assessments because of diaspora goodwill and a more sympathetic view of the Caribbean country's economic challenges and efforts. Potential diaspora investors, however, might encounter obstacles with respect to both inward and outward capital transactions, the regulatory frameworks in the Caribbean, and inefficiencies within the Caribbean financial system in transacting cross-border business. Furthermore, it would be wise to assume that many diaspora investors are risk savvy and that diaspora bonds would have more appeal if there were evidence of sound management of the economies, good governance, and improvements in the functioning of local capital markets.

Financing strategies must address the requirements of the business sector because the level and nature of business sector activity is central to economic growth, fiscal capacity, and the nature of public expenditures, for example the proportion of the public budget that might be deployed in employment creation programmes. Part of the financing strategies for the business sector is to create an institutional and policy framework conducive to the supply of funds. The framework can consist of special purpose institutions such as development banks and venture capital funds to supplement the operations of commercial banks. Development of credit risk appraisal institutions might also make it easier for private financial institutions to manage the risks of providing business finance.

Credit unions are a possible source of business finance. They have become sizeable components of the financial system in many Caribbean Community countries and have sometimes extended their operations beyond traditional deposit and liability services to their members to include provision of a widening array of banking services. Production and income generating enterprises have become their customers. They tend to have significant outreach in terms of the number and country-wide distribution of their credit clientele. Credit unions, however, face two important challenges. One challenge is to strike a balance between the costs they incur in fund mobilisation and lending and their commitment to provision of affordable credit to their members. To be financially viable they must keep operating costs down or increase interest rates on loans. The other challenge is presented by non-performing loans which comprise dangerously high proportions of asset portfolios in some institutions. This should cause credit unions to refine and further develop their credit risk appraisal, monitoring and management systems, to reconsider the design of some of their credit products, to diversify their asset portfolios to reduce overall risks and strengthen liquidity hedges, and to incorporate protection against credit losses which might occur from natural hazard events. A structured arrangement whereby credit unions are provided with institutional strengthening to enhance their capacity for business credit risk appraisal and risk management and a temporary risk indemnification scheme might induce credit unions to be an important part of the business finance structure.

THE CORRESPONDENT BANKING PROBLEM AND SUSTAINABLE DEVELOPMENT

International banks have engaged in what has been termed "de-risking" in their relationship with commercial banks and other financial institutions in the Caribbean. By de-risking is meant the reduction or termination of correspondent banking services to the institutions in the Caribbean. The implications for Caribbean economies are sufficiently significant to have warranted serious attention by CARICOM Heads of Government, Central Banks, commercial banks, and other private financial institutions which use correspondent banking services. I was invited to make a presentation on the problem and its implications for sustainable development at a symposium organised by the UWI – SUNY Center for Leadership and Sustainable Development and the SUNY Global Center in New York on 13 February 2017.

As I noted, correspondent banking services had been terminated in some Caribbean countries with substantial international financial services, for example Barbados, The Bahamas, Cayman Islands, and the Turks and Caicos Islands, as well as in some countries with mainly domestic financial services industry, for example Belize, Haiti and Guyana. Banking services were suspended to certain categories of business entities, notably international money value transfer service providers such as Western Union and MoneyGram, foreign exchange cambios, and private members' clubs which operate casinos. The consequences of suspension or termination of correspondent banking services include reduced efficiency and higher costs of international payments, reduction of foreign trade, reduced foreign currency earnings, and adversely affected domestic incomes and employment. Curtailment of correspondent banking services to international money value transfer service providers was likely to have impaired the flow of migrant remittances and depressed business, particularly in The Bahamas, Cayman Islands, and in Jamaica where the industry accounted for 46 per cent of sales in Jamaican financial markets and engaged in $47 million of foreign exchange inflows.

The adverse consequences for domestic commercial banks were higher levels of liquidity, reduced ability to diversify asset and liability portfolios and to manage portfolio risks by transactions in short-term foreign assets and liabilities, and lower returns on their earning assets. The reduction in correspondent banking services led to contraction of the International Business Companies industry and the offshore finance industry which had helped to sustain economic growth, notably in Barbados, Cayman Islands and the British Virgin Islands.

De-risking has been driven by foreign banks' re-evaluation of their business model in response to increased costs of risk capital caused by the new global standards for capital and liquidity. In the new business model, correspondent banking services are viewed as low return, balance sheet intensive products. Furthermore, the 2012 Financial Action Task Force (FATF) standard shifted from a rules-based approach to a risk-based approach which required correspondent banks to conduct ongoing customer due diligence on respondent banks, including gathering information on the nature of the respondent's business and their reputation, and on the quality of supervision in their operating jurisdictions. This requirement increased operational costs for correspondent banks. Additionally, there are higher compliance costs associated with bilateral and multilaterally imposed economic and trade sanctions, anti-money laundering and counter-terrorist financing, and tax transparency rules. Correspondent banks intent on preserving reputational capital and avoiding fines, penalties and other sanctions will tend to incur substantial costs in complying not only with FATF requirements but also with the requirements imposed by other national and international standard setting and regulatory bodies.

I noted that the Caribbean policy approach to resolving the correspondent banking problem is mainly political, entailing bilateral and multilateral lobbying efforts aimed at improving understanding of the Caribbean situation and gaining sufficient goodwill for reversing the trend towards de-risking. It is my view that political approaches do not address correspondent bank profitability which is the central issue underlying the crisis in correspondent banking relations. Market approaches which address the costs and returns consideration of the banks should be central to the Caribbean efforts and may be usefully supplemented by political efforts.

Some elements of market approaches were suggested. First, Caribbean countries needed to reduce compliance risks by strengthening regulatory and supervisory frameworks in their own jurisdictions. This would entail, among other things, becoming compliant with the long list of FATF requirements for which they are non-compliant or only partially compliant. Second, Caribbean monetary authorities should establish and monitor Know Your Customer guidelines for commercial banks and other financial institutions. These are critical for identifying and managing compliance risks which might emanate from money laundering and financing of terrorism. Third, Caribbean monetary authorities should establish regulatory and supervisory regimes for international money transfer business. Fourth, Caribbean monetary authorities can attempt to reduce information costs incurred by correspondent banks by assuming a quality assurance role, interposing themselves between correspondent banks and domestic financial institutions as guarantors of regulatory observance and information integrity.

I also counselled that country reputation matters to the behaviour of international banks, foreign governments and international institutions and agencies. Observable and widely publicised weaknesses in narcotics crime detection and control, protracted judicial administration in both criminal and civil matters, and undue legislative delays contribute to perceptions that Caribbean countries have weak governance systems which cannot be fully trusted to act consistently with respect to obligations to the international corporate and government sectors. The overhaul of those aspects of Caribbean governance is a critical requirement for achieving a situation in which there is international confidence in the quality of financial sector regulation, supervision and monitoring, and law enforcement in the Caribbean, thereby expanding the scope and lowering the costs of the Caribbean's interface with the global financial system.

A RETURN TO TERTIARY EDUCATION

I actively re-engaged with tertiary education matters in 2012 and have continued to do so. I accepted an offer in December 2011 to be Executive Director of the Caribbean Centre for Money and Finance for an interim period which was expected to last one year but did not end until December 2014. Since 2012, I have led or served as member of teams commissioned by the Accreditation Council of Trinidad and Tobago to conduct accreditation evaluations of universities, colleges and other tertiary institutions offering academic and professional programmes in Trinidad and Tobago. In most instances, the universities were established in the United Kingdom. On behalf of the St Christopher and Nevis Accreditation Board, I also conducted accreditation evaluations of two offshore medical universities in its jurisdiction. I also made training workshop and conference presentations to professional staff of Caribbean accreditation institutions and universities on institutional governance, funding and quality assurance. In 2017, I chaired a Technical Working Group of Caribbean on Tertiary Education established by the CARICOM. In 2013 and 2014, I chaired a UWI Council Task Force on Tuition Fees. I was also substantively involved in the implementation of the UWI Strategic Development Plan 2017-2022 for the St Augustine campus.

THE CHANGING WORLD OF HIGHER EDUCATION

Part of the framework for my efforts in the period is provided in the Cave Hill Campus Graduation Dinner Address which I gave on 21 October 2011 in the presence of Dr John Holder, Archbishop of the West Indies, and other Honorary Graduates. My topic was "The Changing World of Higher Education". I began by observing that universities all over the world are in a time of momentous change. The change which perhaps most impresses itself upon the consciousness of the public and the university community is the tremendous surge in student enrolment. An important driver of enrolment expansion is a strong philosophical commitment to principles of equality of opportunity and upward social mobility, but philosophical beliefs are not all that motivate the expansion.

For many countries, investment in higher education is an essential component of strategies for economic growth and development, especially now that the "knowledge economy" has become an accepted paradigm. Universities through their teaching and research are central to the creation and dissemination of knowledge. Their weakness, with few comparatively recent exceptions, has been in linking knowledge creation and dissemination to innovation and enterprise. This weakness is generally attributable to the discordance between the interests and goals of researchers and teachers and those of corporate enterprises and the lack within universities of an institutional framework for reconciling them. In developing countries, it is also due to the lesser importance attached to research and development in public and private funding of universities. Some countries have embarked upon a "big push" to simultaneously solve the numbers problem and the quality and relevance problem by creation of research clusters partly modelled on Silicon Valley in California. Late starters in science and technology can try to fast start their development by strategically incorporating foreign institutions into their university sector, as done by Qatar in its Education City.

A significant change in the environment for higher education is economic recession. It presents a severe challenge to the finances of higher education institutions which had embarked upon growth and development programmes funded by fiscal contributions, generous private and corporate donations and large endowments incomes. Faced with decreasing inflows of government subventions and endowment incomes, universities have had to explore other funding options in order to minimise contractions of staff through hiring freezes and negotiated early retirement and to minimise reduction in their capital expenditures budgets. Considerable ingenuity on the part of higher education leaders and a comprehensively cooperative approach by all stakeholders is required to see the institutions through such difficult episodes. Parallels have been drawn with the Great Depression of 1929-1932. In that period, there was tremendous job loss, student drop out, penury of continuing students, staff curtailment and salary cuts, and overall reductions in university budgets. However, as noted by one historian, a cardinal difference between then and now is that public policy is based less on the perspective that higher education is a consumption good enjoyed by elites and is based instead on the belief that it is a requirement for resuscitating and sustaining economic growth.

The change with the most pervasive and longest effects is technology. Education technology is fundamentally transforming the higher education landscape. The growth of online education is one of the more significant consequences. More than 800 universities, including ivy league ones, have active online sites in which much of the content is delivered free of charge. The scale of use is staggering. As early as 2011, there were 300 million downloads a year and 350,000 lectures offered by more than 1000 universities. Online education often combines the intellectual resources of several universities to offer a wide array of lectures and courses, thereby allowing online students the opportunity to be educated by the best regardless of institutional affiliation. There is greater flexibility in hours of student access and no constraints on repetition. The one-to-many model of classroom instruction is giving way to a one-to-one model of digital education. These features are in such marked contrast to conventional university education that in the not-so-distant future conventional universities will have very little competitive advantage.

Another significant change is the re-internationalisation of higher education which started three decades ago but received tremendous boost from countries' adoption of the knowledge economy paradigm and the structural change in distance education technology. Since the 1980s, higher education institutions in the UK, the US and Australia have taken advantage of opportunities for growth and financial strength by offshore provision of education services in Africa, Asia, Latin America and the Caribbean, either working alone or through franchising and other partnership arrangements with local institutions.

Universities in France and other European countries now do likewise. Because of the technology revolution, the early pioneers and latecomers can reach a larger catchment of international students than through franchising arrangements which are subject to physical capacity constraints. Professors have become virtually mobile while students do not have to be geographically mobile. It is this liberating capacity of information technology which more than anything else gives salience to the remark by New York University's President John Sexton that universities and the most talented people in universities will operate beyond sovereignty.

Geographically mobile students are nonetheless part of the desired catchment of universities and governments in developed countries. The incomes earned through tuition fees and other expenditures by foreign students are important to both higher education institutions and the host economies. The economic value of foreign students in the US in 2010 was estimated to be $20 billion. In the UK, tuition fees from non-European Union domiciled students comprised approximately 10 per cent of the incomes of higher education institutions in 2009/2010.

There is a challenge to developing countries' institutions, like the UWI, in this rebirth of internationalisation, particularly in its competitiveness dimensions. They are challenged to become less localised and more international in their academic programmes and in their appeal to students if they are to withstand competition from larger, financially stronger institutions in developed countries, but must do so without weakening their role in national and regional development.

I concluded the Address by stating that it was imperative that the leadership of Caribbean universities in conjunction with their stakeholders, including the general public, fashion and implement effective responses to the changes in the higher education environment. It would be wonderful if there is unity in the pursuit of sustainable growth and development of the Caribbean universities committed to equitable development of Caribbean societies. Then, it could be said in the foreseeable future: "Behold, how good and pleasant it is for brethren to dwell together in unity".

TERTIARY EDUCATION SECTOR GOVERNANCE IN CARICOM

The CARICOM Technical Working Group on Tertiary Education which I chaired had as its other members Professor Densil Williams, Pro-Vice Chancellor for Planning and Development in UWI, as Vice-Chair; Professor Dennis Gayle, Executive Chancellor, The University of the Commonwealth Caribbean; Dr Barbara Reynolds, Deputy Vice-Chancellor, University of Guyana; Dr Kofi Nkrumah-Young, President, Association of Caribbean Higher Education Administrators; Dr Karl Dawson, President, Association of Caribbean Tertiary Institutions; Dr Willie Clarke-Okah, President, New Century-New Compact, Canada; Dr Ronald Brunton, President, Caribbean Area Network for Quality Assurance in Tertiary Education; and Dr Eduardo Ali, Programme Manager, Human Resource Development, CARICOM Secretariat. All the members were experts in various aspects of tertiary education governance.

The remit of the Technical Working Group was regional policy for public funding of tertiary education, investment and labour market linkages, regional governance mechanisms, finance, and research, development and innovation.

The Report "Tertiary Education Sector Governance" submitted in November 2017 noted that tertiary education systems in the Caribbean are situated in market driven economies and that tertiary education sectors provide opportunities for revenue growth in the sector and stimulate economic growth and competitiveness in other sectors of the economies. It noted that the tertiary education sector was very heterogeneous, comprised of many institutions in Jamaica and Trinidad and Tobago, and was large in terms of student enrolment. The sector in the Caribbean experienced expansion in size, capacity, costs and output, but there has been critical consideration of educational quality and institutional performance. The Report acknowledged the efforts of Caribbean governments to develop and implement policies to strengthen their tertiary education systems and suggested that, given financial and human resource limitations, there could be greater assurance of achievement if economies of scale are considered, articulated and governed across multiple Caribbean jurisdictions. It therefore recommended inter-sectoral and multi-country collaborations in policy development, resource allocations and management; more capacity and resources for inter-institutional regional connectivity, collaboration, efficiency and effectiveness; and regional accountability, efficiency and transparency in quality assurance of tertiary education institutions.

The Report had much to say on governance of tertiary education institutions. It stated that full range of operations of tertiary education institutions is affected by their governance arrangements. A distinction was made between systems governance which pertains to the laws, regulations and policies which provide the framework for operations of the institutions within the nation system, and institutional governance which pertains to the rules, regulations, policies, procedures, and practices for efficient, equitable and transparent operations by individual tertiary institutions. One critical element of effective system governance is the capacity of the State to develop a vision and strategy for the tertiary education sector. Another element is the existence of a regulatory framework. A third element would be institutional arrangements for quality assurance. A fourth element, typically applicable only to publicly funded institutions, is the use of performance-based funding criteria. Yet another element is the existence of an accountability framework in which institutions report to the State or its agencies.

Private providers of education because they are profits oriented present challenges to State administered governance frameworks, especially if they are in cooperative arrangements with foreign institutions. The issues to be dealt with are risks of programme instability, quality dilution and how much reliance should be placed on quality assurance and governance oversight in foreign jurisdictions. Six main features of institutional governance were identified in the Report – One: organisational autonomy to determine structure, size and modes of operation; Two: financial autonomy to make decisions on financial resource mobilisation, financial allocation, and financial management; Three: human resource autonomy for institutions to obtain and manage their own human resources; Four: academic autonomy; Five: performance and financial accountability; Six: safeguards for the integrity of academic processes.

The Report also considered issues affecting the contribution of tertiary education to national development and explored the concept of the entrepreneurial university. Considerable attention was given to funding patterns and problems. The Report noted that for government-owned institutions the main sources of funds are annual fiscal grants and tuition fees and other charges on students while for private institutions, tuition fees are the primary source of income. Governments have also been a major source for financing tuition fees to public institutions in most Caribbean countries and in the case of Trinidad and Tobago to students at private institutions.

Fiscal difficulties of governments have eroded their ability to sustain accustomed levels of financial support to tertiary education institutions with consequences of accumulating arrears on their transfers to the institutions for both subventions and student tuition fees. Among the government-owned institutions, concerns have been expressed about equity in the allocation of government subventions and matters have been complicated by the absence of agreed formulae or structures for linking government allocations and disbursements to performance indicators. Tertiary education institutions face the challenge of managing the trade-off between raising tuition fees and sustaining enrolment demand, especially when the macro-economic situation depresses household incomes and the related capacity to pay. Institutional consultancy by the institutions and philanthropic contributions are options explored without marked success.

FURTHER CONSIDERATION OF THE FINANCIAL ISSUES

I gave further consideration to the financial issues in the higher education sector in a paper "Financial Challenges in Providing Quality Higher Education in the Caribbean" in a book *Caribbean Quality Culture: Persistent Commitment to Improving Higher Education* edited by Sandra Ingrid Gift and published by the UWI Press in 2021. I described the cost structure of higher education, noting its labour-intensive nature which makes the cost of labour services the largest component of total operating costs. The cost share of labour services is influenced by decision rules, policies and practices which determine the size and earnings structure of an institution's workforce.

The size of the institutions and the range of their academic programmes are also influences on the structure of their costs. Cost drivers in Caribbean higher education were explored. One applicable line of analysis is William

Baumol's cost disease thesis. It postulates that universities are labour intensive enterprises with little scope for varying their production technology in terms of the ratios of their main production inputs, but they operate in environments in which the wage rates of their employees are indexed to wage rates elsewhere in the economy. This thesis has applicability in the Caribbean because higher education institutions operate in highly unionised environments in which negotiated wage rates are strongly influenced by comparable rates in other sectors and because their academic traditions and norms impart some degree of fixity to their production structures which then limits the scope for minimising the impact of wage increases. Other cost drivers have been student enrolment growth and expenditures to improve the quality of educational services.

I drew attention to the underfunding of the publicly funded institutions using the examples of the University of Trinidad and Tobago and the University of the West Indies to illustrate the deleterious effects on the scale of operations in the former case and the threat to financial viability and weakness in operational efficiency and effectiveness in the latter case. Debt financing has become a financing strategy for some Caribbean higher education institutions, partly to provide working capital when governments are delinquent in meeting their agreed financial subventions and partly to finance capital investments and programme development. There are dangers to be avoided in this strategy. The potential debtor institutions must be careful that projected tuition fee income and other uncommitted inflows of funds are sufficiently large and stable to service and amortise the debt and that their liquidity hedges are not compromised if their short-term financial assets are used as loan collateral.

A PERFORMANCE BASED-FUNDING MODEL FOR UWI

As part of my work in relation to the implementation of the UWI Strategic Development Plan at St Augustine, I proposed a performance-based funding model in March 2018. In making the proposal, I stated that university education and training confers benefits to the entire society and to individual graduates and that recognition of the social and private benefits should mean that the costs of university education should be shared between governments as the natural custodians of social benefits and students as the ultimate recipients of the private benefits. I noted that government decisions about sharing of costs have been shaped by the social philosophy to which governments and citizens adhere, especially equity, equality of opportunity and social justice; by fiscal capacity; by recognition that there are both delivery costs incurred by universities and education acquisition costs incurred by students over and above tuition fees and other service charges; and by differences in levels of household incomes and wealth within countries and associated perceptions about ability of some students to pay for university education.

Universities also contribute social and private benefits through the outcomes of their research and development activities. The business community, consumer society and governments are usually the primary beneficiaries but spill-over benefits to the wider society tend to be substantial and long-lasting. Funding of university research and development (R&D) is not a strong feature of the Caribbean government and business environment.

There are differences in funding patterns across the UWI campuses. The differences reflect variances in policies and practices with respect to government fiscal contributions, deviations from common tuition fee policies, decisions by some governments to separately fund some programmes of special interest to them, and significant cross-campus differences in the scope and efficiency of commercial operations. Whatever the reasons, there is not a ONE UWI funding policy or practice. In my judgement the current funding model based on governments and students sharing of economic costs of service delivery has been damaged beyond repair by persistent and widespread failure by many contributing governments to fulfil their financial obligations in accordance with the cost-sharing decisions made by the University's highest decision body, arbitrary departure by some governments from the agreed uniform tuition fee policies and their self-imposition of caps on tuition fees for their nationals, chronic failure to specifically budget for research and development and to fund it, and the absence of an explicit resource budgeting process for capital investments and developmental initiatives.

The proposal has seven principal features – One: government fiscal contributions for teaching services would be based on agreed annual output of graduates; Two: there would be an agreed breakdown of the annual targets of graduates into major disciplinary groups, and sub-disciplinary groups if desired; Three: agreement on projected efficiency costs of producing a graduate; Four: each contributing government declares upfront what proportion of the agreed efficiency cost it will finance; Five: determination of tuition fees and other income measures by university management; Six: programmed cost allocations for agreed research and development programmes; Seven: separate funding of explicit capital expansion and improvement projects and development initiatives. The proposal ties the provision of government fiscal contributions to a specific performance indicator, namely annual output of graduates. It departs from the input-based, cost-budgeting model currently being used. It has the merit of simplicity and when disaggregated by disciplines or faculty allows for a link between desired composition of graduates and actual composition of graduates.

Cost-efficiency performance indicators for teaching are encapsulated in a variable called 'efficiency costs' of producing a graduate. The actual costs of producing a graduate would reflect cost-efficiency indicators such as capacity utilisation ratios, student-staff ratios, teaching loads, throughput rates, procurement and inventory management, and measures of efficiency in use of utilities. In setting a norm for efficiency costs of producing a graduate, one would in effect be setting a composite performance standard for the university in its teaching activities. The efficiency costs would be inflation-proofed in recognition that the university has no control over general inflation. There would be a problem with labour cost increases stemming from the fact that the university is effectively a price-taker since it is the government of the campus country that determines rates of remuneration negotiated with the representative trade unions.

Output and cost efficiency measures would be built into the funding of research and development programmes because each project would have specified outcomes, prior costing of activities and budgetary limits. The explicit framework for funding capital expansion and development initiatives would similarly entail specification of intended outcomes and cost-efficiency standards for implementation.

The operational processes were outlined in ten steps which include governments determining projected target demands for graduates, committing or contracting to allocate annually the funds required to complete the graduation process for the cohort, and committing to financing their contributions to the agreed R&D programmes and agreed capital investment and development initiatives. With respect to teaching services, the university would estimate new student intake for a specified year and subsequent years consistent with projected demand, calculate efficiency costs per graduate, agree with governments the proportion of efficiency costs that they would finance and calculate the requisite fiscal contribution based on their projected demand for graduates, and determine and publish tuition fees annually. With respect to R&D, capital expansion and improvement projects, and development initiatives, the university would be expected to prepare and approve programmes and projects on a multi-year basis and to seek funding from governments and donors.

The performance-based funding proposed has several advantages. It sets goals for the university, contributing governments and other stakeholders in terms of output of graduates and of research and development outcomes which are the source of added value to the economies and societies rather than solely in terms of inputs into the teaching and research process. It allows for the possibility of a closer calibration between identified knowledge and skills needs and the output of the university system. It ensures predictability of funds for teaching and research and development. It encourages greater internal and external focus on the efficiency of the university enterprise and can provide stimuli for efficiency gains. It allows scope for autonomous financial decision-making by the university on tuition fees which are a matter of critical importance to financial viability. It provides a more attractive and better managed framework for financial contributions from entities other than the contributing governments.

APPENDIX

Honours, Awards, Professional Recognition, Boards, Committees and Working Groups

HONOURS

Order of Excellence (O.E.), Cooperative Republic of Guyana
Doctor of Laws (LLD), University of the West Indies
Compton Bourne Street, University of Guyana, Main Campus
Compton Bourne Building, University of the West Indies, St Augustine Campus

DISTINGUISHED AWARDS

Caribbean Studies Association Distinguished Service Award
The American Foundation for the University of the West Indies Award for Outstanding Contribution to the Caribbean
The National Coalition on Caribbean Affairs International Service Award for Outstanding Contribution to Caribbean Development
Accreditation, Council of Trinidad and Tobago Lifetime Award for Excellence in Higher Education
Caribbean Money Market Brokers Award for Development of Caribbean Capital Markets

PROFESSIONAL RECOGNITION

Professor Emeritus, University of the West Indies
President, Caribbean Studies Association
Vice-President, Caribbean Agro-Economic Society
Fellow, Caribbean Academy of Sciences

MEMBERSHIP OF BOARDS

Member, Board of Directors, National Savings Committee, Jamaica, 1975-1980
Commissioner, Port Authority of Trinidad and Tobago, 1981-1983

Member, Board of Directors, Central Bank of Trinidad and Tobago, 1987-January 2000

Member, Board of Directors, Trinidad Publishing Company, 1997-2001

Vice-Chairman, UNESCO Institute for Higher Education in Latin America and the Caribbean, 2000-2002

Chancellor, University of Guyana, 2009-2012

MEMBERSHIP OF AD HOC COMMITTEES AND WORKING GROUPS

1975	Member of Committee (self plus Managing Director and Deputy Managing Director, East Caribbean Currency Authority) to recommend re-alignment of EC$ to US$
1975	Member of CARICOM Special Technical Group on Training and Banking
1977	Working Group on Emergency Production Plan, Jamaica
1988-1989	Chairman of Cabinet-appointed Committee on Technical Aspects of the Relationship between the International Monetary Fund and Trinidad and Tobago
1988	Member of Cabinet-appointed Committee on the Working of Monetary Policy in Trinidad and Tobago
1988	Member of Cabinet-appointed Group on Restructuring for Medium -Term Economic Recovery Programme for Trinidad and Tobago
1993	Member of Cabinet-appointed Committee on Student Loan Scheme, Trinidad and Tobago
1994-1997	Member of CARICOM Working Group on Capital Market Development
1994	Member of Commonwealth Secretariat Working Group on Human Resource Development Policies
2000-2001	Deputy Chairman, Caribbean Trade and Adjustment Group, the Caribbean Regional Negotiating Machinery and the Caribbean Community Secretariat
2003	Chairman, Technical Group on Automaticity of Financing of Caribbean Community Institutions established by Caribbean Community Heads of Government and State.
2004	Member, Caribbean Commission on Health and Development established by Caribbean Community Heads of Government and State
2009	Chairman, Council of Finance and Planning Task Force on

	Regional Strategies for Mitigating the Effects of the Global Financial Crisis on the Caribbean
2009-2011	Chairman of CARICOM Advisory Group on Caribbean Regional Strategic Development Plan
2014	Chairman of University West Indies Council Task Force on Tuition Fees
2017	Chairman, CARICOM Tertiary Education Working Group

SELECTED BIBLIOGRAPHY

Adams, Nassau, "Imports Structure and Economic Growth in Jamaica, 1954-1967". Social and Economic studies 23, 1971.

Bascom, W.O., A Brief Note on the History of Cooperative Credit Banks in Guyana 1914-1954. Unpublished. October 1968.

Bascom, W.O., The Role of the Guyana National Cooperative Bank. Georgetown, Guyana: Guyana National Cooperative Bank, 1969.

Brewster, H.R. and Thomas, C.Y., *The Dynamics of West Indian Integration*. Kingston, Jamaica: University of West Indies, 1967.

Bryant, Ralph C., *Money and Monetary Policy in Interdependent Nations*. Washington, D.C.: The Brookings Institution, 1980.

Burnham, Jessie, *Beware My Brother Forbes*. Ruimveldt, Guyana: New Guiana Co. Ltd, 1964.

Burnham, Linden Forbes Sampson, Towards a Cooperative Republic. Address to 12th Annual Delegates Conference, Peoples National Congress, Georgetown, Guyana, 6 April 1969.

Burnham. Linden Forbes Sampson, Guyana Bauxite. Address to the Nation, Georgetown, Guyana, 28 November 1970.

Burnham, Linden Forbes Sampson, To Own Guyana. Address to the 14th Annual Delegates Conference of Peoples National Congress, Georgetown, Guyana, 18 April 1971.

Burrowes, Reynold A., *The Wild Coast: An Account of Politics in Guyana*. Cambridge, Massachusetts: Schenkam Publishing Co. Inc, 1984.

Burrowes, Reynold A., *Revolution and Rescue in Grenada*. New York: Greenwood Press, 1988.

Collier, David, *The New Authoritarianism in Latin America*. New Jersey: Princeton University Press, 1979.

Demas, William G., *The Economics of Development in Small Countries*. Montreal, Canada: McGill University Press, 1964.

Demas, William G., *Essays on Caribbean Integration and Development*. Kingston, Jamaica: Institute of Social and Economic Research, 1976.

De Tocqueville, Alexis, *Democracy in America*. Chicago: University of Chicago Press, 2000.

Ferguson, Tyrone, *To Survive Sensibly or to Court Heroic Death*. Georgetown, Guyana: Public Affairs Consulting Enterprise, 1996.

Giddens, Anthony P., *The Third Way: Renewal of Social Democracy*. Cambridge: Polity Press, 1998.

Girvan, Norman P., "The Guyana-Alcan Conflict and the Nationalization of DEMBA". New World Journal, V, 4, 1971.

Girvan, Norman P., "Why we need to nationalise bauxite and how to do it". Reprinted in Girvan, Norman and Jefferson, Owen (eds), *Readings in the Political Economy of the Caribbean*. Mona, Jamaica: New World Group, 1971.

Hirschman, A.O., *The Strategy of Economic Development*. New Haven: Yale University Press, 1958.

Holder, Carlos and Worrell, DeLisle, "A Model of Price Formation for Small Economies: Three Caribbean Examples". Central Bank of Barbados Research Department, January 1984.

Hope, Kempe R., "National Cooperative Commercial Banking and Development Strategy in Guyana". American Journal of Economics and Sociology 34, July 1975.

Hope, Kempe R., "Cooperative Socialism and the Cooperative Movement in Guyana" Review of International Cooperation 68, No.2, 1975.

Hope, Kempe R., *Development Policy in Guyana: Planning, Finance and Administration*. Boulder, Colorado: Westview Press, 1979.

Joefield-Napier, Wallace, "Trinidad and Tobago's Economic Growth and the Balance of Trade, 1954-1968". Social and Economic Studies 27, 1978.

Joefield-Napier, Wallace, *The Demand for Imports*. Kingston, Jamaica: Institute of Social and Economic Research, 1982.

Kane, Edward J., "Good Intentions and Unintended Evil: The Case Against Selective Credit Control". Journal of Money, Credit and Banking, 9, 1977.

Kane, Edward J., "Accelerating Inflation, technological Innovation and Decreasing Effectiveness of Banking Regulations". Journal of Finance 36, 1981.

Kwayana, Eusi, "PM Being Messed Up". *Guyana Graphic*, May 7, 1971.

Kwayana, Eusi, *The Bauxite Strike and the Old Politics*. A 1996 publication referenced in Ferguson 1996.

Lewis, W. Arthur, *Theory of Economic Growth*. London: Allen and Unwin, 1952.

Lewis, W. Arthur, "Economic Development with Unlimited Supplies of Labour". Manchester School, Vol 22, 2, 1954.

Mandle, Jay R., *Big Revolution Small Country*. Maryland, USA: The North-South Publishing Company Inc., 1985.

Manley, Michael, *Struggle in the Periphery*. London: World Media Limited, 1982.

McIntyre, Alister, "Decolonisation and Trade Policy in the West Indies" pages 189-212 n F.M. Andic and T.G. Mathews (eds), *The Caribbean in Transition*. Puerto Rico: Institute of Caribbean Studies, University of Puerto Rico, 1965.

McIntyre, Alister, *The Caribbean and the Wider World*. Kingston, Jamaica: The University of the West Indies Press, 2016.

Nurske, Ragnar, *Problems of Capital Formation in Underdeveloped Countries*. Oxford: Basil Blackwell, 1953.

Posner, Richard A., "Theories of Economic Regulation". Bell Journal of Economics and Management Science 2, 5, 1974.

Report of a Commission of Enquiry into Disturbances in British Guiana in February 1962. London: Her Majesty's Stationery Office, 1962.

Rosenstein-Rodan, Paul, "Notes on the Theory of the Big Push" in H.S. Ellis and Henry C. Wallich (eds), *Economic Development for Latin America*. New York: St Martins Press, 1961.

Sen, Amartya, *Development as Freedom*. New York: Anchor Books, 1999.

Singer, Hans, "The Concept of Balanced Growth and Economic Development: Theory and facts". University of Texas Conference on Development, 1958.

Stephens, Evelyn Huber and Stephens, John D., *Democratic Socialism in Jamaica*. London: Macmillan Education Ltd, 1986.

Stone, Carl, *Power in the Caribbean Basin*. Philadelphia, USA: Institute for the Study of Human Issues, 1986.

Sue-A-Quan, Trev, *Cane Rovers: Stories of the Chinese-Guyanese Diaspora*. Vancouver, Canada: Cane Press, 2012.

Thomas, Clive, Sugar Economics in a Colonial Situation. Georgetown, Guyana: RATOON Studies in Exploitation, Number 1, 1970.

INDEX